# Class and News

# Class and News

Edited by
Don Heider

ROWMAN & LITTLEFIELD PUBLISHERS, INC.
Lanham • Boulder • New York • Toronto • Oxford

ROWMAN & LITTLEFIELD PUBLISHERS, INC.

Published in the United States of America
by Rowman & Littlefield Publishers, Inc.
A wholly owned subsidary of The Rowman & Littlefield Publishing Group, Inc.
4501 Forbes Boulevard, Suite 200, Lanham, MD 20706
www.rowmanlittlefield.com

P.O. Box 317, Oxford OX2 9RU, UK

British Library Cataloguing in Publication Information Available

**Library of Congress Cataloging-in-Publication Data**

Class and news / [edited by] Don Heider.
    p. cm.
  Includes bibliographical references and index.
  ISBN 0-7425-2712-3 (cloth : alk. paper) — ISBN 0-7425-2713-1 (pbk. :
alk. paper)
  1. Social classes—United States. 2. Social stratification—United
States. 3. Social classes—Press coverage—United States. 4.
Television broadcasting of news—Social aspects—United States. 5.
Journalism—Social aspects—United States. I. Heider, Don (Donald
Bruce)
  HN90.S6C563 2004
  305.5'0973—dc22

                                                    2004000304

Printed in the United States of America

∞™ The paper used in this publication meets the minimum requirements of
American National Standard for Information Sciences—Permanence of Paper
for Printed Library Materials, ANSI/NISO Z39.48-1992.

I tell you the truth, whatever you did for one of the least of these brothers of mine, you did for me.

—Jesus

You must be the change you wish to see in the world.

—Mohandas Karamchand Gandhi

# Contents

# Illustrations

## FIGURES

# TABLES

# Acknowledgments

A word of thanks goes to the contributors who worked with me to put this volume together, all of whom accepted suggestions and crafted their pieces to fit this book.

Thanks to Steve Reese, Chuck Whitney, and Dustin Harp, who offered valuable suggestions and advice.

Thanks to Brenda Hadenfeldt at Rowman & Littlefield for her patience with me and faith in the project. Thanks also to those who reviewed the proposal and offered helpful feedback and constructive criticism.

Thanks to Jeanne, Anna, Ella, and Cole for inspiration and support every step along the way.

# Introduction

*Don Heider*

I'd see him on my way to the Metro, the subway system in Washington, D.C. He was a large man, clad in many layers of clothes to fight off the cold. He was pushing a shopping basket full of his possessions. I would see him near the Tenleytown stop, where I'd be going to or from American University to my job at a news bureau near the capital.

There are a magic few months when you move to a new city. Magic because you have fresh eyes. You see things as an outsider, as a newcomer. As you live somewhere for a while, what becomes familiar begins to fade into the background and often times you're not as observant of your surroundings. But when you're new, you notice things.

One thing I noticed when moving to Washington was the enormous number of homeless people. They seemed to be everywhere. They were on the mall. They were near Union Station. They were on almost every street. You really couldn't help but notice them. If I'd stop for fast-food breakfast near the bureau, I would occasionally buy an extra coffee and biscuit for someone sitting on the curb between the restaurant and my workplace. But I worried most about the man near Tenleytown.

Because I saw him regularly, he caught my attention and his life captured a bit of my imagination. Where did he sleep? How did he survive? Had his life always been like this? Whose son was he? Whose brother?

I had moved to D.C. from Nashville. There were homeless people in Nashville, to be sure. But because I spent so little time on foot in Nashville, they were not as noticeable, not as tangible. The only time I was conscious of them was when a group of friends and I volunteered two or three times at the rescue mission.

Journalists report what they see and they report what they know. I had done very, very few stories on the homeless, very few stories about people who were poor. I didn't know many poor people. I did know upper- and middle-class people. They were friends and sources and subjects of my stories.


## NEWS AS A CULTURAL PRODUCT

A quarter of a century back, sociologist Herbert Gans noted in his study of four major national news organizations: "the news especially values the order of the upper-class and upper-middle-class sectors of society" (Gans 1979, 61).

Journalists these days are mostly college educated. They often live in the suburbs. They report what they see and what they know. That brings us to *Class and News*.

When I decided to conduct a study focusing on how news workers conceptualize class and how those ideas are manifested in day-to-day news coverage, my first surprise was to find how little had been published previously on the subject. I became convinced that a book would be a good idea.

News as a cultural product has been examined closely by scholars for the past several decades. Sociologists and media scholars have successfully looked at news for ideological content, including how news may shape readers' and viewers' ideas about politics, gender, and race.

One area that has not been explored deeply by U.S. scholars is how news may influence an audience's ideas about class. In American culture in general and in media specifically, class is a concept not often explored. Yet we all have some awareness of class distinctions within the culture. Even though we like to think of our society as egalitarian, most people have learned to distinguish between class groups.

How the news media in particular deal with class may contribute greatly to citizens' ideas about class. This book brings together some current scholarship to help illuminate how this might take place. This collection does not strive to be the definitive work on the subject but weaves together some good pieces on class and news to spur conversation, debate, and more work.

I wish I could, in this introduction, offer a simple, straightforward definition of class. I can for news. In the case of this book, news is primarily but not exclusively a journalistic product; the world of nonfiction information. But explaining class is a weightier proposition. Class is something we all live with daily. One can argue it's an awareness, an economic reality, and a form of power. And perhaps all three simultaneously. At its most basic level, I would argue, class is another way (like gender or race/ethnicity) by which we carve up the world—a method by which we distinguish between groups of people, most often between ourselves and some other group. Each contributor in this volume wrestles with the issue of precisely what class is in the midst of their respective chapters, and I invite you to grapple with them.

Beyond trying to define class, most of the contributors are trying to better understand and help us better understand the way in which class may be fleshed out in some type of media or media practice. The news media is just one way we get information about our culture, but over the past century, it has become an increasingly important way. As we talk to each other less and spend more time watching television and surfing the Net, what we watch and what we see on these flickering screens may influence what we believe and how we act.

This book is interested in symbolic meaning. When we interact with media, whether a newspaper, magazine, radio, whatever, we aren't experiencing firsthand an event or a story. We are experiencing a mediated form of communication. The words and pictures symbolize what has happened, or what might have happened or what might yet happen. So in this project what we are concerned with is the way in which meaning is constructed in news and information products.

The chapters in this volume employ a wide variety of methodologies. Analyzing constructed meaning is rarely a simple task. Therefore a variety of methods is appropriate and welcome. In some case the use of statistics can be crucial to making sense of a media product. In other cases, a close reading of a media text might be more helpful. In still others, entering into a setting where news products are produced might also reveal additional insights. An examination of historical documents might produce further helpful information. So the choice was made at the outset to be open to many approaches; as a result, the totality of the work offers a rich variety of approaches, all useful in different ways.

No discipline has the corner on knowledge about class, or media, or both. Therefore the decision was made to try to be ecumenical. You will find authors here who work in all varieties of journalism and communications fields, as well as political science, sociology, and English. This was an intentional act, with the hopes of finding richness from different points of view and different scholarly traditions.

## FOUNDATIONAL RESEARCH

Although the literature on class and news is sparse, some significant work has been done abroad. Karl Marx and Max Weber, two seminal theorists on class, were gone before our modern media era. But people working in their traditions have done important work in relations to media and its influence. Antonio Gramsci and Louis Althusser both worked to update and refine Marxism, with Althusser attempting to reconcile Marx's ideas with structuralism. Frankfurt School scholars working from a Marxist tradition, especially Max Horkheimer and Theodor Adorno, were very interested in ideas about popular culture and its impact on audiences. Others also contributed. Pierre Bourdieu's development of the idea of *habitus* was a revealing way of thinking about the way in which social status is unconsciously expressed in cultural practices. Those who founded and worked in the cultural studies tradition in Great Britain focused a great deal of time and attention on the influence of literature and media on culture. Richard Hoggart, Raymond Williams, E. P. Thompson, and Stuart Hall, along with the Birmingham Centre for Contemporary Cultural Studies, all played significant roles in trying to formulate the relationship between media and power in contemporary cultures, often in regard to class. Is this sense, they undertook a project to make ideology more visible and less transparent. These efforts, all helpful and significant, might best be summarized by John B. Thompson, who wrote that "ideology, broadly speaking, is meaning in the service of power" (1990, 7). Many of these scholars have analyzed how institutionalized power works to keep control, often allowing little voice for those with limited power or economic clout. The Glasgow Media Group has also produced an impressive body of work, often concentrating on class. Among their findings, the group found that in the coverage of a dramatic strike in Scotland, the media all but ignored the workers' and union's reasons for striking. This is but one example of a rich research tradition abroad that has done much to make class and its relationship with media more apparent. Two scholars in Latin America deserve mention here because of their contributions to ideas about media, class, and culture. In *Pedagogy of the Oppressed* Paulo Freire wrote about how cultural invasion—the process of devaluing local culture and replacing it with the goals and values of the invaders—is both the instrument of and result of domination. Jesús Martín-Barbero wrote about a nation as a market, and how cultural differences that stood in the way of the free flow of products and services have been squelched in favor of the construction of a national culture. In this way, those in power determine the national culture. All of these scholars have helped in trying to dissect and interpret the way in which media operate in regard to class.

## CLASS AND RACE

Finally, I want to discuss briefly the relationship between race and class. I began my research about class and news to help myself better understand the way in which class and ideas about class were manifested in daily news routines. This followed on a research project where I had spent quite a bit of time thinking and writing about race and local news (see *White News*, 2000). What I wanted to understand better, and what I think I do now understand better, is that though class and race considerations sometimes intersect, they are very separate ideas, very separate social constructions. Assuming that *class trumps race* or that by taking class into account we no longer need consider race, I think is a complete fallacy. Both of these powerful ideas are used to make distinctions between people and are often used as the basis of discrimination and prejudice. Although a person's racial identity may on occasion imply a class identity, that does not mean that race and class are always conflated. Furthermore, attempts to analyze inequalities in media representation or practice cannot simply dismiss race in favor of thinking about class. Class is one of several important concepts or social constructions that help us focus on how media operate to create or reinforce social values or norms. The more we research, discuss, and explore both class and race, the better we might understand our own culture, our own social systems, and the way in which power operates.

On three different occasions during the time I lived in Washington, D.C., I went in search of the man who lived near the Metro stop. My goal, if I could find him, was to give him groceries. I wanted to buy him fruit, bread, canned goods; anything I could think of to help him survive the winter. I never found him. Alvin Gouldner wrote that, in essence, all research is autobiographical (1970, 484). If that's true, this is my way of continuing that search.

## REFERENCES

Gans, Herbert J. 1979. *Deciding What's News: A Study of CBS Evening News, NBC Nightly News, Newsweek, and Time.* New York: Vintage.

Gouldner, A. 1970. *The Coming Crisis of Western Sociology.* New York: Avon.

Heider, D. 2000. *White News: Why Local News Programs Don't Cover People of Color.* Mahwah, N.J.: Lawrence Erlbaum Associates.

Thompson, J. B. 1990. *Ideology and Modern Culture.* Stanford, Calif.: Stanford University Press.

# 1

# Media, Class, and Power: Debunking the Myth of a Classless Society

*Deepa Kumar*

In the United States there is a powerful myth that most people belong to the middle class. Unlike older European societies with long feudal histories, the United States, we are told, is a classless society. While there are some rich people, such as Bill Gates and Ted Turner, as well as celebrities, film stars, and sports stars, and there are some poor people, the vast majority of citizens belong to the middle class. Thus, the argument goes that there are no real class differences in the United States—only a large mass of individuals all aspiring to the American Dream. The mass media play no small role in constructing this notion of class. For instance, most newspapers have a business section but not a corresponding labor section. This gives the impression that news written from the point of view of business is of value to all Americans, and there are no conflicts based on different and competing class interests. Yet the reality could not be further from this picture. In this chapter, I discuss the reality of classes in the United States and the role of the media in obscuring these class differences.

Since the early 1970s, significant numbers of people have been affected by declining or stagnant wages, with male workers being affected disproportionately. The bottom 80 percent of males have taken cuts in real wages, and overall household income declined for the bottom 60 percent (Thurow 1996). The decline in household income occurred despite a greater number of married women entering the workforce. Women with young children, who in previous decades had worked primarily at home, became the fastest growing group that entered the paid workforce after the 1970s (Coontz 1997). By 1993, working women in families contributed 41 percent of the family income and most families needed two earners, working longer hours, to maintain their living standard (Coontz 1997). However, this has been a losing battle for the bottom 60 percent whose income continued to fall. The upshot is that most families and individuals are earning less, while they are working longer hours (Schor 1992).

A number of economists have arrived at similar conclusions (Thurow 1996; Gordon 1996; Mishel et al. 1999). According to economist David Gordon who calculated "real spendable hourly earnings," which is the amount left over from the hourly wages of a worker after deducting income and social security taxes and adjusting for inflation, average wages fell by nearly 1 percent from the early 1970s. This is true across the board and includes groups that had previously not seen drops in wages, such as middle-wage women, college-educated workers, and white-collar workers.

While wages did go up for a few years after 1997, this does not even begin to compare with the economic condition of the richest 1–3 percent who have seen their lot improve dramatically, both in terms of income and total wealth. Those at the very top of society, the CEOs (chief executive officer) have seen their income grow by leaps and bounds. While CEO to worker salary was 42 to 1 in the early 1980s, by 1998 it was 419 to 1 (Zweig 2000). In other words, a CEO worked a fraction of a day to make what an average worker earned in a whole year. But income and salary do not tell the whole story. This rise in inequality and class polarization is seen most clearly in wealth distribution (wealth being defined as the value of assets minus liabilities/debt). At the end of the 1980s, the "greed decade," the total wealth of the top 1 percent of society was greater than it had been in the previous sixty years (Wolf 1995). Between 1983 and 1989, the top 20 percent of wealth holders received 99 percent of the total wealth gain (Wolf 2000). The trend continued in the 1990s. In 1995 the top 1 percent held 39 percent of total wealth and the top 20 percent, 84 percent of all wealth (Wolf 2000). The rest of the 80 percent of American society held a grand total of 16 percent of all wealth. This gap is even more stark when you examine financial assets, where the top 1 percent control 47.2 percent, while the bottom 90 percent have 17.1 percent of all financial assets (Mishel et al. 1999). The richest 10 percent almost exclusively own income-generating assets like stocks, bonds, private business equity, and other financial assets, whereas the type of wealth held by the bottom 90 percent is primarily homes and life insurance (Mishel et al. 1999).

Thus the economic growth of the 1980s and 1990s reflected in the increases in GDP found their way to a tiny percentage of people at the top. If all Americans belong to the same class, how do we explain these disparities? How do we also explain the fact that most people are working longer than they did just a decade ago and for lower wages? When we ask these questions, we are forced to confront the fact that the interests of the vast majority of Americans run counter to those of the minority at the top of society. In fact, it points to the conclusion that there are at least two distinct groups or classes in this society and that they have different interests; when one group/class loses ground economically, the other gains ground. The recent corporate scandals have only amplified this point. Although Enron CEO Kenneth Lay sold large amounts of his stock and made a substantial profit before their value plummeted, his employees lost their jobs when the company folded, as well as their life savings and retirement invested in Enron stocks. This raises important questions about who has power in our society and who controls the conditions of work. To address these questions one needs to have an understanding of the nature of class in a capitalist society.

## WHAT IS CLASS?

Some people try to explain class by looking at lifestyle, or the status of a person's job, or even income. Before I define class, I want to explain why these ways of understanding the nature of class are inadequate. First, let us look at the lifestyle definition of class. According to this view, the kind of clothes that one wears, the furniture and household appliances that one has, or the automobile that one drives define whether or not one has "class." Such a definition is superficial in that it views individuals in terms of their consumption patterns. It doesn't ask what this consumption is based on, how it is financed and supported, or even if this lifestyle can be sustained over a period of time.

In the previous section, I discussed how since the 1970s wages for males in the bottom 80 percent of society have been declining. In order to compensate and to maintain their lifestyle, married women have taken jobs outside the home. Additionally, families have taken on longer work hours and have gone into debt. If we were to look merely at lifestyle, we would conclude that things hadn't changed much for the vast majority of Americans over the past three decades. This would be quite wrong. When we look behind the lifestyle and examine how it is being financed, we find a significantly different picture than one of a vast middle class enjoying the fruits of consumer capitalism. When this is combined with the fact that many lower-income families have experienced personal bankruptcies, mortgage foreclosures, and automobile repossession in the late 1990s, you begin to see that lifestyles are quite transient (Andrews 2003). This is why it is important to go beyond the superficial patterns of consumption and look at source of income and the conditions of employment.

However, looking at income alone does not tell the whole story. Wealth- and income-based definitions of class are merely descriptive, lacking much explanatory power. Sociologists who employ this method of discussing class slot individuals along an income gradation, dividing the populace into three classes—upper, middle, and lower. While such a schema might describe where along the income ladder individuals fall, it fails to adequately explain why they belong to a particular class and how individuals may move from one class to another. In short, a descriptive schema can only reflect the existing order of society without providing a means by which to understand change. This is also true of definitions based on the social status of various jobs. For instance, theories of class based on status and income would be hard pressed to explain how the job of a clerk could change over the course of a century. In the nineteenth century, clerical work was a high-status, relatively well-paid occupation dominated mainly by men; but by the mid-twentieth century it had become a low-paying job mainly for women. How do we explain this transformation? Merely looking at income or status tells us little about the process of change.

Harry Braverman (1998) argues that this change in the nature of clerical work corresponds to changes in the structure and organization of capitalism over the past century. He explains that profound changes starting to take place at the turn of the twentieth century led to a reorganization of the conditions of production. This new stage, known as monopoly capitalism, saw businesses grow into large corporate firms. Although earlier the owners of business could hire a few clerks (with whom they usually shared a close personal relationship) to help manage the business, this was no longer possible. The tasks of accounting, recordkeeping, payroll, planning and scheduling, and so on, now took on a scale that could no longer be handled by the owner and a handful of clerks. This gave rise to the "office" in modern corporations, where all these functions of management were handled by various departments and branches of the enterprise. This new division of labor meant that the tasks handled by clerks in various departments required less skill and women, who could be paid less, were hired in these positions. Thus the transformation of clerical work from a high-paying, high-status, predominantly male job a century ago to a low-paying, low-status predominantly female job today is a product of changes in the organization of capitalism.

We can more adequately understand class if we view it in terms of the overall system of production that a society employs. This allows us to understand what classes are as well as how they change over time. Class so defined is understood as a *relation* to the means of production, rather than through static concepts of income, lifestyle, or status. Additionally, this relationship is understood to be based on power. For instance, while some of Enron's employees earned a good wage and led an expensive lifestyle, this could not prevent them from losing their jobs and savings. In short, they had little power over their conditions of work. Such an understanding of class derives from the theories of Karl Marx, who wrote about the system of capitalism and class structures in the nineteenth century. Since then several scholars have developed Marx's explanation of class to account for the existence of classes in today's society. Sociologist Erik Olin Wright explains that within "the Marxist tradition of class analysis, class divisions are defined primarily in terms of the linkage between property relations and exploitation" (1997, 17). Putting it another way, economist Michael Zweig writes that class is "first and foremost a product of power asserted in the production process. This means power over what goes on at work; who will do which tasks at what pace for what pay, and the power to decide what to produce, how to produce it, and where to sell it" (2000, 12).

Based on the above definitions, people who have social power because of their ownership or control over the means of production are referred to as the capitalist class. Those who sell their ability to work for a wage, and have little power at work, are members of the working class or the "proletariat." In between these two classes is the middle class that consists of individuals who work for a living but are not part of the working class, in that they have some power over their conditions of work. While they are subordinate to the capitalist class, they have authority over others lower than themselves and can make decisions of hiring and firing, disciplining, and so on. Additionally, they are given wages higher than workers' and have a "management stake" in the corporation. In the following section we will look at how American society is divided among these three classes and what sorts of jobs fall into each of these classes.

## THE COMPOSITION OF THE MAJOR CLASSES

Based on the above definitions, Zweig conducted a study of the occupation breakdown provided by the U.S. Department of Labor to determine the percentage of the employed population that belongs to each class. Of the 133.9 million people who were employed in 1996, he found that 82.8 million were part of the working class and 51.1 million were part of the middle class and above. In terms of percentages, the working class comprises 62 percent of the working population, the middle class 36 percent and the capitalist class 2 percent (Zweig 2000). These numbers and percentages are not fixed in time; rather, according to our definition of class, the composition of classes changes as the economy changes. With the onset of the 2001 recession, the various corporate bankruptcies, not to mention the deflation of the stock market bubble and the melt-down of the dot-com industry, large sections of the middle class have found themselves in the category of unemployed or working class. Additionally, in many professions considered part of the professional middle class there has been an erosion of the control that employees once had. For instance, with the rise of HMOs (health maintenance organizations) doctors and nurses have lost, and are continuing to lose, autonomy over their conditions of work and are becoming proletarianized. Thus the middle class is likely to have shrunk from 36 percent at the time of Zweig's study, increasing the numbers of the working class.

### The Capitalist Class

By definition, the capitalist class consists of those of who own and control businesses of all sizes. However, there is a vast difference between the owners/CEOs of Fortune 500 companies and a family-run beauty salon. The two don't have the same social power and are not part of the same class. The vast majority of small businesses consist of no employees at all except the owner. Typically, these businesses are meant to supplement the income that the owner receives from his or her working-class job. Only 13 percent of all businesses in the United States have any employees beyond the owner. The owners and managers of these companies compose the capitalist class and amount to 2 percent of the employed population (Zweig 2000).

Even in this bracket, there is a difference between businesses that employ fewer than 500 people and are considered by the U.S. Department of Commerce to be small businesses and those that employ more than 500 workers. The latter (i.e., big business) comprises only 0.2 percent of all businesses in the country but wields power far greater than its numbers. This power is derived from the vast amount of assets and resources that these individuals control: the top 1 percent has 39 percent of all wealth. These "captains of industry," some of whom sit on multiple boards of directors, number about 200,000, and form the core of the capitalist class (Zweig 2000).

All other business owners fall into the middle class. Their very existence, the terms of their growth and their ability to compete, is restricted by the capitalist class. For instance, many small businesses arise in the gaps left by major corporations. They can afford to take risks because of the small amount of capital investment. However, newcomers find it almost impossible to compete with the established corporations. Additionally, due to their scale and size they are vulnerable to the vicissitudes of the market and can go bankrupt or get bought up by larger firms. There are some exceptions to this, such as when a company with a high stock market value acquires larger, more established firms. AOL, a much newer and smaller company, bought Time-Warner in what was then the largest media merger.

### The Middle Class

The middle class, sandwiched between the capitalists and workers, faces pressure from both sides. Small business owners are pressured by the capitalist class but share an interest in keeping workers' power to a minimum. At the same time, they share an interest with workers in trying to find security in an economic landscape dominated by the capitalist class. During times of recession many small business owners find themselves in the working class.

Another segment of the population, managers and supervisors, are like the working class in that they do not own the means of production, have no independent economic existence, and depend on the capitalist class for employment. Supervisors and managers make up a significant portion of the middle class. They monitor the labor of workers and enforce discipline. They are usually paid above the wages of the average worker in return for their loyalty.

Wright argues that managers and supervisors are not a distinct class in as much as they occupy "contradictory locations within class relations" because they "combine the inherently antagonistic interests of capital and labor" (1997, 20). Those at the upper end have a closer relationship to the capitalist class, those at the bottom with the working class. A characteristic of this group is the lack of a clear demarcation at the upper and lower edges and a degree of fluidity. For instance, lower-level supervisors have far less control over the process of production and take their orders from those higher up in the hierarchy. To ensure the trust of these employees, even the lower-level managers, the capitalist class disburses a "loyalty rent" (Wright 1997, 21). The loyalty rent consists of relatively higher earnings derived from a redistribution of profits, opportunities for individual advancement, and relative control over workplace decisions. This layer of managerial and supervisory employees increased substantially over the last quarter of the twentieth century in the United States due to corporate restructuring that demands greater surveillance over the workforce (Gordon 1996). The end result, according to Gordon's (1996) empirical investigation of "managerial bloat," is the creation of "fat and mean" corporations.

The middle class also consists of professionals such as computer engineers, college professors, researchers, lawyers, doctors, and so on. These individuals are not part of the working class because they have a degree of autonomy over their work—they control how they work and what they produce. However, they have no control over investment, recourse allocation, or the physical means of production. Typically they command wages well over what they need to survive. Wright refers to this as "skills rent" (Wright 1997, 22). Like managers, employees who possess certain scarce skills or expertise are in a position to appropriate a part of the profits that accrue from the labor of the working class.

Broadly speaking, the middle class consists of small business owners, managers and supervisors, and professionals. But individuals who are part of this class are never secure in their position. Small business owners can go bankrupt and managers and supervisors are fired from time to time in waves of downsizing. Additionally, changes in the structure and organization of various professions have in the past turned middle-class jobs into working-class jobs, as in the case of clerical work. Computer programmers furnish another example. While their skill was in scarce supply, programmers had a degree of autonomy over their work. However, with the increasing application of scientific management techniques to this area, programmers find themselves subject to working-class conditions (Braverman 1998). Above all, the middle class, and classes as such, must be seen as relations that change with the changing conditions of production. As Braverman notes, "the class structure, the social structure as a whole, are not fixed entities but rather ongoing processes, rich in change, transition, variation and incapable of being encapsulated in formulas, no matter how analytically proper such formulas may be. The analysis of this process requires an understanding of the internal relations and connections which serve as its move force, so that its direction as a process may be understood" (282–83).

## The Working Class

The vast majority of people in United States and around the world belong to the working class. These individuals must sell their ability to work for a wage and have little or no control over their conditions of work. In the common stereotype, only blue-collar workers (i.e., manual laborers) are seen as part of the working class. However, both white-collar and blue-collar workers fall into this class.

Zweig finds that service occupations are "overwhelmingly working class" (2000, 29) and include firefighters, dental assistants, nursing aides, private guards, hairdressers and cosmetologists, janitors, waiters, and waitresses. Although the Department of Labor defines several groups of workers such as respiratory, speech, and physical therapists as "professionals," Zweig argues that are a part of the skilled working class, based on their conditions of work and lack of power.

It has been argued that because the number of workers involved in goods production (i.e., manual blue-collar workers) has declined as a percentage of the workforce, the working class has ceased to exist. There is ample evidence to suggest that the bulk of white-collar jobs are working class in that white-collar workers make products, tangible or intangible, that can be sold for a profit. Furthermore, they receive paltry wages and have almost no control over their work. Zweig's study of Labor Department statistics and occupational categories establishes this point. Wright's (1997) research yields similar results as Zweig's. Based on how skill and authority at work are operationalized, Wright finds that between 39 and 61 percent of the labor force consists of skilled and nonskilled workers. Both studies show that the worker class is a majority of the population and continues to exist as a class.

## RACE AND GENDER COMPOSITION OF THE MAJOR CLASSES

There is a long-held stereotype that the working class consists of white men in hard hats. Zweig's study shows that white men make up less than half the working class, about 46 percent. The majority of the working class consists of white women, and men and women of color. According to Wright's calculations, these figures are even higher. He finds that only 39 percent of the working class consists of white males. See figure 1.1 for a breakdown of the working class based on race and gender composition (information for all the diagrams are taken from Wright). We find that the majority of the working class consists of white females, and black females and males.

When we look at class distribution among African Americans, we find that the vast majority belong to the working class. Among black men, 77 percent are part of the working class while among black women the figure is 87 percent (see figures 1.2, 1.3). A much smaller percentage, 8 percent and 2 percent, of African American men and women belong to the category of expert

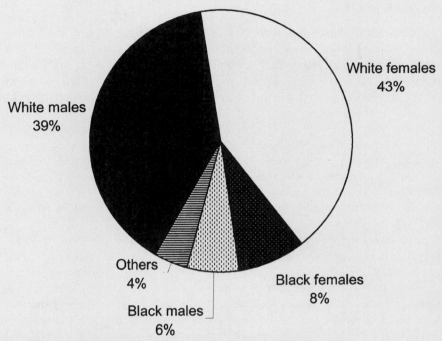

**Figure 1.1.    Race and Gender Distributions in the Working Class**

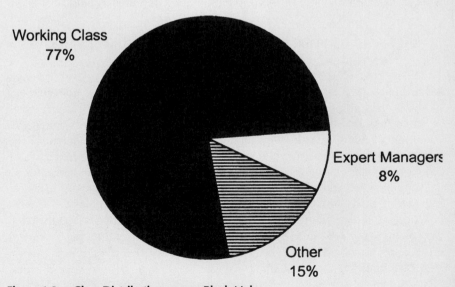

**Figure 1.2.    Class Distribution among Black Males**

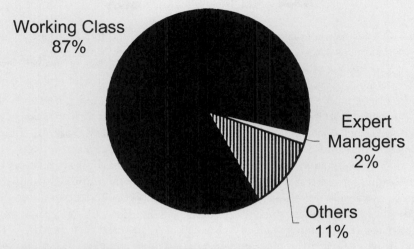

**Figure 1.3.   Class Distribution among Black Females**

managers. There are no African Americans in the capitalist class (see figure 1.4). figure 1.4 also shows that 81 percent of the capitalist class consists of white males. What we find from this race and gender distribution among the major classes is that while the working class is a heterogeneous group consisting of men and women, and members of various races, the capitalist class tends to be overwhelmingly white and male. This, as we will observe in the next section, impacts the discussion of class both in society at large and in the media in particular.

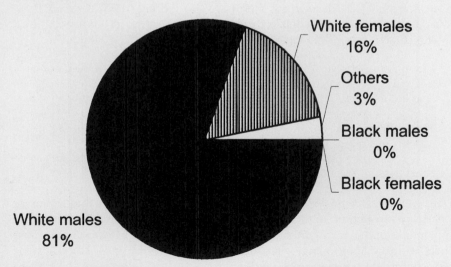

**Figure 1.4.   Race and Gender Distribution in the Capitalist Class**

## MEDIA AND CLASS

The bulk of mass media in the United States and around the world are owned by a handful of large corporations—AOL Time Warner, Sony, News Corporation, Viacom, Vivendi, and Bertelsmann (McChesney 2001). These multibillion-dollar conglomerates are global in reach and scope, with the upshot that a few loud voices tend to dominate. For instance, in the U.S. newspaper industry, about half a dozen major chains have monopolistic control over newspapers that serve metropolitan areas. In radio, Clear Channel, which owns 1,225 radio stations, dominates the audience share in 100 out of 112 major markets. This level of concentration of ownership has been facilitated by laws such as the Telecommunications Act of 1996, which removed many of the regulations on media ownership. Prior to 1996, a media corporation could not own more than forty stations. However, since then, companies like Clear Channel have taken advantage of the atmosphere of deregulation to increase their holdings. The end result is the formation of large, highly profitable media conglomerates and a corresponding decrease in the diversity of voices heard in the media. Media scholar Robert McChesney in his book *Rich Media, Poor Democracy* explains the contradictions between the democratic needs of a society based on a free press, and the interests of the owners/managers of these media giants. He argues that when the media are concentrated in the hands of a few large conglomerates that place profits before open and free communication, the tenets of democracy are severely weakened (McChesney 1999). This is especially true when it comes to class and class interests in the media.

Overwhelmingly, the news tends be biased in favor of the capitalist class. A vast amount of research demonstrates that the news media overrepresent the interests of the elites (Herman and Chomsky 1988; Kellner 1990; McChesney 1999; McChesney and Herman 1997; Eldridge 1995; Entman 1989; Mazzocco 1997). In this context the interests of the working class are at best marginalized. As George Lipsitz observes:

> For almost twenty years, working people and their interests have been absent from most public discussions about our national political and cultural life. As deindustrialization and economic restructuring have radically transformed U.S. society, the people and communities most immediately affected by these changes have been virtually erased. Business initiatives dominate the economic, political, and social agenda of the nation, while labor's perspectives and needs remain almost invisible within most of the country's mainstream media and economic institutions. (1994, 1)

This trend has been developing over the past fifty years with the decline of the labor movement. In the 1930s and 1940s, at the height of the labor movement, a full-time labor editor or beat reporter was the norm among newspapers with medium-to-large circulation. Today, however, most labor news is covered in the business pages and few reporters are assigned exclusively to cover working-class issues. Most daily newspapers, although they have a business section, lack a corresponding labor section.

The picture is not that different in broadcasting. National television, including PBS, offers dozens of business and investor programs but not one regular show on labor or consumer rights. Even though stock ownership has become more widespread, 60 percent of households own no stock at all (Mishel et al. 1999); the top 10 percent of American society owns 88.4 percent of all stocks and mutual funds (Mishel et al. 1999). Thus economically speaking, the public interest—the interest of the vast majority of Americans—in the stock market is minimal. However, cable channels like CNBC are completely dedicated to the coverage of Wall Street; CNN, MSNBC, and other channels have slots in regular programming for stock updates and business perspectives on the economy; similar working-class slots or channels do not exist. It is hardly surprising that on key issues corporate views tend to dominate in the news.

However, the power that the capitalist class has over the news is neither absolute nor direct. During periods of class struggle pressure can be exerted on the media to represent labor issues more accurately. For instance, during the UPS strike of 1997, when 185,000 workers around the country went out on strike, the initial coverage of the strike was biased in favor of corporations. However, as the strike progressed a majority of Americans came out in support of the striking workers—55 percent of the public sympathized with the issues raised by the workers. This put tremendous pressure on the news media to be fair in their representation of the strike. The result was that during the second week of the strike, some media outlets like the *New York Times, Washington Post,* and ABC switched the tone of their coverage to accommodate working-class issues (Kumar 2001). Even though the news generally has a pro-corporate bias, it can be shaped and influenced during periods of struggle.

Media owners do not directly control the news. Rarely do they interfere with the production of news or dictate to reporters what they should or should not say. The mechanisms of control are indirect and structural and derive from the economic priorities of a for-profit media system and the ways in which production is organized to meet this goal. In what follows, I will briefly highlight some of these mechanisms of control. By no means is this meant to be a comprehensive account of the media industry and its practices; rather, it is a discussion of *some* of the key factors that shape the news.

A for-profit media industry is geared around increasing revenues and decreasing costs. The main source of revenue for the media is advertising. General circulation magazines obtain about 50 percent of their revenues from advertising, newspapers 75 percent, and broadcasting nearly 100 percent. Advertising is thus the backbone of the media industry, and an estimated $200 billion a year is spent on advertising in the United States (Cardona 1997). Because of its dependence on advertising, the media industry has had to tailor its content and structure to suit the needs of advertisers. When the Tribune Company bought the Times-Mirror corporation, the logic was to "create a network of regional media hubs where advertisers are matched with audiences through newspapers, television broadcasts and Internet sites" (Barringer and Holson 2000). When attracting and retaining advertisers is one of the key economic imperatives, then the content of the news media is shaped accordingly. It is therefore not surprising that the news media rarely print or broadcast anything that offend advertisers.

When journalists cross the line they are often disciplined and brought in line with the owner's management prerogatives. In 1998, the *Cincinnati Enquirer* ran a detailed story exposing Chiquita Brands International's unethical overseas practices. Chiquita sued the newspaper because some of the information for the story was obtained illegally by a reporter from voice mail messages. While the truth of the story was never disproved, the *Enquirer* fired the reporter, recanted the story, and paid Chiquita $10 million (McChesney 1999). Rupert Murdoch's New Corporation fired reporters Steve Wilson and Jane Akre for a dispute over an investigative series about a Monsanto chemical supplement. At the heart of the dispute was whether reporters or managers controlled the content of news stories. Monsanto, a huge multinational conglomerate that buys advertising time, threatened action against the station employing Wilson and Akre, forcing the Fox affiliate in Tampa to carefully examine what information would and would not appear in an investigative series about milk. As a News Corp. executive put it, "We paid $3 billion for these TV stations. We will decide what the news is. The news is what we tell you it is" ("We paid" 1998, 1). Although this sort of direct intervention by parent companies like Disney, News Corp., and AOL Time Warner happens from time to time, it is not a regular feature and, arguably, does not need to be. This is because the possibility of such intervention hangs like the sword of Damocles over the heads of journalists and producers—a sword that could fall any time they crossed the line. This has a chilling effect far greater than actual acts of censorship by the owners of the mass media. Rather than face the prospect of being blacklisted and jobless, journalists are driven to exercise "restraint" and self-censorship.

One cannot underestimate the pressure of job insecurity on journalists. As part of the plan to keep operating costs down, media conglomerates have fired a large number of reporters over the past decade. The first to be fired are those perceived as trouble makers. Another consequence of keeping costs down is that with fewer reporters news media institutions have become more dependent on cheap, reliable sources of information. The two main sources of such information are corporate public relations departments and the state, with its various departments from the Pentagon to the White House (Herman and Chomsky 1988). Vast amounts of information reach the news media through these two sources. An estimated 40–70 percent of the news is based on press releases and PR-generated information (Carey 1996). Procorporate think tanks like the Heritage Foundation and the American Enterprise Institute provide the media with a steady, convenient supply of "experts." The end result of the business imperatives to keep revenues high and costs low is a system of news production that is biased in favor of the capitalist class.

For the most part, what we hear, read, or view about class in the media is based on myths and misconceptions. This is true, to a greater or lesser extent, in countries around the world. For the last quarter of the twentieth century, class inequality has grown tremendously on a worldwide scale. The promise of globalization—that free markets would lift whole countries out of poverty—has failed to materialize. The vast majority of people in advanced capitalist countries have seen their wages stagnate or decline while social programs have been cut. In developing countries in Asia and Latin America the debt burden has been devastating, and in sub-Saharan Africa conditions have deteriorated alarmingly.

Not everyone has been affected in the same way. While the working class, peasants, and agricultural workers have experienced worsening conditions, some segments of the world's population have benefited enormously. A U.N. study found that the wealth of the richest 225 people was nearly equal to the combined annual income of 47 percent of the world's poorest people (*Human Development* 1998). It is estimated that the world's wealthiest 20 percent now receive 86 percent of the world's gross domestic product (GDP), the middle 60 percent 13 percent, and the poorest 20 percent a mere 1 percent (Tabb 2001). This is the *reality* of classes today, a reality that has largely been ignored by the media.

## CONCLUSION

In American social life there is little or no discussion of the concept of class and the existence of antagonistic class interests. This is due in large part to the myth of class mobility, based on the notion of the American Dream. If we only worked hard enough, if we took a few risks, and if we dared to dream of a better life, then we could achieve it. By extension, if we fail, then we have no one to blame but ourselves. Yet, as this chapter shows, despite the vast majority of American's working harder and taking on longer work hours, they have failed to increase their wealth or even keep up with inflation. This predicament has little to do with individual effort or talent; rather, it is the result of a system that fosters inequality. In contrast to workers, the capitalist class has greatly increased its share of wealth without necessarily working harder. Behind the myth of the American Dream lies the very real existence of classes and competing class interests.

Every now and then a few individuals rise to wealth and power from humble origins, but this is the exception and not the rule. The ability to succeed financially depends in large measure on the power and control that one wields over the system of production. The capitalist class, which owns and controls the means of production, has the power to set the terms on which society organizes its productive processes. This small minority, barely 2 percent of the working population, exercises a good deal of authority over our society. In contrast, the working class, which sells its ability to work for a wage, has little power over the system. Yet this class makes up the majority of the working population. It would not be far off the mark to estimate that the working class is about 70 percent of American society. This class is made up of men and women of all races. In between these two classes is the middle class, which consists of small business owners, managers and supervisors, and professionals. This class is not nearly as big as we are led to believe. Contrary to the myth that the United States consists of a vast middle class with a few rich people at the top and a few poor people at the bottom, the middle class is in fact a much smaller percentage of the overall population.

However, this is not the picture we get from the mainstream media. For instance, television presents American society as an oasis of middle-class consumerism. Overwhelmingly, we are presented with the images and lifestyles of the middle class in both news and entertainment. Such an atmosphere is appealing to advertisers, on whom the for-profit media conglomerates depend quite heavily. The outcome of a for-profit media system is news that disproportionately serves the interests of the wealthy and marginalizes those of the working class. If we claim to live in a democratic society where the majority should have a stake in decisions about social life, we need to challenge this state of affairs. Debunking the myth of a classless society and exposing the reality will allow us to articulate demands for economic justice and organize ourselves around issues of equality.

# REFERENCES

Andrews, Edmund. 2003. "Economic Inequality Grew in 90s Boom, Fed Reports." *New York Times*, January 23, C1.

Barringer, Felicity, and Holson, Laura M. 2000. "Tribune Company Agrees to Buy Times Mirror." *New York Times*, March 14, A1.

Braverman, Harry. 1998. *Labor and Monopoly Capitalism*. 25th anniversary ed. New York: Monthly Review Press.

Cardona, Mercedes. 1997. "Coen: Ad Spending in '98 Will Outpace Overall Economy." *Advertising Age,* December 15.

Carey, Alex. 1996. *Taking the Risk out of Democracy*. Champaign: University of Illinois Press.

Coontz, Stephanie. 1997. *The Way We Really Are: Coming to Terms with America's Changing Families*. New York: Basic.

Eldridge, J., ed. 1995. *Glasgow Media Group Reader*. Vol. 1. New York: Routledge.

Entman, Robert. 1989. *Democracy without Citizens*. New York: Oxford University Press.

Gordon, David. 1996. *Fat and Mean: The Corporate Squeeze of Working Americans and the Myth of Managerial "Downsizing."* New York: Martin Kessler.

Herman, Edward, and Chomsky, Noam. 1988. *Manufacturing Consent: The Political Economy of the Mass Media.* New York: Pantheon.

*Human Development Report.* 1998. New York: Oxford University Press.

Kellner, Douglas. 1990. *Television and the Crisis of Democracy.* Boulder, Colo.: Westview.

Kumar, Deepa. 2001. "Mass Media, Class, and Democracy: The Struggle over Newspaper Representation of the UPS Strike." *Critical Studies in Media Communication* 18, no. 3: 285–302.

Lipsitz, George. 1994. *Rainbow at Midnight: Labor and Culture in the 1940s.* Urbana: University of Illinois Press.

Mazzocco, Dennis. 1997. *Networks of Power: Corporate TV's Threat to Democracy.* Boston: South End.

McChesney, Robert W. 1999. *Rich Media, Poor Democracy: Communication Politics in Dubious Times.* Urbana: University of Illinois Press.

———. 2001. "Global Media, Neoliberalism, and Imperialism." *Monthly Review* 10, no. 52: 1–19.

McChesney, Robert, and Herman, Edward. 1997. *The Global Media: The New Missionaries of Corporate Capitalism.* Washington, D.C.: Cassell.

Mishel, Lawrence, Bernstein, Jared, and Schmitt, John. 1999. *The State of Working America 1998–99.* Ithaca, N.Y.: ILR Press.

Schor, Juliet. 1992. *The Overworked American: The Unexpected Decline of Leisure.* New York: Basic.

Tabb, William. 2001. *The Amoral Elephant: Globalization and the Struggle for Social Justice in the Twenty-First Century.* New York: Monthly Review Press.

Thurow, Lestor. 1996. *The American Corporation Today.* New York: Oxford University Press.

"We Paid $3 Billion for These TV Stations. We Will Decide What the News Is." 1998. *Extra! Update,* June, 1.

Wolf, Edward. 1995. *Top Heavy: The Increasing Inequality of Wealth in America and What Can Be Done about It.* New York: New Press.

———. 2000. "Recent Trends in the Distribution of Household Wealth." In Ray Marshall, ed., *Back to Shared Prosperity: The Growing Inequality of Wealth and Income in America,* 57–63. New York: Sharpe.

Wright, Erik Olin. 1997. *Class Counts: Comparative Studies in Class Analysis.* Cambridge: Cambridge University Press.

Zweig, Michael. 2000. *The working class majority: America's best kept secret.* Ithaca, N.Y.: ILR Press.

# I

---

# CLASS IN PRINT

Any organizational scheme for a book like this is, of course, somewhat arbitrary. I issued invitations to authors and made an open call to find good work on the topic. Once the work arrives, it's up to the editor to decide what goes where, but, of course, any system is imperfect. I chose to stick with tradition in this case and began the book with chapters addressing the press—the printed word.

Many Americans still rely, in large part, on reading news for an idea of what is going in the world around them. We still esteem the printed word in a way we do not the spoken or broadcast word. This means that newspapers and newsmagazines continue to have a significant role in shaping our ideas about class. The following three chapters help us understand how that takes place.

Newspapers in many ways remain at the center of our ideas about what news is and what news looks like, as do newsmagazines. So it seemed logical to begin with three pieces that examine the printed journalistic word.

More than thirty years ago, William Ryan pointed out in his book *Blaming the Victim* how the public had been systematically convinced that poor people were in large part responsible for their own poverty. Janet Blank-Libra continues in this line of work by examining in detail how newspapers perpetuate the myth of the welfare mother as a person responsible for her own poverty. Martin Gilens documents in detail how African Americans continue to be overrepresented in newsmagazine coverage of poverty. Julie Newton and her colleagues discover that in newspaper photographs, white males dominate and are often associated with higher wealth and status compared to people of color. All three pieces help pave the way for us as we begin thinking about the roles news media play in constructing ideas about class.

# 2

# Choosing Sources: How the Press Perpetuated the Myth of the Single Mother on Welfare

*Janet Blank-Libra*

Statistics show that single mothers—women who hold primary responsibility for their family's economic well-being—tend to be poor. Given the milieu existing at the turn of the twentieth century, single mothers, many working as unskilled laborers, faced difficult odds. The nation's employers used more temporary and part-time workers than ever before in U.S. history, and those who worked in the lower levels of these areas tended to be women, most of whom received no health insurance, sick pay, or other benefits (McClure 1994, 23). According to the Washington, D.C.–based Institute for Women's Policy Research (IWPR), 42.4 percent of female workers were employed in technical, sales, and administrative support occupations, which tended to be low paying (*Status* 1996, 21). As Schein wrote, "No matter how you examine the statistics, they say the same thing. To think single mother is to think poverty" (1995, 4).

Such realities did not dissuade Congress in 1996 from eliminating AFDC (Aid to Families with Dependent Children), a guaranteed safety net for poor families, to make room for TANF (Temporary Aid for Needy Families), a state-based program focused on time limits and mandatory work requirements. When the federal government dismantled AFDC in 1996, it dismantled a program that had entitled states, which participated on a voluntary basis, to unlimited federal funds "for reimbursement of benefit payments, at 'matching' rates" (*Green Book* 1996, 384). Congress's argument for change was predicated, as the act's title indicates, on the belief that welfare recipients needed to become responsible for their family's economic well-being, the implication being, of course, that they as individuals had been irresponsible.

Welfare recipients have always needed to defend their integrity. Arguments about the viability or necessity of AFDC typically focused on whether single mothers, the primary recipients of AFDC, needed or deserved government assistance. Given the history of welfare in the United States and in Great Britain (where the U.S. system has its roots), it can be said that welfare, in and of itself, stigmatizes. The notion that only bad people need to use welfare, that there is something inherently wrong with the individual who must succumb to becoming a welfare recipient has deep historical roots. The implications are that the poor reject the work ethic, as well as other "mainstream" ways of behaving. Framed in this way, their behavior, not the system's performance, becomes the "problem." The recipient is, somehow, flawed.

AFDC's roots were intertwined with the roots of federal welfare in this country. Pushed by a depressed economy, the government established as part of the Social Security Act of 1935, Aid to Dependent Children, a cash grant program that enabled states to provide aid for needy, fatherless children. Eventually, the program was renamed Aid to Families with Dependent Children, and the emphasis shifted to allowing aid for needy children and their adult caretakers. By the early twentieth century most states had established nonmandatory pensions for the blind, aged, and widows. Mothers' Aid pensions were designed to keep single mothers, who in the early years of the program were primarily widows, from having to leave their children to make a living. The well-being of children constituted the focus of the program.

Times, however, have changed, and so has the perspective of the nation. Today, single mothers on welfare are apt to be unmarried, divorced, or separated, and thus no longer "deserving" in the way that widows were. They are expected to support their children through participation in the labor force, no matter the standard of living achieved or achievable. Over time, AFDC came to be seen as an entitlement given to the undeserving.

Lamentably, single mothers on welfare are not understood as real individuals but through the prevailing welfare mythology, which goes something like this: Promiscuous, young, single females, probably teenagers, have children to make themselves eligible for AFDC or to get more AFDC—"free money." Once on AFDC, the recipient and her family receive an income that allows them to live "high on the hog." Because a full-time, low-wage job is supposed to support a family, these women are said to be lazy, preferring to live in a culture of dependency. They are said to lack fundamental American values, particularly regarding the application of a work ethic and sexual mores. According to this characterization, these women pass their weaknesses on to their children, thus perpetuating the culture of poverty.

It has been generally agreed that references made to "welfare" prior to 1996 were references to AFDC rather than to welfare in general or to the concept of simply living a good life (Handler 1995, 1; Rose 1995, 1). For that reason, references to welfare recipients in general have been translated by citizens, as well as by politicians, as references to single mothers on welfare. It takes little research to dispel the myths surrounding these women. They need simply to be compared with the reality of life for single mothers in the mid to late 1990s: (1) The average family size of those on AFDC decreased from the 1970s to the 1990s, sliding from an average of four members in 1970 to three members in 1980 to 2.8 members in 1995 (*Green Book* 1996, 386). (2) Contrary to popular belief, most recipients of AFDC were not, at any one time, teenage mothers (*Green Book* 1996, 473). (3) Most single women receiving AFDC survived on total family incomes that fell below the poverty line. (4) Recipients were not women who desired to stay on welfare because they lacked the proper work ethic; rather, participation of recipients prior to reform was contingent on the waxing and waning of the economy. Studies have generally shown that single mothers, whether skilled or unskilled, have cycled between work and welfare (Edin and Lein 1997; Harris 1993; Spalter-Roth, Burr, Hartmann, and Shaw 1995). Their decisions have reflected the state of the economy, that is, its ability—or not—to provide a living wage. Ultimately, welfare was not designed to lift recipients out of poverty. It was designed to provide a standard of living that would force women to leave welfare for work (*Green Book* 1996, 435).

Congress, in passing the Personal Responsibility and Work Reconciliation Act of 1996, made a conservative vision of family values a part of its legislative point of view, a decision that led inevitably to many legislators' moralizing about single mothers and the alleged disintegration they brought to society with their "chosen" way of living. The legislation directly maintains that states should promote marriage (Seiler 2002, 1). Critical to this perspective was the argument that AFDC was not inviolate, that it had enabled single mothers to choose an unhealthy lifestyle and thus needed to be eliminated so that these women could be helped. Relief, it was said (and always has been said), encouraged idleness.

Reporters turned to these politicians and their perspective in 1995–1996 for information. Rather than focus on economics, these sources framed welfare as a moral and a political issue. These women needed to be rescued because their souls had become "corrupted" (Shogren 1996b). Because this point of view dominated, reportage suggested (if not point-blank said) that poverty is caused by the individual, not the system. Authors of welfare-related texts, particularly those who have argued that the system is unjust, have often addressed the role of the news media in covering welfare, sometimes just in passing, other times at greater length, but generally depicting the news media as perpetuators of myths about single mothers on welfare (Colby 1989, 17; Eyer 1996, 65; Gans 1995, 36; Gans 1979, 47; Harris 1997, 4; Jarrett 1996, 371; Jencks 1997; Katz 1989, 10; Kluegel 1987, 97; Nelson-Pallmeyer 1996, 118; Piven and Cloward 1993, 169–70, 331; Rivers 1996, 200–201; Sidel 1996, 171; Turner and Starnes 1976, 145).

This study allowed for the examination of front-page reportage of welfare-related stories produced by four newspapers during the year prior to welfare reform in an effort to answer three questions: (1) Who were the sources to whom these reporters turned? (2) Did these sources contribute to the existing mythology that stereotypes single mothers on welfare? (3) If so, how were these mothers characterized? Ultimately, this study shows that four newspapers stereotyped single mothers and failed to give citizens information that would enable them to understand AFDC and those receiving it.

## THE ROLE OF MYTHOLOGY

People have created myths to explain the world since the dawn of time. Although myths may spring from something actual, they are unquestionably entangled in flawed explanations and half-truths. Nonetheless, myths perform the duties of truth: They inform everyday life. For this reason they are dangerous, each a veritable current that energizes a way of seeing. Thus the ideologies they uphold are unquestionably flawed products of distorted knowledge. Here a myth is defined as an unproved collective belief that is accepted uncritically and is used to justify a social institution. Although myth typically justifies social institutions by maintaining a particular interpretation of reality, it may be that in the case of welfare, myth was employed to dismantle a social institution—AFDC.

Myths about single mothers embody the potential to stigmatize individuals through the use of stereotypes. Into a myth wander stock characters: heroes, villains, victims. To say that the news media cast welfare recipients as characters in myth is to say that these recipients embody particular roles in the story. They function as stereotypes, simple to understand and easy to use when telling a story or explaining a situation. The study of news itself as myth has slowly gained ground. Bird and Dardenne wrote with certainty that "one of the most productive ways to see news is to consider it as myth, a standpoint that dissolves the distinction between entertainment and information" (1988, 336). They noted that Bird's argument in an earlier study (1987) was not that individual news stories function as myth but that news as a communication process can function as myth and folklore.

When addressing the role of the news media in the perpetuation of myth and thus stigmatization, welfare experts who are authors generally say that journalists most often stigmatize welfare recipients who are single mothers, and even more so welfare recipients who are black single mothers. Though little research has been done to consider the truth of such accusations, Wilson found through content analysis that five major daily newspapers framed welfare recipients as personally responsible for their economic difficulties, as opposed to suffering because of structural influences, "from circumstances largely beyond their control" (1996, 413). The homeless and migrant laborers, on the other hand, were not likewise stigmatized, but were instead considered the victims of a structural influence (425).

The work of Golding and Middleton examined the way in which the British press labeled and stigmatized welfare recipients, among others. They found that press coverage targeted recipients as deserving or undeserving. Who was deserving? The old and the disabled were held less accountable for financial misfortune. Who was unworthy? Those who received supplementary aid were perceived as having engaged in "irresponsible family planning" (1982, 91).

## JOURNALISTS AND THEIR SOURCES

Obviously reporters' sources can influence the reportage. Often discussed in the literature and of direct relevance to the way in which individuals (i.e., single mothers) are characterized by the media is journalists' propensity to seek out official sources. Studies have consistently confirmed that journalists, as a result of organizational practices, turn to legitimized officials for news more than any other category of news source (Brown et al. 1987; Gans 1979; Sigal 1973). Gans noted that they do so even when "ordinary people" are present in order to save time and avoid complications (1979, 139–40). Lichter, Rothman, and Lichter suggested that journalists at large publications are attracted to power and the sources who wield it (1986, 112).

Their suggestion is hardly new. Tuchman argued that the individual whose sources are people of note may well gain power from the affiliation, for "the higher the status of sources and the greater the scope of their positions, the higher the status of the reporters" (1978, 69). Sigal worried that reporters, who are inclined to accept the perspectives of "authoritative sources" (1986, 22), might eventually come to share a source's perspective and perhaps "portray [the source] sympathetically in print" (29).

An affinity for using official sources in news stories can result in the construction of flawed or inadequate symbolic realities. For example, Paletz, Fozzard, and Ayanian found that stories in the *New York Times* about violent organizations were grounded in the opinions of public officials: "While almost 75 percent of the stories used no sources from the groups or their supporters, over 75 percent cited one or more authority holders. When a violent source did appear, it was often surrounded by a host of authority figures who served to undermine its credibility" (1982, 167).

These scholars chose to study coverage of the Irish Republican Army (IRA), the Red Brigade, and the Fuerzas Armadad de Liberacion (FALN) because the three groups differ in history, ideology, goals, and tactics (Paletz, Fozzard, and Ayanian 1982, 163). In the end they found that "only in the case of the Red Brigade did the paper provide even a modicum of analysis of group motivations, organization, objectives, or goals" (170). What readers came to know about these organizations rested on how authorities chose to portray violence: "Authorities hold the greater influence over how violence is portrayed in *Times* stories, both because of the frequency with which they are sources and of the interpretations that they offer" (170). For these reasons "the causes of violent groups are denied legitimacy by the authorities and hence by the *New York Times*" (170).


## METHOD

A method devised by David Altheide (1996), ethnographic content analysis, provided a way to examine the influence of journalists' sourcing patterns on newspaper characterizations of welfare recipients. ECA allows for relevant data to emerge from textual analysis; thus, the coding scheme changes as the research progresses, allowing for all salient data to be included in the analysis. To complete the study, four newspapers (*Washington Post, Chicago Tribune, Houston Chronicle,* and *Los Angeles Times*) were selected for the following reasons:

Each of these newspapers possesses a circulation in excess of 500,000; thus, they represent four major media voices in the nation. Three of the four are published in states that in 1996 ranked among the top five for highest caseloads of AFDC recipients. The fourth, the *Washington Post,* was used because it is the hometown paper of the policy makers. Daily newspapers with the top circulations in the United States are the following: *New York Times,* 1,071,120; *Los Angeles Times,* 1,095,007; *Washington Post,* 789,198; *Chicago Tribune,* 655,522; *Houston Chronicle,* 553,387 (Mallegg 1998). The four states leading in caseload numbers in August 1996 were, from greatest to least number of recipients, the following: California, New York, Texas, and Illinois (*Statistical Abstract* 1998, 390). Thus, the *Los Angeles Times,* the *Chicago Tribune,* and the *Houston Chronicle* are used specifically because those newspapers represent populations that included the nation's greatest populations of AFDC recipients. In addition, they represent different regions of the country. The *Washington Post,* as noted, is used rather than the *New York Times* expressly because the *Post* is the local newspaper of the policy makers. In addition, it represents the eastern part of the country.

This research was completed by one researcher—myself—who coded eighty stories (20 per newspaper) at least four times each—more in the case of particularly complex or long stories. Only elected officials were counted as public officials/politicians. Individuals who spoke for public officials—a White House aide, for example—also counted as public officials. Though other categories of sources were coded, the only other one discussed in this chapter is the single mother on welfare. This is the case simply because the sources consulted were overwhelmingly politicians, and their attention was riveted throughout the election year on welfare reform and their desire to make single mothers on welfare responsible for themselves and their children—hence, the Personal Responsibility Act. The coder followed protocol and took copious notes, paying particular attention to the following: the source's stand on reform, the general content of his or her statements, and the relationship of those comments to myths about welfare recipients.

Though slightly modified, and with some categories collapsed, Altheide's steps for ethnographic content analysis were used as follows: The Dialog database provided access to twenty full-text, front-page news stories from each of the newspapers analyzed. Using the following terms in a Boolean search, stories were downloaded onto disk: single mother, single parents, welfare, welfare reform, public welfare, AFDC, welfare mothers, welfare recipients, teen, teen mother, unwed mother. Because these stories were selected from campaign-year reportage, they were often framed, to lesser and greater degree, in a political context. Although it is true that focusing on stories written during the campaign year led to there being sufficient stories available for a study such as this, it is also true that the year under study provided stories that were flavored by an unavoidable political context.

Stories were selected from those generated only if they contained some emphasis on welfare reform and/or single mothers. While the theses of the stories studied were sometimes focused dominantly on women on welfare, they were sometimes not. Single mothers on welfare, for example, may have been used to support points being made in a story whose emphasis was welfare reform. Further, while stories focused on food stamps or Dole's desire to stop male predators from preying on young women may not have been focused dominantly on women and welfare, they nonetheless contained material that spoke to single mothers' relationship to the item under discussion. "Women on welfare," if not the dominant theme in each story, became a subtheme that could be examined in any given story. The *Houston Chronicle* varied from the other three newspapers in that it had not produced twenty stories that easily met these basic qualifications. For that reason, a story on a children's rally in Washington, D.C., for example, was used in the analysis (Children's Rally 1996), for it did contain references to women's poverty. All story selections were made so as to produce a body of stories that had something to say about women as welfare recipients. In pursuing this method, stories relevant to the economy but not single mothers, for example, were bypassed. For example, one *Los Angeles Times* story focused on the working poor and shed considerable light on the plight of the citizen as worker (Labor Revival 1995).

## FINDINGS

Quantitative Results: A total of 262 public officials were consulted for the eighty stories analyzed. Of those, twenty-nine (11 percent) were female and 233 (88 percent) were male. A total of forty-five female welfare recipients were consulted for the eighty stories. Recipients tended to be clustered in groups of three or four in stories; thus, the forty-five were not evenly distributed throughout, as were public officials. For example, no single mothers were used as sources by the *Houston Chronicle* in the twenty stories analyzed.

Of the 262 public officials, 185 expressed opinions about welfare. (Some simply supplied information.) Of those 185 officials, 79 percent expressed pro-reform sentiments, and 21 percent expressed anti-reform sentiments. Sixty-two of these individuals, or 23 percent of the officials consulted, expressed positions that in some way reflected the recipient, not the system, as responsible for her poverty. Fifty-two of the officials consulted, or 20 percent, expressed concern about reform. Obviously the fact that Congress is predominantly male would have influenced these numbers, given that politicians were the preferred source pool.

A total of forty-five recipients were consulted for these stories. The *L.A. Times* turned to twenty-five single mothers for information or opinions, the *Chicago Tribune* to twelve single mothers as sources, the *Washington Post* eight, and the *Houston Chronicle* none.

## INTERPRETATION

The bottom line: The voice of the male public official holding a conservative point of view was significantly dominant. This finding is more important than any other, for these individuals' comments supported their political agenda—welfare reform—and affected the very tone of the reportage, most notably defining the recipient as dependent (91 percent of stories).

If this perspective had been balanced with information about the state of the job market, readers could have at least considered the issue from a perspective focused on economics. However, in 55 percent of all stories analyzed, no specific discussion was made of the job market. The reality, however, was that work paid less than welfare in 1996. Edin and Lein's study of 379 low-income single mothers, who were either wage- or welfare-reliant, showed that the absence of affordable health insurance, affordable (and good) child care, and affordable housing made it impossible for poor single mothers to succeed in the workforce (1997, 5). Welfare at least made it possible to provide health care for their children, since recipients tended to be eligible for Medicaid and food stamps.

That public officials possessed the strongest voice in this reportage was not a surprise, given that 1996 was an election year. Nonetheless, the overwhelming dominance of this type of source reveals the absence of a multiperspectival approach in the reportage—reportage that arguably possessed at least indirectly the ability to affect legislation. If citizens believed, given the newspapers' emphasis on a conservative perspective, that reform was necessary, they would have had no reason to counter the government's agenda, through their votes or their voices. (Of the four newspapers, the *Los Angeles Times* clearly presented the more balanced selection of voices.) Of course, how much a newspaper's reportage might have affected an individual's perspective would have depended on that person's knowledge of welfare as well as his or her personal life experiences.

Both the formal language of legislative deliberation and the language of the reporter depicted women as dependent in this story. For example, the four newspapers gave considerable attention to congressional deliberation of the necessity of time limits (71 percent of stories) and mandatory work (68 percent of stories)—two discussion points that supported the notion of dependency. On the other hand, not one story made mention of the fact that single mothers on welfare tended to cycle on and off assistance, their status at any time dependent on the viability of the market place. Tim, in *Current Population Reports*, a publication produced by the Department of Commerce, described well this relationship between recipients and welfare: "Generally, program participation rates are related to poverty and business cycles—rising along with poverty rates during periods of economic contraction, and falling during periods of economic expansion" (1996, 2). Nonetheless, the journalistic reportage on congressional deliberations noted that Congress wished to "move," "force," "steer," or "prod" (words that transform people into objects) people from welfare to work. Obviously these women would not willingly get jobs.

Though the voices of public officials spoke for and, to a much lesser extent, against reform, they were united in their acceptance of dependency as fact. It was said that states would have to get "tough" (Jeter and Hsu 1996) and that recipients would have to be "steered toward training and work rather than simply handed a check" (Vobejda 1996). The prevailing point of view was that women stayed on welfare for reasons that had nothing to do with the job market and wages; thus reform would save them. Clinton proclaimed that "our nation's answer to this great social challenge will no longer be a never-ending cycle of welfare" (Welfare overhaul 1996). Representative Bill Archer (R-TX) announced that reform would transform "today's welfare trap for the needy into a trampoline to self-sufficiency" (Jouzaitis 1995), and Sen. William V. Roth Jr. (R-DE) proclaimed that reform would replace "the hopelessness of the current system . . . with the hope that comes from self-reliance" (Shogren 1996b). In short, their goal was to rescue these flawed women from themselves. These politicians were knights in shining armor.

Reporters' voices often affirmed congressional sources' presentation of dependency as fact, thus affirming and strengthening the stereotype. One reporter noted that "the White House, Congress and the nation's leading governors all played a role in developing the new welfare framework, which attempts to break the culture of dependency by requiring recipients to work instead of providing them with an open-ended source of subsistence-level support" (Shogren 1996a). The existence of such a culture was simply stated as fact. In another story, a reporter noted that "[AFDC] mostly serves the children of women who are unmarried and unable or unwilling to work" (Richardson 1996). Another reporter noted that recipients were on a "trek toward self-sufficiency" (Alvarez 1996). An aura of facticity surrounded this reportage.

In the end, none of these comments questioned the basic direction. The system was not at any point indicted for being incapable of supporting all citizens with a decent, living wage. The watchdog, apparently, felt there was nothing to be watched.

The emphasis of this reportage was distinctively affected by the opinions offered by welfare recipients who were undeniably placed in an awkward position as sources. Their voices did little to debunk the stereotype of the dependent mother. To present themselves as antireform, for example, was to risk presenting themselves as lacking a work ethic; why else would a recipient, someone defined as dependent, not support legislation designed to lift people such as herself into lives of self-sufficiency and integrity?

The comments by recipients were emotion laden and often served to distance the source from her peers on welfare. In effect, these women's comments set up a me–them dichotomy that supported myth, for their comments shifted attention away from themselves and onto others characterized as less deserving. The message was that while others might be dependent mothers, they were not. For that reason, readers were likely to perceive these recipients as supportive of welfare reform. Examples from the stories reveal that recipients' voices ranged from those who supported reform (and thus protected their own integrity) to those who denigrated the AFDC recipient to those who wanted to work yet feared the outcome of welfare reform. Recipients who rallied behind reform distanced themselves from recipients in general. One woman stressed her optimism, saying, "I believe you've got to try, and this reform thing will make a lot of people try. It will open up a lot of eyes" (Finn 1996). Another recipient relayed that she was "disgusted with what she [felt was] rampant lying among welfare recipients" (Callender 1995), and yet another said she could not "just sit here and take and take and take" (Callender 1995). Yet another woman interviewed for this story said of welfare reform: "I think it's good. There are people who have kids just to get bigger checks" (Callender 1995). These comments all fly in the face of the reality: that low-wage jobs do not make it possible for individuals, particularly those raising families, to make ends meet. They also fail to reveal that recipients tended over time to move on and off welfare based on the viability of the job market (Tim 1996, 2). Further, they support the myth that says single mothers on welfare are lazy and willing to lie, fallacies easily debunked by the literature.

Some women, like some officials, represented a sort of middle ground, generally a more realistic interpretation of the situation. They were only opposed to welfare reform that did not provide sufficient funds for child care. One twenty-six-year-old recipient said, "I'm willing to work—no problem. I don't like welfare at all. But I need help with my daughter. She's just 10 months old. It's hard to find decent baby-sitting nearby" (Stein 1995). Another recipient moved to Minnesota, hoping to find a job and get off welfare, but she said, "I need some help. Child care is where they should be helping me" (Shogren 1996c).

Of the forty-five recipients given a voice in this story, only three expressed point-blank opposition to reform, at least two in such a way that their comments simultaneously denigrated and stigmatized recipients. One said, "I don't see how people who have never worked a day in their lives are going to do this" (Kuczka 1996). Despite having applied for fifty jobs, she had found no employment. Another woman who opposed reform was portrayed in a way that stigmatized, in this case through the reporter's voice as well as her own. This woman, 17, had one child and had earned her GED. She was unable to find work. The reporter wrote that she spoke in "a slow monotone" (Havemann 1996), words that certainly imply stupidity. A third woman, who had done "a short stint on welfare" but at the time of the story was working three jobs, noted that the system simply did not work (LaGanga 1995). The opportunity for the reporter to discuss why this woman needed three different jobs to survive (and how it was that she could work three jobs and be present as a parent) was bypassed.

The use of single mothers as sources, certainly a crucial reportorial approach for this reportage, unfortunately led to the gathering and use of anecdotal information that reinforced the stereotype. The lead to one story represented women on welfare through a recipient whose life "happily, was cooking, cleaning, shopping, television and sitting in her well-worn armchair." Although her husband left her, "the basic rhythm of her life remained unchanged, thanks to the welfare benefits that she then began to receive." The next paragraph continued in this way: "But now another world—as she sees it, a forbidding one with time clocks and bosses and rules—is closing in. The 32-year-old Loudoun County woman would just as soon stay home." And the third paragraph drove home the depiction of a lazy welfare recipient: "I like it here," she says. "I've got my television shows, my video games. I can get up and go out shopping. I'm here in the afternoon when my kid gets home. When my husband was here, I had dinner ready for him" (Finn 1996).

This well-written lead set the tone for the story and hinted at the thesis. The lead of any story is integral to the creation of meaning. The woman selected to represent welfare recipients spoke of her lifestyle as a chosen one. What reader would interpret her behavior as anything other than lazy? In addition, the portrayal is sexist, drawing a parallel between the life of the homemaker and the life of a recipient: both lives, this says, represent easy lives.

The story went on to depict a second woman, also poor, who had only recently gone on AFDC. Prior to the birth of her second child, this woman was "pulling double shifts six or seven days a week to provide for herself and her daughter." She represented the extreme opposite of the first recipient, but managed nonetheless to support the characterization of the first woman, saying that "welfare is like an addiction, tempting you to sit at home" before commenting on her children: "My babies are my life. They are what push me. They make me get out and do what needs to be done, not stay at home and do nothing" (Finn 1996). (Again, the work of the homemaker and mother is trivialized.) Clearly this nineteen-year-old woman who worked double shifts six or seven days a week was the hero in this construction that focused on the work ethic. One might ask, though, why the reporter failed to challenge other questions of value raised by the description. What kind of time could this second woman, forced to work these kinds of hours just to stay off AFDC, have been able to give her first child, three years old at the time the story was written? This mother's words affirm the work ethic and in doing so separate her from "others" who "stay at home and do nothing." Depicted as heroic, she becomes a role model. What does her situation say about the lives of children whose mothers would, after reform legislation passed, have to seek work that would sustain them and their families? Would they too have to work double shifts six or seven days a week?

The second woman depicted could not be characterized as lazy. In fact, one could read her story as exemplifying the difficulties that recipients would face. The story goes on to note that "willing or not" (Finn 1996) recipients in Virginia would have to find jobs as mandated by new statewide welfare legislation. While welfare recipients in this story are held responsible for their poverty, the job market goes unexamined until the final paragraph of the story when the first recipient described asks, "What will happen if you lose your job and you can't find another one" (Finn 1996)? The question goes unanswered. Readers are left to believe that only the lazy recipient will be unable to cope. What was the thesis of this story? Women can make it if they try. And the thesis—in this story if not in reality—is well supported. It is not, however, a fair one, for its cogency comes at the cost of balance.

In short, these women were not given a significant voice regarding their actual experiences in the job market. Only one was described in a depth that enabled an understanding of a recipient's life. At twenty-seven, this woman was raising two children and desired to continue college. But she lost her job and was unable to find another. The reporter described how much this woman made, how much she needed, and why it was difficult for her to overcome her circumstances (Gladwell 1996). The reporter's story gave a voice and a face to someone who would be affected by reform.

These dynamics offer a possible reason for reporters' inability to interview single mothers or decision to interview so few single mothers. The mothers themselves may have been reluctant or felt themselves put in a defensive position. The public official, on the other hand, is more easily represented. Such individuals want their ideas circulated and can be reached via fax, phone, or e-mail. Such circumstances, of course, cannot explain the reasons behind a reporter's choice of either the source or the quotes used for a story.

## REASONS FOR THE THEMATIC CONTENT OF THE WELFARE REPORTAGE

Can we blame the press for its depiction of single mothers on welfare as dependent people who chose not to take "personal responsibility" for the economic well-being of their families?

Clearly Congress resolved to discuss welfare, recipients, and its belief in the necessity of reform during the year before legislation passed. Toward that end, members talked about what was on the agenda: moving welfare recipients toward taking personal responsibility by legislating that they join the paid workforce. Given that, one might argue that the newspapers merely reported on the work of Congress. But it's not as simple as a one-way chicken-and-egg debate. The watchdog did two things: First, it chose to represent more strongly the voices of those who favored reform. Second, it chose not to counter the argument that recipients would be able to find work that would enable them to earn a living wage, that once off reform they would be able to secure a decent-paying job with benefits.

Many explanations for why newspapers reinvigorated a negative stereotype in their reportage are possible. Is it possible that journalists simply relied on the stereotypes embedded in myth to create this story? Perhaps reporters plugged into myth in deciding how to approach stories about welfare. In doing so, they would have applied—and did—a moral frame that left little room for variation in the depiction of mothers on welfare. The printed stories were peopled with collectively known types—archetypes. As Schudson (1989), Swidler (1986) and Best (1991) have shown, the press's decision-making process leads reporters to cast its characters in known roles—villains, heroes, victims. Such was the case here. Mothers played the villains (and sometimes the heroes if they overcame their dependency), children the victims, and politicians the heroes.

Further, the newspapers' dominant point of view, framed by a conservative political and economic perspective, supports leftist hegemony theorists who say journalists, and/or the institutions they work for, choose to ignore or give scant attention to conflict in an effort to maintain the status quo. In supporting the current economic order by failing to critique it, these newspapers recreated again and again the perspective that no alternatives to a capitalistic structure exist. In doing so, they participated in the ongoing maintenance of the current order, which calls for a body of low-wage workers as an enduring part of the picture. In short, these stories did not challenge the fundamental premises of the marketplace. This reportage supported big business—and journalism is big business. It is possible that journalists who pursued this perspective were deferring to unspoken newspaper policy.

The most plausible explanation is that journalists' coverage represented their personal belief in and support of the capitalist system. In other words, they entered the institution of journalism as individuals willing to defend its way of being. The work of Lichter, Rothman and Lichter showed that the "media elite" believed strongly in the fairness of the free enterprise system (70 percent of those surveyed) (1986, 29). Later surveys have shown that "journalists around the country seem to echo the media elite's strong support for private enterprise" (42). Journalists, elites or not, are fairly conservative when it comes to economics, despite describing themselves as liberal in orientation regarding social issues (Lichter, Rothman, and Lichter 1986, 31). Some journalists may have unconsciously packed their belief in the virtues of capitalism into the stories they wrote. They simply took for granted the validity of their belief that work, even low-wage work, would lift people out of poverty. That was their worldview.

Lichter, Rothman, and Lichter found that the majority of the media elite described themselves as liberal in orientation (1986, 31), while Weaver and Wilhoit found that about 47 percent of journalists (1996, 15) considered themselves as such. Lichter, Rothman, and Lichter's work showed that journalists generally support or sympathize with underdogs (95), an alliance that implies a caring attitude, not a detached one. Not so with single mothers.

Perceived as a menace to the nation's economic stability, single mothers on welfare, who stood in contradiction to reporters' belief in the fairness of free enterprise, became villains of a sort, not underdogs. Is "villain" an extreme choice of word? No, for to describe these women as lacking a work ethic when the American Dream is said to be within anyone's grasp was to hold them in contempt. They were shown as standing against a desirable national norm. To validate their experience as low-wage earners would have been to indict the system of free enterprise.

Consciously or not, when reporters failed to challenge welfare reform, they supported enlarging a body of low-wage workers, "undeserving" women, for the continuation of the system. Such an outcome reflects the concerns of Piven and Cloward, who argued that the rescinding of benefits generally coincides with a desire to increase the low-wage labor force (1993, 345). By using a moral frame, journalists and their sources held mothers up as responsible for poverty. The average journalist in the United States has been raised according to a national work ethic—one that colored reporters' perception of the plight of single mothers on welfare. From this point of view, mothers could only be perceived as having "failed" unnecessarily.

## CONCLUSION

These results invite one to consider how the press contributes to the public's ability to understand and think about an issue such as welfare. In what ways does reportage such as this compromise the democratic process? At the end of the day, good journalism should reconstitute reality in as much of its complexity as possible and lead the reader to a better understanding of the world.

The study shows that these newspapers perpetuated the myth of the welfare recipient as flawed and therefore responsible for her poverty. Just as those causes which motivated the Red Brigade were denied legitimacy, so was the life of the welfare recipient denied legitimacy. These newspapers' built-in ability to define this situation and the actors within it gave them an opportunity to disseminate and promote a particular perspective, one that supported the capitalist economic system, private enterprise, free markets, and a Republican congressional agenda—all at the expense (literally) of single mothers and children. Shoemaker and Reese described the power of sourcing when they noted that "we depend on secondhand sources for our knowledge about that part of the world beyond our immediate perceptual grasp, which is most of it" (1991, 34–35). This reportage did not make it possible for the average citizen to grasp the reality of the single mother on welfare.

The press failed on at least two levels: (1) Journalists created reportage that stereotyped recipients, largely a result of a journalistic propensity to interview official, conservative sources for information; (2) journalists presented incomplete reportage, most noticeably neglecting to evaluate whether the job market would, as politicians argued, support single mothers and their children. Because the system went unindicted, single mothers shouldered full responsibility for their poverty. Should a newspaper be held responsible for what it does not say? Yes. An incomplete story is not a fair story. Certainly the statistics on women and children in poverty reveal a need for a more profound understanding of welfare in the United States. In 1996, when reform was enacted, children constituted 40 percent of the poor in the United States, despite their being but 27 percent of the total population (Weinberg 1997, 2). Between 1959 and 1996 the poverty rate for female-headed households remained above 35 percent and close to or over 40 percent (*Green Book* 1998, 1304).

It is essential that citizens understand the lives of welfare recipients. As Gans put it, "Major policy decisions are . . . being made on the basis of massive stereotyping" (1995, 25). By 2002 it became clear that the reform measures enacted in 1996, founded on the fallacious argument that recipients would find adequate financial support in the job market, were failing to alleviate poverty. As of winter 2001–2002, statistics showed that welfare recipients who had lost assistance were struggling to make ends meet during a recession that was dealing blow after blow to the labor market. The healthy economy of the late 1990s did enable many former welfare recipients to find low-wage jobs. Findings suggest, however, that after 1995 "declines in the effectiveness of the safety net in reducing poverty among families headed by working single mothers offset the effect of the improving economy, halting the reduction of the poverty rate for these families and pushing those who remained poor deeper into poverty" (Porter and Dupree 2001, v, 17). Despite a strong economy at the close of the 1990s, the loss of benefits foiled any positive effects a healthy economy might have produced (Porter and Dupree 2001, 17).

As the country moved into a new century, it also crossed the threshold into a recession that saw increases in 2001 both in the general poverty rate and the number of poor, from 11.3 percent and 31.6 million to 11.7 percent and 32.9 million (Proctor and Dalaker 2002, 1). Boushey, a researcher for the Economic Policy Institute, a nonpartisan, nonprofit economic think tank, described the consequences for recipients: "The economy's slide into recession and the fallout from the September terrorist attacks have led to considerable job losses in the very industries in which many welfare recipients had found employment. It will now be difficult for these workers to maintain their tenuous foothold in the labor market, and those who lose their jobs will find a much-weakened safety net available to break their fall into poverty" (2001, 1). Boushey noted that recipients' place in the job market was a "tenuous" one at best, before going on to note that "job losses in most of these industries [namely personnel supply services and the hotels and lodging industries] predated the terrorist attacks" (2). Further, she noted many of these recipients now faced lifetime eligibility limits of fewer than five years (Congress mandated a five-year lifetime limit but gave states leave to set their own limits) as well as state budgets that had "diverted [TANF funds] into programs such as child care and transportation" (3). The result: only 43 percent of TANF block-grants actually provide cash assistance (3). The safety net had disappeared.

According to the reportage examined for this study, poverty follows a poor work ethic. Sadly, such beliefs interfere with efforts society makes to mitigate the effects of poverty or eliminate it entirely. Within this reportage the repetition of stereotypes reinforced inaccurate cultural beliefs about single mothers on welfare. Such beliefs must be debunked to make room for new and better understandings and relationships—and possibly new and better legislative decisions. Myth denies the complexity of life for single mothers struggling to raise children. The myth of the "welfare mother" must be removed as a force; only then will productive change ensue.

## REFERENCES

Altheide, D. L. 1996. *Qualitative media analysis*. Thousand Oaks, Calif.: Sage.
Alvarez, F. 1996. County report: What to do with welfare? *Los Angeles Times*, July 21, A1.
Best, J. 1991. "Road warriors" on "hair-trigger highways": Cultural resources and the media's construction of the 1987 freeway shootings problem. *Sociological Inquiry* 61: 327–45.

Bird, S. E. 1987. Folklore and media as intertextual communication processes: John F. Kennedy and the supermarket tabloids. In M. L. McLaughlin, ed., *Communication yearbook*, vol. 10. Newbury Park, Calif.: Sage.

Bird, S. E., and Dardenne, R. W. 1988. Myth, chronicle, and story: Exploring the narrative qualities of news. In D. Berkowitz, ed., *Social meanings of news: A text-reader*, 333–50. Thousand Oaks, Calif.: Sage.

Boushey, H. 2001. Last hired, first fired: Job losses plague former TANF recipients. *EPI Issue Brief*. Washington, D.C.: Economic Polity Institute.

Brown, J. D., Bybee, C. R., Wearden, S. T., and Straughan, D. 1987. Invisible power: Newspaper news sources and the limits of diversity. *Journalism Quarterly* 64: 45–54.

Callender, E. 1995. Drawing the line: Even some welfare mothers call "family cap" a good idea. *Los Angeles Times*, August 2, A1.

Children's rally attracts 200,000 in Washington. 1996. *Houston Chronicle*, June 2, A1.

Colby, I. C. 1989. *Social welfare policy: Perspectives, patterns, insights*. Chicago: Dorsey.

Edin, K., and Lein, L. 1997. *Making ends meet: How single mothers survive welfare and low-wage work*. New York: Russell Sage Foundation.

Eyer, D. 1996. *Mother guilt: How our culture blames mothers for what's wrong with society*. New York: Random House.

Finn, 1996. Changing welfare: The next test as job rules kick in: One northern Virginia mother is optimistic, another is anxious. *Washington Post*, March 25, A1.

Gans, H. J. 1979. *Deciding what's news: A study of CBS Evening News, NBC Nightly News, Newsweek, and Time*. New York: Vintage.

———. 1995. *The war against the poor: The underclass and antipoverty policy*. New York: Basic.

Gladwell, M. 1996. A precarious balancing act, a smaller net: As social spending contracts, many fall. *Washington Post*, May 25, A1.

Golding, P. and Middleton, S. 1982. *Images of welfare. Press and public attitudes to poverty*. Oxford: Martin Robertson.

*Green Book*. 1996. Committee on Ways and Means, U.S. House of Representatives Report. 104-14. Washington, D.C.: Government Printing Office.

———. 1998. Committee on Ways and Means, U.S. House of Representatives Report. 105-7. Washington, D.C: Government Printing Office.

Handler, J. F. 1995. *The poverty of welfare reform*. New Haven, Conn.: Yale University Press.

Harris, K. M. 1993. Work and welfare among single mothers in poverty. *American Journal of Sociology* 99: 317–52.

———. 1997. *Teen mothers and the revolving welfare door*. Philadelphia: Temple University Press.

Havemann, J. 1996. Welfare reform for teens runs into harsh reality; live-at-home rule assumes home is suitable. *Washington Post*, June 4, A1.

Jarrett, R. L. 1996. Welfare stigma among low-income, African American single mothers. *Family Relations* 45: 368–74.

Jencks, C. 1997. The hidden paradox of welfare reform. *American Prospect*, May-June, 33–40. http://epn.org/prospect/32/32jenkfs.html.

Jeter, J., and Hsu, S. S. 1996. Va. and Md. chart own welfare course, but federal government guides D.C.'s. *Washington Post*, August 2, A1.

Jouzaitis, C. 1995. House OKs Republican welfare bill; veto expected if Senate passes it. *Chicago Tribune*, December 22, A1.

Katz, M. B. 1989. *The undeserving poor: From the war on poverty to the war on welfare.* New York: Pantheon.

Kluegel, J. R. 1987. Macro-economic problems, beliefs about the poor attitudes toward welfare spending. *Social Problems* 14: 82–99.

Kuczka, S. 1996. Wisconsin welfare recipients skeptical of reform. *Chicago Tribune,* May 25, A1.

LaGanga, M. L. 1995. Race, welfare reform join economy as central issues. *Los Angeles Times,* November 6, A1.

Lichter, S., Rothman, S., and Lichter, L. 1986. *The media elite.* Bethesda, Md.: Adler & Adler.

Mallegg, K., ed. 1998. *Gale directory of publications and broadcast media.* Detroit: Gale Research.

McClure, L. 1994. Working the risk shift. *Progressive* 58: 23–27.

Nelson-Pallmeyer, J. 1996. *Families valued: Parenting and politics for the good of all children.* New York: Friendship.

Paletz, D. L., Fozzard, A., and Ayanian, J. Z. 1982. The I.R.A., the Red Brigades, and the F.A.L.N. in the *New York Times. Journal of Communication* 32: 162–71.

Piven, F. F., and Cloward, R. A. 1993. *Regulating the poor: The functions of public welfare.* New York: Vintage.

Porter, K., and Dupree, A. 2001. Poverty trends for families headed by working single mothers: 1993 to 1999. Washington, D.C.: Center on Budget and Polity Priorities.

Proctor, B., and Dalaker, J. 2002. Poverty in the United States: 2001. *Current Population Reports,* P60-219. Washington, D.C.: U.S. Department of Commerce, Bureau of the Census.

Richardson, L. 1996. Welfare reforms outlined. *Los Angeles Times,* July 24, A1.

Rivers, C. 1996. *Slick spins and fractured facts: How cultural myths distort news.* New York: Columbia University Press.

Rose, N. E. 1995. *Workfare or fair work: Women, welfare, and government work programs.* New Brunswick, N.J.: Rutgers University Press.

Schein, V. E. 1995. *Working from the margins: Voices of mothers in poverty.* Ithaca, N.Y.: Cornell University Press.

Schudson, M. 1989. The sociology of news production. *Media, Culture, and Society* 11: 263–82.

Seiler, N. 2002. *Is teen marriage a solution?* Washington, D.C.: Center for Law and Social Policy.

Shoemaker, J., and Reese, S. D. 1991. *Mediating the message: Theories of influences on mass media content.* New York: Longman.

Shogren, E. 1996a. Clinton accepts broad welfare changes as "last best chance." *Los Angeles Times,* August 1, A1.

———. 1996b. Senate approves welfare reform. *Los Angeles Times,* July 24, A1.

———. 1996c. Child-care needs dash dreams of leaving welfare. *Los Angeles Times,* September 5, A1.

———. 1996d. Values program for teen mothers tries to stop cycle. *Los Angeles Times,* August 7, A1.

Sidel, R. 1996. *Keeping women and children last: America's war on the poor.* New York: Penguin.

Sigal, L. V. 1973. *Reporters and officials: The organization and politics of newsmaking.* Lexington, Mass.: Heath.

———. 1986. Sources make the news. In R. K. Manoff and M. Schudson, eds., *Reading the news: A pantheon guide to popular culture*, 9–37. New York: Pantheon.

Spalter-Roth, R. M., Burr, B., Hartmann, H., and Shaw, L. 1995. *Welfare that works: The working lives of AFDC recipients*. A report to the Ford Foundation. Washington, D.C.: Institute for Women's Policy Research.

*Statistical Abstract of the United States*. 1998. Washington, D.C.: U.S. Department of Commerce, Bureau of the Census.

*Status of women in the states: Politics, economics, health, demographics*. 1996. A report funded by the Ford Foundation. Washington, D.C.: Institute for Women's Policy Research.

Stein, S. 1995. 8,000 on welfare are told to get a job or lose benefits. *Chicago Tribune*, November 2, A1.

Swidler, A. 1986. Culture in action. *American Sociological Review* 51: 273–86.

The labor revival. 1995. *Los Angeles Times*, September 3, A1.

Tim, J. 1996. Who gets assistance? *Current Population Reports*, P70-58. Washington, D.C.: U.S. Department of Commerce, Bureau of the Census.

Tuchman, G. 1978. *Making news: A study in the construction of reality*. New York: Free Press.

Turner, J. H., and Starnes, C. E. 1976. *Inequality: Privilege and poverty in America*. Santa Monica, Calif.: Goodyear Publishing.

Vobejda, B. 1996. After 60 years, a basic shift in philosophy. *Washington Post*, August 1, A1.

Weaver, D. H., and Wilhoit, G. C. 1996. *The American journalist in the 1990s: U.S. news people at the end of an era*. Mahwah, N.J.: Lawrence Erlbaum.

Weinberg, D. H. 1997. Press briefing on 1996 income, poverty, and health insurance estimates. Washington, D.C.: U.S. Department of Commerce, Bureau of the Census.

Welfare overhaul becomes law by signing a bill ending dole as we know it; Clinton hopes to do same to opponent Dole. 1996. *Chicago Tribune*, August 22, A1.

Wilson, G. 1996. Toward a revised framework for examining beliefs about the causes of poverty. *Sociological Quarterly* 37: 413–28.

# 3

# Poor People in the News: Images from the Journalistic Subconscious

*Martin Gilens*

Accuracy remains a high priority for America's news reporting organizations. For most mainstream news media—whether print or electronic—a reputation for factual reporting is an important asset and journalists strive to provide accurate information to their audience. But the standards for truth and accuracy that are applied to the text of news stories are often not extended to the images that those same stories contain.

In this chapter, I contrast the generally accurate representation of American poverty in the text of newsmagazine stories with the strong racial biases in the pictorial representation of the poor. I argue that in their impact on readers' perceptions, pictures are indeed worth a thousand words. After documenting the changing racial imagery of the poor in American newsmagazines, I assess a variety of possible explanations for the misrepresentation of the poor in the news. I conclude that the racial distortions in poverty coverage are best explained by news professionals' subconscious stereotypes of African Americans. Finally, I make use of the research literature in social psychology to identify the conditions under which subconscious stereotyping can be overcome. I argue that racial biases are not inevitable, and that deliberate efforts to monitor the pictorial representation of poverty can help to combat—rather than reinforce—Americans' misperceptions of the poor.

The analyses of media content contained in this chapter are based on my examination of stories on poverty published between 1950 and 1992 in *Time, Newsweek,* and *U.S. News and World Report.* I chose these newsmagazines because they are widely read, are national in coverage and distribution, and have been published continuously for many years. In addition, they contain many pictures, an especially important consideration in studying the racial portrayal of the poor. Finally, my more limited analysis of television news coverage of poverty suggests that the patterns found in the newsmagazines are shared by network television news (see Gilens 1999 for more details of the newsmagazine analysis as well as comparative analysis of television news).

To assess newsmagazine poverty coverage, I examined every story indexed under the headings "poor," "poverty," "welfare," and "relief," as well as cross-referenced topics in the *Readers' Guide to Periodical Literature* (see Gilens 1996a, 1999). In all, I collected 1,256 stories that included pictures of 6,117 poor people. I was able to determine the race of about three-quarters of the poor people pictured in these stories, with an intercoder reliability of .87 (see Gilens 1999 for details).

## RACE AND POVERTY IN AMERICA

My analysis of news coverage of poverty focuses on the racial representation of the poor for a simple reason: the public's attitudes toward poverty and welfare are strongly shaped by perceptions of African Americans and beliefs about the racial composition of the poor. Among whites, the belief that blacks are lazy is strongly related to the perception of welfare recipients as undeserving, and both of these attitudes are powerful predictors of opposition to welfare (Gilens 1996b, 1999).

Even white Americans' perceptions of the simple demographic composition of the poor predicts their attitudes toward welfare recipients. One survey question, for example, asked what is more to blame when people are on welfare: lack of effort or circumstances beyond their control. Among white Americans who think that most welfare recipients are white, fully 50 percent attribute welfare use to "circumstances beyond their control." But among whites who think that most welfare recipients are black, only 26 percent blame circumstances while 63 percent attribute welfare use to a lack of effort.[1]

## THE POWER OF PICTURES

Pictures of poor people can powerfully convey the texture of poverty and the experience of deprivation, as Dorothea Lange's remarkable photographs from the Great Depression do. While most news images of the poor do not rise to this level of expressive power, they do convey important information to readers or viewers. Whatever their artistic or emotional content, pictures of poor people in the news almost always communicate a more specific kind of information: the age, sex, and race of the poor.

There is good reason to think that magazine readers' perceptions of the racial composition of America's poor are shaped more by the images they encounter in the news than by the text of the stories that accompany those images. First, most newsmagazine stories on poverty include photographs of poor people while only a small minority of stories include textual information about the demographic composition of the poor.[2] Second, even when factual information about the racial makeup of the poor is included in the text of a news story, there is good reason to think that readers will be more swayed by the images that accompany that information. Research has shown that people are more likely to remember the pictures in a news story than the words, and more likely to be swayed by examples of individuals than by statistical information.[3]

Finally, most newsmagazine readers do not read each issue cover to cover. Instead they skim through the magazine, looking at pictures and headlines, and read only the articles (or parts of articles) that they find particularly interesting. Thus even readers who do not read a particular poverty-related story are still likely to be exposed to the pictures of the poor that the story contains.

Pictures are simple and immediate, and the race of those pictured can be absorbed at a glance. Processing words takes more time and effort. And even when factual information is attended to and remembered, the power of vivid examples will often outweigh the factual information contained in dry statistics. In short, it would be unrealistic to expect the occasional factual statements within the text of news stories to correct the racial misrepresentation of American poverty reflected in the pictures of the poor that those stories contain.

## NEWSMAGAZINE PORTRAYALS OF THE POOR

Throughout most of American history, public discussions of poverty ignored the African American poor. From the first scientific efforts to document the country's poor in the late nineteenth century to the emergence of poverty as a national issue in the early 1960s, the black poor were conspicuous only by their absence.

During the mid-1960s, however, poor blacks emerged from obscurity to become the focus of public attention to poverty. This dramatic transformation is evident in the photographs that accompanied newsmagazine stories on poverty. During the 1950s fewer than 20 percent of the poor people pictured in newsmagazines were African American (figure 3.1). This proportion increased slightly during the early 1960s and then accelerated, rising from only 27 percent in 1964 to 49 percent in 1965 and 72 percent in 1967.

As the thin line in figure 3.1 shows, the change in the racial representation of the poor during the 1960s cannot be explained by any true change in the proportion of blacks among the poor. Instead, three kinds of factors help to explain the racialization of poverty in the news media.

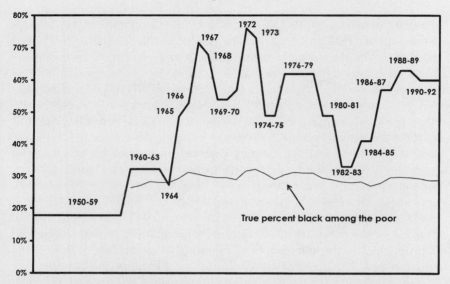

**Figure 3.1. Percentage of African Americans in News Magazine Pictures of the Poor, 1950–1992**

First, a number of broad social changes set the stage for changing racial imagery of the poor. One such change was the widespread migration of rural southern blacks to northern cities. At the beginning of the twentieth century, over 90 percent of African Americans lived in the South, primarily in rural areas.[4] As a result of migration, the population of northern, urban blacks grew steadily during the 1940s and 1950s, and continued to grow, though at a slower rate, in the 1960s.[5] But as figure 3.1 shows, the racialization of public images of the poor occurred quite suddenly and dramatically between 1965 and 1967. Clearly there is no simple connection between the growth of African American communities in northern cities and public perceptions of the poor as black. Nevertheless, the growth of the black population in the North facilitated the shift in media images and public attention that occurred during the mid-1960s.

A second change that paved the way for the racialization of poverty images was the changing racial composition of AFDC, the nation's most conspicuous program to aid the poor. At its inception in the 1930s, only 14 percent of ADC (Aid to Dependent Children, as it was then called) beneficiaries were African American (Lieberman 1995). Over the next three decades, however, the proportion of blacks among ADC recipients rose steadily in response to legislative, judicial, and economic developments. The percentage of African Americans among ADC/AFDC recipients increased steadily from about 14 percent in 1936 to about 45 percent in 1969, after which the proportion of blacks declined slowly until it reached about 36 percent in 1995. (Blacks currently comprise about 39 percent of the beneficiaries of Temporary Assistance to Needy Families, the successor to AFDC.)[6]

During the mid to late 1960s, then, African Americans made up a substantial minority of AFDC recipients. Yet the pattern of change in the AFDC caseload also makes clear that the sudden shift in images of poverty during the 1960s cannot be attributed to any sudden change in the makeup of the welfare population. The proportion of blacks among AFDC participants had been growing steadily for decades. Like black migration to the North, the changing racial composition of the welfare roles constituted a background condition that contributed to the changes in public perceptions of the poor, but it did not serve as a precipitating cause of those changes. After all, the proportion of blacks among welfare recipients was nearly as high in 1960 as it was in 1967, yet public concern in 1960 was still focused on poor whites, in particular, the rural white poor of Appalachia.

Two other factors were more proximate influences on the changes in the media's racial representation of the poor: the urban riots that erupted in American cities in the summers of 1965 through 1968 and the shift in focus of the civil rights movement from the fight against legal inequality to the battle against economic inequality. Economic inequality had long been a concern of the country's black leaders, but this struggle had been largely eclipsed during the 1950s and early 1960s by the effort to end Jim Crow segregation and to secure black voting rights in the South. By the mid-1960s, however, important victories had been made in ending legal discrimination and in 1966 Martin Luther King and the Southern Christian Leadership Conference turned their attention to Chicago, where they organized demonstrations and rent strikes to dramatize the dire economic conditions facing blacks throughout the country.

The urban riots, the shifting focus of the civil rights movement, and the rise of a new generation of militant black leaders contributed to the public visibility of the black poor. Yet as dramatic and important as these events were, they cannot explain the timing of the racialization of poverty in the news since the numbers of poor blacks in news stories jumped even before the shift in focus of civil rights leaders or the urban riots became prominent.

## THE WAR ON POVERTY AND CHANGING
## MEDIA PORTRAYALS OF THE POOR

President Johnson launched the War on Poverty in January 1964, and media attention to poverty jumped dramatically. The number of newsmagazine stories on poverty increased fivefold from the years immediately preceding the Johnson administration's initiatives (Gilens 1999, 113). But this early coverage of the war on poverty remained focused on poor whites.

A good example of poverty coverage from this time is the twelve-page cover story that *Newsweek* ran on February 17, 1964. The cover of the magazine showed a white girl, about eight or ten years old, looking out at the reader from a rustic shack, her hair disheveled and her face covered with dirt. This story profiled poor people from around the country: an elderly couple from Portland, a family of ten living without electricity or running water in rural Georgia, a "Main Street wino" in Los Angeles, young students in a one-room school in West Virginia. Of the fifty-four poor people pictured in this story, only fourteen were black.

This story was typical of War on Poverty coverage during 1964 in its substantial focus on rural poverty, its emphasis on images of poor whites, and its generally neutral tone toward the Johnson administration's antipoverty efforts. The expansion of news coverage that accompanied the War on Poverty did not coincide with the racialization of poverty images; at its inception at least, the War on Poverty was associated more with poor whites than poor blacks.

## THE RACIALIZATION OF POVERTY IN THE NEWS

The turning point in the racialization of poverty in the news came in 1965. Coverage of poverty in that year remained focused primarily on the War on Poverty, but the tone of coverage changed. Instead of offering neutral stories describing the Johnson administration's new antipoverty initiatives or broad portraits of the American poor, poverty stories in 1965 were much harsher examinations of the government's antipoverty efforts and much more critical portraits of the poor. And these stories included far larger numbers of African Americans than stories on the War on Poverty from the year before.

News stories about the Job Corps, one of the first War on Poverty programs to get off the ground, illustrate the negative coverage of the War on Poverty during this period. These stories focused on problems such as poor screening of participants, high dropout rates, the irresponsible behavior of Job Corps members, and the tension between Job Corps centers and nearby towns. In sharp contrast with stories on the War on Poverty from 1964, the negative reports about the Job Corps, as well as other aspects of the War on Poverty, were illustrated primarily with pictures of African Americans.

The increasing focus on the black poor that began in 1965 continued over the next few years. As figure 3.1 shows, newsmagazine stories on poverty contained even higher proportions of African Americans in 1966 and 1967. During a period in which the true percentage of African Americans among the poor hardly changed at all, but in which poverty discourse became decidedly more negative, blacks came to dominate images of the poor in the media. In the decades that followed, the racial representation of the poor in these magazines fluctuated, but the tendency to over-represent blacks was strong. In the twenty-five years between 1967 and 1992, 57 percent of newsmagazine images of poor were black, almost twice the true rate of 29.5 percent over this period.

## CHANGING RACIAL IMAGERY OF THE POOR

The tendency of the news media to associate blacks with negative stories on poverty and whites with neutral or positive stories is not limited to the war on poverty. During the decades since the 1960s, the proportion of African Americans in poverty stories has risen and fallen; the highest percentage of blacks have appeared in periods when the media discourse on poverty is most negative, and the lowest percentage in the more sympathetic coverage that tends to accompany economic downturns. As figure 3.1 shows, the highest proportions of blacks among the poor were found in 1972 and 1973, while the images of poverty appearing during the economic recessions of 1974–1975 and 1982–1983 were much whiter.

Coverage of poverty during 1972 and 1973 focused primarily on problems with welfare and efforts at welfare reform. Between the mid-1960s and the mid-1970s, spending on welfare increased dramatically and by the early 1970s, the expansion of welfare had come to be viewed as an urgent national problem. Stories published during 1972 and 1973 almost invariably referred to this situation as the "welfare mess" and the weekly newsmagazines offered story after story focusing on mismanagement in welfare bureaucracies or abuse of welfare by people who could be supporting themselves. This sustained negative coverage of welfare was accompanied by the highest proportions of blacks of any point during the entire forty-three-year period examined.

In stark contrast to the negative poverty stories of the early 1970s, newsmagazine poverty coverage during the "Reagan recession" of the early 1980s was extremely supportive of the country's poor. Focusing on the faltering economy and the Reagan administration's efforts to "trim the safety net," these stories contained the smallest proportion of blacks since the racialization of poverty in 1965.

A good example of this sympathetic coverage is *Newsweek's* prominent story titled "The Hard-Luck Christmas of '82," which proclaimed, "With 12 million unemployed and 2 million homeless, private charity cannot make up for federal cutbacks." This story went on to describe the desperate condition of poor families living in tents or in automobiles, portraying them as noble victims "who are paying the price of America's failure of nerve in the war on poverty." Reflecting the general lack of black faces in these sympathetic poverty stories, "The Hard-Luck Christmas of '82" included only seventeen African Americans among the ninety poor people pictured.

It is not surprising that poverty is portrayed in a more sympathetic light during economic hard times. What is noteworthy, however, is that shifts in the tone of news reporting on the poor are accompanied by shifts in the racial mix of the poor people in news stories. The true proportion of blacks among America's poor remained virtually constant throughout these decades, but the racial portrayals of the poor in newsmagazines shifted dramatically as media attention turned from highly critical coverage of welfare during the early 1970s to highly sympathetic stories on poverty during the recession of the early 1980s.

## NEWSMAGAZINE PORTRAYALS OF POVERTY SUBGROUPS

As we've seen, black faces in news stories become more numerous when the discourse on poverty becomes most critical of the poor, and less numerous when outlooks on poverty become more sympathetic. A similar tendency is found in comparisons of news stories about different poverty subgroups: black faces are most likely to be found in stories about the least sympathetic subgroups of the poor, while whites are found more frequently among the most sympathetic groups.

One example of a clearly deserving subgroup is the working poor. Their willingness to work shows that their poverty is not a result of indolence, and that they share the "middle class" commitment to responsibility and self-support. In reality, poor blacks are less likely to be working than the non-black poor, but the difference is small (42 percent versus 54 percent). In newsmagazine stories, however, poor nonblacks were over twice as likely to be shown working as poor blacks.[7]

Another sympathetic group among the poor are the elderly, who are not expected to be working. Once again, poor blacks were portrayed more negatively and less accurately than nonblacks. Although black faces made up a majority of the working-age poor in these magazines, less than one-fifth of older poor people in newsmagazines were black. Once they reach retirement age, poor blacks seem to disappear from the news even more completely than poor whites.

African Americans were scarce in news portrayals of the working poor and the elderly poor, but there was one group of poor people in the news where black faces were the only ones to be found. In newsmagazine stories about the underclass published between 1950 and 1992, every single poor person pictured was African American. Of all the subgroups of the poor, the underclass—associated with crime, drugs, out-of-wedlock births, and "welfare as a way of life"—is perhaps the least sympathetic. And in news accounts, it is the most black.

These patterns of media coverage are not wholly divorced from reality. Compared with nonblacks, African Americans *are* disproportionately found among the underclass,[8] and blacks are slightly underrepresented among the elderly poor and the working poor. Similarly, the proportion of blacks among welfare recipients is somewhat higher than the proportion among the poor as a whole (41 percent versus 29 percent for the period studied). But the real-life racial differences are small in comparison to the huge differences in news images. Readers who relied on these magazines for their information about the American poor would likely believe that there are few blacks among the working poor or those of retirement age, and that African Americans entirely account for America's underclass. The media's demographic misrepresentation of the American poor reflects negatively on the poor as a whole, but it reflects even more negatively (and less accurately) on poor blacks.

## EXPLAINING MEDIA MISREPRESENTATIONS OF THE POOR

In recent decades, African Americans have been dramatically overrepresented in newsmagazine images of the poor. More importantly, perhaps, African Americans were consistently associated with the least sympathetic subgroups of the poor and were most prominent in these magazines during periods when the discourse on poverty was most negative.

Why do journalists—traditionally regarded as politically liberal and sympathetic to disadvantaged groups—create news stories that distort American poverty and portray the black poor in an unfairly negative light?

One might suppose that the location of news bureaus in large cities could explain the tendency to over-represent the black poor. But contrary to popular perceptions, most poor people in large cities are not black. In the nation's ten largest metropolitan areas, for example, blacks make up 32 percent of all poor people, only slightly higher than their representation among America's poor overall.[9]

It is true that in the poorest neighborhoods of the country's largest cities, the proportion of blacks is higher. But even these inner-city neighborhoods contain large numbers of nonblacks. If news photographers, producers, and editors truly sought a more balanced racial portrayal of the poor, it would not be hard to achieve—even if they restricted themselves to the poorest neighborhoods of the country's largest cities.

Most tellingly, racial distortions in poverty coverage vary dramatically over time and across subgroups of the poor. The concentration of poor blacks in inner cities cannot explain the sudden "whitening" of poverty images when news coverage of the poor becomes more sympathetic. Nor can it explain the lack of black faces in stories about sympathetic subgroups like the elderly or the working poor.

If the racial geography of America's poor cannot explain the racially distorted coverage of poverty, we must consider the *perceptions* of the poor held by those who produce the news. Surveys show that most Americans exaggerate the extent to which blacks compose America's poor. When asked on one survey whether most poor people in this country are black or white, 55 percent of respondents chose blacks and only 24 percent white.[10] When another survey simply asked what proportion of America's poor are black, the median response was 50 percent.[11]

We might expect the journalists who work in elite news media to have more accurate perceptions of social conditions than the average American.

To assess whether journalists' own misperceptions could explain the racial distortions of the poor in newsmagazine photographs, I interviewed the photo editors responsible for stories on poverty at *Time, Newsweek,* and *U.S. News and World Report.* Newsmagazine stories on American poverty appear primarily in either the national news section, which tends to contain hard news stories such as government poverty or unemployment statistics, or the society section, which contains softer news like stories on runaways, welfare hotels, and so on. At each magazine, I spoke with the senior photo editors in charge of these two sections.[12]

I asked each of the editors I contacted what percentage of all the poor people in America they thought were black. As a group, these photo editors shared the public's misperceptions regarding the racial composition of the poor, but not to the same degree. On average, the six photo editors I spoke with estimated that 42 percent of America's poor people are black, less than the public's estimate of 50 percent, but still higher than the true figure of 27 percent. To some extent, then, the overrepresentation of blacks in newsmagazine stories on poverty might reflect the misperceptions of the news professionals who produce these images. But in newsmagazine stories from the time period of these interviews, blacks composed fully 62 percent of all poor people pictured, so the misperceptions of the photo editors who choose these images is a partial explanation at best.

More importantly, perhaps, blacks were not simply overrepresented in poverty stories; they were differentially associated with the least sympathetic aspects of poverty. As already noted, journalists' reputation as political liberals would seem at variance with the unfairly negative portrayals of the black poor documented above. But even liberal whites, surveys show, often harbor the same negative racial stereotypes as other white Americans.

When a recent survey asked white respondents to place blacks as a group on a scale from hard-working on one end to lazy on the other, far more whites chose the lazy side of the scale. Even whites who called themselves liberals more often labeled blacks "lazy" than "hard-working."[13]

Journalists may differ in their racial views from other liberal whites, of course, and may be less likely to consider African Americans lazy. But stereotypes function at the subconscious as well as the conscious level, and the choice of examples with which to illustrate stories on poverty may depend as much on subconscious judgments about which pictures "work best" as on conscious evaluations of blacks and the poor.

## THE PSYCHOLOGY OF STEREOTYPING

Psychologists have shown that even people who consciously reject a particular stereotype may nevertheless use that stereotype subconsciously to evaluate social groups. The notion of a subconscious stereotype draws on the idea that people hold a variety of beliefs and perceptions that guide their behavior but of which they are normally unaware. When people act purposefully and reflectively, their conscious beliefs guide their actions, but when they act on impulse, their implicit or subconscious stereotypes can influence their decisions.

One technique that psychologists have used to measure implicit stereotypes is to subconsciously prime experimental participants to think about blacks, but the priming is done in such a way that the participants are unaware that they have been exposed to a racial prime. For example, in one influential study, Patricia Devine used a tachistoscope, a device that flashes words on a screen so briefly that observers cannot consciously make out what words have been presented (Devine 1989). Devine randomly divided her (all-white) subjects into two groups, one of which was shown words associated with blacks (e.g., "Negroes," "blacks," and "Africa") while the other was shown neutral words unrelated to race (e.g., "number," "said," and "sentences"). She then presented both groups with a description of a hypothetical individual named Donald engaging in a number of behaviors that might or might not be judged to be hostile (such as refusing to pay his rent until his apartment is repainted). Donald's race was not indicated in the description, with the expectation that those subjects who were exposed to race-related primes would apply their own stereotypes of blacks when interpreting Donald's behavior, while subjects who were exposed to race-neutral primes would not. After reading the description of Donald's actions, the subjects were asked to evaluate how hostile they thought he was.

Devine found that subjects who were subconsciously exposed to the black-related words judged Donald's behaviors to be more hostile than those exposed to the non–race related primes. This difference emerged despite the fact that subjects were unable to tell what words they had been exposed to via the tachistoscope. Devine interpreted this finding as showing that racial stereotypes (in this case the stereotype of blacks as hostile) can be activated subconsciously, without the person holding these stereotypes being aware. By being subconsciously made to think about blacks, the white subjects applied their existing negative stereotypes in evaluating the ambiguous behavior of the hypothetical "Donald." Those subjects exposed to the non–race related primes, however, did not interpret Donald's actions in the context of race, and consequently saw his ambiguous behavior as less hostile.

Another aspect of Devine's experiment is even more significant for our purposes. When Devine separated her subjects into those who scored high on a survey-type measure of racial prejudice and those who scored low, she found that both groups were equally affected by the racial priming. By subconsciously making blacks salient to her subjects, Devine caused both the ostensibly high-prejudice and the ostensibly low-prejudice subjects to apply negative stereotypes of blacks to their evaluations of Donald's behavior. In contrast, when simply asked to list their (conscious) thoughts in response to black Americans, Devine found that high-prejudice subjects were much more likely than their low-prejudice counterparts to include themes like hostile, violent, or aggressive. When thinking consciously about blacks, the low-prejudice subjects rejected the stereotype of blacks as hostile, but when reacting subconsciously, they drew on this stereotype nonetheless.

Devine and other "implicit stereotyping" researchers theorize that most people in our culture are exposed to a set of stereotypes about blacks (and other social groups) that they internalize to varying degrees. Because these stereotypes are internalized, those who consciously reject them must make a deliberate effort to disregard these stereotypes in their everyday lives. When acting subconsciously, however, these same rejected stereotypes can influence people's perceptions and behaviors. The profound implication of this research is that goodwill toward blacks and a conscious rejection of negative stereotypes are not enough to guarantee that the insidious beliefs about African Americans that are part of our culture will not influence behavior. In order to rise above these negative stereotypes, we must become conscious of their operation and purposefully act to defuse their influence over our judgments. Of course, not everyone holds the same subconscious stereotypes of blacks, or of any other group.[14] But studies of implicit stereotyping suggest that negative stereotypes of blacks (and others) are widespread and can influence the behavior of even those who explicitly reject these stereotypes.

This account of the shaping of news images as a subconscious process is bolstered by the fact that none of the photo editors I talked with had any clear idea about the racial breakdown of the photos of poor people that appeared in their magazines. When told that newsmagazine pictures of the poor over the previous five years were about 62 percent black, many expressed considerable surprise.

## AVOIDING SUBCONSCIOUS STEREOTYPING

To overcome the influence of subconscious stereotypes, news professionals, like other Americans, must consciously "monitor" their reactions to racially charged stimuli. To avoid stereotyping, the subconscious process must be made conscious. One series of experiments that nicely illustrates both the tendency toward subconscious stereotyping and the conditions under which it can be avoided used a "false memory" paradigm to assess racial bias (see Banaji and Bhaskar 2000).

In the first version of this experiment, subjects were given a list of names, some of which, they were told, were the names of criminals that they might remember having heard in the news. In fact, none of the names were of criminals, but were instead chosen as "white-sounding" or "black-sounding" names (for example, Frank Smith and Adam McCarthy on the one hand, Tyrone

Washington and Darnel Jones on the other). Subjects were then asked to try to identify which of the names on the list belonged to criminals. Under these conditions, almost twice as many "black names" as "white names" were identified as criminals, showing the operation of racial stereotyping. As was true in the "Donald" experiment described above, the bias against African Americans emerged for white subjects who expressed positive conscious attitudes toward blacks just as it did among those who expressed negative conscious attitudes.

In order to assess the conditions under which subconscious stereotyping could be eliminated, the next version of the experiment "warned" a random subset of the subjects about the possibility of subconscious stereotyping. These subjects were told that "people have been found to associate criminality with African Americans more than with whites, Asians, or other ethnic groups. This is true for people who believe they have race prejudices (people who are racist) as well as for those of us who believe we are not prejudiced. Please try not to be influenced by the race of the name in making your judgments."

Unlike the subjects in the first experiment, those who had been warned to avoid racial stereotyping identified equal numbers of black and white names. By making the "hidden" racial dimension of the task salient, subjects were able to use their conscious control to combat the effect of subconscious stereotypes.

The process of choosing images to accompany news stories operates at many levels at once, and varies from individual to individual and story to story. At times, the process can be quite deliberate while at other times it is primarily subconscious or intuitive. Among the photo editors I talked with, some expressed a strong concern that the images they produce accurately reflect the reality of the topic. These editors expressed their determination to avoid stereotyping. When I asked one editor at *U.S. News and World Report* how pictures are selected for stories on poverty, he said "I begin by approaching things in the negative. I have little voices in the back of my head reminding me of things that I don't want to do. I don't want to do a dishonest portrayal. . . . In particular, we're very careful about racial issues. . . . I guess if I had to put it all in one word its clearly fairness."[15]

This concern with fairness in general, and an honest racial representation of the poor in particular was shared by some of the other photo editors I talked with, but not all. For other editors, what mattered was the emotional power of the image. As an editor at *Time* magazine put it "I will pick the picture that's most moving, disturbing, dramatic or graphic. . . . Race doesn't come into the decision in terms of I may choose one picture over another if its black or white."[16]

As the experimental literature in psychology shows, without the "little voices in our heads" reminding us not to draw on our (subconscious) stereotypes, racial biases are likely to find expression in the judgments we make. The first condition, then, necessary to improve the racial representation of the poor in the news is to make fairness and accuracy a more universal concern among photographers, editors, and others responsible for the production of news images.

But psychologists' experiments with subconscious stereotypes also suggest that the motivation to avoid stereotyping is not in itself enough. Sufficient cognitive resources must also be available to allow the conscious efforts at overcoming stereotypes to succeed. One of the reasons people use stereotypes is because they simplify decision making. Rather than attend to the specifics of an individual or group, relying on a stereotype provides a cognitive shortcut. Consequently, psychologists have shown that people are more likely to use stereotypes when they are pressed for time or face other limitations on the cognitive resources they can devote to a decision (Macrae, Hewstone, and Griffiths 1993; Macrae, Milne, and Bodenhausen 1994; Payne 2001).

The ability of time constraints to interfere with efforts to avoid stereotyping was also shown in the criminal names experiments. In a final version of this experiment, both the subjects who were provided with an explicit warning about stereotyping and those who were not were then divided further. One half of each group were told that they must complete the "criminal identification" task within one minute, while the other half were allowed to take as much time as they liked.

Among the self-paced subjects, the stereotype warning worked as before: those who received the warning showed no racial bias and those who did not receive the warning identified more black than white names as belonging to criminals. But among the time-pressured subjects, *both* groups—those who were warned about stereotyping and those who were not—revealed a racial bias in their selection of names. In other words, even those motivated to avoid racial stereotyping were unsuccessful in doing so if they were pressed for time.

Time pressure is, of course, a common part of the news business. The weekly newsmagazines have a somewhat more relaxed schedule than the daily (or more frequent) deadlines of television and newspapers, but even at the newsmagazines the time pressure is substantial (e.g., Gans 1979). In order to avoid the negative stereotypes of blacks which my analysis of newsmagazine images reveals, the process of selecting these images must be made more deliberate *and* the time necessary to do so in a conscious and considered manner must be available. In short, the standards of care and accuracy that are routinely applied to the text of a news story must be extended to the images as well. Few journalists at the country's elite media organizations would be willing to produce a story that inaccurately reported the racial composition of America's poor. But photographs are not held to the same standards, and their selection consequently reflects the subconscious judgment process through which negative racial stereotypes emerge.

Combating negative racial imagery takes effort, but it can be done within the constraints faced by news organizations. In response to concerns about the images of minorities in the news, some news organizations have instituted "photo audits" to systematically track the way minorities (or women) are portrayed. For example, in 1988 the *Seattle Times* began to count photographs of minorities appearing in positive, neutral, and negative contexts, and found that negative images of minorities outnumbered positive images by 4 to 1.

In response to this dismal portrayal of minorities and to the discussion and consciousness-raising that ensued among the news staff, coverage changed. In the following year, positive images of minorities outnumbered negative images. By 1990, the *Times* published twice as many photographs depicting minorities positively as negatively (a ratio that closely approximated the portrayal of whites in the *Times* coverage). As the experience of the *Seattle Times* shows, when a news organization makes the fair representation of different social groups a priority and takes concrete steps to monitor its own news content, substantial change can be accomplished in a short time.

As we have seen, the largely subconscious process of choosing examples to illustrate news stories on poverty results in a particular pattern of racial imagery: not only is poverty coverage dominated by black faces, but the racial mix of examples varies depending on the subgroup of the poor being covered. As one of the photo editors I spoke with suggested, only some kind of "subtle racism" can explain these patterns of racial misrepresentation of poverty in the American news media.

Journalists are professional observers and chroniclers of our social world. But they are also residents of that world and are exposed to the same biases and stereotypes that characterize society at large. Both psychology experiments and news organizations' real-world experience show that with sufficient effort the influence of journalists' subconscious biases on news images can be eliminated. But when the motivation or resources are insufficient, journalists' stereotypes will inevitably creep into news stories, distorting the public's perceptions of the poor and perpetuating misperceptions that unfairly burden African Americans.

## NOTES

This chapter has been expanded from earlier work appearing in *Why Americans Hate Welfare*.

1. CBS/New York Times poll, December 1994. These differences remain when statistical controls are added for respondents' age, education, sex, family income, and liberal/conservative ideology (see Gilens 1999, 140).

2. In a sample of newsmagazine stories on poverty published between 1960 and 1990, less than 5 percent included any concrete information on the racial composition of the poor or on any subgroup of the poor such as AFDC recipients or public housing tenants (Gilens 1999, 112).

3. On the impact of photographs, see Graber 1987, 1990, and Kenney 1992. On the tendency to be swayed by specific examples rather than statistical information, see Brosius and Bathelt 1994, Hamill, Wilson, and Nisbett 1980, and Kazoleas 1993. For a general discussion of the importance of visual images in television news coverage of poverty, see Entman 1995.

4. Meier and Redwick 1970, 213.

5. *Report of the National Advisory Commission on Civil Disorders*, 240. Reprinted in Piven and Cloward 1993, 190.

6. U.S. Department of Health and Human Services, Office of Family Assistance, *Fifth Annual Report to Congress on Temporary Assistance For Needy Families (TANF), Characteristics and Financial Circumstances of TANF Recipients*. www.acf.hhs.gov/programs/ofa/annualreport5/chap10.htm#_Toc25546983.

7. Forty-two percent of poor blacks work compared with 54 percent of the non-black poor (U.S. Bureau of the Census, *Poverty in the United States: 1988 and 1989*, Current Population Reports, series P-60, no. 171. Washington, D.C., 1990). In newsmagazine stories published between 1988 and 1992, 12 percent of blacks and 27 percent of nonblacks were identified as working (Gilens 1996a, 524).

8. Social scientists disagree about how to define the underclass, and even about whether it is a useful concept at all. But no matter how we define the underclass—no matter what combination of poverty "indicators" we pick—the underclass includes substantial numbers of nonblacks. By most definitions, blacks constitute a minority of the underclass. Yet the underclass in the news was portrayed as exclusively black.

9. The ten largest metropolitan areas (based on 1980 population) and the percentage of blacks among the poor are New York, 34.9 percent; Los Angeles, 13.0 percent; Chicago, 49.9 percent; San Francisco, 19.3 percent; Philadelphia, 45.4 percent; Detroit, 52.9 percent; Boston, 15.7 percent; Washington, 51.4 percent; Dallas, 32.4 percent; Houston, 33.6 percent (1990 United States Census of the Population, Summary Tape File 3A).

10. CBS/New York Times Survey, 1994.

11. National Race and Politics Study, 1991.

12. I am grateful to Guy Cooper and Stella Kramer at *Newsweek*, Richard L. Boeth and Mary Worrell-Bousquette at *Time*, and Richard Folkers and Sara Grosvenor at *U.S. News and World Report* for their time and cooperation. These interviews were conducted in October 1993.

13. General Social Survey, 2000.

14. For example, Fazio et al. (1995) found that white subjects varied in the extent to which they responded negatively to racial primes consisting of images of black faces, and that this variation was related to subjects' racial beliefs as measured by surveys and to their interactions with a black experimenter.

15. Rich Flokers, personal communication to author, October 8, 1993.

16. Mary Worrell, personal communication to author, October 1, 1993.

## REFERENCES

Banaji, M. R., and Bhaskar, R. 2000. Implicit Stereotypes and Memory: The Bounded Rationality of Social Beliefs. In D. L. Schacter and E. Scarry, eds., *Memory, Brain, and Belief*, 139–75. Cambridge, Mass.: Harvard University Press.

Brosius, H.-B., and Bathelt, A. 1994. The Utility of Exemplars in Persuasive Communications. *Communication Research* 21, no. 1: 48–78.

Devine, P. G. 1989. Stereotypes and Prejudice: Their Automatic and Controlled Components. *Journal of Personality and Social Psychology* 56, no. 1: 5–18.

Entman, R. M. 1995. Television, Democratic Theory, and the Visual Construction of Poverty. *Research in Political Sociology* 7: 139–59.

Fazio, R. H., Jackson, J. R., Dunton, B. C., and Williams, C. J. 1995. Variability in Automatic Activation as an Unobtrusive Measure of Racial Attitudes: A Bona Fide Pipeline? *Journal of Personality and Social Psychology* 69, no. 6: 1013–27.

Gans, H. J. 1979. *Deciding What's News*. New York: Pantheon.

Gilens, M. 1996a. Race and Poverty in America: Public Misperceptions and the American News Media. *Public Opinion Quarterly* 60, no. 4: 515–41.

———. 1996b. "Race Coding" and White Opposition to Welfare. *American Political Science Review* 90, no. 3: 593–604.

———. 1999. *Why Americans Hate Welfare: Race, Media, and the Politics of Antipoverty Policy*. Chicago: University of Chicago Press.

Graber, D. 1987. Television News Without Pictures? *Critical Studies in Mass Communication* 4: 74–78.

———. 1990. Seeing Is Remembering: How Visuals Contribute to Learning from Television News. *Journal of Communication* 40, no. 3: 134–55.

Hamill, R., Wilson, T. D., and Nisbett, R. E. 1980. Insensitivity to Sample Bias: Generalizing from Atypical Cases. *Journal of Personality and Social Psychology* 39: 578–89.

Kazoleas, D. C. 1993. A Comparison of the Persuasive Effectiveness of Qualitative versus Quantitative Evidence: A Test of Explanatory Hypotheses. *Communication Quarterly* 41, no. 1: 40–50.

Kenney, K. 1992. Effects of Still Photographs. *News Photographer* 47, no. 5: 41–42.

Lieberman, R. 1995. Race and the Organization of Welfare Policy. In P. E. Peterson, ed., *Classifying by Race*, 156–87. Princeton, N.J.: Princeton University Press.

Macrae, C. N., Hewstone, M., and Griffiths, R. J. 1993. Processing Load and Memory for Stereotype-Based Information. *European Journal of Social Psychology* 23: 77–87.

Macrae, C. N., Milne, A. B., and Bodenhausen, G. V. 1994. Stereotypes as Energy-Saving Devices: A Peek Inside the Cognitive Toolbox. *Journal of Personality and Social Psychology* 66, no. 1: 37–47.

Meier, A., and Redwick, E. 1970. *From Plantation to Ghetto*. New York: Hill & Wang.

Payne, B. K. 2001. Prejudice and Perception: The Role of Automatic and Controlled Processes in Misperceiving a Weapon. *Journal of Personality and Social Psychology* 81, no. 1: 181–92.

Piven, F. F., and Cloward, R. A. 1993. *Regulating the Poor: The Functions of Public Welfare*. 2nd ed. New York: Vintage.

# 4

# Picturing Class: Mining the Field of Front-Page Photographs for Keys to Accidental Communities of Memory

*Julianne H. Newton, Dennis J. Dunleavy, Chad Okrusch, and Gabriela Martinez*

> You always get the sense in the back of your head that things would be different if you looked a certain way or had a certain amount of money.
>
> —Chastity Davis (Scott 2003)

> The reality we have in common, and in which we find ourselves, is . . . a world itself brought forth by our ways of communicating and joint action.
>
> —Baerveldt and Verheggen 1997

A mid-twentieth-century bas-relief sculpture atop the journalism building at the University of Oregon portrays the press as a bare-breasted female figure striving to unify the working classes and social elites. How interesting that an image intended to be highly visible stressed the need to bridge the classes and proclaimed that an unfettered press was to be that bridge. Although we can find clear efforts in twenty-first-century media to speak to and for all people, few studies have examined the ways in which newspaper photojournalism mediates our understanding of class. The events surrounding September 11, 2001, brought a number of class-related issues to the front page: the importance of civil servants such as firemen and police officers, the reliance on political leaders for assurance, the central role of journalists during times of crisis, the strength of friendship and everyday family relationships, and the vast differences between American and Middle Eastern cultures. The costumes were not new. The stage set was. In horror and disbelief North Americans watched a reality play with ramifications for social and class upheaval of local and global magnitudes. Aware of the power of imagery to frame our understanding of the world, we thought newspaper images published in fall 2001 would prove a rich source of insight into class-related issues.

A November 2002 (Bumiller) article painted a word picture that exemplified the types of images we expected to find in 2001 publications. The article reported President Bush's signing of legislation requiring the federal government to pick up insurance losses for the September 11 attacks:

"With this new law, builders and investors can begin construction in real estate projects that have been stalled for too long, and get our hard hats back to work," said Mr. Bush, who was flanked on the East Room stage by a group of construction workers in T-shirts and blue jeans. Mr. Bush asserted that a lack of terrorism insurance had held up or caused the cancellation of more than $15 billion in real estate transactions.

Astute in the use of images to sway public opinion, the President's staff had recognized an opportunity to associate the Bush administration with the working class. Focusing attention on construction workers clothed in the costume of T-shirts and blue jeans shifted attention away from capitalist interests in protecting insurance companies and shoring up real estate investments, and toward working class concerns about unemployment.

This chapter reports the first stage of a larger study we hope will answer questions about the role media imagery plays in the construction of perceptions of class.

## LITERATURE REVIEW

Although we found no systematic investigation of newspapers' visual coverage of class, we found a number of intriguing studies in which image and class intersected. Grabe (1996), for example, determined that tabloid newsmagazine programs are more likely than traditional programs to present criminals as belonging to the middle or upper class, while traditional shows are more likely to present criminals as belonging to the working class. In their study of likability, Lott and Lott (2001) examined complex interactions among gender, race, and winner/loser status in people's responses to newspaper articles. Several experimental conditions included accompanying photographs. Placing their work in the context of established research, Lott and Lott concluded that status (defined as social class, occupation, winner or loser) can sometimes provide more influential cues than gender and race in the assignment of likability and positive or negative stereotypical attributes.

One rich source of class-related imagery is documentary photography, often credited with effecting change by making visible the previously invisible. A recent *New York Times* article, "There Go the Neighborhoods" (Scott 2003), was somewhat reminiscent of Jacob Riis's classic *How the Other Half Lives* (1971), which examined the living conditions of the poor in New York City. Other documentary classics include Agee's and Evans' *Let Us Now Praise Famous Men* (1966), which sought to comprehend the lives of tenant farmers in Alabama, and Charles Moore's *Powerful Days* (1991), a book about 1960s discrimination against African Americans. Especially interesting is Jim Goldberg's (1985) photographic exploration of the lives of the rich and the poor, a sociological project that ultimately resulted in a personal examination of his perceptions about different groups in society.

## DEFINING CLASS

To arrive at our theoretical definition of class, we looked to classical Western literature. Western civilization was built by the hands of those who largely existed outside the economically determined social ranking system. The seeds of our commonsense economic definition of class were planted in Rome almost 2,600 years ago, when the Servian Constitution codified a ranking system for citizens (landholding males) on the basis of one's wealth. Noncitizens (slaves, women, and the landless) were not included. We looked for the major themes that emerged from theories of class: Ricardo's identification of the role of the classless masses in the accumulation of wealth, conceptualizing labor in both economic and social categories; Thompson's (1824) and Hodgskin's (1825) development of Ricardo's ideas into a comprehensive economically based theory of class division; and Marx's (1968) argument that class was determined, not by one's wealth (or lack of wealth), but by one's relationship to the production process—whether a person sold his labor or profited from the labor of others. Marx problematized a strictly economically determined notion of class by focusing on the struggle for power inherent in the class system.

Weber, who further problematized the concept of class, distinguished class, power, and prestige—three semiautonomous but connected facets of class (Edgar and Sedgwick 1999). Weber's definition is flexible and acknowledges that one can belong to the working class and still have access to power and/or social prestige. Gramsci added another important consideration to understanding class and society. Through his concept of hegemony, Gramsci focused on how power manifested as dominance over ideas, institutions, and values.

Contemporary economist Michael Zweig (Lee 2002), who founded the Group for the Study of Working Class Life, offers a contemporary conceptualization of class in terms of power. Zweig points out that 62 percent of the U.S. labor force "are working-class people, by which I mean people who do not have much control or authority over the pace or the content of the work and they're not a supervisor and they're not the boss. We're talking about white-collar workers, like bank clerks or cashiers; we're talking about blue-collar workers and construction and manufacturing."

Zweig notes that after the September 11 attacks, firefighters, emergency medical technicians, and ironworkers were viewed as American heroes. He cautions, however, that hero status did not guarantee economic benefits: "There is a double message: the workers are heroes but the workers didn't get help. Tens of thousands of people lost their jobs in the airlines but the workers did not get extensions of their benefits—but the airlines got $15 billion in aid."

This cursory overview of major themes in the development of our understandings of class underscores the fluidity of the concepts we know as *class*. Although class is defined differently in different geopolitical and historical contexts, three broad, defining categories associated with class emerge: wealth, power, and status (prestige). We chose these as the basis for our analysis of newspaper imagery related to class.

## OTHER THEORETICAL THEMES

In addition to historical perspectives on class theory, our theoretical approach is grounded in anthropology and visual perception.

### Anthropology

New work in anthropology supports a redefinition of the *field* for *fieldwork* as a kind of community located in human memory—fleeting, dynamic moments in time in which people's lives intersect, forming temporary, unique communities located in the memories of those who lived the moments. In *Anthropological Locations* (Gupta and Ferguson 1997), Laurie Malkki explores the concept of "accidental communities of memory," particularly as mediated through news. By community of memory, Malkki refers to the "biographical, microhistorical, unevenly emerging sense of accidental sharings of memory and transitory experience," rather than to a local or national community (1997, 91). Malkki offers such examples of accidental communities of memory as: "people who have experienced war together . . . who have lived in a refugee or internment camp together for a certain period . . . who are stricken by a particular illness; or . . . who worked together on a particular humanitarian or development project" (92). Such communities "bring together people who might not otherwise, in the ordinary course of their lives, have met" (92). Malkki suggests that "these accidental, shared contexts" are significant beyond memory or psychological process, or traces in people's heads: "These memories—even when not very much narrativized— can powerfully shape what comes after. Who one is, what one's principles, loyalties, desires, longings, and beliefs are—all this can sometimes be powerfully formed and transformed in transitory circumstances shared by persons who might be strangers" (92).

Malkki stresses the critical role of journalism in providing anthropological evidence about accidental communities. We want to link Malkki's concepts of news as evidence about accidental communities to conceptualize news imagery as an accidental community that can play important roles in memory, reality construction, and subsequent human interaction. Lutz and Collins (1993) expressed a related notion through their concept of a photograph as an intersection of gazes. We are primarily concerned about how a photograph's content can provide artifacts of memory that can be drawn on in subsequent interaction with actual people. We argue that front-page images foreground aspects of reality in such a way that viewers intuitively feel they themselves are witnessing the events portrayed and therefore become for fleeting moments part of accidental communities.[1] Artifacts of those viewing experiences live on in their memories and affect subsequent conceptualizations of the world. This theoretical framework echoes Berger and Luckmann's (1966) social construction of reality theory, but focuses attention on news photographs as the source of information from which constructions are made, as well as on the effects of that information on people's attitudes about and interactions with others.

Photojournalists believe their primary role is to be eyewitnesses of history for those who cannot see events for themselves. Malkki notes shifts in anthropology from ethnographic description to witnessing, or "a form of a caring vigilance" (Hebdige in Malkki 1997, 94). Also important is Moore's (1987; in Malkki 1997) assertion: "Events may equally be evidence of the ongoing dismantling of structure or of attempts to create new ones. Events may show a multiplicity of social contestations and the voicing of competing cultural claims" (Malkki 1997, 87). It is not a big leap then to theorize that images obtained through the kind of "caring vigilance" many photojournalists view as their raison d'être, images that record moments of "social contestations," might play an important role in the construction of the reality through viewers' perceptions.

## Visual Perception

Our rationale also is based on research about how humans interact with external images. Recent studies indicate that people remember the visual better than the verbal (Sargent and Zillmann 1999), that the visual short-circuits rational mental processing (LeDoux 1986, 1996), that people use images of various kinds to negotiate strategies for living (Bechara et al. 1997; Winson 2002), and that human memory systems do not distinguish memories obtained through media from memories obtained through lived experience (Barry 2003). Much of this visual activity takes place beyond conscious mental processing. One way to conceptualize the complex set of variables inherent in visual perception is through an ecology of the visual (Newton 2001), an interdependent, symbiotic system of psychological/physical and cultural/societal responses. Within this living system, humans create, interpret, use, and respond to external and internal visual stimuli. These interactions are personal and individual, yet part of the larger sphere of human visual behavior (Newton 2001).

Researchers also have examined human perceptual interaction with news images. Studies show, for example, that news images command attention by directing a viewer's attention through the page (Garcia and Stark 1991). The larger the image, and the more dominant the placement above the fold of the newspaper, the greater the perceptual influence and persuasive impact it may have. Garcia and Stark determined that readers process photographs 75 percent of the time, compared with headlines 56 percent of the time and text 25 percent of the time. In other words, not only are news photographs likely to get and hold our attention, but they are likely to become memories on which we base everyday behaviors.

Sociologists link everyday imaging about class-related issues through the concept of class imagery: the "commonsense or everyday beliefs about social class that are held by ordinary members of society" (Marshall 1998, 76). For our study, class imagery is formed by visual cues about the three essential aspects of class outlined above: wealth, status, and power. We wanted to examine the role media images—especially newspaper images—play in constructing people's "everyday beliefs about social class." The first step then was to determine if indeed newspaper imagery communicates about class, and if so, what it communicates. We were primarily concerned with *what* newspaper images convey about class-related issues as the ground from which readers/viewers mine artifacts for the construction of class imagery.

## Theoretical Summary

Applying these ideas to our study of class imagery in newspapers, we argue that news photographs provide both evidence of and locations for participation in fleeting accidental communities that result in memories on which people base attitudes and behaviors. The event of social contestation, which can range from the traumatic to the mundane, is witnessed by actual participants, as well as by the participant observer—a photojournalist. The photojournalist represents the event through his or her images, which then are selected or eliminated through the editorial process for publication on the front page. The viewer/reader, who can be an original participant, a journalist, or other viewer/reader, then becomes a participant observer through the field of the photograph and the newspaper front page.[2] On one level, those who are drawn together into accidental communities continue their communal sharing through images of the events in which they participated. On a second level, news workers such as photojournalists and editors continually add building blocks of the communities of memory through the news production process. On a third level, newspaper readers add their own building blocks drawn from their repositories of personal experience, at once receiving, participating in, and projecting understandings of their social worlds. Our class imagery—whether derived from common experience, professional journalistic responsibility, or personal perception of self, others, and images of self and others—undergoes a constant process of participation in accidental communities of memory through a visual, ecological system of mediation, negotiation, and construction in which media images invariably play a major role. Newspaper front-page images are particularly influential in this process of reality construction for a number of reasons: (1) newspapers typically are considered the most credible source of news, (2) editors typically assign what they consider to be the most important news to the front page, (3) viewers/readers have been trained through experiences of reading to expect the most important news to appear on the front page, and (4) front-page images often are more compelling due to size, color, composition, and content. For these reasons, editors typically select front-page images very carefully, with consideration of potential story frames, interpretations, and effects. The newspaper is a complex continuum of message-making and meaning-making processes, a field in which accidental communities are reported and created, resulting in communities of memory through which readers and viewers negotiate their understanding of and relation to class in society. As such, we propose the following questions:

Do front-page newspaper images represent class?
If so, what visual indicators of class typify reportage?
Are there patterns to the reportage?
How might those patterns maintain or challenge viewers' understanding of class?
How might those patterns maintain or challenge an increasingly global society's broader construction of an image of class?
What do those patterns suggest about class and news in the twenty-first century?

## METHOD

Because of our interest in class in relation to the attacks of September 11, 2001, pivotal data for our study were published in autumn 2001. We believed studying September 11 imagery as reported in the Pacific Northwest would offer important insight into a region of the United States that was seldom in the limelight during that critical time in our history. How did Oregon newspapers report issues related to our major interest of study, class, during this unique time in U.S. history?

Oregon is a particularly interesting state to study for a number of other reasons. Oregon's traditions are rooted in railroad and logging culture, which brought scores of immigrants to the state in the early and mid-1900s. Oregon is known nationally as a state supporting assisted suicide, legalized marijuana for medical treatment, and same-sex partners. Oregon also has more hungry residents than most other states, one of the highest unemployment rates in the country, and low representation of minority groups. Oregon is known nationally as progressive and homogeneous, regionally as a state with low church attendance, and locally as one in which citizens often refuse to raise taxes to support progressive initiatives. Two key sites in Oregon are Eugene, nationally known as the home of anarchists and one of the most socially active universities, and Portland, a city distinguished by Oregon's most diverse population and as a center for high-tech industry.

Oregon's newspapers range from the *McKenzie River News*, which provides regular (though unintended) entertainment for residents of higher socioeconomic status via its weekly sheriff's report (which features residents some readers presume to be of lower socioeconomic status), to the *Oregonian*, a major daily that won the Pulitzer Prize for Public Service in 2001. Because we had ready access to the *Register-Guard*, Eugene's major daily newspaper, and the *Oregonian*, Portland's largest daily, that is where we began our study. We drew a constructed week sample, using simple random sampling, as specified by Riffe et al. (1993), of the two newspapers from September 1 through December 31, 2001, obtaining a sample of fourteen front pages (seven issues from each newspaper) from the total population of 244 issues (122 from each newspaper).

We decided to conduct both quantitative and qualitative content analyses— quantitative in order to determine in a reliable manner key patterns of manifest visual coverage and qualitative in order to delve more deeply into the subtle, latent discourse elicited through individual perception of visual information.[3]

We assigned five values for the overall category of class: 1 = lower, 2 = lower middle, 3 = middle, 4 = upper middle, 5 = higher. As explained above, we broke class down into three primary categories: wealth, status, and power. Each was measured using a 5-point scale with 1 as low and 5 as high. Wealth was operationalized as access to resources, environment (home, office, recreation), grooming, and material goods, such as clothing and products manifested in a photograph. We operationalized status as recognizeability, role (leader, sports, entertainer, civil servant), and position in a hierarchy. Power was operationalized as command of resources (human or material), societal strength, and role or position (authority, influence). Looking for possible correlations between sex and class, and between race and class, we included categories for each. Sex was coded as a dichotomous variable with 1 for female and 2 for male. Most uncomfortable trying to code race based on visual information, we decided instead to code for shade of skin, with a scale ranging from 1 for lighter and 5 for darker.[4] We also included a category for noting citizenship where possible from caption information, in order to determine possible correlations between class and nationality.

Coders were instructed using examples of front pages from 2003 issues of the *Register Guard* and *Oregonian*. Categories were discussed, and a sample coding sheet was provided. The code sheet provided a blank rectangle in the proportion of a broadsheet page, with dotted lines indicating three sections: nameplate and teasers (A), area above the fold (B), area below the fold (C), and bottom of the page (D). Coders were instructed to draw and number rectangles within the larger rectangle indicating the location and relative size of photographs. Then they were to draw and number circles indicating the position of each person imaged in a photograph. This process provided a system for indicating on an adjoining chart which person in a photograph was being coded. For example, a person might be indicated as "A1.1," which stood for "Section A (top), Image No. 1, Subject No. 1." The code sheet then provided spaces for indicating the coder's judgment as to level of wealth, status, and power (on a scale of 1 to 5), sex (on a scale of 1 or 2), shade (on a scale of 1 to 5), and citizenship (verbal description). Two individuals coded all fourteen newspapers. A third individual examined eleven newspapers.

We also employed a qualitative content analysis based on a grounded, inductive, "context-sensitive scheme" (Schwandt 1997) through which we could identify emerging patterns, themes, and concepts. With a qualitative analysis of the same fourteen issues we drew at random for the quantitative coding, we hoped to probe beyond obvious characteristics, identifying subtle social indicators we might not have considered. After quantitatively coding the pages, each coder was asked to review, in detail, two issues of the newspapers qualitatively, examining the photographs in the context of the whole page along with its headlines, text, and juxtapositions.

Two coders read newsprint pages. One coder read scanned versions of the newsprint pages projected on a computer screen. Three pages were coded via microfiche enlargement because print versions were not available.

## RESULTS

### Quantitative

Close to 38 percent ($N = 102$) of individuals imaged were coded as middle class in terms of wealth; lower middle class was the next largest group (25 percent, $N = 68$). In terms of status, a majority of people fell into either the middle-class category (29 percent, $N = 79$) or the lower-class category (28 percent, $N = 76$). In terms of power, people fell into lower, lower-middle, and middle-class categories in roughly equal numbers (25 percent, $N = 67$ in lower; 26 percent, $N = 71$ in lower-middle; and 27 percent, $N = 74$ in middle). A majority of people were coded as having lighter-toned skin (55 percent, $N = 144$). Nineteen percent ($N = 49$) had light-toned skin, 13 percent ($N = 33$) had middle-toned skin, 7 percent ($N = 19$) had darker-toned skin, and 6 percent ($N = 15$) had dark-toned skin. Most people imaged were male (81 percent, $N = 240$).[5]

Means for wealth, status, and power fell between lower and middle class, with an overall mean of 2.61 ($N = 270$) on a scale of 1 (lower) to 5 (higher). Mean score for wealth was 2.74, for status 2.58, and for power 2.53, on scales of 1 (lower) to 5 (higher). Mean score for shade was 1.89 ($N = 260$) on a scale of 1 (lighter) to 5 (darker).

Correlation between wealth and status was .74, between wealth and power .67, and between status and power .7. All were significant at the $p <$ .01 level. Correlation between wealth and shade was $-.26$, between status and shade was $-.21$, and between power and shade was $-.28$. All were significant at the $p < .01$ level.

In summary, our quantitative findings indicate that a majority of people imaged on the front pages of the *Oregonian* and the *Register-Guard* in the fall of 2001 fell into the middle-class category in terms of wealth, status, and power. Most people were male, and most people had lighter to light shades of skin tone. Most people were judged to be from the United States, with thirty being from Afghanistan, and a few from Ireland (1), Vietnam (1), England (1), and two unknown.

Overall intercoder agreement was 78 percent, which Riffe, Lacy, and Fico (1998) indicate is sufficient when developing new coding categories and methods.

## Qualitative

Three coders each analyzed four pages qualitatively, by which we mean each engaged in a personal hermeneutic through which he or she derived evaluative conclusions about observed themes and patterns. The pages studied in this manner were the September 21, 2001 (see figure 4.1), and October 23, 2001 (see figure 4.2), issues of the *Oregonian* and *Register-Guard*, selected because they kept coming up in our discussions. We include below a few key selections from the coders' qualitative analyses.

### Coder A

The September 21 *Register-Guard* front page portrayed President Bush, who obviously ranks pretty high all across the board. He belongs to the upper class. His status and power are major. This picture features Bush all by himself. It represents the wealth, status, and power of the United States in one person. Bush's facial expression symbolizes the pain of the American people, who are going through a mourning process since the events of September 11. But at the same time, by showing him in a high to medium angle and standing alone and holding in his hand a badge from a dead policeman, it means that all these deaths are not going to be accepted and that he has the power for taking revenge.

**Figure 4.1.    September 21, 2001. Used with permission.**

The fact that he is portrayed alone demonstrates that he has risen in the so-cial consciousness of the American people. He deserves now a full or at least a half page just with him in the picture where he can stand by himself and lead the nation through hard times and on to victory against the wrong doers. His picture, although showing certain emotion, seems to be saying that he is the one chosen by destiny to re-establish the balance of order in our world.

In contrast to the picture of Bush that occupies almost the entire front page, at the bottom of the page, we have very small pictures. One shows Oregon Governor Kitzhaber, who also is wealthy but not as wealthy as Bush. In terms of status and power, if we look at Kitzhaber in relation to Bush's presence in this front page, Kitzhaber cannot rank beyond the average. His facial expression indicates worry or concern. The other pictures in this sec-tion reflect the entertainment that appeals to the average American: sports and film. One is a baseball player, whom I'm assuming is wealthy but of less status than Kitzhaber or Bush.

The September 21 *Oregonian* (see figure 4.1) main picture is full of symbols and visual rhetoric to produce a sense of "we hold the power" and "God is on our side." I would say that the framing used by the photographer is a frame within a frame, since besides the picture frame, the subjects in the picture are

Figure 4.2.    October 23, 2001. Used with permission.

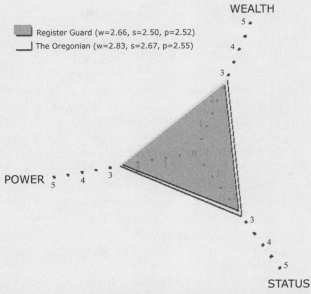

Figure 4.3.    A representation of how coders quantitatively interpreted *Register Guard* and *Oregonian* front-page photographs in Fall 2001 in terms of class, defined by wealth, status, and power. 1 = lower class, 2 = lower middle class, 3 = middle class, 4 = upper middle class, 5 = upper class.

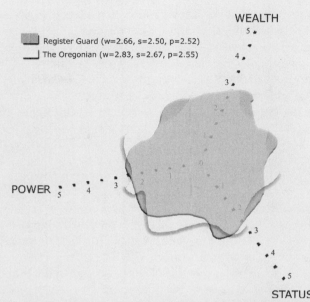

WEALTH

■ Register Guard (w=2.66, s=2.50, p=2.52)
⌐ The Oregonian (w=2.83, s=2.67, p=2.55)

POWER

STATUS

**Figure 4.4. A representation of how coders qualitatively interpreted *Register Guard* and *Oregonian* photographs in terms of class. Graphics by Chad Okrusch.**

framed within powerful architectural boundaries: two imposing columns. On top the words "In God we trust" serve as a rhetorical device to communicate the moral and spiritual stance of the subjects in the picture, a stance they feel gives them the right to "save" the world from evil. The way the subjects are positioned in the picture provides a well-known Christian paradigm: the Sacred Trinity. It is a perfect triangle, it is a perfect number, and it is the three people with the most power to either forgive or punish those who go against "good" and "freedom."

The flag represents the American institution of the presidency and the power conferred to the president. But notice that it is placed below the big words "In God we trust," indicating it is God who protects and guides the power of the institution symbolized by the flag. The two gray-haired men may represent wisdom, but more than that they represent power to back up the president. The president has been photographed in a high angle, and he seems to be looking at the horizon as if foreseeing his mission to crusade in the name of the God he trusts in and the God who has given to the American people the values and ideals that encompass freedom.

In the dominant photograph in the October 23 *Oregonian* (see figure 4.2), most people are in their work uniforms, which tells me their line of work—postal workers. This indicates to me that they are middle lower class. They all seem to be of the same status, except for the only white person in the picture, who is the only one not wearing a uniform. This white person may earn more money, and perhaps he is in a managerial position and therefore has more status in that context. They all look powerless and not necessarily too happy. The man in the very front looks concerned.

In contrast, the two images toward the lower half of the page show people who have higher income, look more happy, and are less concerned. They both are wearing suits. One of the people is in a position of some power as a professor or someone who is teaching about a part of the world that most people in America know very little about. He owns knowledge: cultural capital.

At the bottom of the page is a photo of a man I cannot recognize. He seems to be someone with certain wealth and he is speaking with a posture of power, as if he has the right to say whatever he is saying.

In the October 23 *Register-Guard* (figure 4.2), the main picture shows me class through these two postal workers, whose body language tells me of their concerns and uniforms tell me that they are working class. They belong to the lower middle class, having no status for lack of being recognizable persons or within their own working context.

The photo below them shows soldiers in action, which gives them some power in the context of war. But their power is limited since they are receiving orders; so I think in the context of the army, they rank in the middle in terms of power. They both share the same status and probably in terms of wealth they are just common soldiers who make less than what Colin Powell would make. At the top of the page is a photo of someone I ranked a 4 in terms of wealth, assuming he is a professional player, but uncertain of status and power in his team, I am assuming he ranks average.

### Coder B

By the time these newspapers were published, ten days had passed since 9/11. The mass media had extended the boundaries of our accidental community to an unprecedented scale. The entire planet shared the common experience of reliving the horror hundreds upon hundreds of times. Those images, as so many have noted, crashed, like the passenger jets, into our collective consciousness and impacted us in profound ways.

As I reexamine these front pages, I relive the days following the attacks. I'm struck by two dynamic concepts that apply to our definition of stratified class: descent and ascent.

Descent. The jets descended from atmospheric heights to the uppermost heights of humanity's built environment. People descended en masse through the towers' stairwells, and the most desperate, out of skyscraper windows. And the towers—one by one—made the most dramatic descent of all. We collapsed, too, each time we relived that day. The stock market collapsed materially, manifesting our collapsing hopes and fears. The old world collapsed into smoking mountains of concrete, office debris, and humanity.

But in a McLuhanesque tetradic twist, some ascended as the world collapsed around them. New York City's first responders—firefighters, police officers, and emergency workers—ran up and into the flaming towers, running past the sea of frightened faces they were there to help.[6] Their ascent translated into, what in retrospect seems a brief period, adulation and admiration, from the public: a kiss, hug, and ephemeral rise in status. Talk shows, evening news programs, and newspapers featured these working-class heroes, temporarily elevating their status by placing them on a heroes' perch.

Politicians ascended and descended in interesting ways. Rudy Giuliani, for example, rose to the status of a god because of his compassionate descent into ground zero. *Time* magazine named him Person of the Year for 2001 and pictured him standing atop the Manhattan skyline in place of the missing towers. Paradoxically, Giuliani ascended by descending.

George Bush, as pictured on the front page of both the *Oregonian* and the *Register Guard,* appears larger than life. The photo in the *Oregonian* pictures him from below, flanked by powerful men. Above him, military personnel prepare and a fighter jet ascends on some path to ensure, as the headline reads in bold type, "Justice will be done."

In the *Register Guard,* once again, class hierarchies are entangled in interesting ways. An obviously emotional President Bush, the most powerful man in the world, holds up the police shield of New York police officer George Howard. Howard died saving others as the towers collapsed.

The world post 9/11 was turned inside out and upside down, as were the towers. Some descended, some ascended, and as Giuliani showed, some ascended because of their descent. Of the three aspects of class we've focused on, it seems status is the most dynamic—and ephemeral. Wealth and power are firmly entrenched. Status, we can more easily confer.

*Coder C*

An observation for me came about as I thought about the materiality represented in the content categories. Clearly, wealth and status can be thought of in terms of materiality, but power may not be as clear-cut. When I was coding, if there was a gun in the image, I associated the bearer not with wealth or status per se but with power. How does this fit with a discussion of class?

Images stand in relation to the context in which they are applied through the news. Through repetition, images of power serve as mnemonic devices which become anchored or embedded within the pathways of collective consciousness. We learn to read presidential power images without giving them a second glance or additional scrutiny. The language of the visual is a subtle and extremely complex communicative process that requires a synergy of rational and intuitive thinking. In a comparison between similar front pages, the ideals of power are displayed through the juxtaposition of images and text. The eye moves between what we think the image says to us about presidential power and what we are told it represents through the headlines "We will not fail," and "Justice will be done."

Editors construct front pages through what they consider to be the most salient and conspicuous selection of verbal and visual representations of an event. In analyzing presidential imagery, framing becomes a critical and essential visual dynamic. The American flag in this instance serves to frame the president's position rhetorically through connotation and symbolism. Deductively, the reader is given the equivalent of a visual frame supported by such symbolic elements as the flag or the shield. What do colors signify in these images? Do gray-haired politicians signify wise elders? Does the flag signify patriotism and freedom? Does a civil servant's shield signify sacrifice? How does the rhetoric of such sound bites as "Justice will be done" and "We will not fail" contribute to the meanings we construct around these images?

Analyzing the front-page displays of two *Oregonian* newspapers illustrates visual processes. The anthrax scare and deaths of U.S. postal workers, coinciding with the attacks on the World Trade Center and the Pentagon on September 11, 2001, received prominent display in both dailies five weeks later. Although the images selected as dominant differ somewhat in content, what is signified here communicates emotional and intellectual appeals. While the image of the line of postal workers boarding buses after being screened for toxins (*Oregonian*, figure 4.2) signifies the event quantitatively, therefore lending credibility to the seriousness of the event, another selection (*Register-Guard*, figure 4.2) suggests a more qualitative mood. In this image, pensive postal workers seated on a bus communicate to the reader a sense of despair through intimacy and gesture. Choice of focal length, framing, selective focus, and vantage point contribute significantly to any subsequent readings along with image placement and positioning on the page.

Additionally, in this example the dominant or lead images of the anthrax poisonings are juxtaposed against smaller images providing visual cues for a reader's coherence of events. The external social and cultural frames communicating perceived threats to national security are signified through these ancillary images. In one instance (*Register-Guard*) U.S. military personnel are shown loading ordinance onto an aircraft carrier's jet. It is presumed in this case that the juxtaposition of an image depicting a domestic threat, as illustrated in the postal worker photograph, has some relation to the secondary image and text on the page—one that depicts U.S. military retaliatory preparedness overseas.

Through these images, civil servants (postal workers) are represented as hapless, powerless, and vulnerable victims on one hand and patriotic, powerful, and resistant on the other hand. Further, the images symbolically convey the normalized societal value of national security and independence over personal sacrifice. Similarly, the *Oregonian*'s selection of postal workers is juxtaposed by an image of a college professor, originally from Afghanistan, gesturing in front of a map of the world. The visual cues provided by the confluence of dominant and secondary imagery on the page suggest an alignment of informational hierarchies. The animated professor gesturing to a class contrasts sharply with the impression provided by the image of postal workers boarding a bus. Although in all cases the reader is viewing "action" photographs, the visual cues offered in the images about social class or status are distinctly different. From this perspective, perceptions of class associated with predominantly African American postal workers differ from associations made with military service personnel or an Afghani college professor.

## DISCUSSION

This chapter reports our examination of the media's role in defining and maintaining social class through front-page newspaper images. We were curious about effects of the events of September 11 on social stratifications as visualized through newspaper imagery, and about whether we could discern class differences in that imagery. As a quantitative measure, we coded the visual content of front pages of two Oregon newspapers published in fall 2001. Our data indicated that the majority of front-page photographs featured middle-class, light-skinned males from the United States. For a qualitative measure, we subjectively analyzed the entire content of four front pages published in fall 2001. Our qualitative interpretations focused on the upholding of political power in the hands of white males over the relative powerlessness of black civil servants. We will discuss our findings in answer to the questions posed earlier.

*Do front-page newspaper images represent class?* Yes, although systematically assessing class imagery is complicated. Our intercoder agreement percentage, 78 percent, is significant in that most of the data coded was on a five-point ordinal scale.

*If so, what visual indicators of class typify reportage?* Despite the complexity of our definition of class as an inextricably knotted triad of wealth/status/power, our coders repeatedly assigned very similar values in each category to photographic subjects. Although each coder used the same structural criteria, each subjectively interpreted visual elements communicated by the photographs. This speaks not only to the complexity of picturing class, but also to the complexity of analyzing visual imagery—we each engage the visual in a subjective way. Our personal histories, values, and ways of seeing the world inevitably affect our cognitive processing of the visual information we perceive.

For example, while we may agree that power is roughly defined as relative command of resources, we each interpret visual representations of this command in unique ways. A gun in the hand of a police officer certainly represents power to some, but the relative lack of autonomy of the average police officer—the rigid behavioral codes, legal structures, and hierarchy ("chain of command") of power within which he or she works, for example—can also be viewed as a lack of power. Our South American coder often saw the photos in terms of story context, her perceptions about America, and her knowledge of video documentary. One North American coder interpreted the photographs in terms of self-image, the relative nature of personal power, and his own working-class upbringing. The other North American coder interpreted the images in terms of how people make meaning from looking at pictures, separately and in juxtaposition.

Nevertheless our methods of analysis were successful in mining artifactual evidence of wealth, status, and power to help us determine general quantitative information, as well as information specific to context and viewer perception.

*Are there patterns to the reportage?* Yes. Lighter-skinned males dominate front-page news.

*How might those patterns maintain or challenge viewers' understanding of class?* The patterns affirm lighter-skinned males as the most newsworthy, which could be associated with higher wealth, status and/or power in the minds of readers/viewers. The patterns also affirm darker-skinned males as possessing less wealth, status, or power. Women of any class continue to be minimally visible when it comes to front-page news.

- Wealth. Our coding resulted in a standard bell curve, which seems to support the idea that most Americans are middle class. But, as Zweig maintained, that is not the case—it is myth. It may be a more truthful statement to say that most Americans are lower to lower-middle class—especially in Oregon.
- Status. When compared to the wealth data, our status data are peculiar. Lower class is highly represented, then lower-middle-class numbers dip, followed by a rise in middle-class numbers. Why the dip? Can this be explained in light of increased international representation, especially of seemingly poor Afghanis?
- Power. The power data are skewed toward a significant representation of lower- to middle-class images.
- Shade. This seemingly skewed distribution appears to fall in line with the predominantly white makeup of Oregon. Furthermore, when we analyzed the papers individually (i.e., the *Oregonian* vs. the *Register Guard*), shade numbers rose slightly for the Portland paper—which makes sense in that Portland is a somewhat more diverse population.
- Sex. Ironically, we began this chapter by referencing the "bare-breasted female" embodiment of the press fixed atop the UO journalism building. The most astonishing set of numbers in our dataset is that 81 percent of subjects were male. How could this be true at the dawn of the twenty-first century? Oregon may be considered progressive, but if its

two main papers are reporting the news correctly, women are not newsmakers, something we find hard to believe.

*How might those patterns maintain or challenge an increasingly global society's broader construction of an "image of class"?* Regular juxtaposition of powerful Americans, who typically were light-skinned, male, and middle class, with images of Afghanis, who typically were dark-skinned, hungry, grieving, fighting or captured, affirmed a view of a successful first world (or first-class) nation as superior to an embattled third world (or third-class) nation. The events of 9/11 elevated class consciousness to a global magnitude in a specific, significant manner. September 11, 2001, posited the figure of twenty-first-century capitalism, imaged through the World Trade Center towers ascending toward the heavens, against the background of twenty-first-century agrarianism and religious conviction—then reversed the image to posit third-world anger and frustration against a more than leveled first world made painfully conscious of its wealth.

*What do those patterns suggest about class and news in the twenty-first century?* Twenty-first-century news workers need to consider the multiplicity of a global society in determining what is the most significant news and how to portray that news. Readily available and comfortable images of political leaders may seem intuitively significant, but they are not the whole story. Not all voices speak with high wealth, status, and power. If, as reporter Flynn McRoberts said, the role of journalism is to give "voice to people . . . to give a picture, an image, of what life is . . . let's allow their voices to shape the picture we give" (Ettema and Peer 1996).

## IMPLICATIONS

It is important to stress that this study reports data from two newspapers during an extraordinary four months of American history. It is not offered here as support for making generalizations about all newspapers. We can, however, suggest a few evocative conclusions.

Our study offers proof of the fluidity of the concept of class. From a critical structuralist perspective (cultural materialist), the study demonstrates the elite's ability to manipulate means of mental production to, at the very least, parade images in front of our eyes that send covertly encoded political messages: "we're all in this together," "trust me," "I feel your pain," and so forth. From a poststructuralist perspective, the study offers proof that socially constructed structures such as class do not exist as some unchanging Platonic ideal but are constantly in a state of becoming in the ecological system of human visual behavior.

This study provides a baseline for evaluating not only how a newspaper portrays class through its images, but also how news itself is part of the process of maintaining societal norms and constructing social change. As part of established institutions, the front pages of at least two newspapers in fall 2001 reinforced class distinctions by imaging people and issues through filters reminiscent of centuries-old ideologies concerning class, race, and gender. If we look beyond the cloaks of news values, we find visualizations indicating rivers of difference continue to flow through human interactions involving wealth, status, and power. We all participate in these rivers of difference through accidental communities of memory constructed in part from the artifacts we mine from viewing newspaper photographs.

Any meaning derived from news images must be subjected to the problematic interrogation of an interstice of power and knowledge in society. On one level, images serve as informational gateways in which people organize their daily lives according to the immediacy and relevancy of events. On another level, images also reinforce public perceptions, stereotypes, and cultural norms associated with power and social class in society. It is through the confluence of visual and textual communication that implied and overt displays of power become actualized in the news. We developed a novel method for studying class as news within a living systems approach to understanding complex mediated visual phenomena. We sought to take seriously the complexity of our task while striving to find ways to deduce useful insight that would advance the study of class and news.

The common ground shared among the researchers in this study is concomitant with an attempt to negotiate the ambiguities of defining social order through visually mediated messages. There exists within this paradigm an implied understanding that multiple realities and perspectives of the interpreters are valued in providing a richer and more humanistic context for any conclusions that may be drawn. Qualitative interpretations do not entirely assume the intersubjectivity of an agreed bias toward or basis of socialized knowledge. Instead, the conditions of knowing that inform these interpretations may be viewed as emergent, dynamic, and motivated by human agency and experience. It is presumed here that the common ground of differing interpretations resides, as Filstead (1979) suggests, with "social meanings" and can only be examined within a context of human interaction.

Although the coverage was predominantly of light-skinned males, it does not mean the *Oregonian* and *Register-Guard* ignore women and minorities. Fall 2001 was an extraordinary time in U.S. history. The two newspapers put on the front page the news that editors deemed was most significant for readers. The fact that the news continues to be dominated by light-skinned males is not solely determined by the editors, however, given the reality of U.S. society through which light-skinned males continue to dominate. The means for class indicate the majority of the two papers' coverage did not focus on the upper class, but rather struck a balance in terms of class. What needs to be determined, however, through analysis of other parts of the papers, is how class is portrayed through the newspapers. Both newspapers, for example, feature local/regional news in other sections. Even if we find a fair representation of class throughout the newspapers, that finding will not change the significance of the fact that front-page news—the most important news—featured light-skinned males predominantly. That means that all other members of society usually were of lesser importance, according to news judgment. We do not have to stretch that conclusion very far to reason that nonwhite, nonmale news protagonists are, at least metaphorically, second class. Social order can be actualized through the repetition, placement, and positioning of visual mediated messages. Social hierarchy and class dominance is legitimized through "the taken for granted" agencies of news imagery and editorial control.

Then the question becomes: Should newspapers feature more photographs of women and people of color on the front page, how will they be portrayed in terms of wealth, status, and power? The first step is that women and people of color have to get *on* the front page. If our accidental communities of memory usually are composed of artifacts of white male power, wealth, and status, we have little room for empowering images of those relegated to the back of the bus via the newspaper. Journalism then is in effect a class act, even while trying to do its best to cover significant news appropriately.

It is not surprising that newspapers known for their egalitarian coverage of multiple voices would return to imagery that reinforces traditional power structures in the United States. In times of crisis old scripts can take over. Many Americans, for example, returned to nationalistic flag waving, spiritual solace, and family bonds in the face of the crises of the fall of 2001. Yet it was an extraordinary time when the actions of ordinary people representing a wide range of wealth, power, and status revealed first-class strength. And that makes good news.

## NOTES

1. For an extended discussion of viewer interaction with subjects in photographs, see Newton 2001, chapter 10, "The Problem of Real People."

2. See Newton 2001, chapter 3, "From Instinct to Practice," for an extended explanation of a model of photography that incorporates observer and observed interacting at various stages of image creation and interpretation.

3. See Babbie 1998 for a discussion of manifest and latent content; and Altheide 1987 for discussion of combining types of data collection.

4. See Keenan 1996 for a seminal study of skin tones and physical features of blacks in magazine advertisements.

5. The number of cases coded was lower for shade and sex due to differences in media used for coding. For example, three pages necessarily were coded via black-and-white microfiche, which made measuring shade and sex occasionally problematic but allowed for a general reading of a photograph's content.

6. See McLuhan and Powers 1989 for a discussion of the tetrad.

## REFERENCES

Agee, J., and Evans, W. [1940] 1966. *Let us now praise famous men*. New York: Ballantine.

Altheide, D. 1987. Ethnographic content analysis. *Qualitative Sociology* 10, no. 1: 65–77.

Baerveldt, C., and Verheggen, T. 1997. Paper presented at the seventh conference of the International Society for Theoretical Psychology, Berlin, April–May 1997. Updated August 2000. http://watarts.uwaterloo.ca/~acheyne.

Babbie, E. 1998. *The practice of social research*. 8th ed. Belmont, Calif.: Wadsworth.

Barry, A. M. S. 2003. Mediated memory: The impact of media experience on emotional memory. Paper presented at Visual Communication: Rhetorics and Technologies, William A. Kern Conference in Communications, Rochester Institute of Technology, Rochester, N.Y., April 5.

Bechara, A., Damasio, H., Tranel, D., and Damasio, A. 1997. Deciding advantageously before knowing the advantageous strategy. *Science* 275: 1293–295.

Berger, P. L., and Luckmann, T. 1966. *The social construction of reality: A treatise in the sociology of knowledge*. Garden City, NY: Doubleday.

Bumiller, E. 2002. Government to cover most costs of insurance losses in terrorism. *New York Times*. Accessed on November 27, 2002, at www.nytimes.com/2002/11/27/politics/27BUSH.html?todaysheadlines.

Edgar A. and Sedgwick P., eds. 1999. *Key concepts in cultural theory*. London: Routledge.

Ettema, J. S., and Peer, L. 1996. Good news from a bad neighborhood: Toward an alternative to the discourse of urban pathology. *Journalism and Mass Communication Quarterly*, Winter, 835–56.

Filstead, W. J. 1979. Qualitative methods: A needed perspective in evaluation research. In Cook, T., and Reichardt, C., eds., *Qualitative and quantitative methods in evaluation research*. London: Sage.

Garcia, M., and Stark, P. 1991. *Eyes on the News*. Poynter Institute for Media Studies.

Goldberg, J. 1985. *Rich and poor*. New York: Random House.

Grabe, M. E. 1996. Tabloid and traditional television newsmagazine crime stories: crime lessons and reaffirmation of social class distinctions. *Journalism and Mass Communication Quarterly*, Winter, 926–46.

Gupta, A., and Ferguson, J. 1997. *Anthropological loations:* Boundaries and ground of a field science. Berkeley: University of California Press.

Hebdige, D. 1993. Going global: Culture in the nineties. Multimedia presentation to the Department of Anthropology Colloquium Series, University of California, Irvine, 16 March.

Hodgskin, T. 1825. *Labour defended against the claims of capital*. London.

Keenan, K. L. 1996. Skin tones and physical features of blacks in magazine advertisements. *Journalism and Mass Communication Quarterly* 73, no. 4: 905–12.

LeDoux, J. 1986. Sensory systems and emotion. *Integrative Psychiatry* 4: 237–43.

———. 1996. *The emotional brain*. New York: Simon & Schuster.

Lee, F. R. 2002. Welcome to the working class! Interview with Michael Zweig. *New York Times*. Accessed on January 12, 2003, at www.utoronto.ca/soc101/info/article_11.html.

Lott, B. 2002. Cognitive and behavioral distancing from the poor. *American Psychologist* 57, no. 2: 100–11.

Lott, B., and Lott, A. J. 2001. Likability of strangers as a function of their winner/loser status, gender, and race. *Journal of Social Psychology* 126, no. 4: 503–11.

Lutz, C. A., and Collins, J. L. 1993. *Reading National Geographic*. Chicago: University of Chicago Press.

Malkki, L. H. 1997. News and culture: Transitory phenomena and the fieldwork tradition. In Gupta, A., and Ferguson, J., eds., *Anthropological locations: Boundaries and grounds of a field science*, 86–101. Berkeley: University of California Press.

Marshall, G. 1998. *A dictionary of sociology*. 2nd ed. Oxford: Oxford University Press.

McLuhan, M., and Powers, B. 1989. *The global village: Transformations in world life and media in the 21st century*. New York: Oxford University Press.

Marx, K. [1849] 1968. Wage labour and capital. In K. Marx and F. Engels, *Selected Works*. London: Lawrence & Wishart.

Moore, C. 1991. *Powerful days: The civil rights photography of Charles Moore*. New York: Stewart, Tabori & Chang.

Moore, S. F. 1987. Explaining the present: Theoretical dilemmas in processual anthropology. *American Ethnology* 14, no. 4: 727–51.

Newton, J. H. 2001. *The burden of visual truth: The role of photojournalism in mediating reality*. Mahwah, N.J.: Lawrence Erlbaum.

Riffe, D., Aust, C. F., and Lacy, S. R. 1993. The effectiveness of random, consecutive, and constructed week sampling in newspaper content analysis. *Journalism Quarterly* 70, no. 1: 133–39.

Riffe, D., Lacy, S., and Fico, F. 1998. *Analyzing media messages: Using quantitative content analysis in research*. Mahwah, N.J.: Lawrence Erlbaum.

Riis, J. A. [1890] 1971. *How the other half lives: Studies among the tenements of New York*. New York: Dover.

Sargent, S. L., and Zillmann, D. 1999. Image effects on selective exposure to news stories. Paper presented to the International Communication Association annual convention, San Francisco, May.

Scott, J. 2003. There go the neighborhoods: Rich and poor, side by side. *New York Times*. Accessed on March 5, 2003, at www.nytimes.com/2003/03/05/nyregion/05LIVI.html?ex = 1047865883&ei = 1&en = 7f9ee62a697ce584.

Schwandt, T. A. 1997. *Qualitative inquiry, a dictionary of terms*. Thousand Oaks, Calif.: Sage.

Thompson, W. 1824. *An inquiry into the principles of the distribution of wealth most conducive to human happiness*. London.

Winson, J. 2002. The meaning of dreams. *Scientific American: The Hidden Mind* 12, no. 1: 54–61.

# II

## CLASS ON TELEVISION

When polled, Americans routinely report that television is their primary source for news. This is a disturbing fact, even for those of us who worked in and still work in television news. When you remove commercial time and time designated for weather, sports, and teases, most late evening half-hour newscasts contain between twelve and fifteen minutes of actual news. In that amount of time, providing context for stories is, to say the least, difficult.

Local news is more heavily watched by most people than is network news. That is why I decided to venture back into a local newsroom to better understand how news workers were dealing with questions of class. The findings are not encouraging. Our chapter begins this section and is followed by two pieces dealing with network newsmagazine programs. Elizabeth Grabe discovered that there are lines of demarcation between magazine and tabloid programs, and these lines interestingly run along class boundaries. Jennie Phillips takes a closer look at the language and images used in magazine programs in an effort to shed light on the more nuanced messages about class contained in these programs.

Finally, televised sports provide a great deal of content that can draw large audiences and great viewer interest. The sportscasters, often also journalists, provide the descriptions and analysis of these events for viewers. James Rada and Tim Wulfemeyer continue their work in analyzing sports content by looking at the way in which sports commentary constructs a culture of poverty often associated with African American athletes.

# 5

## Class and Local TV News

*Don Heider and Koji Fuse*

> Two nations; between whom there is no intercourse and no sympathy . . .
> as if they were in different zones, or inhabitants of different planets.
>
> —Benjamin Disraeli

Class, as a concept in American culture, does not seem to carry very far. It is not a term that comes up often in day-to-day conversation. Does this mean America is a classless society?

"Any social system that involves economic inequality will generate social classes" (Jackman and Jackman 1983, 8). There is ample evidence of economic inequality in the United States, especially given that this society is based on an economic system that does not espouse any principle of fiscal equality. Further evidence points out that the gap between the rich and the poor is widening in the United States. Between 1970 and 1990, average income for families in the bottom fifth of the income scale dropped 5 percent. Meanwhile, income among the top fifth shot up 33 percent. According to the *New York Times*, the median value of assets owned by families with incomes less than $25,000 fell between 1995 and 1998, while those families with higher incomes saw their assets soar (Stevenson 2000, 3). In addition, larger numbers of clerical, sales, and service workers cannot be automatically construed as an expansion of the middle class, because they have been subjected to the same deskilling process that metamorphosed traditional craft workers into blue-collar workers. The average income of lower-level white-collar workers is much less than that of blue-collar factory workers, which indicates a further proletarianization of the working class in general. Even the so-called new middle class, including managers and professionals, may be in the same predicament as the working class. The abundance of unemployed Ph.D.s has changed the hiring policy in academia, forcing them to accept low pay and heavy course loads (So 1995).

America is obviously a society where there is considerable class diversity, whether it is publicly acknowledged or not. How do the news media deal with the question of class? In other words, how do media workers themselves conceptualize class, and how do those constructions manifest themselves in news coverage? To answer these questions we thought it would be appropriate to examine, in depth, how one news organization dealt with the idea of class. For this study, the decision was made to enter into a local television newsroom as an observer to begin examining the way in which news was constructed in light of these questions. By observing news decision making in a naturalistic setting, some insights might be gained unavailable through other methods. During the study period, newscasts were taped and researchers completed a content analysis of those newscasts to help triangulate findings. The results offer some initial insight into local news and the issue of class.

## CONSTRUCTING CLASS

*Class* is one of those terms that is rarely defined in American culture. It is much like the term *race*. People use both, but if pressed might not be able to provide an exact set of operational definitions for either. Yet citizens lead lives based on certain assumptions about both. There seem to be innate and often unspoken beliefs about what it means to be black or what it means to be middle class. Even though most people may not know or agree on what exactly distinguishes one class from the next, it remains clear that each of us lives with beliefs about class, which social class we fall into, and where others fall as well. "Social classes and class structure are the most decisive forces that affect us in most everything we do in our lives," argues Berch Berberoglu (1994, vii). According to research, since the 1940s Americans have consistently identified themselves strongly with a social class (Jackman and Jackman 1983).

If class distinctions exist, how does one go about defining a social class? Two of the most influential social theorists, Marx and Weber, both set forth models of how class systems work; each has been widely debated. Both perspectives add greatly to the way we think about class. Suffice it to say that each time a theorist tries to set forth qualifications to define boundaries for different class groups, such as the ownership of land, life chances, or income levels, exceptions to those qualifications can be found. Therefore the boundaries are almost always imperfect.

In this chapter we will not talk about social classes as rigid, well-defined groups. Instead, building on work of theorists such as Jackman and Jackman, we define class as the way in which people make distinctions between themselves and others, based primarily on perceptions about income, inherited wealth, status, and vocation. Jackman and Jackman (1983, 217) have written in their study of class awareness that "classes take shape in public awareness as clusters of people with similar socioeconomic standing." Specifically in regard to the newsroom studied, class was not ever overtly discussed, let alone defined. Yet it most often manifested itself in the way news workers talked about people's income level.

Underlying Americans' class identification are various lines of both visible and invisible class struggles, such as race, gender, and age. Demands for pay equity, antidiscrimination in employment opportunities and the workplace, and government support for affirmative action all point to economic infrastructural deficiencies of the society (Spector 1995). Furthermore, as Patricia Hill Collins (1990) argues, these divisive lines of struggles intersect to engender more subtle systems of oppression.

## CLASS AND NEWS

In general, these are ideas Americans spend time thinking about more than talking about. "Class is not discussed or debated in public because class identity has been stripped from popular culture," writes Gregory Mantsios (1998, 202).

There are, however, ways in which news media do refer to class. Researchers recently have begun dissecting class questions in news coverage by looking specifically at coverage of issues that are tied to more easily identifiable lower classes. For instance, there are news stories, often in print media, about the poor. But researchers have found this coverage is not always fair and accurate. A. Scott Henderson found in a review of media coverage of the poor and public housing in popular periodicals since 1965 that the press presented a distorted image of public housing, portraying an underclass made up of young African Americans who were most often socially dysfunctional. "In this respect, by associating public housing with poverty, crime, racial homogeneity, the popular press conveyed unambiguous messages to its readers, most of whom were white, middle-class, and suburban" (1995, 47).

Another way of dealing with class in an indirect manner is to talk about hunger. When it comes to news media's coverage of this issue, Dan McMurray (1991) has written that coverage has been extremely uneven, from periods of great attention to periods where the subject disappears from view. McMurray contends that political climate, rather than the seriousness of the issue, is responsible for varied interest in the topic.

Homelessness is a topic that has received more coverage in recent years than have others related to class. Gary Blasi wrote that "images and issues relating to 'the homeless' seemed to have a power that issues of 'poverty' or 'housing the poor' did not" (1994, 565). In looking at *New York Times* cover-age of homelessness, Blasi observed that early articles revealed the horrors of homelessness, then stories began detailing efforts to provide assistance, then coverage shifted to deficiencies of the assistance programs and of the persons expected to use them, and finally, more recent stories focused on subgroups of homeless such as mentally disordered and substance abusers, and on backlash against the homeless. In other words, as time passed cov-erage became more cynical.

Welfare is a program that also symbolizes class. Martin Gilens (1999) in an earlier work took a detailed look at Americans' perception of welfare, which he concludes is often negative in no small part due to media coverage. Gilens concludes that because of Americans' persistent stereotypes of African Amer-icans as lazy, there continue to be negative perceptions about welfare.

Ettema and Peer's study of newspaper coverage of two Chicago neigh-borhoods revealed that the coverage of an affluent neighborhood was much more extensive than that of a poorer neighborhood. In addition, when it came to topics of stories, the poorer neighborhood had twice the amount of crime stories than the affluent neighborhood, despite a lower overall crime rate. Even when good news was reported in the poorer neighborhood, the story was reported as a response to some bigger, ongoing pathology.

Though few U.S. media studies have dealt precisely with class, these stud-ies do provide insight as to problems in regard to coverage of poverty, homelessness, and welfare.

## METHOD

As mentioned earlier, both qualitative and quantitative methods were em-ployed in this study. A researcher traveled to Denver, Colorado, a top-25 me-dia market, and spent one month in a television station newsroom as a par-ticipant observer. The researcher who visited the newsroom had spent ten years working in television newsrooms, and therefore negotiating the setting was a relatively easy task. The researcher sat in on all weekday news meet-ings, observed behavior and conversations in the newsroom, went out on stories with reporters and photographers, and conducted nineteen in-depth interviews with news workers. "Qualitative interviewers listen to people as they describe how they understand the worlds in which they live and work" (Rubin and Rubin 1995, 8). For each interview, a basic set of questions served as a starting point, but as much as possible the interview was con-ducted in a manner constructed to simulate a conversation. This allowed the news workers the greatest flexibility in speaking about what was important to them in regard to news coverage, news decision making, and class. Anonymity was guaranteed to those interviewed as well as others observed in the newsroom.

To examine how the issue of class permeated in news stories, the researchers taped 5:00 P.M. and 10:00 P.M. newscasts aired on this Denver station in July 1998. This content analysis included newscasts that are considered to be the station's primary news products: 5:00 P.M. and 10:00 P.M. newscasts that aired Monday through Friday. These newscasts receive the most resources and scrutiny from station personnel. In short, we analyzed what the station itself considers its best news programs. Weekday newscasts were examined that aired between July 6 and July 28. All news stories in a newscast were examined and coded by two trained graduate students.

This content analysis placed a primary focus on the relationships between story topic, story location, demographic characteristics of a person covered in a news story, and the tone of his or her portrayal. Story topics included crime, disaster, human rights, the needy, the environment, education, politics/government, consumer, health, economics/business, weather, feature, and sports. Particular attention was paid to crime, the needy, and economics/business news stories because those story topics were expected to relate to class issues.

Up to four people mentioned in a story were investigated regarding their race (whites, blacks, Hispanics, Asians, Native Americans, or others), estimated age (under ten years old, teens, twenties, thirties, forties, fifties, or sixties and over), gender (male or female), occupation (government, business, education, homeowner, professional, manual labor, clergy, or unemployed), and the tone of their portrayals (positive, neutral, or negative). In addition to basic demographic differences, the study also focused on the target-audience age categories (twenties, thirties, and forties), and white- versus blue-collar workers.

Other variables included newscast time (five o'clock or ten o'clock), geographic level of story topic (national or regional), running time in seconds, reference to class (yes or no), and reference to residence (yes or no).

The intercoder reliability ranged from .71 (story topic) to 1.00 (newscast time and reference to class). The average intercoder reliability was .91.

In total we had 672 news stories. Those stories made up dataset 1. Because more than one person could appear in a single news story, we created a second dataset. Dataset 2 was based on the total number of people appearing in all of the news stories coded. In total, there were 660 people who appeared in news stories. Univariate characteristics and bivariate relationships were examined. This study, though exploratory, reported inferential statistics to observe strengths of such relationships.

## RESULTS

From spending time listening to conversations in the newsroom and discussions in news meetings it became clear early on that class is a topic that is almost never mentioned. That does not mean, however, that there are not ways in which class is implied through more covert means. Through observing the editorial decision-making process ideas about class become more readily apparent. Specifically, the most obvious ways in which the idea of class became apparent was in seeing how news workers conceptualized their audience, and then, in light of that, what groups should therefore receive more news coverage. This two-step process had a large impact on what stories were and were not covered.

One of the most obvious ways of examining how a news operation deals with the idea of class is to closely look at story selection and the story selection process. In this newsroom, like other newsrooms observed, news decision-making power resided in the hands of a few managers. In any television newsroom, the news director generally sits atop the organizational chart. In this newsroom the news director had a set of managers directly under him, with four most directly affecting news decision making. They were the assistant news director, the executive producer, the night-side executive producer, and the assignments manager. These four, in consultation with the news director, controlled most of the content on a day-to-day basis. Two or three of these four would most often attend two daily news meetings, one in the morning and one in the afternoon. Attending these meetings, along with the managers, were the newscast producers. Each producer was responsible for a particular news program, for instance the noon show, or the 5:00 P.M. or 10:00 P.M. news. These producers had some decision-making power in regard to the content of their particular program. The managers would select the big stories of the day with input from others in the meetings, and it was often up to the show producers to fill in shorter, less significant stories that would make up the remainder of their newscasts.

## Targeted Story Selection

In regard to class, in the month the newsroom was observed, there were stories that often fit into one of two classifications: those that were deemed worthy because of audience appeal and those that were not. Clearly the news workers in this newsroom had a very specific idea of an audience. Stories often were not selected with regard to a broad, wide-ranging, and diverse viewership (which is, in fact, the audience of most local television affiliates with the major networks). Instead news workers had a very specific sense of a particular audience they were trying to appeal to. This first became apparent in listening to discussions in news meetings. Exchanges like the following were not uncommon:

> PRODUCER: I've got another Beanie Baby story off the feed.
> EXECUTIVE PRODUCER: Perfect. That's your demo.
> ASSISTANT NEWS DIRECTOR: Get those women watching.

What was meant by demo was demographic. In other words, a particular viewer profile composed of basic information like age and gender. In the nineteen interviews conducted with station personnel, seventeen were with people who worked in the newsroom. Of those seventeen, fifteen identified, when asked, a particular demographic profile of viewers they were trying to attract. The majority said women, though not all agreed on the age parameters of this group of women:

> PRODUCER: Women eighteen to forty-nine is the target.
> REPORTER: It's women in the twenty-five to forty-five bracket or thirty to fifty or something.
> PRODUCER: Women my age—twenty-five to fifty-four.

Women were perceived to be important because of a belief that they controlled decision making when it came to household spending. Several of those interviewed also mentioned characteristics suggesting that class elements made this audience group desirable. "It's females, often young professionals, who make a pretty good living, who live in the suburbs" (assignment editor).

> PRODUCER: Primarily adults eighteen to fifty-four with a socioeconomic level that has been stressed to us. They want families with an income I guess of $30,000 and above and with 2.1 kids and four-wheel drive in the garage. You know stations will boast about how much better their demographics are and how they have the higher demographics and the higher income.
> ASSIGNMENT EDITOR: Suburban, basically, people who are fairly young and have disposable income and children.

The language here points to a fairly specific class profile: a middle- or upper-middle-income family, homeowners who live in the suburbs and have disposable income. Many of those interviewed also had an idea of why this was considered to be an important part of the audience.

> PRODUCER: I guess it is always the eighteen- to forty-four-year-old women, because they tend to buy everything and it's what people sell the advertisers.
> MANAGING EDITOR: Women twenty-five to fifty-four. It's the demo to bring in dollars. One, for sales and two, to raise the ratings. It's the business side of things. We make personnel changes for that reason; we select stories for that reason.

The purpose of targeting this particular group is clear: the "demo to bring in dollars." Television stations have traditionally tried to convince advertisers that they have the highest ratings—the most viewers in their market—and that those viewers are an attractive group of potential customers. In other words, the pitch from station salespeople to advertisers is: if you buy a spot in our local news, this group of people with this profile will see the spot and buy your product or service. The problem lies in whether stations can really deliver audiences that are that specific. Television was traditionally attractive to advertisers because it offered one of the widest and largest markets available. But with the advent of cable, the market became more segmented, especially as cable channels sought to target specific audiences to make up for a lack of sheer audience numbers.

Now it seems, in at least this one newsroom, that having a target market audience has become part and parcel of how a newscast is put together. This is at odds with the traditional view of the purpose of national and local broadcast news. Broadcast news in television was offered initially as a public service, specifically to help stations meet the FCC requirement that stations, since they were broadcasting over public airwaves, serve the public interest. Early on, norms of traditional print journalism were adopted. Eventually broadcast journalists developed their own codes of ethics, and one version was codified by the Radio and Television News Director's Association. It states that broadcast journalists "will evaluate information solely on its merits as news, rejecting sensationalism or misleading emphasis in any form" (RTNDA 1987). In a recent revision of the code, adopted in 2000, this statement is included: "Understand that any commitment other than service to the public undermines trust and credibility" (RTNDA 2000). Yet given what news workers reported here and what was observed in the daily news meetings, there is ample evidence that each and every story is not evaluated on its merits primarily as news, and there was clearly another commitment apparent in news decision making. Once you introduce the idea of a target audience, that becomes a filter through which decisions are made.

Other scholars have identified ways in which economics might influence news judgment. Ben H. Bagdikian (2000) postulated that the concentration of media ownership would negatively influence journalistic freedom and that media corporations would use their power to repress public information when their most sensitive economic issues are at stake. J. Herbert Altschull (1994) has written that local stations' news coverage often generally supports capitalism, reflecting station owners' personal ideology. But what we found in this market shows how, in great detail in at least this one newsroom, the influence of economics is more direct, in that it is overtly discussed by news workers and adopted by them as an acceptable set of criteria by which news decisions should be made, despite ethical codes or other standards of professional practice.

The news director defended his station's practice, arguing that the major news of the day remained untainted: "I would say that doesn't affect the basic coverage plan of the day." He argued that demographic considerations only came into play in the less important news of the day.

NEWS DIRECTOR: Every day there's a series of stories that are elective. You know: do you want to do this, or do you want to do that? And I think from a business standpoint we have gotten people to think about running those stories through a filter—is this story interesting to people who we would like to watch our news more often?

But at least one news staffer disagreed with the news director's assessment. An assignment editor felt identifying a target audience was not in line with journalistic principles:

ASSIGNMENT EDITOR: I think sometimes in catering to target audiences you fail to present a fair and accurate portrayal of news. And let me say I don't think it is primarily a crime of culmination. It is a crime of omission. I think that a lot of times there is bias and it's not that the stories that are aired should not be aired.

An example of this during the period studied was a number of stories and live shots that were done on an annual event in Denver called the Parade of Homes, which centers on the promotion and sales of new homes. The only possible news value to the story was that the parade was taking place at an area that had been a military base but was now opened up to new development. None of the homes featured in the parade were priced under $150,000, so it would be hard to argue that this was a story that was of interest to each and every viewer. Each day producers and managers dedicated resources and news time to covering the home show that could have been spent on other news stories. But it was easily rationalized because the marketing of attractive new homes fit easily into the idea of what was believed would be interesting to the station's target demographic: well-to-do professionals.

Over ten years ago Phyllis C. Kaniss (1991) took a close look at media coverage in one city and found that because so many people, especially people with income, had moved into the suburbs, news coverage of the suburbs had increased, leaving a void of coverage of the inner city. Our findings support what Kaniss found, but in this case news coverage wasn't targeted just by the urban/suburb split, but also by the perceptions of what class of audience might be most interested in the story. John H. McManus (1994), in his study of local television news, found support for his idea of a system of market-driven journalism. Some news decisions were influenced by market forces, such as the cost of covering certain stories, and/or whether stories would attract the largest possible audience. What we observed offers general support for his theory, but what we found in our interviews with news workers was a much more overt orientation toward market forces. There seems to have been a fairly significant shift in the years since his study was published, in that attracting the largest audience is no longer as desirable as attracting an upscale targeted audience, and news workers are not now so reluctant to talk openly about how this orientation impacts day-to-day coverage.

Two separate but not necessarily unrelated phenomena took place in news decision making that affected news coverage with regard to class. The first, discussed above, demonstrates how news managers and producers often actively selected stories on the basis of whether they believed the story would appeal to a certain demographic profile of a viewer. We call this *targeted story selection*. The news staff has a target audience in mind—middle- and upper-class viewers—and news decisions are made in an effort to target those audience members in an effort to increase ratings and sell this more attractive audience to advertisers. The second phenomenon taking place comes in looking at not what stories are selected but what stories are not selected.

## Story Avoidance

As mentioned earlier, class is not a topic that often comes up in daily conversations, let alone in news meetings. As other researchers have described, one way class manifests itself is in the way we think and talk about the poor. Therefore it became interesting to note what attention was given to lower socioeconomic areas in Denver, or how much attention was given to topics that would directly impact poor people.

During the four weeks of the study several stories were discussed that directly impacted what would be considered economically lower-class people in the station's viewing area. In each case, news workers opted not to cover the story. One particularly illuminating example came when the Environmental Protection Agency announced it was holding a meeting to discuss the results of soil testing with residents of a Denver neighborhood. The testing had taken place in a part of Denver called Swansea, an area that had a high crime rate and was populated by the very poor. There was also recent historical significance to the story. In another area, Globeville, soil sampling had revealed high levels of contamination, and through litigation the American Smelting and Refining Company eventually paid out $38 million for a cleanup. The EPA event was discussed at the morning news meeting. Several of the younger producers in the room did not know where Swansea was. The executive producer asked, "Does anyone even speak English down there?" There was scattered laughter. This was a reference to the belief that the population was believed to be recent Spanish-speaking immigrants to the area. In regard to the story one producer said, "It doesn't blow my hair back." No one was assigned to the story and it was not covered. What was never reported by this station was that results from 3,550 soil samples showed in some properties in that area levels of arsenic and lead high enough to prompt the EPA to promise an extensive cleanup. By almost any journalistic standard, this event constituted a news story. About seventy-five neighbors attending the meeting had heated questions about their and their children's safety. The story was timely, it had conflict, it reflected impact on people, and it took place in the proximity of the station's coverage area. But this story did not fit one criterion: It might not have been appealing to an upper-class demographic and did not occur in an area that impacted the news workers making this decision. No one in that meeting, let alone in the station's newsroom, lived in Swansea. Therefore, there was not a sense of urgency or fear among those making the coverage decision. The story did not impact them directly and seemed far removed from the locations of their own homes, which they perhaps assumed were not built on soil full of contaminants. We call this phenomenon story avoidance: a story comes up that by a number of different traditionally held news values should be covered, but is not.

Another example came in the way a story was covered. During the study period Denver suffered a long streak of 100-degree days, a fairly unusual occurrence. The station did extensive coverage, especially in regard to energy use. That much heat for that many days meant that the city's energy use was breaking records. During the heat wave, each day in the morning meeting producers, managers and reporters would try to brainstorm what new angles they could cover. Because of the forecast and the presence of meteorologists at the station, they knew in advance what the daily temperature was likely to be. During this period, only one story—about how firefighters were distributing free fans for anyone who needed them—touched indirectly on how poor people were affected by the heat. Day after day, the station covered different aspects of the story without ever considering the impact on the group arguably most directly impacted by dangerously high temperatures: people who lacked air-conditioning.

One of the station's two parking lots was located a short distance from the building. Each day, many news employees had to walk half a block from their cars to the station. They passed directly in front of two apartment buildings, neither of which had central air-conditioning. During the heat wave, residents were often sitting on the front steps of the building, apparently trying to escape the heat inside the apartments. Despite the fact that journalists passed these people daily, it was never suggested in a news meeting that talking to some of these people or others so directly affected by the heat would be newsworthy. The station at one point did a live shot and reporter story about how the local zoo was taking care of animals in light of the high temperatures. This seemed particularly ironic, considering many zoo animals come from hot, arid regions of the world.

It would be difficult to argue that how poor people were impacted by a heat wave is not a newsworthy story. Yet the story was never discussed in a weekday news meeting and was never covered.

Robert W. McChesney argues:

[T]he corporate media cement a system whereby the wealthy and powerful few make the most important decisions with virtually no informed public participation. Crucial political issues are barely covered by the corporate media, or else are warped to fit the confines of elite debate, stripping ordinary citizens of the tools they need to be informed, active participants in a democracy. (1999, 281)

Although McChesney makes a powerful argument for this by tracing media history, what this study offers is evidence to the same conclusion on a micro and not a macro level. The heat story was shaped into coverage that was neither helpful nor important to the majority of the audience watching. It was instead narrowly focused for what was perceived to be the station's most attractive, elite audience. In this case, public participation, or at least public interest, was thwarted by a group of news workers who avoided any stories about certain segments of the audience. Those news workers were also assuming that stories affecting the poor were of no interest to the general public, an assumption based on no specific or verifiable evidence. It is assumed that the middle and upper classes are as crass and uncaring as this group of journalists themselves.

## News Content

Our content analysis conducted of the newscasts during the study period provides additional evidence of the lack of coverage of the poor.

First, dataset 1, which consists of 672 total news stories, was analyzed to examine various story features including news topics. Regional-level news accounted for 65.2 percent, about twice as many as national-level stories. The average broadcast time was 69.5 seconds, but 59.2 percent of news stories were less than one minute long. Its median was 45 seconds.

Table 5.1 shows the distribution of TV news stories according to topics. One of our focal topics—crime—was the top news topic, representing more than one-fifth of news stories. Economics/business came fourth, which was dealt with in more than 10 percent of stories. 'The needy,' however, had the second smallest share of news stories, accounting for only 1.9 percent. Furthermore, only nine (1.3 percent) out of 672 stories made direct references to class. None of the nine stories, however, mentioned people's residences. These results seem to substantiate our qualitative findings of newsroom decision-making processes to avoid class stories in general.

**Table 5.1.   Frequencies of Story Topics**

| Topic | Number of Stories (N = 672) | Percentage |
|---|---|---|
| Crime | 147 | 21.9 |
| Sports | 80 | 11.9 |
| Weather | 75 | 11.2 |
| Economics/business | 69 | 10.3 |
| Consumer | 59 | 8.8 |
| Feature | 53 | 7.9 |
| Politics/government | 51 | 7.6 |
| Disaster | 39 | 5.8 |
| Health | 35 | 5.2 |
| Environment | 32 | 4.8 |
| Human rights | 13 | 1.9 |
| The needy | 13 | 1.9 |
| Education | 6 | 0.9 |

Next, analysis of dataset 2 delved into the issue of class in demographics of people who appeared in news stories; 352 news stories referred to at least one person, containing 660 people in total. Table 5.2 shows distributions of demographic characteristics of those people. They were predominantly white and male. The largest age category was the thirties, and the professional-occupation category represented more than a half of people in news. Their portrayals were mostly positive. These characteristics represented the most typical combination of attributes of people mentioned in news stories, accounting for 7.6 percent (*N* = 50). Regarding age, the TV station's target audiences, who were in their twenties, thirties, or forties, accounted for approximately three-quarters (72.4 percent), although the percentage of people in their twenties was quite small. Manual laborers constituted a small portion of people in news (4.7 percent), which reflects the diminution of traditional blue-collar workers in our society.

Due to a small frequency of each nonwhite category, the variable race was dichotomized into whites and nonwhites. Contrary to our expectation, minority members were not strongly associated with such "class" topics as crime, the needy, and economics/business.

However, older white males seemed to occupy the focal attention in the TV representation of the world, which signifies their high status in the hierarchical class ladder. As table 5.3 shows, whites tended to be older while nonwhites were more likely younger. The largest racial difference was among people under twenty. In addition, the mean broadcast time was longer for whites than nonwhites. See table 5.4. Similarly, males received the longer mean broadcast time than females, although the difference was not as great as that of race.

**Table 5.2. Demographic Characteristics of People Who Appeared in News**

| Race (N = 655) | Age (N = 623) | Gender (N = 653) | Occupation (N = 387) | Portrayal (N = 629) |
|---|---|---|---|---|
| Whites 81.5% | >10 1.6% | Male 72.7% | Professional 56.1% | Positive 61.5% |
| Blacks 11.0% | 10s 10.6% | Female 27.3% | Government 28.9% | Neutral 22.4% |
| Hispanics 5.8% | 20s 5.0% | | Manual labor 4.7% | Negative 16.1% |
| Asians 1.2% | 30s 41.3% | | Business 4.4% | |
| Native Am. 0.5% | 40s 26.2% | | Education 2.1% | |
| Others 0% | 50s 12.7% | | Homeowner 2.1% | |
| | 60s & over 2.7% | | Clergy 1.3% | |
| | | | Unemployed 0.5% | |

**Table 5.3.    Cross Tabulation of Age by Race**

| Age | Whites n = 510 | Nonwhites n = 109 |
|---|---|---|
| Younger than 20 | 10.4% | 21.1% |
| | (n = 53) | (n = 23) |
| Between 20 and 49 | 73.5% | 67.0% |
| | (n = 375) | (n = 73) |
| Fifty and older | 16.1% | 12.0% |
| | (n = 82) | (n = 13) |

$\chi^2$(Pearson) = 9.930, d.f. = 2, $p$ = .007; total $N$ = 619.

Yet gender did affect which age category one would be in. As table 5.5 shows, males tended to be older, the largest difference observed among people under twenty. Although less than 10 percent of males were younger than twenty, approximately one-quarter of females were in this age category.

Contrary to our expectation, manual laborers were not associated with class news topics. Whereas only one (5.6 percent) out of eighteen manual laborers appeared in these types of news, 140 (38.2 percent) out of 367 white-collar workers were included. The largest news topic was human rights (33.3 percent, $N$ = 6) for manual laborers, and crime (27.3 percent, $N$ = 100) for white-collar workers. Also only two (11.1 percent) manual laborers appeared in news stories that made direct references to class. The vast majority of those blue-collar workers were white (94.4 percent, $N$ = 17) and male (83.3 percent, $N$ = 15), who received positive coverage (77.8 percent, $N$ = 14).

In order to examine bivariate demographic relationships for class news topics, people who appeared in crime, the needy, and economics/business stories were examined ($N$ = 283). Table 5.6 shows the relationship between age and race. Compared to table 5.3, which exhibited for all news topics the largest racial difference in the youngest age category, it was the oldest age category that had a disproportionately higher percentage of minorities than whites (27.3 percent vs. 11.8 percent). On the other hand, the category of people between twenty and forty-nine showed a much higher percentage of whites than minorities (71.8 percent vs. 54.6 percent).

**Table 5.4.    Mean Broadcast Time by Race and Gender**

| Race | Mean Air Time in Seconds (Standard Deviation) | T-value |
|---|---|---|
| Whites (n = 534) | 110.5 (66.6) | 3.16, d.f. = 653, p = .002 |
| Nonwhites (n = 121) | 89.5 (63.5) | |
| Gender | | |
| Male (n = 475) | 109.1 (69.9) | 1.83, d.f. = 382.6, p = .069 |
| Female (n = 178) | 99.2 (57.6) | |

**Table 5.5.    Cross Tabulation of Age by Gender**

| Age | Male<br>n = 446 | Female<br>n = 171 |
|---|---|---|
| Younger than 20 | 7.9%<br>(n = 35) | 23.4%<br>(n = 40) |
| Between 20 and 49 | 74.0%<br>(n = 330) | 68.4%<br>(n = 117) |
| Fifty and older | 18.2%<br>(n = 81) | 8.2%<br>(n = 14) |

$\chi^2$(Pearson) = 33.086, d.f. = 2, $p$ = .001; total $N$ = 617.

Table 5.7 shows the relationship between age and gender in class news topics. Similar to table 5.5, males tended to be older than females in class topics. Differences in news topics did not seem to affect this bivariate relationship.

These findings alone might not have been very telling, but linked with the observations made in the newsroom, they seemed to confirm that, as least at this station during the study period, stories on the poor were avoided and coverage of whites was disproportionately strong.

### Content-Reality Comparisons

After examining the station's news coverage, we compared it to demographic data to see how the coverage had deviated from actual demographic distributions. The statistics used here are based on the Denver, Colorado, PMSA (Primary Metropolitan Statistical Area), the area that is served by the station. Although there are some time-frame differences between our study and the demographic data we used, we chose the data as close to our study period as possible.

The most striking finding was a contrast between the station's virtual indifference to 'the needy' and the proportion of those living below the poverty level. In 1997, the total population of the area was a little over 1.9 million. This

**Table 5.6.    Cross Tabulation of Age by Race in "Class" News**

| Age | Whites<br>n = 220 | Nonwhites<br>n = 44 |
|---|---|---|
| Younger than 20 | 16.4%<br>(n = 36) | 18.2%<br>(n = 8) |
| Between 20 and 49 | 71.8%<br>(n = 158) | 54.6%<br>(n = 24) |
| Fifty and older | 11.8%<br>(n = 26) | 27.3%<br>(n = 12) |

$\chi^2$(Pearson) = 7.744, d.f. = 2, $p$ = .021; total $N$ = 264

**Table 5.7.   Cross Tabulation of Age by Gender in "Class" News**

| Age | Male $n = 193$ | Female $n = 72$ |
|---|---|---|
| Younger than 20 | 11.9% ($n = 23$) | 29.2% ($n = 21$) |
| Between 20 and 49 | 70.5% ($n = 136$) | 65.3% ($n = 47$) |
| Fifty and older | 17.6% ($n = 34$) | 5.6% ($n = 4$) |

$\chi^2$(Pearson) $= 14.921$, d.f. $= 2$, $p = .001$; total $N = 265$

is a metro area where the median income in 1994 was only estimated at a little over $24,000 annually and where as of 1993, slightly over 10 percent were living under the poverty line (U.S. Bureau of the Census 1998, 61, 91, 97). However, only 1.9 percent of all news stories during our study period were devoted to the needy. Furthermore, while the 1996 unemployment rate was 3.8 percent (U.S. Bureau of the Census 1998, 103), only 0.5 percent of people in the news whose occupations were known belonged to the unemployed category.

This tremendous discrepancy signifies not symbolic misrepresentation of the poor, but rather, in its literal sense, what Gaye Tuchman (1978) calls "symbolic annihilation." In other words, as far as the station's coverage and representations are concerned, the issue of class seems to occupy a distinctly different stage or be making much slower progress than that of other social-inequality variables such as race, gender, and sexuality.

Looking at the history of media representations, we know that people of color, particularly African Americans, struggled for more representation when their images were almost nonexistent in the first half of the twentieth century. As mass media presented more and more images of African Americans, the goal of the fight shifted from an increase of media representations to an elimination of negative stereotypes and a creation of more positive images. Similarly, women and gay communities have demanded that mass media represent them fairly, accurately, and positively (see, e.g., Croteau and Hoynes 2000, chap. 6). However, the lower classes, specifically the poor, continue to suffer from nonrepresentation by the media.

Why this utter void of media attention to the lower classes? History unequivocally points to the persistent profit motive behind the dynamics of media industry. James Curran (1979), for example, describes how the British radical, working-class press, which thrived in the first half of the nineteenth century and whose primary revenue source was readership or circulation, declined due to tough economic competition posed by less political middle-class papers that relied on advertising. As Croteau and Hoynes state, "To advertisers, reaching smaller numbers of upper- or middle-class readers seemed to be a better sales strategy than reaching large numbers of working-class readers who did not have the necessary resources to buy many of the advertised goods and services" (2000, 68). Now that the middle class has become predominant in contemporary society, the lower classes seem to have almost no value to advertisers or the mass media. This is the nature of commercial media, and local television stations are no exception.

As of 1996, the state of Colorado had 98.4 males per 100 females (U.S. Bureau of the Census 1998, 4), which basically indicates an equilibrium between two genders. Assuming that this ratio was the same as that of the Denver, Colorado, PMPA, we found that the station's news coverage was highly skewed toward male dominance. Males predominated news stories, tended to get longer coverage, and were more likely older than females (see tables 5.2, 5.4, 5.5).

In 1996, whites constituted 90.1 percent of the population of the Denver metro area (U.S. Bureau of the Census 1998, 67). While nonwhites received more representation than this demographic statistic indicted, their mean airtime was far less than their white counterparts (see tables 5.2, 5.4).

Finally, in 1996, people between fifty-five and sixty-four accounted for 8.0 percent of the population, and people sixty-five or older 9.4 percent (U.S. Bureau of the Census 1998, 67). However, our content analysis showed that 12.7 percent of people in news were in their fifties, and only 2.7 percent in their sixties (see table 5.2). In contrast, people in their thirties and forties received disproportionately greater coverage than the older groups. Again, the same economic logic of mass media, which attempts to attract people with disposable income, seems to apply.

In sum, the issue of class seemed to persist in the station's news coverage, especially in terms of its nonrepresentation of the lower-class segment of society. The title of the ABC profile of its viewing audience issued in the 1970s succinctly summarizes this trend: "Some People Are More Important Than Others" (Croteau and Hoynes 2000, 216).

## Class and Local Broadcast News

This brings us to consider why and how news decisions were made in regard to class. The newsroom, through discussions and decisions, constructed two classes: those who were in the target market, which we could call a privileged class, and those who were not. Those who were not in the target audience did not have the economic clout to be considered in news decisions. Some decisions were based on the emphasis of trying to appeal to a certain part of the audience. Even when a target demographic did not enter into the spoken discussion of a story idea, there was another dynamic at work. In morning and afternoon editorial meetings, in discussions in the newsroom, and in management meetings, one group was never represented: the poor. One reporter put it this way: "It's just not a view that's represented at our

editorial meetings. It just isn't something we consciously forget or actively ignore. It's just sometimes it can be a very difficult viewpoint to get advanced."
This newsroom, like many newsrooms, was staffed by people who could
easily be classified by almost any method as middle- or upper-middle class.
Every person interviewed was college educated, and an analysis of home addresses of news employees revealed that the vast majority lived in the suburbs in areas identified by census figures as middle- and upper-middle income neighborhoods. Weaver and Wilhoit (1986, 6) have concluded in a
sample of U.S. journalists that most come from the "established and dominant cultural groups in the society."

> PRODUCER: A lot of us don't come from poor backgrounds. A lot of us don't
> understand that and don't think those people watch. You know, we do home-
> less stories when the weather gets cold and so forth because it is something we
> can feel compassion for. But on a day-to-day basis we aren't going to do a lot of
> those stories.

When questioned about it, news workers themselves were aware of the coverage deficit.

> ASSIGNMENT EDITOR: As a general rule no, I don't think we cover poor peo-
> ple very well. Since none of us are poor we don't think of them. We don't think
> of what they are doing in the heat or in cold weather, for example.

It comes down to whether each day, as managers and other newsroom personnel consider what might be covered, they are concerned with people
who are from different class backgrounds, who live different experiences,
who face a different set of daily realities especially economically.

> MANAGING EDITOR: I don't think we run from it but I don't think we think
> about it. It's not like we're committed to helping them improve their lives or get
> the assistance they need. If a story comes up and fits into our day where we can
> go and cover it we might pick it up. But I can't even tell you the last package
> we've done on it.

What became evident in observing the newsroom, sitting in on news meetings, and interviewing station workers, was there was a consistent lack of
knowledge, and in some cases care, about people with lower-class economic backgrounds. A young news writer at the station seemed to have a full
understanding of the problem:

> NEWS WRITER: It strikes me as we just don't know. Or some of us do know but
> aren't at the morning meetings to say anything which is a mistake. Somehow
> we've got to get that knowledge or get our hands on that knowledge of we don't
> know it and that knowledge comes in various ways. It comes culturally, it comes
> through various contacts whether environmentally or politically or whatever.

You can never have enough people who have that knowledge, and that's something we have to work on.

## CONCLUSION

Several decades ago, sociologist C. Wight Mills (1956) in *The Power Elite* wrote that the men who controlled the media are among the most important in culture because of their ability to influence a mass society. In 1979 Herbert J. Gans published a seminal study of news decision making titled *Deciding What's News*. Gans studied two networks' news programs and two national newsmagazines. He found that "the news especially values the order of the upper-class and middle-class sectors of society" (Gans 1979, 61). Because of journalists' own positions in the middle and upper-middle classes, Gans wrote that they represent best their own perspective and not those of the lower classes.

In this study we found evidence to support Gans's contention on a local television news level. Because of phenomena such as targeted story selection and story avoidance, we contend that news coverage of the poor specifically and of the lower classes in general in this one market was sorely lacking. Because many of these news workers had worked in other stations in other markets and reported similar attitudes and philosophies, this may not be an isolated case. Others such as Bagdikian (2000), Altschull (1994) and McChesney (1999) have argued persuasively about the negative impact generally of economics on news coverage. This research looked at one specific newsroom and demonstrated how news workers themselves may be now aiming coverage at one particular demographic—the well-to-do—and away from the less fortunate. McManus (1994) argued forcefully how an economic model negatively influences news coverage decisions, but his work dealt with more the economic workings of news organization in an era when stations were still trying to attract the largest possible audience to help build ratings. In this newsroom, we saw a clear shift from the desire for a wide audience to a very economically elite and gender-specific audience.

We began this chapter with a quote from Disraeli about two nations that know nothing of each other: the rich and the poor. Toward the end of the twentieth century the American economy was enjoying record gains. Whether those gains were helping America's poor, or whether this era meant a larger disparity between the haves and the have-nots, the public might have difficulty knowing, if they depend on local news and if what was found in Denver is replicated in other television news operations around the country. In this market, at this station, news was constructed as a product aimed primarily at those who had disposable income, lived in the suburbs, and had significant purchasing power.

# REFERENCES

Altschull, J. Herbert. 1994. *Agents Of Power: The Media and Public Policy*. 2nd ed. White Plains, N.Y.: Longman.

Bagdikian, Ben H. 2000. *The Media Monopoly*, 6th ed. Boston: Beacon.

Berberoglu, Berch. 1994. *Class Structure and Social Transformation*. Westport, Conn.: Praeger.

Blasi, Gary. 1994. "And We Are Not Seen: Ideological and Political Barriers to Understanding Homelessness." *American Behavioral Scientist* 37, no. 4: 563–86.

Collins, Patricia Hill. 1990. *Black Feminist Thought: Knowledge, Consciousness, and the Politics of Empowerment*. Boston: Unwin Hyman.

Croteau, David, and William Hoynes. 2000. *Media/Society: Industries, Images, and Audiences*. 2nd ed. Thousand Oaks, Calif.: Pine Forge.

Curran, James. 1979. "Capitalism and Control of the Press, 1800–1975." In James Curran, Michael Gurevitch, and Janet Woollacott, eds., *Mass Communication and Society*, 195–230. Beverly Hills, Calif.: Sage.

Gans, Herbert J. 1979. *Deciding What's News: A Study of CBS Evening News, NBC Nightly News, Newsweek, and Time*. New York: Vintage.

Gilens, Martin. 1999. *Why Americans Hate Welfare: Race, Media, and the Politics of Antipoverty Policy*. Chicago: University of Chicago Press.

Henderson, A. Scott. 1995. "'Tarred with the Exceptional Image': Public Housing and Popular Discourse, 1950–1990." *American Studies* 36, no. 1: 31–52.

Jackman, Mary R., and Robert W. Jackman. 1983. *Class Awareness in the United States*. Berkeley: University of California Press.

Kaniss, Phyllis C. 1991. *Making Local News*. Chicago: University of Chicago Press.

Mantsios, Gregory. 1998. "Class in America: Myths and Realities." In Paula S. Rothenberg, ed., *Race, Class, and Gender in the United States: An Integrated Study*, 131–43. 4th ed. New York: St. Martin's.

McChesney, Robert W. 1999. *Rich Media, Poor Democracy: Communication Politics in Dubious Times*. Urbana: University of Illinois Press.

McManus, John H. 1994. *Market-Driven Journalism: Let the Citizen Beware?* Thousand Oaks, Calif.: Sage.

McMurray, Dan. 1991. "The Several Faces of Hunger: A Review of the Amount and Types of Information Available to the Public on Domestic Hunger, 1967–1990." *National Journal of Sociology* 5, no. 2: 92–109.

Mills, C. Wright. 1956. *The Power Elite*. London: Oxford University Press.

RTNDA. Code of Ethics. 1987. Unanimously adopted by the RTNDA board of directors.

———. Code of Ethics. 2000. Adopted September 14, 2000, by the RTNDA board of directors.

Rubin, Herbert J., and Irene S. Rubin. 1995. *Qualitative Interviewing: The Art of Hearing Data*. Thousand Oaks, Calif.: Sage.

So, Alvin Y. 1995. "Recent Developments in Marxist Class Analysis: A Critical Appraisal." *Sociological Inquiry* 65, no. 3–4: 313–28.

Spector, Alan J. 1995. "Class Structure and Social Change: The Contradictions of Class Relations in Advanced Capitalist Society." *Sociological Inquiry* 65, no. 3–4: 329–38.

Stevenson, Richard W. 2000. "The Nation: In a Time of Plenty, The Poor Are Still Poor." *New York Times*, January 23, sec. 4, p. 3.

Tuchman, Gaye. 1978. "Introduction: The Symbolic Annihilation of Women by the Mass Media." In Gaye Tuchman, Arlene Kaplan Daniels, and James Benét, eds., *Hearth and Home: Images of Women in the Mass Media*, 3–38. New York: Oxford University Press.

U.S. Bureau of the Census. 1998. *State and Metropolitan Area Data Book, 1997–98*. Washington, D.C.

Weaver, David H., and G. Cleveland Wilhoit. 1986. *The American Journalist: A Portrait of U.S. News People and Their Work*. Bloomington: Indiana University Press.

# 6

# The Social Stratification Potential of Tabloid and Highbrow Newsmagazine Programs

*Maria Elizabeth Grabe*

Tabloid journalism has been discussed with much fervor over the past decade. Carl Bernstein characterizes one pole of this public debate when he refers to tabloid journalism as public discourse turned into a kind of news "sewer" perpetuating an "idiot culture" (Bernstein 1992, 22, 28). At the heart of this outrage are three popular concerns about the tabloids: they violate notions of good taste, displace socially significant stories, and are viewed as a newly sprung drift into excessiveness. A number of scholars have refuted these three concerns.

First, regarding notions of good taste, the practice of journalism must be positioned in terms of the high and low culture distinction. According to Gans (1974), high culture refers to the music, art, literature, and other symbolic products that are preferred by members of the educated elite, and to the styles of thought and ways of living associated with those who are "cultured." Mass, popular, or low culture refers to the symbolic products associated with the poor, uneducated, working, "uncultured" classes. Tabloid news, like any other popular culture artifact, presents the supposedly unsophisticated version of the highbrow ideal. Tabloid newspapers were developed with two goals in mind: to achieve commercial success and to serve nonelite citizens. Until the development of the penny press in the 1830s, American newspapers mostly served an elite audience consisting mainly of politicians and businesspeople. The penny press generated popular and affordable papers that appealed to the masses but provoked critical outrage among elites. The intention to serve ordinary people continued with the Pulitzer and Hearst newspapers. The two newspaper tycoons claimed to promote democracy by featuring the views and issues central to the lives of common people. Today there are indications that the content (story topics) of tabloid newspapers such as the *National Enquirer* caters to ordinary people. When we condemn popular culture, including tabloid news, as fit only for those with poor taste, we are reinforcing the divisions in society that our democratic pursuits have attempted to eliminate (see Shusterman 1992).

Second, in response to the argument that the tabloids displace news that is truly important to an informed citizenry, scholars have pointed out that stories about family conflicts, substance abuse, violence, disaster, and other disruptions of everyday life are more significant to the lives of ordinary people than the traditional political and economic issues that elites prescribe as important information for the masses (Bird 1992; Grabe 1997; Stevens 1985). Shusterman (1992, 187) calls this denial of the legitimacy of problems facing ordinary people a "convenient strategy for the privileged and the conservative to ignore and suppress the realities of those they dominate." Like the penny press papers of the 1830s, today's tabloids have made news accessible and popular among nonelite audiences, perhaps serving a democratizing function.

Finally, historians have pointed out that the discontent with the current state of journalism in America stems from mostly unsupported nostalgia about the profession's supposed exemplary past. Bernstein's (1992, 25) argument that "for the first time in our history the weird and the stupid and the coarse are becoming our cultural norm, even our cultural ideal" lacks historical insight. Sensational news stories date back to news books and news ballads in Europe during the late 1500s (Bird 1992; Shaw and Slater 1985; Stevens 1985). Since then public outrage about sensational journalism has become a periodic ritual. Reactions to the penny press of the 1830s, "yellow journalism" at the end of the nineteenth century, and the findings of the Hutchins Commission after World War II strongly resemble the damning tone of current public discourse about sensationalism in news (Altschull 1990; Tannenbaum and Lynch 1960). The recent preoccupation with tabloid news should therefore be put into historical perspective rather than presented as an issue unique to contemporary times.

The recurrence of moral panic about tabloid journalism signals its ritualistic function in society. It is not unreasonable to argue that this perennial debate is functional to the complicated process whereby societies reaffirm social class distinctions. When tabloid journalism is repeatedly and publicly condemned as a tasteless and inferior news source, those who consume news from such sources are cast at lower levels of the social hierarchy. But the *content* of tabloid and highbrow journalism is also suspected of containing narrative elements to promote social class segregation among their respective viewing publics. Thus, through exposure to the content of a specific news genre an audience acquires the sensibilities that find expression in that news genre. Bourdieu (1989) offers comprehensive evidence that this socialization process takes place though the consumption of media and consumer products. Put simply, social class distinctions between members of a social system are drawn through what they consume. Mass media use plays a substantial role in this process. Bird (1992) argues that tabloid newspaper stories subtly suggest a separation of lower-class tabloid readers from the upper-middle and upper classes (see also Grabe 1997; Grabe, Zhou, and Barnett 1999). For example, although tabloid news is preoccupied with celebrity news, it does not cover stories about famous icons in high fashion or art circles. Tabloid television is politically cynical and morally conservative. It emphasizes the corruption, self-interest, and greed of the politically powerful and the upper class, while simultaneously promoting traditional, religious, blue-collar values (Bird 1992; Knight 1989). Bird (1992) also argues that tabloid newspaper content has always provided hope for working-class readers with its heavy doses of "rags to riches" stories, while simultaneously offering consolation in its emphasis on "money can't buy happiness" narratives (Bird 1992; Knight 1989).

Using data from two studies of television newsmagazine programs, this chapter offers systematic evidence to buttress the notion that the content of tabloid and highbrow news stories differs and that these patterned disparities support the socialization of audiences at different levels of the social order. The argument that tabloid news poses a threat to highbrow sensibilities by debasing all, or most of, the news landscape is directly contradicted by this data. In fact, the findings reveal several distinctions between highbrow and tabloid news content and suggest that the line that separates these two news formats is robust. This conclusion is drawn from examining two narrative mechanisms through which social hierarchy is expressed.

The first study comparatively examined the socioeconomic status of news sources on *Hard Copy* and *60 Minutes*. The opportunity to speak, symbolically deems sources as important. The questions addressed in this study are whether the two newsmagazine programs (1) favored news sources from a specific socioeconomic group and (2) varied in this favoritism. People in lower-middle and lower classes are more likely to watch tabloid newsmagazines while the audience of highbrow shows such as *60 Minutes* are mostly members from the upper-middle and upper classes. If the demography of news sources appearing on the two programs reflects the same class division, the potential for strengthening social class distinctions through variant sourcing patterns becomes evident.

The second study looked specifically at the social class of criminals and victims on a larger selection of highbrow and former tabloid newsmagazine programs. Crime stories offer a unique opportunity to observe the promotion of distrust among demographic groups. If a specific social class dominates in the role of the criminal wariness of that group is a likely outcome, especially if the audience resembles the socioeconomic status of the most prominently reported victim. Again, the question is whether the two magazine formats, tabloid versus highbrow, vary in the demographic profile of whom they present in the role of criminals and victims. If that is the case, newsmagazine shows promote classism in their respective audiences.

Newsmagazine programs provided the most comprehensive format for showcasing the demography of news sources as well as criminals and victims. Unlike the brief segments of nightly newscasts, the longer newsmagazine format allows for more in-depth development of news stories and more opportunity for interviews with news sources. Moreover, magazine programs are prominent on the network prime-time schedule, and have larger audiences and are rated as more trustworthy than any other source of news in America. While the national and local television news audience has shrunk from 30 percent in 1993 to 15 percent in 1998, the newsmagazine audience has held steady since 1996 (Pew Research Center 1998). For the first week of 1998, the nightly network newscasts on ABC, CBS, and NBC averaged 12.5 million viewers per night while *60 Minutes* alone drew 19.8 million viewers in the same week (Mifflin 1998). Newsmagazine programs apparently have also become the most trustworthy source of news information for Americans: 51 percent of the audience trust the information of newsmagazine programs, whereas 43 percent trust the information on nightly newscasts and 37 percent trust national newspapers (Sawyer 1998).

## STUDY 1:THE SOCIAL CLASS OF VOICES IN THE NEWS

Schudson (1978) asserts that news making begins with news sources and that if journalism indeed provides the first rough draft of history, news sources are the first drafts people.[1] In a society that places a high premium on equality and democracy, the demographic makeup of those who have their voices represented in the news is expected to be diverse. Yet a number of scholars point out that journalists routinely select a small group of empowered elite voices to serve as society's experts, analysts, and commentators (Berkowitz 1987; Brown, Bybee, Wearden, and Straughan 1987; Gans 1979; Sigal 1973, 1986).

Berkowitz (1987, 513) argues that sources play a large part "in shaping information from which people unconsciously build their images of the world." Research on this topic reveals that in newspapers and television news alike, Washington-based, institutional, white, male elites dominate as news sources who shape viewers' images of the world. Depending on operational definitions and the specific news publication, between 55 and 78 percent of news sources in print media are local, state, national, and international government officials (Brown et al. 1987; Gans 1979; Sigal 1973), while approximately 49 percent of television news sources are government officials (Berkowitz 1987; Whitney et al. 1989). Sigal (1973) and Brown et al. (1987) also point out that journalists show preference for elite sources in the commercial realm. More than a quarter of news sources in newspapers are part of a business enterprise. Particularly troubling is that these elite sources from the world of business and government are used to cite "facts" without further investigation (Ericson,

Baranek, and Chan 1989).[2] As Soloski (1989) argues, news sources take the position of society's reifiers of "fact" turning what is essentially a product of human creation into perceptions of fact.[3] The dominance of those in power to speak and be heard contradicts the very notion of a pluralistic society in which journalists have a social responsibility to safeguard the rights of individuals and to assume the role of a watchdog over government and big business. If journalists engage in a symbiotic relationship with government sources their self-imposed role as scrutinizers of government actions is compromised.[4] Parenti (1986) points out that this relationship between journalists and government sources "continually recreates a view of reality supportive of existing social and economic class power." Gans (1979) refers to this relationship as a conspiratorial dance against the public where sources mostly do the leading.

Yet a number of scholars don't view journalists' reliance on government officials as willful or consciously biased actions. Sigal (1973) argues that efficiency dictates newsgathering through routine channels. Journalists are merely striving to meet deadlines and thereby rely on those news sources who are available for comments (Epstein 1974; Gans 1979; Gandy 1982; Tuchman 1978). Government agencies, aware of the time and financial constraints on news organizations provide journalists with news releases ready for publication, close to deadlines. This leads to a strong affiliation with government institutions (Dominick 1977; Whitney et al. 1989)[5] and perhaps an unhealthy dependence on official government sources (Brown et al. 1987; Gans 1979; Sigal 1973).

What is not debated in this body of literature is that ordinary citizens are assigned a much different position in terms of prominence and prevalence in the news. Whitney et al. (1989) report that only 25.7 percent of news sources in network news are private individuals. Similarly, Gans (1979) found that only one-fifth of news sources in CBS News and *Newsweek* were ordinary people and they were most likely to be rioters, strikers, or victims of some sort. Gans (1979, 15) remarks that "most ordinary people never come into the news, except as statistics. How ordinary people work, what they do outside working hours, in their families, churches, clubs, and other organizations, and how they relate to government and public agencies hardly ever make the news." According to Hallin (1992) the mean duration of a sound bite of the "average citizen" is four seconds, whereas the mean for elite sources is nine seconds. Yet Hallin (1986) argues that the evening news in the United States shows much stronger focus on the lives of ordinary citizens than news in most other countries. The research focus for the first study is to assess if *Hard Copy* and *60 Minutes* favored sources from a specific social class and if the two programs varied in whom they gave voice to.

## Method

A content analysis of twenty-seven weeks of *Hard Copy* and *60 Minutes* programs was conducted. *Hard Copy* and *60 Minutes* were chosen because they exemplify the two poles of the tabloid/respectable television news-magazine genre (see Briller 1993; Rapping 1992; Rosenberg 1989).[6] The mother of the newsmagazine format, *60 Minutes*, reaches a larger audience than any other news program in the history of American journalism (Campbell 1991). The program's historical importance, critical acclaim, and credibility with the news audience mark it as a cornerstone of respectable television journalism (Campbell 1991; Keller 1993; Freedom Forum 1998; Sawyer 1998). In public debate *60 Minutes* is often held up as the antithesis of *Hard Copy*. For example, in 1997 CBS executives decided to scrap an interview with Bill Cosby about an extramarital affair that would have aired on *60 Minutes* after *Hard Copy* featured Cosby's admission of the affair (Levin 1997). The producers of *60 Minutes* expressed concern that they would be accused of stooping to tabloid tactics. Don Hewitt, the executive producer of *60 Minutes*, stated that the program "is too important a franchise to get caught up in that kind of circus" (Levin 1997). In 1996, a panel of twenty-four television executives, chaired by Jack Valenti, was confronted with the question: What is a news program? (Farhi 1996). The panel decided to reserve the news label for "traditional news programs" including *60 Minutes* but specifically excluding *Hard Copy* and thereby positioning the two programs at opposite ends of the news landscape in terms of respectability (Farhi 1996).

A little more than twenty-five hours of television newsmagazine stories (excluding advertisements, logos, promotions, and anchor chatter) were analyzed. A six-month (July 1, 1996, to December 31, 1996) census of *60 Minutes* programs was used for the analysis. The same period was used for sampling *Hard Copy* programs. Because *Hard Copy* was broadcast five days a week on local stations, one *Hard Copy* program per week was randomly drawn for analysis.

Individual news sources were used as the unit of analysis. They were analyzed in terms of their prominence, namely, the frequency and duration of their appearance, whether they were introduced with voice-over narration and visual material, the frequency with which they were cited in voice-over narrations, and the number of times that reporters interrupted news sources. The institutional affiliation[7] and the position from which sources contributed information to the news story were also coded.[8] The demographic analysis of news sources focused on social class and education.

This study's coding instrument for social class was based on what DeFleur (1964), Estep and MacDonald (1983, 1985), and Greene and Bynum (1982) used in their content analyses of television characters. Sources were coded as belonging to the upper class when they were presented as members of the "old rich" or the "nouveau riche" successful elite. Members of this class are financially independent (have no need to work) or exemplify the gold-collar occupational level (i.e., executives or proprietors of large concern, major professionals or celebrities, and professional athletes). A higher education was considered in coding a source as belonging to the upper class but not to the exclusion of the relatively uneducated "nouveau riche."

The middle class was identified by comfortable living standards without extraordinary riches and mention of a higher education. Members of this class fall into a group between the gold- and blue-collar occupational levels. In other words, the middle class includes white-collar occupations such as technicians (i.e., computer programmers, laboratory technicians), minor professionals (i.e., nurses, school teachers, salespeople), farmers of medium production, and small proprietors. The coding instrument did not distinguish between upper and lower levels of the middle class.

The working class was identified by the depiction of a lifestyle of just getting along or barely making ends meet. Members of this class are from the blue-collar occupational level, including semi-skilled or unskilled workers (i.e., manual laborers, artisans, and kindred workers). The homeless, unemployed, and destitute were coded using the "at poverty level" option, whereas coders used the "undetermined" choice when they could not determine the social class of news sources.

The highest education level of sources was coded using the following options: Ph.D., other graduate degree (e.g., M.A., M.F.A., law, medical doctor in general practice), B.A., high school only, high school not completed, undetermined.

Three coders with graduate degrees in mass communication who worked as broadcast journalists participated in data collection. After a coding manual was developed, three coder training sessions were held. These sessions also helped refine and revise the categories for this study. Material from recorded programs that were not included in this study's population was used during training sessions. The coding for this study was completed over a six-month period. The overall reliability for this study is .93 (Krippendorff's alpha). Evaluative categorical items, which involved qualitative judgment (i.e., social class) yielded agreement of .85, while the reliability for simple categorical counts (i.e., duration of source appearances) was .97.

## Results

A total of 184 *Hard Copy* news stories were analyzed, yielding 416.87 minutes of program time. The mean duration of a *Hard Copy* segment was 2.27 minutes. The total program time of the 107 *60 Minutes* stories was 1,101.58 minutes with a mean duration of 10.30 minutes per story. Altogether sources occupied 24.76 percent of program time and the mean duration of a source appearance was 33.52 seconds. *60 Minutes* lent more prominence to sources than *Hard Copy*. The mean duration of source appearances on *60 Minutes* was 51.57 seconds compared to 15.47 seconds on *Hard Copy*. *60 Minutes* sources also took up noticeably more program time (30.9 percent) than *Hard Copy* sources (18.61 percent). Also noteworthy is the fact that *60 Minutes* lent more latent prominence to sources than *Hard Copy*: just over 91 percent of *60 Minutes* sources were introduced with voice-over narration and video material prior to their sound bites and 34.6 percent of *60 Minutes* sources were cited in the reporter's voice-over narration. By comparison, 43.5 percent of *Hard Copy* sources were introduced with voice-over and 17.9 percent were cited in the reporter's voice-over.

## Demography of News Sources

The education level and social class of news sources were not always clear. The education level of 61 percent and the social class of 24.3 percent of sources were coded as unknown (see table 6.1). Yet among the remaining cases a discernible demographic profile emerged for the most cited news sources. In fact, 78 percent of sources with determined education levels had some form of higher education and about 80 percent of those with identified social class were coded as belonging to the upper or middle class. It is noteworthy that *60 Minutes* (32.8 percent) was more likely than *Hard Copy* (9.3 percent) to feature news sources with graduate degrees whereas *Hard Copy* featured more than twice (7.6 percent) as many sources who had a high school or less education than *60 Minutes* (3.3 percent). Similarly, *Hard Copy* featured working-class people (15.9 percent) far more regularly than *60 Minutes* (3 percent), while *60 Minutes* relied more heavily on upper- and middle-class sources than *Hard Copy* (73.2 percent compared to 57.5 percent).

## Institutional Affiliation and Contribution

*Hard Copy's* tendency to give voice to ordinary people more willingly than *60 Minutes* is also evident from how often vox pops (person on the street opinion bites) were featured in both programs. Approximately 21 percent of

**Table 6.1. Demography of News Sources on *Hard Copy* and *60 Minutes***

| Variable | Hard Copy Percentage | 60 Minutes Percentage | Total Percentage |
|---|---|---|---|
| Education | | | |
| Ph.D. | 3.0 | 11.1 | 7.6 |
| Other graduate degree | 6.3 | 21.7 | 15.1 |
| B.A. | 10.3 | 11.9 | 11.2 |
| High school | 5.6 | 1.8 | 3.4 |
| Less than high school | 2.0 | 1.5 | 1.7 |
| Undetermined | 72.8 | 52.0 | 61.0 |
| Social class | | | |
| Upper | 11.0 | 32.3 | 23.1 |
| Middle | 46.5 | 40.9 | 43.3 |
| Working | 15.9 | 3.0 | 8.6 |
| At poverty level | 0.0 | 1.3 | .7 |
| Undetermined | 26.5 | 22.5 | 24.3 |

*Hard Copy* segments featured vox pop bites, whereas only 12.9 percent of *60 Minutes* segments presented the voice of ordinary people on the street. Moreover, a total of forty-two individual vox pop voices, or 0.39 per segment, were presented on *60 Minutes*. By contrast *Hard Copy* featured 158 individual vox pop bites, averaging 0.86 per segment.

A growing body of research is critiquing newspapers and prestigious television newscasts for perpetuating the opinions of elite news sources while ignoring the voices of ordinary people. From this body of literature on news sources, particular concern about the dominance of government officials as spokespeople is apparent. Table 6.2 shows that government officials made up a considerable portion of the newsmagazine source pool (10.2 percent) yet were less prominent than in nightly television newscasts (49 percent). Only 2 percent of *Hard Copy* sources were government officials, compared to 16 percent of the sources in *60 Minutes*.

Both programs featured relatively few sources from the world of business. Approximately 2 percent of *Hard Copy* sources were businesspeople, whereas 5.1 percent of *60 Minutes* sources were business professionals. The largest percentage of sources in both programs (*Hard Copy* 23.3 percent, *60 Minutes* 23.7 percent) came from the nonbusiness professional category (doctors, teachers, lawyers, etc.). Journalists made up 13.2 percent of all sources in the two programs and appeared three times as often on *Hard Copy* (22.6 percent) than *60 Minutes* (6.1 percent). More academic sources were used in *60 Minutes* (7.8 percent) than in *Hard Copy* (2 percent), whereas celebrities appeared more often on *Hard Copy* (11.3 percent) than *60 Minutes* (1.5 percent).

**Table 6.2.   Institutional Affiliation of News Sources**

| *Variable* | Hard Copy *Percentage* | 60 Minutes *Percentage* | *Total Percentage* |
|---|---|---|---|
| Elite | 29.6 | 53.0 | 41.3 |
|    Government | 2.00 | 16.4 | 10.2 |
|    Business Professionals | 2.3 | 5.1 | 3.9 |
|    Nonbusiness Professionals | 23.3 | 23.7 | 23.5 |
|    Academics | 2 | 7.8 | 5.3 |
| Celebrities | 11.3 | 1.5 | 5.7 |
| Journalists | 22.6 | 6.1 | 13.2 |
| Interest groups | 4.3 | 10.4 | 7.7 |
| Nonelites | 12.3 | 3.5 | 7.3 |
|    Industrial workers | 1.7 | 1.5 | 1.6 |
|    Service workers | 10.6 | 2 | 5.7 |
| Housewives | 4.3 | 4.0 | 4.2 |
| Students | 2 | 2 | 2 |
| Vox pops | 21 | 12.9 | 16.5 |
| Undetermined | 11.3 | 11.11 | 11.2 |

*Note:* The above categories are not mutually exclusive.

When government officials, business professionals, nonbusiness professionals, and academics are viewed together as elite sources, it becomes clear that both programs under investigation relied heavily on elites (41.3 percent). Yet *60 Minutes* used elite sources far more often (53 percent) than *Hard Copy* (29.6 percent). At the same time *Hard Copy* was more likely than *60 Minutes* to use nonelites as news sources. Industrial workers made up 1.7 percent and service workers 10.6 percent of the sources in *Hard Copy*. A mere 1.5 percent of sources (in *60 Minutes*) were industrial workers; 2 percent were service workers. Special interest groups were given voice just under one-tenth of the time (8 percent), and there were more sources speaking on behalf of special interest groups on *60 Minutes* (10.4 percent) than *Hard Copy* (4.3 percent). Housewives (4.2 percent) and students (2.0 percent) were seldom used as sources in either program and tended to be evenly distributed between the two shows.

Using the interrupt variable, which is an indication of how reporters assert themselves over sources, a cross tabulation with the institutional affiliation[9] of sources was performed to assess who was interrupted. Overall, 62.1 percent of all government sources, 32.6 percent of elite sources, and 30 percent of nonelites were interrupted during interviews. Sources were seldom interrupted on *Hard Copy* (1.2 percent overall or six cases in total), which makes cross tabulation analysis inappropriate. Looking at *60 Minutes* alone, nonelites encountered the highest interruption rate of all sources (80.0 percent) whereas 72.6 percent of government sources and 72.3 percent of elite sources were interrupted on this program.

Sources contributed on different levels to news stories by fulfilling different roles in news stories. For example, 47.5 percent of news sources had either personal experience or were witnesses to the topic, 9 percent either shared hearsay or gossip about the topic, 13.2 percent were experts on the topic, 13.1 percent expressed nonexpert opinions on the issue, 8.4 percent spoke as potentates, 1.7 percent were victims of some sort, 2.8 percent were the subjects of a profile story, and 2.2 percent were accused or sentenced for committing crime (see table 6.3). There were also noteworthy differences and similarities between *Hard Copy* and *60 Minutes* in terms of source roles. The two programs did not differ much in the frequency of featuring sources as experts, victims, criminals, or the subject of a profile story. However, *Hard Copy* and *60 Minutes* differed markedly in their use of sources who witnessed or had personal experience with an issue (39.5 percent versus 55.5 percent respectively), shared hearsay or gossip (17.3 percent versus 3 percent respectively), gave nonexpert opinions about the topic (17.3 percent versus 8.8 percent receptively), and occupied official positions of power, here referred to as potentates (4.3 percent versus 12.4 percent respectively). Most strikingly, blue-collar workers could be presented as experts on matters of their trade. However, on *60 Minutes*, not a single expert source was a blue-collar worker. By contrast, 9.3 percent of experts on *Hard Copy* were blue-collar workers.

**Table 6.3. The Role of News Sources in News Stories**

| Variable | Hard Copy Percentage | 60 Minutes Percentage | Total Percentage |
|---|---|---|---|
| Firsthand experience or witness | 39.5 | 55.5 | 47.5 |
| Hearsay or gossip | 17.0 | 3.0 | 9.0 |
| Expert | 14.3 | 12.1 | 13.2 |
| Opinion | 17.3 | 8.8 | 13.1 |
| Potentate | 4.3 | 12.4 | 8.4 |
| Victim | 2.0 | 1.3 | 1.7 |
| Accused/criminal | 1.3 | 4.0 | 2.2 |
| Profile | 3.0 | 2.5 | 2.8 |
| Other/undetermined | 1.3 | 0.3 | 0.8 |

## Conclusion

Government sources are less prominent in newsmagazine programs than in nightly newscasts, but there is evidence that other elites, including major professionals, academics, and people from the business world, appear more than five times as often as blue-collar workers on newsmagazines. The findings therefore suggest that together the two newsmagazine programs did favor a specific socioeconomic profile for news sources. This supports Parenti's (1986) argument that through sourcing news reaffirms the social and economic positions of those in power, particularly in the case of *60 Minutes*. In fact, the most striking findings of this study emerged from comparing *Hard Copy* and *60 Minutes* news sources on socioeconomic variables. *Hard Copy* continued the 170-year-old tabloid journalism tradition of giving voice to those on the periphery of socioeconomic power by using more members of the working class and those without graduate degrees as news sources and expert news sources than *60 Minutes* did. Indeed, this tabloid program provided a rare public outlet for the voices of nonelites. Overall, this study provides evidence of patterned variation in the socioeconomic status of sources across the two newsmagazine programs.

## STUDY 2: WHO VICTIMIZES WHOM?

According to Gerbner et al. (1979) demographic profiles of criminals and their victims have the narrative potential to communicate a society's class divisions to its members. Research on fictional narratives reveals the marginalization of lower socioeconomic groups. In fact, emphasis on lower socioeconomic groups as society's criminals promotes suspicion and distrust of this social class (Barrile 1986; Halloran 1978; Haney and Manzolati 1981; Kerner 1969; Sheley and Ashkins 1981). Gerbner and colleagues also argue that the portrayed repercussions of criminal actions often demonstrate power relations to society's members by communicating "who gets away with what against whom" (Gerbner et al. 1979, 181). In this sense the narratives of crime stories (fictional or nonfictional) cultivate a "scary view" of the world and produce suspicion among demographic groups. The goal of the second investigation was to determine (1) if newsmagazine programs favor specific social classes in the role of criminal and victim and (2) if favoritism varies across tabloid and highbrow programs. If the socioeconomic status of the scary criminal differs across the two magazine genres, there is potential for promoting distrust between social classes.

## Method

*A Current Affair, Inside Edition, American Journal,* and *Hard Copy* were the tabloid newsmagazine programs under investigation in the second study.[10] The specific highbrow programs were *Dateline NBC, Primetime Live, Turning Point, 48 Hours, Eye to Eye with Connie Chung, 60 Minutes, Day One,* and *20/20.* Tabloid magazine programs were half-hour weekday broadcasts and typically featured three stories per program. Highbrow magazine programs were usually hour-long weekly broadcasts that featured between three and five stories. A census of highbrow and tabloid broadcasts aired during a six-month period (October 1, 1994, to March 31, 1995) were analyzed and yielded 272 hours of material. An additional week of television broadcasts (April 1–7, 1995) was used in coder training sessions and coder reliability pretests.

The analysis was conducted on four levels. First, by focusing on the newsmagazine program as the sampling unit, the general prevalence and prominence of crime was documented. Categories enabled an assessment of how many program segments featured crime as well as the portion of program time taken up by crime stories. The position of crime stories in the program lineup was also documented.

Second, a crime story was defined as a program segment that featured one or more acts of breaking the law as central to the narrative. The type of crime, the motivation behind it, and two aspects related to the aftermath of the crime were recorded. By recording crime types the coding instrument produced data for comparing socioeconomic groups in terms of the kinds of offenses they were associated with, as both criminals and victims.[11] Coders were also instructed to code reported motivations for crime.[12] By providing a rationale for a criminal's behavior, news stories have the potential to frame criminals as acting in self-interest or because of personal flaws (e.g., greed, jealously, substance abuse) or as a result of a dire situation beyond their control (e.g., protecting themselves or stealing because of poverty that results form racism or other social-structural causes). The aftermath of the crime provides insight into power relations between demographic groups. The prevalence of the *crime does not pay* message was recorded and stories in which the criminal justice system was presented as inadequate were identified. Through these categories the notion of Gerbner et al. (1979) of "who gets away with what against whom" could be assessed.

Third, three separate coding sheets dealt with the criminal(s), victim(s), and crime(s) of each crime story. Social class and the occupational status of suspects and victims were recorded. The coding instrument for social class, used in study 1, was also used in this study. The criminal was identified as the person, group, or organization suggested, suspected, accused, charged, or found guilty of a crime and who was central to the crime narrative. The victim was identified as the person or group that suffered due to criminal actions. Three important aspects were considered when coding a victim. As with the criminal, the victim had to be central to the crime narrative. Stories often feature criminals without victims. In such instances only the presented criminal was coded. Moreover, when animals were presented as the victims of a crime, the "other" option was used in demographic variables. Finally, in order for someone to be coded as a victim, he or she had to be a direct or primary victim of the criminal act. Acquaintances or family members of the primary victim who were portrayed as secondary victims (e.g., they lost the murdered family member) were not coded as victims.

A primary coder and two secondary coders, serving as coder reliability checks, participated in this content analysis. A week before the coder training started, coders were provided with the codebook. During a practice coding session the instrument was applied to an additional week of sampled program content. A few options within variables were added to improve exhaustiveness. Using the Krippendorff (1980) Canonical Matrix Formula, an acceptable level of coder agreement (83 percent) was established at the end of the training period. The same formula was used in a post hoc assessment of coder reliability. Ten percent of the six-month sample (3 weeks) was randomly selected and coded by all three coders. The overall agreement among the three coders in this study was .91. Because demographic items involved some qualitative evaluation, coder agreement was slightly lower on these items (.89) than on simple frequency items such as duration of segments (.93).

## Results

Because tabloid and highbrow programs did not feature the same number of crime stories, percentages were used to make comparisons. A larger percentage of tabloid program segments was devoted to crime than was the case with highbrow segments. Approximately 43 percent of tabloid segments and 25 percent of highbrow shows were coded as crime stories. Moreover, almost half (49.2 percent) the tabloid program duration was taken up by crime stories, while 26.9 percent of the total highbrow content duration was coded as crime stories.

The common accusation that tabloid reporters practice *body bag journalism* is thus supported by this study's results and consistent with Knight's (1989) argument that the tabloid news genre is more concerned than highbrow news with crime, scandal, and human tragedy. Yet, when tabloid and highbrow shows covered crime, they featured these stories with approximately the same prominence. The notion *if it bleeds it leads* is not an exclusive trademark of tabloid newsmagazine programs. The coded positions of the first crime segment in a program were used to investigate the comparative prominence with which tabloid and highbrow newsmagazine programs presented crime. In both news shows crime made up well beyond half (60–70 percent) of lead stories.

## Demographic Profiles

Overall, the newsmagazine program criminal is most likely to be a legitimately employed (66.7 percent) member of the upper class (50 percent). The demographic profile of the most prominent victim of crime was the same: legitimately employed (36.8 percent) and belonging to the upper class (40.6 percent). But there were noteworthy social class differences between highbrow and tabloid victims and criminals. Class separatism is prominent at the most basic level: on tabloid shows the upper-class criminal was most prominent (55.2 percent versus 29.9 percent on highbrow shows); whereas on highbrow programs the working-class criminal prevailed (49.7 percent versus 30.5 percent on tabloid programs). Moreover, highbrow shows were far more likely (17.1 percent) than tabloid shows (3.3 percent) to present criminals as unemployed. Therefore, on tabloid shows the wealthy dominated as criminals, while on highbrow shows the opposite was communicated: Unemployed working-class people were most likely to be featured as criminals. Tabloid and highbrow programs also varied in the social class of the most likely victims of crime. Highbrow shows were more likely (36 percent) than tabloid shows (22 percent) to portray the victim as belonging to the middle class. Tabloid shows were more likely (35 percent) than highbrow shows (20 percent) to present the victim as a homemaker.

From table 6.4 it is clear that across tabloid and highbrow shows the class of criminals and their victims mostly corresponded. In other words, in tabloid and in highbrow shows members of the upper class seem to be the most likely victimizers of members of their own class. In the same way middle- and lower-class criminals dominated as the perpetrators of crime against their own class. Yet subtle differences deserve discussion. On tabloid shows working-class criminals were much less likely to victimize the middle and upper classes than on highbrow shows. At the same time, on tabloid shows working-class victims were almost three times more likely to be victimized by the upper class than on highbrow shows.

*Maria Elizabeth Grabe*

**Table 6.4. Who Victimizes Whom on Tabloid versus Highbrow News Magazine Programs?**

| Victim Class | Criminal | | |
| | Percentage Upper | Percentage Middle | Percentage Working |
| --- | --- | --- | --- |
| Tabloid | | | |
| Upper | 88.8 | 2.8 | 8.3 |
| Middle | 67.5 | 18.1 | 14.4 |
| Working | 8.3 | 17.1 | 74.7 |
| Highbrow | | | |
| Upper | 69.3 | 5.7 | 25.0 |
| Middle | 27.2 | 22.3 | 50.5 |
| Working | 2.8 | 16.7 | 80.6 |

The difference between tabloid and highbrow class portrayals was also evident from analyses of the criminal's social class and crime types (see table 6.5). As far as property crime is concerned, tabloid shows presented the middle class, and highbrow shows presented the working class, as the most prominent perpetrators. This means that tabloid shows were most likely to present the middle class as thieves to their mostly working-class viewers. On the other hand, the mostly middle- to upper-class highbrow audience was presented with an image of the working class as thieves. Cross tabulations of tabloid and highbrow portrayals of motivations for crime and the demography of the criminal were also performed. Tabloid programs (46.8 percent) more often than highbrow programs (28.2 percent) portrayed the middle class as committing crimes because they were greedy. The inverse is true for working-class criminals who were reportedly motivated by greed. On highbrow shows 41 percent of greedy criminals were working-class people whereas on tabloid shows only 27 percent of criminals acting in greed were members of the working class.

Working-class criminals were most likely to commit sex crimes in both newsmagazine genres. Interestingly, highbrow programs were more likely than tabloid programs to portray the middle class as victims of these sex crimes. About 22 percent of sex crime victims on tabloid shows and only 12.5 percent of victims on highbrow shows were from the working class (see table 6.5).

## The Aftermath of the Crime

Both tabloid and traditional news genres clearly delivered the lesson that crime doesn't pay (73 percent of crime stories in both shows). Yet it is fair to argue that tabloid shows were more likely than highbrow shows

**Table 6.5.  Who Perpetrates What Kind of Crime against Whom?**

| Criminal/Victim | Percentage Tabloid | Percentage Highbrow |
|---|---|---|
| Criminal | | |
| Property Crimes | | |
| Upper class | 2.9 | 3.2 |
| Middle class | 24.8 | 10.3 |
| Working class | 16.6 | 30.2 |
| Victim | | |
| Sex Crimes | | |
| Upper class | 6.0 | 2.5 |
| Middle class | 9.8 | 21.4 |
| Working class | 21.6 | 12.5 |

to suggest that law enforcement is serving society's members. Tabloid (11 percent) programs were less likely than highbrow (31 percent) programs to report that the law enforcement system is inadequate. Highbrow shows (31 percent) were also more likely than tabloid shows (11 percent) to present working-class criminals as being involved in crimes where law enforcement was portrayed as inadequate (see table 6.6). Interestingly, highbrow shows were more likely than tabloid shows to present the middle class as the victims of such crimes. Tabloid shows were more likely than highbrow programs to emphasize the upper-class criminal in crimes where law enforcement failed to serve justice while highbrow shows were most likely to present the working-class criminal in situations where the law enforcement system was inadequate. These portrayals of the justice system as failing a particular class of people in favor of criminals from the opposing class inscribe social class divisions.

**Table 6.6.  Demography of Criminals and Victims in Stories in Which Law Enforcement Was Presented as Inadequate**

| Class | Percentage Tabloid | Percentage Highbrow |
|---|---|---|
| Criminal | | |
| Upper class | 39.8 | 16.4 |
| Middle class | 21.4 | 20.9 |
| Working class | 38.8 | 62.7 |
| Victim | | |
| Upper class | 29.9 | 18.2 |
| Middle class | 32.7 | 58.2 |
| Working class | 37.4 | 23.6 |

## Conclusion

This study provides evidence of dominant socioeconomic profiles for criminals and victims. Moreover, there is variance across tabloid and high-brow newsmagazine programs in these profiles and other narrative elements associated with the motivations and types of crime as well as the aftermath of crime. These contradictory portrayals offer evidence of varied vilification across newsmagazine genres.

## DISCUSSION

Considering the demographically distinctive viewing audiences of tabloid and highbrow news, the findings of the two studies presented here suggest strong potential for the guardianship of social class distinctions. The Simmons Market Bureau's (1996) documentation of tabloid and traditional newsmagazine audiences reveals that the social class (education, income, and occupation) of *60 Minutes* viewers is typically upper-middle and upper class. *Hard Copy* attracts viewers from the lower-middle and working classes. When the socioeconomically privileged audience of *60 Minutes* is exposed mostly to elite sources and is reminded of the views of working-class people, less than 4 percent of the time, social class separation, not integration, is promoted. Similarly, the mostly working-class audience of *Hard Copy* hears working-class views three times more often and elite views less than half as often as *60 Minutes* viewers. This variance in sourcing patterns across tabloid and traditional newsmagazine programs suggests that their viewing publics are prompted to affiliate with people from different levels of the social hierarchy.

In the same vein crime narratives that plot social classes against each other in ways that make suspicion among them a likely outcome, contribute to the social class cleavage. By focusing on working-class criminals, highbrow shows suggest to its upper-middle to upper-class audience that people at lower levels of the socioeconomic order should be distrusted. Similarly, by emphasizing middle- and upper-class criminals tabloid shows vilify rich folks to their mostly lower-middle and lower-class audience. Most strikingly, the tabloid audience, as the underclass with most reason to rebel against the social order, was more likely to be exposed to lessons promoting faith in the mechanism that officially upholds law and order in society. Despite the lip service given to the promise of equal opportunity in democratic social systems, there is reason to question if all members of a society are accommodated in the same way or to the same extent. Functionalists like Merton (1949) argue that social systems strive for differentiation, division, and exclusion in order to produce functional hierarchical relations of dependency, inequality, and control. On the other hand this differentiation produces resistance and opposition from system members. In reaction the system manages this threat to social stability by striving to incorporate, consensualize, and normalize (Durkheim 1915, 1933; Knight 1989).

This study's results do not suggest that conspiratorial powers are at work, but that two maintenance functions are present in newsmagazine content. On the one hand class distinctions are reaffirmed by communicating to the mostly elite audience of highbrow news shows that working-class people are most likely to commit crimes against them, and get away with it, and by telling the mostly working-class audience of tabloid shows that upper-class people are criminals who should be distrusted. Yet the social system also overcomes this division. By communicating to all newsmagazine program viewers that crime is unprofitable and by cultivating trust in its law enforcement system among the mostly working-class tabloid audience, the system normalizes the resentment among members of different social strata.

This study is certainly not an exhaustive examination of content differences between tabloid and highbrow news formats. Yet it provides some support for the thesis that mass media content functionally caters to different segments of the population to promote social stratification and maintain the status quo. While the content of different newsmagazine formats internally supports social class separatism, the criticism of tabloid journalism that periodically preoccupies public debate, as discussed in the opening paragraphs of this chapter, provides external fortification of these class distinctions. By calling tabloids a new phenomenon, one that threatens the journalistic mission to serve democracy, tabloid critics add urgency to their publicly expressed concerns. When tabloids are described as tasteless, the line between highbrow and lowbrow culture is publicly drawn in terms of journalism, and members of the news audience are cued to consume news congruent to their social status. The consequent social stratification in exposure to news outlets brings the audience in contact with news content that, as revealed by this study's findings, further supports class separatism.

## NOTES

1. News sources are defined as individuals who appeared in voice or visually in the news. Journalists theoretically also rely on sources such as databases, documents, books, and so on. Yet it is noteworthy that Hansen, Ward, Conners, and Neuzil (1994) report that, despite the introduction of supposed revolutionary electronic information technologies, almost half of all newspaper stories don't make reference to written or electronic documents.

2. See also Hansen et al. 1994, who found that the majority of statements of newspaper sources (78.3 percent) went unexamined. Only 16 percent of stories revealed journalists who attempted to question the statements of news sources.

3. See also Koch 1990; Whitney et al. 1989.

4. Weaver and Wilhoit (1986) point out that a small group of journalists view their role as adversarial, directed at government (20 percent) or business (15 percent).

5. Dominick (1977) found that half of television news came from Washington, D.C., and Whitney et al. (1989) found that the District of Columbia, with 0.3 percent of the U.S. population, accounted for 30 percent of network news sources.

6. Other news genres include (1) local and national broadcasts; (2) talks shows, of which *Face the Nation* and *Meet the Press* exemplify the "proper" type and *Montel Williams* and *The Jerry Springer Show* the tabloid versions; (3) eyewitness programs such as *Cops* and *American Detective*; (4) reenactment programs including *Rescue 911* and *America's Most Wanted*; and (5) celebrity programs such as *Entertainment Tonight* and *Extra*. The last three genres all typify tabloid and have no "respectable" counterparts.

7. Separate categories included occupational roles such as senator, congressperson, government official, political candidate, member of law enforcement or the military, corporate executive, employee of large corporation, independent small businessperson, interest group representative, academic, noncorporate/business professional, service worker, industrial worker, housewife, student, celebrity, journalist, social/labor position undefined.

8. This category included the following options: firsthand personal experience of topic, witness to topic, hearsay about topic, gossip about topic, expert on topic, potentate, victim, accused, criminal, personal opinion, subject of a profile story, unknown, other.

9. Categories of sources were collapsed to compute new variables called government sources, elite sources, and ordinary people. Government sources include senators, representatives, politicians, and law enforcement officers. Elite sources are executives, employees of large corporations, business owners, academic experts, professionals, and celebrities. Ordinary people include service and industrial workers as well as housewives.

10. The three shows that epitomize tabloid news (*A Current Affair, Inside Edition*, and *Hard Copy*) were all on the top 15 syndication list; each reached approximately 20 million homes in America.

11. The categories were property crime, sex crime, violent crime, and financial crime. Yes and no options were used for each of the crime types because they are not mutually exclusive.

12. Individual motivations for crime, such as greed, revenge, substance abuse, and psychological instability, provoke viewers to assign blame for crime to perpetrators, thereby vilifying individuals (Iyengar 1994). By ignoring possible structural causes for crime (such as poverty or racism), this individualized (or sometimes called personalized perspective of crime) frames criminals as society's irrational enemies who deserve little sympathy because they presumably act as a result of their own will (Barrile 1986).

## REFERENCES

Altschull, J. H. 1990. *From Milton to McLuhan: The ideas behind American journalism*. New York: Longman.

Barrile, L. G. 1986. Television's "bogeyclass"? Status, motives, and violence in crime drama characters. *Sociological Viewpoints* 2: 39–56.

Berkowitz, D. 1987. TV news sources and news channels: A study in agenda-building. *Journalism Quarterly* 64: 508–13.

Bernstein, C. 1992. The idiot culture: Reflections of post-Watergate journalism. *New Republic,* June, 22.

Bird, S. E. 1992. *For inquiring minds: A cultural study of supermarket tabloids*. Knoxville: University of Tennessee Press.

Bourdieu, P. 1989. *Distinction*. London: Routledge.

Briller, B. 1993. The Tao of tabloid television. *Television Quarterly* 26: 51–61.

Brown, J. D., Bybee, C. R., Wearden, S. T., and Straughan, D. M. 1987. Invisible power: News sources and the limitations of diversity. *Journalism Quarterly* 64: 45–54.

Campbell, R. 1991. *60 Minutes and the News*. Urbana: University of Illinois Press.

DeFleur, M. L. 1964. Occupational roles as portrayed on television. *Public Opinion Quarterly* 28: 57–74.

Dominick, J. 1977. Geographic bias in national TV news. *Journal of Communication* 27: 94–99

Durkheim, E. 1915. *The elementary forms of the religious life*. New York: Free Press.

———. 1933. *The division of labor in society*. New York: Free Press.

Epstein, E. J. 1974. *News from nowhere*. New York: Vintage.

Ericson, R. V., Baranek, P. M., and Chan, J. B. L. 1989. *Negotiating control: A study of news sources*. Milton Keynes: Open University Press.

Estep, R., and Macdonald, P. T. 1983. How prime-time crime evolved on TV, 1976–1981. *Journalism Quarterly* 60: 293–300.

———. 1985. Crime in the afternoon: Murder and robbery on soap operas. *Journal of Broadcasting and Electronic Media* 29: 323–31.

Farhi, P. 1996. Panel must decide what rates as news. *Washington Post*, December 16, C1.

Freedom Forum. 1998. *The Newseum celebrates the 30th anniversary of CBS's 60 Minutes*. Arlington, Va.: C-SPAN.

Gandy, H. O. 1982. *Beyond agenda setting: Information subsidies and public policy*. New Jersey: Ablex.

Gans, H. J. 1974. *Popular culture and high culture: An analysis and evaluation of taste*. New York: Basic.

———. 1979. *Deciding what's news*. New York: Pantheon.

Gerbner, G., Gross, L., Signorelli, N., Morgan, M., and Jackson-Beeck, M. 1979. The demonstration of power: Violence profile no. 10. *Journal of Communication* 29: 177–96.

Grabe, M. E. 1997. Tabloid and traditional television newsmagazine crime stories: Crime lessons and reaffirmation of social class distinctions. *Journalism and Mass Communication Quarterly* 73: 926–46.

Grabe, M. E., Zhou, S., and Barnett, B. 1999. Sourcing and reporting in newsmagazine programs: *60 Minutes* versus *Hard Copy*. *Journalism and Mass Communication Quarterly* 76: 293–311.

———. Explicating sensationalism in television news: Content and the bells and whistles of form. *Journal of Broadcasting and Electronic Media* 45: 635–55.

Greene, J. R., and Bynum, T. S. 1982. TV crooks: Implications of latent role models for theories of delinquency. *Journal of Criminal Justice* 10: 177–90.

Hallin, D. C. 1986. We keep America on top of the world. In T. Gitlin, ed., *Watching Television*, 9–41. New York: Pantheon.

———. 1992. Sound Bite Democracy. *Wilson Quarterly*, Spring, 34–37.

Halloran, J. D. 1978. Studying violence and the media: A sociological approach. In C. Winick, ed., *Deviance and the mass media*, 287–305. Beverly Hills, Calif.: Sage.

Haney, C., and Manzolati, J. 1981. Television criminology: Network illusions of criminal justice realities. *Human Behavior* 12: 278–98.

Hansen, K. A., Ward, J., Conners, J. L., and Neuzil, M. 1994. Local breaking news: Sources, technology, and news routines. *Journalism Quarterly* 71: 561–72.

Iyengar, S. 1994. *Is anyone responsible: How television frames political issues.* Chicago: University of Chicago Press.

Keller, T. 1993. Trash TV. *Journal of Popular Culture* 26: 195–206.

Kerner, O. 1969. *Report to the National Advisory Commission on Civil Disorders.* New York: Bantam.

Knight, G. 1989. Reality effects: Tabloid television news. *Queen's Quarterly* 96: 94–108.

Koch, T. 1990. *The news as myth: Fact and context in journalism.* New York: Greenwood.

Krippendorff, K. 1980. *Content analysis: An introduction.* Beverly Hills, Calif.: Sage.

Levin, G. 1997. 60 Minutes pulls Cosby interview. *Washington Post,* January 31, C6.

Merton, R. 1949. *Social theory and social structure.* Glencoe, Ill.: Free **Press**.

Mifflin, L. 1998. "No. 1 Ratings for '60 Minutes.'" *New York Times.* March, E7.

Parenti, M. 1986. *Inventing reality: The politics of the mass media.* New York: St. Martin's.

Pew Center for the People and the Press. 1998. Available at www.people-press.org.

Rapping, E. 1992. Tabloid TV and social reality. *Progressive* 56 (August): 35–37.

Rosenberg, H. 1989. *Hard Copy*: By any other name it's still tabloid. *Los Angeles Times,* September 27, sec. 6, p. 1.

Sawyer, D. 1998. 3,000 Minutes. *New York Times Magazine,* September 20, 89–94.

Schudson, M. 1978. *Discovering news: A social history of American newspapers.* New York: Basic.

Shaw, D. L., and Slater, J. W. 1985. In the eye of the beholder? Sensationalism in American press news, 1820–1860. *Journalism History* 12: 86–91.

Sheley, J. F., and Ashkins, C. D. 1981. Crime, crime news, and crime views. *Public Opinion Quarterly* 45: 492–506.

Shusterman, R. 1992. *Pragmatist aesthetics: Living beauty, rethinking art.* Cambridge, Mass.: Blackwell.

Sigal, L. V. 1973. *Reporters and officials: The organization and politics of newsmaking.* Lexington, Mass: Heath.

———. 1986. Sources make the news. In R. K. Manoff and M. Shudson, eds., *Reading the News,* 9–37. New York: Pantheon, 1986.

Simmons Market Research Bureau. 1996. *Studies of Media and Markets.* New York: Simmons Market Research Bureau.

Soloski, J. 1989. Sources and channels of local news. *Journalism Quarterly* 66: 864–70.

Stevens, J. D. 1985. Sensationalism in perspective. *Journalism History* 12: 78–79.

Tannenbaum, P. H., and Lynch, M. D. 1960. Sensationalism: The concept and its measurement. *Journalism Quarterly* 37: 381–92.

Tuchman, G. 1978. *Making news: A study in the construction of reality.* New York: Free Press.

Weaver, D. H., and Wilhoit, G. C. 1986. *The American journalist: A portrait of U.S. news people and their work.* Bloomington: Indiana University Press.

Whitney, D. C., Fritzler, M., Jones, S., Mazzarella, S., and Rakow, L. 1989. Geographic And Source Biases in Network Television News, 1981–1984. *Journal of Broadcasting and Electronic Media* 33: 159–74.

# 7

# Constructing a Televisual Class: Newsmagazines and Social Class

*Jennie Phillips*

This chapter foregrounds an often overlooked pattern in critical U.S. media studies: a general failure to conceptualize social class as a primary variable rather than a component of the more salient constructions of race and gender. This, in conjunction with the U.S. commercial broadcasting system and the popular mythology that Americans live in a "classless" society, suggests that the relationship between social class and television may be a fertile but untapped area of study demanding further attention.[1]

In 1995, Paula S. Rothenberg edited an integrated study of race, class, and gender in the United States. The following passage by Gregory Mantsios appeared in his chapter focused on the issue of social class in America:

> We don't speak about class privileges, or class oppression, or the class nature of society. These terms are not part of our everyday vocabulary, and in most circles they are associated with the language of the rhetorical fringe. Unlike people in most other parts of the world, we shrink from using words that classify along economic lines or that point to class distinctions. (1995, 131)

Mantsios offers an explanation for this sociological phenomenon by stating, "Class is not discussed or debated in public because class identity has been stripped from popular culture" (1995, 131). Surveys of the literature broadly related to popular television representations of class further confirm the virtual absence of scholarly work specifically examining issues of social class in the United States.[2]

In this chapter I argue that studying television, particularly the newsmagazine format, reveals much about the current state of class values in the United States. Misdirected critiques have functioned in tandem with subtle textual narratives to perpetuate the misconception that class has been stripped from popular culture. However, I suggest that social class, particularly any semblance of the upper-middle class, is so firmly entrenched in television programming that its complete normalization masks its presence. It is not that class is absent from television, but rather that it appears as virtually transparent. I utilize a textual analysis to posit that articulations of social class may be rendered transparent, but they nevertheless embody the very essence of the televised newsmagazine.

## NEWSMAGAZINES AS A SITE OF POPULAR CULTURE

We rarely consider news as a site of popular culture, and that might be a mistake. Magazine programs such as *48 Hours* and *Primetime Live* (in contrast with tabloid magazines like *Inside Edition* and *Extra*) are produced by the network news divisions and have therefore been traditionally associated with informational more than entertainment fare. But, let me assert that newsmagazines entered the realm of popular culture through the networks' prime-time schedules. Don Hewitt, executive producer and creator of *60 Minutes,* has stated that television newsmagazines tell stories by packaging reality in the way that Hollywood constructs fiction. So, to understand contemporary popular culture, perhaps we should begin by destabilizing the tacit association of news as information. News is also entertainment.

In the 1990s, the television newsmagazine format grew increasingly popular and pervasive in prime-time programming. Not only was there an increase in the number of newsmagazines, but there was also a substantial increase in how frequently the shows were aired. These developments changed the face of prime-time programming, blurring the line between the seemingly discrete categories of "information" and "entertainment." Entertainment programming strategies have influenced the production of newsmagazines, and vice versa, as supported by the current explosion of reality (i.e., nonfiction) productions in lieu of fictional series in the network schedules. Commanding respectable ratings, these low-cost alternatives challenged standard television genres in the prime-time lineups.

The conceptualization of news as entertainment serves as a reminder that "non-fiction" in no way implies the absence of industrial conventions and constructions. NBC's entertainment division head told the *New York Times*, "There is no show more important to us than 'Dateline.' I look on 'Dateline' as a hit show the same way I look on 'E.R.' as a hit show" (Carter 1998).[3] Newsmagazine producers strategically arrange their shows to keep audiences watching. Stories addressing women's health issues, for example, run opposite *Monday Night Football*, male-oriented features are used to counterprogram shows that target a largely female audience, and especially dramatic stories are reserved for broadcast during sweep weeks (McClellan 1995; Carter 1998; Miller 1998; Stroud 1998). More than the traditional dramas and situation comedies, which often rapidly appear and disappear from television schedules, a newsmagazine like ABC's *20/20* can be used to brand a network for audiences across decades of programming. Television journalists are personalities or celebrities that audience members are expected to identify with (Brill 1998; Landow, Hewitt, and Wallace 1998). They package the news, rather than report it, contributing an air of familiarity in the process (Reibstein, Brant, and Biddle 1994; Brill 1998; Consoli 1998; Turner and Hosenball 1998). Increasingly, coverage sounds more like dramatic narrative than traditional journalism (Campbell 1991; Sawyer 1998). Therefore, we might regard newsmagazine journalists as characters in our repertoire of dramatic entertainment.

The newsmagazine genre bridges the principles of informational and entertainment formats, so failing to recognize its position in popular culture is ignoring an important segment of the television landscape. This is particularly significant when one is concerned with the construction and representation of social class, as the tension between traditionally highbrow (informational) and historically lowbrow (entertainment) programming is fundamentally rooted in class distinction. Although traditional broadcast news and entertainment programs are abundantly investigated, newsmagazines are less frequently researched. In this chapter, I argue that newsmagazines are rich sources of dramatic narratives and televisual constructions from which to explore questions of class.

## PAST APPROACHES TO THE STUDY OF SOCIAL CLASS ON TELEVISION

How have past media researchers studied social class? Most of the literature addressing constructions and representations of class in critical U.S. studies must actually be extracted from research on other topics. Considerations of class issues are most typically woven into larger discussions, particularly with regard to race and gender, where class is treated as a symptom or manifestation of some other variable or combination of variables. Generally speaking, class is not examined as a topic worthy of study in and of itself,[4] and there are surprisingly few critiques of this omission.[5]

Historically, attention to class issues, as they intersect with the study of television, has fundamentally been associated with one of four general categories of methodological inquiry. The first of these categories, content analysis used to quantify the representation of class, has primarily been restricted to the examination of dramatic, fictional programming. Class, in this thread of research, is typically equated with occupation and very few projects specifically address social class beyond coding for employment. Recent studies have expanded into the news arena, but newer prime-time formats such as newsmagazines and reality programs remain distinctly underexplored.

Textual analyses of class-based story lines compose the second major category of methodological inquiry. Although researchers have extensively analyzed dramatic texts, only a minute portion of those inquiries have explored class-inspired narrative themes in any systematic way. Insights into class issues gleaned through a text-based framework of analysis typically come in the form of afterthoughts. In fact, there is a tendency for scholars to overlook issues of class in the vast majority of texts.

The third and smallest category consists of empirical analyses that incorporate class as a mediating variable, and on occasion as a suppression variable. Richard Butsch observes:

> Rarely has class been considered a variable in research seeking to identify specific effects resulting from television viewing. This research tradition has concentrated on generalizations about psychological processes rather than on group differences. In a major bibliography of almost 3,000 studies of audience behavior only seven articles on television effects and thirteen on use patterns examined class. (1997, 1525)

The final category, composed of reception analyses that treat social class as an independent variable (and occasionally as an antecedent variable), characterizes the majority of the most recent research. Nevertheless, reception studies, more than any of the other research categories, seem to examine class as a function of purportedly larger, more significant variables. Much of these discussions are focused around gender and race or ethnicity; however, topics such as family use patterns of media are also included here.

## Operationalizing Class: Quantitative Analyses

Multiple and varied conceptualizations of social class are required if we hope initially to recognize the presence of class in media texts and subsequently to capture the dimension and full significance of class-based issues in contemporary popular culture. One of the earliest approaches to the study of class on television was to determine, through a content analysis, the distribution of television characters' social classes (Gentile and Miller 1961). This study operationalized social class with regard to occupation, speech, consumption, style, and character ethnicity. As the only work of its time studying television content in terms of social class, Gentile and Miller's indices must be considered fairly elaborate.

Content analyses were the most commonly replicated studies in the existing body of research, but the works that followed Gentile and Miller's initial study in the next two decades tended to be much more streamlined by design. Often contrasts were drawn between the resulting distributions and the actual distribution of the U.S. population's social classes. With the exception of the brief era characterized by the social relevance programs of the 1970s (e.g., *All in the Family*), all reported longitudinal findings supported that lower- or working-class characters have consistently remained underrepresented whereas middle- and upper-middle-class characters have consistently remained overrepresented on television.[6] Nevertheless, studies such as these rarely discussed "class." It was necessary for social class to be inferred by the reader, primarily on the basis of the measures for each occupational code.[7]

Similar content analyses eventually invoked the term "social class," but even they continued to rely on occupational data codes to determine the characters' classes (Butsch and Glennon 1983; Butsch 1992). Coding the occupational frequencies for these content analyses generally included several categories that mirrored the U.S. Census Codes, yet operationalizing class in these ways was still clearly limited. Although most indices of class have primarily been based on the head of households' occupations, others have also considered character statements of wealth (Butsch and Glennon 1983). Nevertheless, it follows that these fundamentally unidimensional categories restricted the potential for more nuanced understandings of social class to emerge in relation to televisual culture.

## Qualitative Analyses

Fundamentally, the strength of a content analysis hinges on the simplicity of its coding. In contrast, textual analyses allow researchers to analyze material and tackle questions beyond the reach of indices and quantitative measures. Whereas television content must be organized within the categories specified by a content analysis, textual analyses allow researchers latitude to infer and associate beyond even the boundaries of a single, contained text.

In *Prime-Time America*, Sklar (1980) transcended conceptualizations of class as occupation and incorporated elements of home, dress, class awareness in characters, leisure activities, speech patterns, values/morals, and consumption patterns as signs that could potentially inform his reading of class struggles and class-inspired television story lines. Sklar's research was significant not only for its methodological turn, but additionally because it represented one of the few studies that specifically examined social class as portrayed through class-inspired narratives. More commonly, class issues have been read in analyses of texts that addressed related but different variables.[8] Although the relevance of such studies to the project at hand is indirect, their contributions come through the expanded and extended definitions of class they each suggest.

The reception of television programming across a variety of genres intersects with social class issues in the current literature, primarily because researchers frequently recognize class identification as an independent variable in reception analyses. However, some scholars have argued that the potential of fictional television programming to influence viewers' beliefs and values is greater than that of news (Thomas 1986; Puette 1992). This is based on the assumption that the average viewer filters information during the reception of entertainment programming in a less conscientious manner than he or she does while viewing news programming.

Although this is neither a reception nor an effects analysis, I would like to suggest that the potential for newsmagazines to construct class distinctions is at least as great as with traditional entertainment fare. The current production of dramatic narratives in the newsmagazine genre operates in accordance with the same guiding principles employed by other more established entertainment formats.[9] Perhaps the possibility for newsmagazines to construct class distinctions is even greater than that of fictional programming. As the only portion of news in prime-time entertainment, perhaps newsmagazine content is more likely than fictional content to be read as fact (vs. factual narrative).

## FOUNDATIONAL CRITIQUES

How do we account for those arguments that either ignore the presence or discuss the absence of class on television? Perhaps critics, typically speaking from the ranks of white-collar professionals in the upper middle class, have fallen into the trap of failing to recognize representations of their own social status as televised images of "class." It is as though social class were something reserved to define only "the other."[10]

Consider the following scenario proposed by Jhally and Lewis in their analysis of normalized middle- and upper-middle-class representation on television:

> An alien researching life on Earth would certainly learn a great deal by scrutinizing satellite broadcasts of television from the United States. The inquiring alien might, nevertheless, ponder various curiosities: Who collects the garbage or cleans the streets? Who builds the houses, farms the land, or works on production lines to produce all those delightful gadgets? Strangest of all, How does the economy sustain all those lawyers and doctors, who seem to be everywhere? (1992, 23)

Lawyers and doctors embody class just as fully as the garbage collectors, street cleaners, farmers, and production-line workers typically omitted from televisual culture. Granted, the current representations and portrayals of white-collar professionals on television may bring with them a different set of implications than *Laverne and Shirley* did, for example, in the situation comedies of the 1970s. Nevertheless, the articulations of social class through doctors and lawyers, or accordingly through broadcast journalists like Stone Phillips (of NBC's *Dateline*), for example, are no less present and influential than the articulations of social class through the characters on a situation comedy like *Roseanne*. Yet if class on television is studied, it is primarily only the working class that is recognized as embodying class attitudes and identities. Doctors, lawyers, and news anchors, in contrast, are just "normal," implying they are somehow free of class attitudes and identities. The distinction is not that class has been stripped from popular culture, but rather that its homogenized representation in current television programming masks its presence. Roseanne's social class was apparent not because her class identity was stronger or more significant than an upper-middle-class character, but rather because it clashed with the otherwise homogenized portrayal of social class on television. However, "homogenized" is by no means "eradicated." Critiques that mistakenly suggest the absence of class should instead be redirected toward the current "transparency" of television's dominant social class that has become normalized as neutral, value-free, and seemingly without consequence.

Another explanation as to why critiques have been misdirected toward the "stripping" rather than the "transparency" of class on television may reside in the limited ways we have tended to define and operationalize "class" in previous examples of research. If we see social class only as an occupation, is there any wonder that representations of class remain under-examined? Attempting to reconsider televised representations, informed by Pierre Bourdieu's (1984) notions of distinction and cultural capital and the following conceptualization of class from Langston (1995), could qualitatively transform how we understand the relationship between social class and television.[11]

> Class is about money and it is about more than money. As a result of the class you are born into and raised in, class is your understanding of the world and where you fit in, it's composed of ideas, behavior, attitudes, values, and language; class is how you think, feel, act, look, dress, talk, move, walk; class is what stores you shop at, restaurants you eat in; class is the schools you attend, the education you attain; class is the very jobs you will work at throughout your adult life." (101–2)

It was from this elaborated understanding of class, as a point of origin, that I began to identify current articulations and representations of social class in television newsmagazines.

## METHODOLOGY

In order to address some of the limitations in the current body of scholarship on social class and television, I decided to conduct a textual analysis. This approach was strategic in the sense that I hoped the added flexibility of a textual framework of analysis would enable me to expose more nuanced articulations of class, beyond the traditionally rigid occupational codes employed by past researchers. Newsmagazines surfaced as a logical yet under-examined site of inquiry. They combine traditional news and entertainment conventions to secure, as I have argued, a position in contemporary popular culture. For the purposes of this study, television newsmagazines were conceptualized as hour-long magazine format programs that are produced by the major U.S. broadcast networks' news divisions to be aired in their prime-time television schedules.

As my analysis will suggest, the incorporation of traditional entertainment conventions in the production of television newsmagazines results in a new and perhaps more subtle construction of class representation and distinction. Expanding the conceptualization of social class beyond occupational status to incorporate Langston's considerations of ideas, behaviors, attitudes, values, language, thoughts, and style—essentially as a whole system of existing in, experiencing, and reproducing the world—grants us access to the presence of social class distinctions that have been previously overlooked.

Because this research was intended to expose the presence of class articulations on television, rather than to characterize the entirety of all televisual culture, I chose to conduct my analysis on a non-probability sample of television newsmagazines. Therefore, I make no claims of representativeness or generalizability with this analysis. I drew my sample of taped shows from the month of November 2002, a Nielsen Media Research "sweeps" period, when broadcasters are particularly competitive about commanding the largest, most commercially-attractive audiences possible.[12] I therefore felt that broadcasters' programming standards and priorities were likely to be most pronounced and apparent during this period.

My sample included newsmagazines from the major U.S. broadcast networks: ABC, NBC, and CBS.[13] All shows were produced under the umbrellas of the networks' news divisions and were aired between 7:00 and 11:00 P.M. (eastern standard time)—prime-time viewing hours. Following a pilot test where I inductively read one newsmagazine, I analyzed the various constructions and representations of social class paying particular attention to articulations portrayed through narrative structure, story type, story subjects, journalists, consulted sources, and production techniques that functioned within the narrative or to establish a televisual relationship with the viewers.[14]

## READINGS OF SOCIAL CLASS IN TELEVISION NEWSMAGAZINES

Analyzing my segments of newsmagazines intertextually exposed two key patterns that contributed to constructing the transparency of social class: distancing the poor from the upper middle class and increasing the proximity of the upper middle class to the very elite.[15] It was rare for the segment narratives to explicitly reference social class. If class was mentioned, it was almost always with regard to the very poor. Such references to lower-class status functioned in the narrative to symbolically distance the poor from the upper-middle class, the implication being that lower-class individuals are sociologically isolated and exceptionally rare. In the remainder of segments, upper-middle-class story perspectives, characters, and values predominated but were narrativized as universal to the extent that even those with elite social status could be encompassed by such broad conceptualizations. This functioned to divorce the story perspectives, characters, and values from any precise association with class status or identification. Because these articulations of social class were homogeneously predominant and constructed to seem universal, their presence often appeared to be transparent. Nevertheless, deconstructing the stories and their discourses revealed that class issues were abundantly woven into the narratives of the newsmagazine segments.[16]

## Symbolically Isolating the Disenfranchised

Morley Safer of *60 Minutes* presented "Jackpot Justice," a segment that addressed the problems associated with the litigious actions of class-action lawsuit plaintiffs. Safer describes Fayette, Mississippi, as "the land of jackpot justice. Poverty may be the ruling condition, but there are those who've found a means of escape." The plaintiffs suing corporations in "Jackpot Justice" are people looking for a way out of poverty. They are lower class. Shots of small-town life, with dirty store facades and unpaved streets, pan across the television screen. Small houses are sagging and rundown, with overgrown yards that appear to be taking over the dilapidated structures. The main street of Fayette in Jefferson County, Mississippi, shows no sign of new construction or renovation. Some of the buildings appear to have been abandoned long before the cameras rolled into town. The automobiles pictured are small and old. As these images fade away, a newspaper columnist speaks for the people of Mississippi as he describes this *system of justice*.

> Look at the jurors, these are disenfranchised people. These are people who've been left out of the system, who feel like, hey, stick it to the Yankee companies. Stick it to the insurance companies. Stick it to the pharmaceutical companies. The African Americans feel like its payback for disenfranchisement. And, uh, the rednecks, shall we say, it's like hey, get back at . . . uh revenge for the Civil War. [Knowing glances between the columnist and Safer are exchanged.] So there's a lot of resentment, a lot of class anger, a lot of racial anger. And it's very easy to weave this racial conflict and this class conflict into a big money pot for the attorneys . . . I mean it's very hard if you're lower income and you're struggling to pay your bills and you see these [solicitation ads to join lawsuits] on TV. I mean, most people say, 'Sure, why not?'

In this segment, the Mississippi locals are described as impoverished, uneducated, angry, and conflicted. So, everything that follows this framing of the segment functions to reinforce such images and associations with poor, low-class people (and, simultaneously, *not* with higher-class people like the columnist).

He goes on to describe some of the television advertisements that ask people if they feel tired or get headaches and he jokes, "Yes! [he does]," with the implication being that people like himself would never join one of those lawsuits.

The next cut is to a local florist, now described as a millionaire. The florist is obese and slow-moving; he is also effeminate. Safer does a voice-over, "He took the obesity drug Redux, started complaining of chest pains, and was found to have a major blockage in his heart, which *he says* was caused by the drug . . . He won't say how much he received in the settlement, but admits he hit *paydirt*." The show cuts to the florist who brags in a high-pitched, slow whine, "A fifty-cent diet pill made a lot of people multimillionaires . . . [smiling proudly and laughing] [I've] come a long way. You know, in the area that I'm from, a lot of people dream to be rich and with the diet pill company it has helped them to become whatever they want to be."

Safer's voice-over continues, "His payday may not be over. He's a plaintiff in *yet another* suit, this time against the diet drug Meridia." [Safer is shown in a television studio interviewing the florist.] "You think you are going to do as well with the Meridia?"

"I think I'll do better because not as many people took Meridia," the florist responds, "so therefore we should get more money." The image of the florist contrasts with the columnist and Safer, who are both in suit jackets and ties. They speak assertively with deep voices and confidence in a manner that further emphasizes the florist's comparatively timid persona. The narrative is constructed as a judgment of the plaintiffs' behavior, not with malicious intonations, but rather with pity. The implication is that the poor, uneducated people of Mississippi don't know any better and cannot make connections between the lawsuits and the results of damage awards unsupported by [upper-middle-class] *reason and logic*. A local pharmacist speaks about the resulting increases in property taxes and the inability of the county to keep business and commerce strong.

Then a Mississippi doctor in a white physician's coat, dress shirt, and tie states, "We're all paying the price . . . you can't legislate their [plaintiffs'] morality or their ethics, but the legislature and the court systems can cap this to stop the greed from driving the system." He argues that Mississippi is on the verge of a crisis because physicians are leaving the state and hospitals cannot attract new recruits. Fear of malpractice suits and the inflated rates of malpractice insurance in Mississippi have led to an extreme shortage of healthcare providers.

How does this all relate to the home audience? The narrative tries to bring the audience into the story with the suggestion that Mississippi is setting the national drug policy. The columnist appears again and states:

> The FDA looks at the benefit [of a drug] and looks at the potential death and says the benefit is more than the harm. Then you go to Jefferson County where half the jurors don't have high school degrees and all you do is trot out the fifty deaths and say, "Can you believe these people died?" Time to send a message that they can't kill Mississippians and next thing you know the pharmaceutical company owes $500 million in punitive damages.

The resulting implication is that it does not make sense for drug companies to incur such risks, so they stop producing various drugs. Then, everybody else suffers as a result of the greed of the poor. Safer concludes the segment back at the *60 Minutes* studio (which signifies journalistic detachment and objectivity) with the statement, "Since we began this story, the Mississippi legislature voted to put some caps on awards that a plaintiff can receive against healthcare providers only. The legislature is currently debating the question of further caps against other companies." The narrative conclusion is that the greedy, litigious actions of the low-class poor threaten society as a whole, so much so that legislators are forced to remedy the chaos.

The narrative of "Jackpot Justice" judges the sensibility, motivation, and ethics of the very poor in a manner that discourages the implied reader to distance him- or herself from those societal outcasts (i.e., the very few left behind by a system of equilibrium that the poorest of the poor eventually push into chaos). In "Jackpot Justice," the narrative positions journalists, pharmacists, and doctors as the characters of reason. The plaintiffs' motivations are contextualized as strategies for upward (economic but not social) mobility.

Damage to the florist's heart, for example, was presented merely as his personal assertion. The narrative structure emphasized the florist's greed by asking him to speculate on the cash value of "yet another" jury verdict. The class status of the extremely disenfranchised (the unjustified, according to this narrative) is brought into question (characterized as greed, anger, conflict, and resentment), while the narrative discourse renders transparent the class status of everybody else (i.e., the just but potential victims) that do not sue to hit a jackpot. Although audience members may not be doctors, pharmacists or journalists, those not jackpot plaintiffs are constructed through this narrative as seemingly free of class identification. The story perspective positions everybody but the rare jackpot plaintiff as sharing in its judgment, some sort of universal logic or reason that the narrative disassociates from upper-middle-class values. However, the significance of these articulations of class become even more apparent when juxtaposed with other newsmagazine segments.

## Constructing a Televisual Class: The Universal Upper Middle

On a different evening, Ed Bradley presented a segment, "Not the Best Policy: Unum Provident," which also aired on *60 Minutes*. There were some noticeable parallels between the two stories: both involved unethical practices and law suits with multimillion dollar awards for damages. However, the story perspectives were quite different. Bradley opened the piece by directing the following comment to the home audience, "If you're one of the 50 million Americans who has money deducted from your paycheck to pay for disability insurance, or if you purchased a disability policy on your own, you may think you're covered if you're injured or too sick to work. But don't be too sure." The segment featured Dr. John Tedesco, described as a "successful eye surgeon" who had purchased disability insurance from Unum Provident (the largest disability insurance company in the United States) to pay him a salary in the event that he was unable to work.

Tedesco is consistently referred to as a doctor throughout the piece, and the audience is told he was limited to diagnostic work after he developed a tremor in his hand. He is professional in appearance and conservatively dressed. Tedesco's hair is neatly groomed, he is clean shaven and has well-manicured hands. Images of the doctor in a white physician's coat over a dress shirt and tie cross the screen, with Dr. Tedesco pictured in front of framed diplomas in his office. He talks on the telephone while reviewing charts on his desk. He appears lean and physically fit as he is shown walking down the hospital corridors. He is presented as focused and conscientious as he examines x-ray films in front of light panels. Dr. Tedesco states, "I know that if I tried to operate on somebody, I might hurt them. I might blind them." To legitimate this claim, the camera cuts to a close-up shot of his tremoring hand.

Bradley's voiceover tells the audience Tedesco was diagnosed with Parkinson's disease. He was unable to keep his hand steady enough to do routine eye exams and three physicians attested that he was too disabled to operate. Nevertheless Unum Provident paid disability benefits for only four months before closing Dr. Tedesco's claim, stating he was not disabled and could continue performing surgery. Surveillance video of Dr. Tedesco, shot for Unum Provident, appears on screen showing a man playing football in the lap of suburban comfort. But the videotape is quickly mocked as the audience is told the football player outside Tedesco's home was his son.

Bradley is next presented on a television set interviewing a former Unum Provident claims handler. Three additional former claims handlers join Bradley as they each explain how the company had given dollar figures to claims handlers as targets for what they needed to save monthly by closing or rejecting claims. Class is never discussed directly; however, the women are quite different from Dr. Tedesco in appearance. All four are overweight and pictured sitting passively, rather than in action as Tedesco had been. Their clothes do not fit well, being either too tight or untailored. Two of the women have dark roots showing through bleached hair, two have heavily sprayed, permed, and teased hairstyles, and they are shown wearing thick eyeliner.

As the women answer Bradley's questions (rather than appear to speak unprompted as Tedesco seemed to have done), it is mentioned that the claims handlers have very little authority in an insurance company. Every claim decision needs to be approved by a manager and/or an insurance physician, so the physical cues that differentiate the women from Tedesco are tacitly associated with a class of workers relatively low on the corporate hierarchy. The audience, however, seems to be encouraged to relate to Tedesco (recall the initial audience address by Bradley) and distance themselves from the claims handlers due to their admission of unethical behavior, such as rejecting legitimate claims on technicalities. The women go on to discuss the practice of managers praising handlers who closed large claims for the company and the pattern of bonus checks shortly following such closures. Additionally, the women's comments are represented as suspect because the handlers are each former employees. The journalistic narrative therefore includes a voice-over statement that although the former claims handlers may have been discredited by Unum Provident, allegedly based on instances of dishonesty in their personal lives, upper-level sources have verified each of their assertions as representative of the company's corporate practices.

The audience learns that Dr. Tedesco sued Unum Provident and a jury awarded him $36 million in damages. In order to avoid an extensive appeal process, Tedesco settled with the company for an undisclosed sum. In contrast to the florist and his co-plaintiffs in "Jackpot Justice," the validity of Dr. Tedesco's claim is never questioned. In fact, it is repeatedly supported by frequent shots of his hand tremors. His right to a multimillion-dollar settlement also goes unquestioned and without critique. Instead, the narrative is constructed to suggest that justice was served with the jury verdict because the statement of damages was preceded by verification of the claims handlers' statements and followed by a discussion between Bradley and a government insurance commissioner about the problem with target standards in evaluating policyholder claims.

It is quite interesting to note how the actions of Unum Provident employees are described in the segment. For example, the practice of using target figures is discussed as "standard procedure." The allegation of criminal activity is indirectly made in the piece as Bradley asks a claims handler, "So you were given a target, a dollar figure to save the company that had nothing to do with the validity of the claims?" and the woman responds, "Many times." This allegation is followed by the company's written statement [an excerpt from a letter is displayed on the screen] that occasionally mistakes are made, due to the large volume of claims handled, but Unum Provident works hard to remedy those situations. The claims handlers admit that they have closed what they knew were legitimate claims to meet their targets, yet the language is still quite muted in tone, as demonstrated by the segment title "Not the Best Policy." Dr. Tedesco represents the victim in this narrative and Unum Provident's role as the villain is solidified by the insurance commissioner's statement that the company is breaking the law.

There is, however, no corporate face to attach to this blame as Unum Provident only responded to the allegations through written statements. The viewer is left with contrasting images of Dr. Tedesco as a successful doctor (i.e., the story character whose actions are justified by the narrative) and the claims handlers as shamed but redeemable workers (i.e., the story characters whose actions are not justified by the narrative, only explained as financially motivated by bonus checks). Tedesco speaks with no noticeable accent, his grammar is precise, and his education is verbally and visually cued through the repetition of his title and his diplomas. The claims handlers have Tennessee accents, and one is even portrayed sitting on her porch in what appears to be a rural area. In these ways, class differences are present and extended visually and symbolically through style, intonation, and location, for example, without ever being directly or explicitly referenced as they were in "Jackpot Justice." Instead, these class distinctions are rendered transparent by the narrative as the segment concludes by joining forces together against Unum Provident, the corporate villain.

## Exposing the Transparency of Televisual Class: Intertextual Comparisons

Through another newsmagazine segment that featured cheating, we see even more clearly how the upper-middle class is presented as expansive. Again, class identification in this segment went without reference. But, it is interesting to compare this segment's narrative with the one constructed in "Jackpot Justice."

This particular segment features a professor and students from the University of Virginia, where it was discovered that students were submitting recycled papers as their own work to fulfill course requirements. The professor and students are presented as neatly dressed people who carry handbags and drink bottled water. They have healthy, shiny hair, manicured nails, perfectly straight teeth, and are physically lean. They wear light makeup and understated jewelry (in contrast, for example, to the claims handlers from "Not the Best Policy"). The students and professor are not labeled upper middle class in the way "Jackpot Justice" explained its story characters as rooted in class anger and resentment, but their more elite status is inferred when the journalist describes higher education as "$30–40,000 a pop."

The segment suggests intense competition to manage academic life has led to widespread cheating at American universities, to the extent that students feel it is "no big deal to admit doing it." A panning shot of students working at computers accompanies a voice over that states the current generation of students is "cyber cheating." The journalist reports, "for a few bucks [cheaters need only] point and click." The segment cuts to a close-up of a computer monitor connected to an "online term paper mill" where thousands of papers ranging from "The Sexual Politics of Walden Pond" to "Vietnam and the Crisis of American Empire" are available for about $10 a page. "For $19 a page, they will write you a brand new essay." The journalist selects a paper, reads a description of the seven-page, seventy-dollar paper, and purchases a copy of it by providing his credit card information. This is how paper recycling is done.

This type of cheating is discussed in the segment with regard to the University of Virginia honor code. However, students' nonchalant attitudes about how many people cheat are punctuated in the narrative by "what's the big deal about a little cheating?" especially when juxtaposed with the recent behavior in the government and on Wall Street. Cheating is not excused, but is perhaps justified as the competitive schools are characterized as "academic rat races" where noncheaters feel disadvantaged by cheaters and therefore justify their own subsequent cheating.

The cheating discussed in this particular segment is quite elite with regard to the characters included in the narrative. Government officials, Wall Street professionals, and students who pay $9–19/page for papers and can afford higher education at $30–40,000 a pop are arguably privileged. Nevertheless, unlike the "violations" depicted in "Jackpot Justice," these "violations" are not explicitly tied to a segment of the population embodying a particular class status. Rather, these acts are described as "widespread," "epidemic," "not uncommon": the behavior of a new generation.

Unlike "Jackpot Justice," when the newspaper columnist emphasized the class status of the residents of Fayette, Mississippi, no mention is made of the students' apparent disposable income signified by drinking bottled water, having credit cards, being computer literate, and studying topics like sexual politics or crises of empire. The class status of the upper middle class is rendered transparent in this narrative that characterizes this elite form of cheating as pervasive and associates the behavior with an entire generation of young adults. Boundaries that could be used to distinguish the upper middle class in this segment are not referenced, as though no such boundaries even existed. Whereas the actions of a few plaintiffs in "Jackpot Justice" were constructed as acts that everybody paid for, the effects of widespread cheating on society, or the implications of the wealth required to cheat and remain competitive at today's institutions of higher education are not elaborated on in this segment. Instead, what might be considered an elite phenomenon is constructed as a societal problem in the way that rural poverty, for example, was not constructed in "Jackpot Justice."

## Elite as Ordinary

During the November sweeps, numerous newsmagazine specials were broadcast featuring hour-long interviews with celebrities such as Jennifer Lopez and Justin Timberlake. The in-depth pieces constructed around these popular culture idols described as "multimillionaires" illuminated how newsmagazines are able to construct upper-middle-class narratives expansive enough to include even those with the most elite financial and social status. ABC's Diane Sawyer (for *Primetime*) began her feature on Jennifer Lopez by describing her as "not just a star, a kind of supernova." Sawyer states that Lopez was the first Latina who cracked the $1 million barrier for a movie. Images of J. Lo from her music videos flash across the screen, interspersed with photographs of Jennifer walking the red carpet at award shows and film premieres and documenting her new romance with Ben Affleck.

Although Lopez's status as culturally, socially, and financially elite are foregrounded, the narrative quickly shifts to emphasize how the implied audience can relate to her as an ordinary person. Throughout the feature, promotions for Lopez's film, *Maid in Manhattan*, and her album featuring the hit single "Jenny from the Block" were woven into the interview. Lopez said she could relate to her character in *Maid in Manhattan*, a single mother from the Bronx who worked hard and invisibly as a hotel maid and in a moment of yearning lived out a fantasy, because she was that character.

Sawyer tells the audience about Lopez's "Latina moxie," and how underneath her big hair and makeup was a vivid showstopper. Additionally, Lopez's status as an "entertainment powerhouse" was addressed through the lyrics of "Jenny from the Block" as a clip of the video ran with her singing "used to have a little, now I have a lot . . . I'm still, I'm still Jenny from the block." This is followed by a segment with Sawyer joining Lopez on a trip back to the Bronx, where she visits her old public school and meets her former sixth grade teacher. Lopez gives Sawyer a tour of the neighborhood where her grandmother still lives and they stand in front of the modest, working-class home where she grew up. The two have pizza and Lopez explains how she used to eat it everyday, for every meal as she was struggling early in her career, because it was only a dollar. Lopez talks about her childhood excitement over getting dressed up and taking the train with her mother down to Manhattan to meet her father for lunch in his company's cafeteria. She states she wanted to be a part of that [Manhattan] world to "have an exciting life."

When asked, "How much fun is it to be able to buy anything you want?" Lopez responds, "Fun!" and laughs. Sawyer and Lopez spend some time discussing her favorite dresses, like her strapless, black gown with a full skirt that she wore to the Oscars. Lopez explains how she will never get over having fancy, pretty clothes and a closet full of designer shoes because she was the girl who used to have holes in her shoes. Her parents had very little money to get her the things she needed and that embarrassed her as a child. These devices connect the implied audience to the superstar. Jennifer Lopez is a popular culture idol, but still gets her feelings hurt when the press criticize her fashion or photograph her looking terrible.

The camera shoots a close-up of Lopez's pink diamond engagement ring from Affleck. Lopez describes how she and Affleck are more alike than people think. She says they share the same kind of background, upbringing, family, house, "all that kind of stuff" as photographs of Affleck's childhood are shown side-by-side with photographs from her own childhood. Photographs of the couple kissing on the set of a movie, sailing on a yacht, and eating at an outdoor café are then shown, reemphasizing the couple's superstar status. The narrative concludes with Lopez's statement, "At the end of the day, to have a big house and be by yourself in it is not really the mood, you know, it's really about filling that house up with a lot of love and a lot of family. It sounds corny, but it's just so true."

Sawyer asks, "Is that what you dream about, that moment before you go to sleep?"

"Yes," Lopez answers.

The narrative positions Jennifer Lopez alongside ordinary people by interweaving the poverty of her childhood with her current elite status, and human emotions like looking for love and gaining the approval of others, getting to know yourself, making mistakes, and in the end valuing a family over the trappings of superstardom. In these ways, we can see that the construction of common ground through narrative is extensive enough to bridge the text's implied reader with the story's starring character.

## DISCUSSION

As my analysis suggests, the narrative discourse of the newsmagazine segments constructed the implied reader as upper middle class through the segment perspectives, shared value judgments, and characters.[17] If the real reader interacts with the text in accordance with the narrative form, he or she (independently of class status) symbolically joins the ranks of television's constructed, homogenized, and implied upper middle class. This constructed association is but one way that articulations of social class are present but rendered transparent in televisual culture. In accordance with the narrative structure of shared value judgments, the implied reader of television newsmagazines is left with nothing to identify with but upper-middle-class perspectives and characters.

Although the real reader may be overweight with the unbleached roots of his or her natural hair visible, the moral authority of the magazine segment did not encourage the implied reader to associate with the claims handlers in "Not the Best Policy." The implied audience member that Bradley addressed was the person who rejected the actions of the claims handlers, and who could potentially be victimized (as Dr. Tedesco had been initially victimized) by America's largest disability insurance company.

Conversely, even through the celebrity profile segments, the narrative discourse surrounding J. Lo, for example, did not associate the elite pop superstar with the implied audience. Instead, the segment was structured to meld the multimillionaire, designer-dressed media idol with the Puerto Rican girl, from a working-class neighborhood in the Bronx, who walked around as a child with holes in her shoes. Jennifer Lopez, in her Bronx accent, makes indirect reference to her childhood experiences as she states, "I will be sixty years old and still go into my closet and see my shoes and be like, 'Yes!' [giddy laughter]." Here the implied reader is offered a class hybrid, "Jenny from the block," a narrative construction somewhere between a social elite of unattainable status and a two-year-old girl who knew about having to pay "the bills." Segments like these are saturated with class associations, but the narrative structures function to de-emphasize the class components of the stories in favor of themes such as love and justice that are seemingly detached from class identification.

Newsmagazine narratives reproduce the mythology of America's "imperial middle" while simultaneously communicating class distinctions in increasingly subtle ways.[18] In accordance with Bourdieu's hierarchies of distinction, signs of cultural capital or lack thereof function as markers of social class, even when explicit references are not verbalized. These are the articulations of social class that are abundant in the television landscape, but often get overlooked. In the case of the newsmagazines analyzed, the symbols of status and wealth (or lack thereof) were articulated through clothing, hair styles, physical fitness, food choices, and the cultural geography of housing, and so on. However, class identification was constructed in these newsmagazine segments through narrative devices such as story perspective (i.e., narrating agency), story character, and narrative discourse.[19] As suggested, the potential impact of this construction is magnified when one intertextually considers newsmagazines within the larger televisual landscape. It is therefore difficult to argue that television and popular culture are stripped of social class. A more plausible explanation of our failure to discuss issues of class is the homogenized rendering of class into a normalized degree of transparency.

Critically examining social class through the television newsmagazine provides us with the potential to reveal much about the influence, perhaps unnoticed but no less powerful, of class distinctions in this country and the role of television in contributing to our notions of common sense norms. Of course this research is inherently limited by its scope as well as its approach. As reception analyses have demonstrated, no single interpretative reading can account for the polysemic nature of texts when they interact with audiences. The analysis I have offered is no exception. However, my objective was not to propose "the" (or even an) audience reading. Rather, my intent was to draw parallels between news storytelling and fictional storytelling conventions to argue that reality-inspired class mythologies are constructed in the same manner and hold the same potential to operate culturally as traditional Hollywood narratives. These points in no way detract from the informational programming imperatives and public service critiques embodied in classic journalism as information research. Rather, they are intended to extend notions about the role, impact, and functions of news in the contemporary media environment. Although news is indeed information, newsmagazines are as much a part of the popular culture landscape as dramatic series. To separate the study of information from the study of entertainment may deemphasize the role of news as storyteller and cultural myth maker. Through the reconceptualization of normalized definitions and through the investigation of previously overlooked sites of inquiry, this project has attempted to demonstrate the potential to expose articulations of things seemingly transparent. Exposing such transparencies reveals much about the current manifestations of social class in American media texts.

## NOTES

1. Mythology is used as Hartley (1982) uses myths to discuss society's utilization of characters and events, both factual and fictional, to construct meanings and make sense of the world.

2. Social class has been the conceptual heart of British cultural studies for decades. However, the emphasis on class issues in American cultural studies significantly declined as the focus was refashioned to revolve more frequently around issues of race and gender.

3. This article taken from the *New York Times* was reprinted from a periodical database; therefore page numbers for direct quotations were not available.

4. It is not my intention to suggest that social class is more significant than race and/or gender, nor is it my intention to suggest that these conceptualizations of identity should be severed from each other. Feminist criticism convincingly argues that race, class, and gender cannot be separated. However, the paucity of research that takes class as a primary variable should direct us to question why critical class studies or class criticism components do not typically accompany critical race studies and feminist criticism on the campuses of American universities.

5. Media scholars such as Croteau and Hoynes (1997) and Butsch (1997) have acknowledged this oversight.

6. This is in comparison with the nationwide distributions available at the respective dates that the research was conducted.

7. See studies by DeFleur (1964); Seggar and Wheeler (1973); Greenberg (1980); Greenberg, Simmons, Hogan, and Atkin (1980).

8. These include, but are not limited to, issues of gender and generation (Press 1991), race (Jhally and Lewis 1992), stereotypes (Berk 1977), poverty (Gould, Stern and Adams 1981), social mobility (Freeman 1992), gender (Steeves and Smith 1987), social order (Thomas 1986), and family and happiness (Thomas and Callahan 1982).

9. See Campbell's (1987) comparisons of *60 Minutes* narratives with conventional genre forms.

10. This models the pattern in racial politics where the ethnicity of African Americans, for example, is juxtaposed with the normalized dissociation of ethnicity from the apparent neutrality (or cultural purity) of whites. A similar example can be found in ideological politics that position alternative perspectives as radically present whereas the status quo is "invisible" and seemingly value-free.

11. Bourdieu recognized communicative potential in all aspects of social life ranging from the selection of clothing or home decor to a preference for different types of foods, and so on. He suggested that meaning arises as a choice and is expressed in relation to other potential choices. Categories of culture are not classified as legitimate until contrasted with different, presumably illegitimate and therefore inferior, categories. In this way, the judgments or distinctions are transformed into hierarchies of taste and status, and cultural practices become conceptualized as social resources or cultural capital.

12. During this period, television ratings are compared to demographic viewing information collected in 210 U.S. markets. In large part, advertising rates are based on this data.

13. Networks like Fox and the WB were not broadcasting newsmagazines in prime time during this period.

14. Based on my pilot reading, these were elements I anticipated as potentially significant; however, it was not my intention to focus on them to the extent of excluding additional elements that might emerge from a larger sample and more extensive, in-depth analysis.

15. As discussed by Gray (1995), representation is not understood in isolation but rather through relationships of representations within as well as across media texts.

16. As suggested by Kozloff (1992) in her explication of narrative theory.

17. As taken from Chatman's (1978) delineation of narrative participants.

18. Borrowed from Demott's (1990) analysis of social class in America.

19. Extended from Burgoyne's (1990) discussion of the cinematic narrator.

## REFERENCES

Allen, R. C., ed. 1992. *Channels of Discourse, Reassembled: Television and Contemporary Criticism*. 2d ed. Chapel Hill: University of North Carolina Press.

Berk, L. 1977. "The Great Middle American Dream Machine." *Journal of Communication*, Summer 1977.

Bourdieu, P. 1984. *Distinction: A Social Critique of the Judgment of Taste*. Cambridge, Mass.: Harvard University Press.

Brill, S. 1998. "Q&A: Dan Rather on Fear, Money, and the News." *Brill's Content*, October 1998.

Burgoyne, R. 1990. "The Cinematic Narrator: The Logic and Pragmatics of Impersonal Narration." *Journal of Film and Video* 421: 3–16.

Butsch, R. 1992. "Class and Gender in Four Decades of Television Situation Comedy." *Critical Studies in Mass Communication* 9 (1992): 387–99.

———. 1997. "Social Class and Television." In H. Newcomb, ed., *Encyclopedia of Television,* 3: 1524–27.

Butsch, R., and L. M. Glennon. 1983. "Social Class: Frequency Trends in Domestic Situation Comedy, 1946–1978." *Journal of Broadcasting* 271: 77–81.

Campbell, R. 1987. "Securing the Middle Ground: Reporter Formulas in 60 Minutes." *Critical Studies in Mass Communication*, December 1987, 325–50.

———. 1991. *60 Minutes and the News*. Urbana: University of Illinois Press.

Carter, B. 1998. "The Man Reshaping Prime Time; Television Newsmagazines Keep Spreading. Here's Why." *New York Times*, June 8, 1998.

Chatman, S. 1978. *Story and Discourse: Narrative Structure in Fiction and Film*. Ithaca, N.Y.: Cornell University Press.

Consoli, J. 1998. "All the News That Fits: Television News in Prime Time." *Adweek*, 2219, S12.

Croteau, D., and W. Hoynes. 1997. *Media/Society: Industries, Images, and Audiences*. Thousand Oaks, Calif: Pine Forge.

DeFleur, M. 1964. "Occupational Roles as Portrayed on Television." *Public Opinion Quarterly* 28: 57–74.

Demott, B. 1990. *The Imperial Middle: Why Americans Can't Think Straight about Class*. New York: William Morrow.

Freeman, L. 1992. "Social Mobility in Television Comedies." *Critical Studies in Mass Communication* 9: 400–406.

Gentile, F., and S. M. Miller. 1961. "Television and Social Class." *Sociology and Social Research* 453: 259–64.

Gould, C., D. C. Stern, and T. D. Adams. 1981. "TV's Distorted Vision of Poverty." *Communication Quarterly*, Fall, 309–14.

Gray, H. 1995. "Television, Black Americans, and the American Dream." In G. Dines and J. M. Humez, eds., *Gender, Race and Class in Media: A Text-Reader*. Thousand Oaks, Calif.: Sage.

Greenberg, B. 1980. *Life on Television: Content Analyses of U.S. TV Drama*. Norwood, N.J.: Ablex.

Greenberg, B., K. Simmons, L. Hogan, and C. Atkin. 1980. "The Demography of Fictional TV Characters." In B. Greenberg, ed., *Life on Television: Content Analyses of U.S. TV Drama*, 35–46. Norwood, N.J.: Ablex.

Hartley, J. 1982. *Understanding News*. London: Methuen.

Jhally, S., and J. Lewis. 1992. *Enlightened Racism: The Cosby Show, Audiences, and the Myth of the American Dream*. Boulder, Colo.: Westview.

Kozloff, S. 1992. "Narrative Theory and Television." In R. C. Allen, ed., *Channels of Discourse, Reassembled: Television and Contemporary Criticism*. 2d ed. Chapel Hill: University of North Carolina Press.

Landow, B., D. Hewitt, and M. Wallace. 1998. "60 Minutes Laid Bare." *Brill's Content*, October 1998.

Langston, D. 1995. "Tired of Playing Monopoly?" In M. L. Andersen and P. H. Collins, eds., *Race, Class, and Gender*, 101–2. Belmont, Calif.: Wadsworth.

Mantsios, G. 1995. "Class in America: Myths and Realities." In P. S. Rothenberg, ed., *Race, Class, and Gender in the United States: An Integrated Study*. New York: St. Martin's.

McClellan, S. 1995. "Shapiro's Risk Pays Off with 3-Night Dateline." *Broadcasting and Cable*, May 1.

Miller, S. 1998. "TV Turns Mag Rack: Nets Turn to Newsmags as Rating Pillar." *Daily Variety*, November 20.

Press, A. L. 1991. *Women Watching Television: Gender, Class, and Generation in the American Television Experience*. Philadelphia: University of Pennsylvania Press.

Puette, W. J. 1992. *Through Jaundiced Eyes: How the Media View Organized Labor*. Ithaca, N.Y.: ILR Press.

Reibstein, L., M. Brant, and N. A. Biddle. 1994. "The Battle of the TV Newsmagazine Shows." *Newsweek*, April 11.

Rothenberg, P. S. 1995. *Race, Class, and Gender in the United States: An Integrated Study*. New York: St. Martin's.

Sawyer, D. 1998. "3,000 Minutes." *New York Times Magazine*, September 20.

Seggar, J. F., and P. Wheeler. 1973. "World of Work on TV." *Journal of Broadcasting* 17: 201–14.

Sklar, R. 1980. *Prime-Time America*. New York: Oxford University Press.

Steeves, L., and M. C. Smith. 1987. "Class and Gender on Prime-Time Television Entertainment: Observations from a Socialist Feminist Perspective." *Journal of Communication Inquiry* 111: 43–63.

Stroud, M. 1998. "Can Dateline Thrive on Night no. 5?" *Broadcasting and Cable*, July 13.

Thomas, S. 1986. "Mass Media and the Social Order." In G. Gumpert and R. Cathcart, eds., *Intermedia: Interpersonal Communication in a Media World*, 611–27. 3rd ed. New York: Oxford University Press.

Thomas, S., and B. P. Callahan. 1982. "Allocating Happiness: TV Families and Social Class." *Journal of Communication* 23: 184–90.

Turner, R., and M. Hosenball. 1998. "The Datelining of TV." *Newsweek*, May 4.

# 8

## Calling Class: Sports Announcers and the Culture of Poverty

*James A. Rada and K. Tim Wulfemeyer*

### COLORING CLASS

In seeking to explain the disproportionate number of African Americans found in the socioeconomic condition that has come to be defined as the *underclass*, Oscar Lewis has often been credited with coining the term frequently used to label this disparity—the culture of poverty.

> This culture originated in endemic unemployment and chronic social immobility . . . this culture was typified by a lack of impulse control, a strong present-time orientation, and little ability to defer gratification. Among families it yielded an absence of childhood, an early initiation into sex, a prevalence of free marital unions, and a high incidence of abandonment of mothers and children. (Massey and Denton 1993, 5)

Wilson added to this definition by looking beyond the externally visible symptoms to an exploration of potential causes and cures:

> [C]onservative students of inner-city poverty . . . have focused almost exclusively on *the interconnection between cultural traditions, family history, and individual character*. For example, they have argued that a ghetto family that has had a history of welfare dependency will tend to bear offspring who lack ambition, a work ethic, and a sense of self-reliance. *Some even suggest that ghetto underclass individuals have to be rehabilitated culturally before they can advance in society*. (Wilson 1987, 13; emphasis added)

In the early 1960s, the federal government also investigated the seeming interconnectedness between African Americans and socioeconomic status. *The Negro Family: The Case for National Action*, commonly known as the Moynihan Report, detailed the dissolution of the black family. In noting that many middle-class African Americans were able to "save" themselves from poverty, the report detailed a tangle of pathology that it said had ensnared the African American community. This pathology is characterized by illegitimate births, an overabundance of fatherless households, a dependence on government intervention and programs to sustain themselves, and heightened rates of crime (U.S. Department of Labor, Office of Policy Planning and Research 1965).

While sociologists, scholars, and governmental researchers wrestle to understand the nuanced relationship between race and class, the mass media rarely have had such a dilemma. For the media, the intricacies of this complex phenomenon boil down to a simple explanation.

The black underclass appears as a menace and a source of social disorganization in news accounts of black urban crime, gang violence, drug use, teenage pregnancy, riots, homelessness and general aimlessness. In news accounts . . . poor blacks (and Hispanics) signify a social menace that must be contained. *Poor urban blacks help to mark the boundaries of appropriate middle class behavior as well as the acceptable routes to success.* (Gray 1989, 431; emphasis added)

Portrayals of African Americans found in the news and entertainment media are actually stereotype–ridden misportrayals that show the African American experience to be inextricably linked to the symptoms that symbolize the culture of poverty (see Dates and Barlow 1990; Dixon and Linz 2000; Entman and Rojecki 2001; Romer, Jamieson, and de Coteau 1998; Staples and Jones 1985; U.S. Commission for the Study of Civil Rights 1977; U.S. Riot Commission Report 1968). Perhaps nowhere are these portrayals more evident than in television, where the visual imagery combines with the spoken narrative to paint a picture whereby African Americans are transformed into an iconic representation of the cause of society's ills.

This research sought to investigate whether this relationship holds true in televised coverage of intercollegiate athletics. For the two most popular intercollegiate sports in terms of attendance and television coverage, Men's Division I-A football and basketball, African Americans compose 46 percent and 56 percent of the participants, respectively (Racial and Gender Report Card 2001). The overrepresentation of African Americans on the field and court, combined with the historical *mis*representation of African Americans on television, provides fertile areas for exploration.

Along with its numerical representation on the field, televised sports coverage also carries with it a symbolic representation. Birrell notes that sports serve as a "site for the reproduction of relations of privilege and oppression and of dominance and subordination structured along gender, race, and class lines" (1989, 213).

Others have noted that televised sports coverage helps to define an "urban black masculinity" by describing African American players as deviant, evidenced by an uncontrolled lifestyle off the field or court and a similar style of play on it (Davis and Harris 1998, 160). The coverage often insinuates the cause of this deviance.

> Depictions of African-American athletes as deviant often imply that African American culture and communities are to blame, suggesting that this culture is deviant . . . Media often link the (portrayed) deviance of African American athletes to stereotypes of dysfunctional single-parent families, welfare dependency and drug-infestation associated with African American communities. (Davis and Harris 1998, 161)

What is striking is the consistency associated with how African American players are described. Announcers disproportionately confine their comments about African American athletes to praise of their physical attributes—often credited to god-given ability. When the announcers venture beyond the realm of the athlete as a physical specimen, their comments about African American athletes' off-field endeavors and persona paint a clear picture of these men at odds with the accepted social, moral, and legal norms of society (Lule 1995; Rada 1996; Rada and Wulfemeyer 2001; Rada and Wulfemeyer 2002; Rainville and McCormick 1977).

Such comments, in and of themselves, are problematic in the message they convey, of course, but the impact of the comments becomes magnified when whiteness is the standard, or norm, against which African Americans are compared. Dyer (1997), among others, has noted the power of whiteness. According to Dyer, whiteness serves as the invisible norm by which the behavior of others can be measured. The fact that an announcer chooses to mention one specific aspect of a player's performance or personal life is not, in and of itself, a sign of negativity. Indeed, the information may be factual. A player may have been arrested, been on academic probation, and so on; however, the problem arises when statements are contextualized in such a way that they create a dichotomy between players of different races.

When announcers have a myriad of personal information from which to choose, and they consistently select the positive aspects of a white player's life and the negative aspects of an African American player's life, then we begin to see a pattern wherein the white athlete represents the positive, as expressed through social and moral norms. And, in drawing the lines between appropriate and inappropriate behavior, the media show that the "white" answer is usually the right answer (Brooks and Rada 2002; Omi and Winant 1994).

In sum, the mass media *race* our social reality. As it is used here, the term *race* does not refer to a physical contest of speed. Instead, it refers to a process whereby representations of reality are inextricably entwined with representations of race. The result is a *raced* view of society—and in this case, using skin tone as a referent, darkness equals deviance.

## THE PRESENT STUDY

In our most recent work, we analyzed more than seventy-five hours of televised coverage of intercollegiate football and men's basketball from the 1998–1999 season. Consistent with previous findings, our research found differences across race in comments about a player's intelligence and character. However, the present research also sought to go beyond the numbers into an in-depth analysis of the language behind the numbers. In effect, we sought to understand what was being said and how it contributed to the racial dichotomy drawn by mediated portrayals. While the number of statements in these categories constituted a small percentage of the overall number of comments, they create an image that far outweighs their numbers in the sample.

Our analysis uncovered four themes that appeared throughout the coverage. Three of these themes focus on how African American athletes deviate from the team/collective spirit of athletic competition, the traditional family unit, and established legal/moral norms of society. The fourth theme focuses on how the African American athlete, as a product of his culture, is by himself societally impotent and in need of guidance in the ways of the world; in need of a father figure—which materializes in the form of his coach. We begin by looking at how the African American player is portrayed as deviant from the team/collective spirit of athletic competition.

## THE SELFISH TEAMMATE

Referring back to our prior discussion of the culture of poverty and the portrayal of African American deviance, reference is made to the emphasis on self-gratification, a lack of impulse control, and a self-centered mind-set. As a cultural norm, self-gratification may not be seen as a negative. However, when taken in the context of athletic competition—team competition in which teamwork, cooperation, loyalty, and self-discipline are highly valued (Gantz and Wenner 1991)—then placing one's own interests over those of the team is indeed deviant.

Witness an announcer's comments about an African American football player. As the game unfolded, this player—a backup running back who was having a productive game—became the focus of increased attention. As is often the case, announcers used the on-field activity as an opportunity to segue to a discussion of the person behind the player. It is then we hear of a self-centered individual who lacks the discipline or unselfishness to "go along with the program;" to place the interests of the team above his own.

> Some guys have a hard time getting it all together—they have a hard time marching with everyone else—McCaslin is one of those guys.[1]

A short time later, the announcers offer up a bit of praise for this player. However, the announcers dilute that praise by pointing to his indiscretions:

> Give McCaslin credit. He was suspended for violating team rules but still stayed active in supporting the team.

One could argue that if the player did not want any negative commentary directed toward him, he should not have done whatever he did to get suspended. But compare the previous comments directed toward an African American player to how the announcers use a factual aspect of a white player's history:

> He signals in the plays—loves learning from Spurrier. He wanted to transfer but scored a TD in the spring game. He's an important part of the team in that function. If he makes a mistake, it could be vital.

As with the African American player, there is a verifiable element to this comment. But the difference emerges when we compare how these factual elements are used to segue into a description being crafted by the announcer. Whereas the African American player's on-field contributions are minimized by his off-field activities, the white player's peripheral involvement in the game is maximized.

In a similar vein, during the course of a basketball game, an announcer takes the liberty of speculating on behalf of the team members of a white player—at the time, the only white member of that team's five players on the court. In a previous reference, the announcer described this player as having "an angelic look to him." This time the announcer opines, "Scott Pohlman must be such a delight to play with."

As the white players hold the exclusive access to such positive ruminations, the African American players are left with descriptions of their deviance. This adds one layer to the racial dichotomy. Another layer is added when we look at how the announcers describe the players' lives off the field.

## THE SOCIETAL NORM

It is one thing when announcers describe an African American athlete at odds with his team. It is another to portray him at odds with society. In comments within this theme, the announcers emphasize the player's deviance from legally established or culturally accepted norms. As an African American player stepped to the foul line to shoot two free throws, the momentary pause in the action provided the announcers some time to tell us about this player. We do not hear relevant game-related commentary; instead, we hear the following:

> He's had an interesting off-court session for Weber State—two DUIs, suspended, but now he's back.

Another deviant description refers to an African American player's violation of the established guidelines set forth by the governing body of intercollegiate athletics. This particular athlete played for the University of Kansas. But during the tournament, his team was assigned to play games in New Orleans, Louisiana—the player's home state and home of the school where he was first recruited. Even though the game was at a neutral site, as this particular player entered the game, he was met with a chorus of boos from those in attendance. This provided the announcers a chance to focus on one unsightly aspect of this player's past:

> And a greeting for Lester Earl—if you want to call it a greeting. Earl, a Louisiana native out of Baton Rouge, first recruited and signed with LSU. Later, his recruitment process landed LSU on probation and they're still bitter about that down here in Cajun Country—blaming Earl.

This particular statement carries with it two meanings. The first is the overt inclusion of the player's alleged past indiscretions. The second is the conspicuous exclusion of another participant in this illegality. The announcers name the individual player and say "his recruitment process" was the cause of this particular school being penalized. By depersonalizing the "recruitment process," the announcer draws attention away from at least one other participant in the process—the coach who recruited Earl. This then places the responsibility for the indiscretion squarely, and solely, on the player's shoulders. Later on we will visit the hallowed ground that the announcers allow the coaches to occupy.

Many of the aforementioned comments are fact based and verifiable. Thus it could be said that announcers are "just doing their job" and "telling it like it is." However, once again we see a disparity in the descriptions directed toward white players. Such is the case when we get to hear of a white player's off-court activities.

> Burgess is contemplating going on a Mormon mission at the end of the season.

While only one statement, it carries with it the weight of conformity with a value-laden ideology. We turn to our next theme to see where these values manifest themselves on a larger scale.

## BREAKDOWN OF THE FAMILY UNIT

In the small sample of comments that we uncovered, the overwhelming majority focused on some aspect of the player's family life, or background. Along with the aura of illegality, one of the most prominent features of the culture of poverty is an emphasis on the breakdown of the traditional family unit. This breakdown is characterized by an "absence of childhood, an early initiation into sex, a prevalence of free marital unions, and a high in-cidence of abandonment of mothers and children" (Massey and Denton 1993, 5).

Throughout the course of our research, we uncovered several not so sub-tle references to these characteristics. One such example:

Jason Terry, oldest of ten kids, so he's been a father figure at home.

While not explicitly mentioned, the absence of a father is clear. The indi-rect reference to the lack of a father in the house, evidenced by the fact that the player himself had to fill the role of "father figure," also points to another culture of poverty characteristic—the absence of a childhood. There is also the inferred reference that, with ten children and no father around, the chil-dren have most likely been fathered by different men, and they and their mother have been abandoned.

Another example of a fatherless household:

Another young man on the St. John's team who has it in the right perspective because of the adversity in his life. He lost his mom, April, nine years ago to Leukemia, was raised by his grandmother.

The fact that in the absence of his mother, his grandmother had to step in once again alludes to the lack of the father in the household.

And yet another conspicuous omission in the following:

Postell is from Albany, Georgia. Mom is a security guard at a prison—tough young man—does all the dirty work.

We hear of the mother's work, but not the father's. Once again, there is no reference made to the presence of a father. These references to specific play-ers and their families may not, in and of themselves, symbolize a conscious effort on the part of announcers to portray deviance among the African American players; however, compare them with the descriptions of white players. While we hear, either directly or indirectly of the lack of a father in the lives of African American players; we hear—rather directly—of the pres-ence of a father in the households of white players.

Scott Padgett grew up listening to Wildcat basketball on the radio with his father Wilbur . . . dreaming of one day being a Wildcat, a deep attachment for sure for Scott Padgett.

There's his dad, gotta be very proud . . . all those days they worked in the back-yard, working on that shot.

Gabe Gross—wears number 22 out of respect for his father.

The comparison is not just limited to the presence or lack of a father figure. Several announcers made references to an athlete's entire family. When this is the case, we hear of the presence of the white player's family, and their support as well.

As proud as everybody is about the way this guy's developed as a basketball player, I betcha his parents are even prouder of the way he's developed as a student athlete—all academic SEC.

Swenson—growing up on the family farm in North Dakota—family needs him on the farm, but they don't want to stand in the way of his dream of playing ball.

No such references were made to the families of African American players. Instead, when announcers commented on the family life of the African American players, their commentary built on previous statements pointing to the lack of a father to offer a portrayal of an entire household in a state of disarray.

## A BROKEN HOME IN A BROKEN NEIGHBORHOOD

Just as the juxtaposition of white athletes' portrayal serves to magnify the deviance in the portrayal of the African American athletes, the same effect is achieved when the announcers combine deviant descriptions of African Americans. Such is the case when we hear of the environment in which the following player was raised.

A rough neighborhood, Artest grew up in a five-room apartment . . . from time to time as many as seventeen people in that apartment.

The definition of "a rough neighborhood" is clear. And, while we do not get the specifics of the seventeen people who live in the five-room apartment from time to time, their transience certainly does not infer stability.

Another reference features more family problems for an African American athlete.

Bootsy Thornton's overcome a lot of obstacles—including some problems in the family life. . . . His half brother Travis is in a prison in Maryland serving three years on drug-related charges.

Once again, the information is verifiable. But compare the announcers presentation of verifiable information relating to the African American player with that of a white player. Describing the troubled homeland from which one European player hails, the announcer is more vague about the details, and is quick to offer sympathy and to compliment the player for his ability to overcome adversity.

Savovic—from Montenegro, Yugoslavia—you can imagine what that young man is going through right now in terms of the crisis back in his homeland and still being able to concentrate on basketball.

One of the basketball games we analyzed provided one of the more significant examples of the black/white dichotomy. The two players described are on the same team and the two descriptions came less than five minutes apart in the same game. In the first description, we hear this about a white player:

Pregame ritual—three showers, bagels and eggs. If you look inside his shirt, you'll find the number 44 pinned there—it's in memory of a good friend who died recently. Kid with a tremendous past and an incredible future.

Then, a few minutes later, we hear the story of an African American player:

Raised by his grandmother in Miami. A guy who appreciates his roots and recognizes friendships. Underneath his jersey is another one with double zero—that is to honor a friend who was shot last year.

These two comments create starkly different portrayals. After a discussion of the white player's eating and hygiene habits, the profound leap to his memorializing a friend is made. For the African American player, the introduction mentions the absence of *both* parents. Perhaps the most interesting aspect of this comparison are the references to the tributes to their fallen friends. Both athletes carry the uniform number of their friend as a sign of reverence. However, in the case of the white player, we hear only that his friend "died recently." For the African American player, we hear the cause of death. Clearly, the loss of life is tragic. But when that loss of life is attributed to a shooting, there is a clear insinuation of illegality. Omitting the cause of death for the white player's friend may direct the audience to a sympathetic response. No such sympathy is evoked for the African American player's friend whose cause of death might lead the audience to suspect that he brought it on himself.

There is another interesting point to note about these two descriptions. The announcer refers to the white player's "tremendous past" and then projects ahead to his "incredible future." While announcers certainly cannot be expected to be clairvoyant, and should not be held accountable for inaccurate predictions, it is worth noting that this white player's "incredible future" was derailed when he was suspended from the team his senior year for illegal gambling activities (DiRocco 2001; Pells 2001).

## COACH AS A HERO

Along with a subtle reference to the lack of a father figure, descriptions in this category hearken back to Wilson's observation that "some even suggest that ghetto underclass individuals have to be *rehabilitated culturally* before they can advance in society" (1987, 13; emphasis added). Among those who can contribute to the rehabilitation effort are the coaches.

Some of the announcers have a built-in conflict of interest when it comes to commenting on coaches because many are ex-coaches themselves and they are often asked to participate, with financial compensation, at summer clinics being conducted by current coaches (Anderson 2001; McCallum and O' Brien 1998; Stewart 1990; Wolff and Stone 1995). Thus there can be a distinct lack of objectivity. After repeated references to the culture of poverty associated with African American players, often the announcers take it upon themselves to craft a savior for the poor, misdirected, African American young men. In fact, the announcers often portray the coaches as "Father Flanigan" figures (Miklasz 1991).

> Barnes—a young man who's overcome a lot of tragedy in his life. His mother shot to death during a burglary in his home when he was eight years old. He lost his father when he was in high school—the kind of young man with whom John Chaney will work forever.

> Brokenborough—he's an example of the kind of guy that John Chaney takes and treats so well. That's why I hope John Chaney never retires, cause every year he saves four young men.

The players are African American, as is the coach, John Chaney of Temple University. Perhaps it could be seen as a positive that when the announcers refer to the culture of poverty characteristics of these particular players, they provide a solution in the form of another African American male. However, when taken in context, there are two problematic aspects associated with these statements. The first is that the statements have wrestled control of the player's life away from the player and given it to the coach. A coach who, while he may be African American, is still a representative of two predominantly white institutions—postsecondary education and the coaching profession. In doing so, they reinforce the assumption of the out of control, endemic nature of the culture of poverty.

Second, while we don't know what criteria the announcer uses to proclaim these players "saved" by their coach, it must not take into account their education. Of those four young men the announcer credits John Chaney with "saving" every year, only one of them will graduate (Scouting Reports 2001).

The following comment perhaps serves as the most profound example of an announcer combining the deviance of the African American player with the messianic nature of the coach. In this instance, both coaches being referred to are white.

> Will we see Odom again? It took so long for him to make it into college . . . with the background he has had . . . a very turbulent upbringing. You won't meet a more cordial young man and when you go through what he's gone through . . . the streets of the city . . . there are a lot of classic hangers on that one must deal

with and I think that the balance that Jim Harrick, and his staff have been able to bring to this young man . . . Assistant Coach Jerry DeGregorio who coached at the high school that he played for had a lot to do with that.

Reference to the characteristics of the culture of poverty is obvious, but there is more. Earlier, we discussed a phrase wherein the announcer pointed to the "recruitment process" that landed a player's school on probation. Conspicuously absent from that description was a reference to the role of the coach in that process. In this instance, when the player is noted for his cordiality in the face of difficult circumstances, credit is given to his coaches—both of whom are white. There is a distinct irony to the fact that Jim Harrick, the coach credited with saving the player from "the streets of the city" and bringing "balance" to his life, was fired from his previous coaching job for falsifying documents (Dufresne 1998; Saladino 2001; Schlabach 2002; Wright 1998).

There is one more comment that is worthy of discussion. This comment is unique in that it was not made in response to anything that was happening on the court at the time, but instead refers to an event that took place more than 30 years ago. Still, it serves as an example of how announcers deify the coaches. In this particular instance, announcers were referring to an historic event in the history of college basketball. In 1966, Texas Western (now the University of Texas at El Paso) beat the University of Kentucky for the national championship. What made the event historic was the composition of the two teams. Texas Western's starting lineup was composed entirely of African American players, and Kentucky's was composed of all white players.

One of the announcers minimized the importance of this event by pointing out that previous championship teams, while not composed entirely of African Americans, still had some African American players on them. This announcer then acknowledged the impact of this event. However, he did not mention the players who accomplished this historic feat, but instead directed his praise to their white coach when he said, "Give Coach Haskins a lot of credit."

## AN IMBALANCE OF POWER

By their performance, individual African Americans have empowered themselves on the field/court. But by their coverage of such performances, announcers have disempowered African American athletes off the court. In sports, athletes can be assessed a penalty for their on-field actions. When sports are televised, announcers are assessing penalties based not on behavior, but on race. The extent of the penalty is not measured by yards, foul shots or time in a penalty box, but by distinctions in the minds and hearts of people in society.

Just as African Americans are overrepresented, to the point of being almost exclusive titleholders of the culture of poverty portrayals in the media, American society at large overrepresents the percentage of African Americans who constitute the underclass. Gilens (1999) argues that the media's overreliance on these images of the black underclass serves not only to perpetuate the stereotypes, but also to justify widespread hostility for social policies designed to remedy such circumstances. It is not only the content of these portrayals that creates such a reaction, but the context as well. Gilens notes that specific, detailed anecdotal examples—such as the ones found in this study—are more likely to influence a person even when presented with overwhelming statistical evidence to the contrary.

In a society where race has served as a determinant of life chances (e.g., Gandy 1998), the disparity brought about by racial divisions is magnified by class divisions. By painting a bleak portrait of the underclass, and coloring it black, the media have marginalized the African American community. Zweig (2000) argues that this robs African Americans of their dignity, individuality, and right to self-determination that is an inalienable right—at least according to the Constitution. African Americans now serve as the other, a collective symbol of moral and ethical trespasses against a civilized society. By isolating them from what society considers to be right—which in the media's eyes means white—African Americans have become an acceptable target for fear, loathing, and animosity. Armour (1997) says this has the effect of turning African Americans into targets of another sort when he points out that mediated messages which reinforce the image of African Americans as an inherent threat to society provide a common sense justification for legal actions disproportionately applied to African Americans, such as racial profiling. Even worse, it may lead society to accept such institutionalized inequalities as a necessary means to protect the moral from the amoral. In this scenario, an instance wherein a police officer mistakenly shoots an African American or a jury mistakenly convicts an African American may not actually be judged a mistake. Instead, the perceived threat might be considered a valid explanation for a raced decision.

In sum, class equals power. Those in the upper class are imbued with the moral, material, legal, and political power to effect change. The class-endowed get to determine their destiny and that of others, especially the underclass. Clearly this situation is unlikely to change unless more concerted efforts are made by media practitioners to de-race their coverage and portrayal of African Americans in sports and other aspects of everyday life.

## NOTE

1. All comments quoted in this chapter were transcribed verbatim. Any grammatical or syntactical errors reflect the announcer's spoken commentary.

## REFERENCES

Anderson, W. B. 2001. Does the cheerleading ever stop? Major league baseball and sports journalism. *Journalism and Mass Communication Quarterly* 78, no. 2: 355–82.

Armour, J. D. 1997. *Negrophobia and reasonable racism*. New York: New York University Press.

Birrell, S. 1989. Racial relations theories and sport: Suggestions for a more critical analysis. *Sociology of Sport Journal* 6, no. 3: 212–27.

Brooks, D., and Rada, J. 2002. Constructing race in black and whiteness: Media coverage of public support for President Clinton. *Journalism and Communication Monographs* 4, no. 3: 115–56.

Clawson, R. A., and Trice, R. 2000. Poverty as we know it: Media portrayals of the poor. *Public Opinion Quarterly* 64: 53–64.

Dates, J., and Barlow, W. 1990. *Split Image: African Americans in the mass media*. Washington, D.C.: Howard University Press.

Davis, L. R., and Harris, O. 1998. Race and ethnicity in U.S. sports media. In L. Wenner, ed., *Mediasport*, 154–69. London: Routledge.

DiRocco, M. 2001. Dupay done at UF: Troubled guard ruled ineligible. *Florida Times-Union*, September 8, D1, D7. Retrieved from Lexis-Nexis database.

Dixon, T., and Linz, D. 2000. Race and the misrepresentation of victimization on local television news. *Communication Research* 27, no. 5: 547–73.

Dufresne, C. 1998. College basketball/Chris Dufresne; ultimately, NCAA mediated a family quarrel. *Los Angeles Times*, May 1, p. C1. Retrieved from Lexis-Nexis database.

Dyer, R. 1997. *White*. London: Routledge.

Entman, R. M., and Rojecki, A. 2001. *The black image in the white mind: Media and race in America*. Chicago: University of Chicago Press.

Ford, T. E. 1997. Effects of stereotypical portrayals of African Americans on person perception. *Social Psychology Quarterly* 60, no. 3: 266–78.

Gandy, O. H. 1998. *Communication and race: A structural perspective*. London: Arnold.

Gantz, W., and Wenner, L. A. 1991. Men, women, and sports: Audience experiences and effects. *Journal of Broadcasting and Electronic Media* 35, no. 2: 233–43.

Gilens, M. 1996. Race and poverty in America: Public misperceptions and the American news media. *Public Opinion Quarterly* 60, no. 4: 515–41.

———. 1999. *Why Americans hate welfare: Race, media, and the politics of antipoverty policy*. Chicago: University of Chicago Press.

Gray, H. 1989. Television, black Americans, and the American dream. *Critical Studies in Mass Communication* 6: 376–86.

Hall, S. 1981. The whites of their eyes: Racist ideologies and the media. In G. Bridges and R. Brunt, eds., *Silver Linings*, 28–52. London: Lawrence & Wishart.

Hill, J. R., and Zillman, D. 1999. *The Oprahization of American: Sympathetic crime talk and leniency*. *Journal of Broadcasting and Electronic Media* 43, no. 1: 67–82.

Jackson, D. 1989. Calling the plays in black and white. *Boston Globe*, January 22, A25.

Katz, M. B. 1993. The urban "underclass" as a metaphor of social transformation. In M. Katz, ed., *The "underclass" debate: Views from history*, 3–26. Princeton N.J.: Princeton University Press.

Lapchick, R. E. 2000. Crime and athletes: New racial stereotypes. *Society* 37, no. 3: 14–20.

Lule, J. 1995. The rape of Mike Tyson: Race, the press, and symbolic types. *Critical Studies in Mass Communication* 12, no. 2: 176–95.

Massey, D. S., and Denton, N. A. 1993. *American apartheid*. Cambridge: Harvard University Press.

McCallum, J., and O'Brien, R. 1998. More bull from Billy. *Sports Illustrated,* March 30, 29.

McCarthy, D., and Jones, R. L. 1997. Speed, aggression, strength, and tactical naïveté. *Journal of Sports and Social Issues* 21, no. 4: 348–62.

Miklasz, B. 1991. Even before loss, UNLV was no UCLA. *St. Louis Post-Dispatch*, March 31, F1. Retrieved from Lexis-Nexis database.

Omi, M., and Winant, H. 1994. *Racial formation in the United States from the 1960s to the 1990s.* New York: Routledge.

Pan, Z., and Kosicki, G. 1996. Assessing news media influences on the formation of whites' racial policy preferences. *Communication Research* 23, no. 2: 147–78.

Pells, E. 2001. Florida point guard Dupay ineligible; gambling probe wrapped up. Associated Press, September 7. Retrieved from Lexis-Nexis database.

Person's Tracking Report. 1998. Nielsen Media Research.

Power, J. G., Murphy, S. T., and Coover, G. 1996. Priming prejudice: How stereotypes and counter-stereotypes influence attribution of responsibility and credibility among ingroups and outgroups. *Human Communication Research* 23, no. 1: 36–58.

Racial and Gender Report Card. 2001. *The Center for the Study of Sport in Society: Northeastern University.* Report available online at www.sportinsociety.org.

Rada, J. A. 1996. Color blind-sided: Racial bias in network television's coverage of professional football games. *The Howard Journal of Communications* 7, no. 3: 231-240.

———. 2000. A new piece to the puzzle: Examining effects of television portrayals of African Americans. *Journal of Broadcasting and Electronic Media* 44, no. 4: 704–15.

Rada, J. A., and Wulfemeyer, K. T., 2001. *A picture plus a thousand words: Racial bias in televised coverage of collegiate sports.* Paper presented at the annual conference of the National Communication Association, Atlanta, November.

———. 2002. Color blindsided in the booth: An examination of the descriptions of college athletes during televised games. Paper presented at the Association for Education in Journalism and Mass Communication's National Convention, Miami, August.

Rainville, R., and McCormick, E. 1977. Extent of covert racial prejudice in pro football announcers' speech. *Journalism Quarterly* 54: 20–26.

Romer, D., Jamieson, K., and de Coteau, N. 1998. The treatment of persons of color in local television news: Ethnic blame discourse or realistic group conflict? *Communication Research* 25, no. 3: 286–306.

Saladino, T. 2001. Georgia's Harrick Jr. admits to erroneous bio in media guide. *Advocate* (Baton Rouge, La.), December 21, D6. Retrieved from Lexis-Nexis database.

Schlabach, M. 2002. Friday's game: Georgia vs. Murray State, approximately 10:20 P.M.: On his terms: Georgia's Jim Harrick has courted controversy wherever he coaches, but he always wins. *Atlanta Journal Constitution*, March 14, D1. Retrieved from Lexis-Nexis database.

Scouting Reports. 2001. *Sports Illustrated*, November 19, 96–130.

Staples, R., and Jones, T. 1985. Culture, ideology and African American television images. *Black Scholar*, May-June, 10–20.

Stewart, L. 1990. Packer, Tompkins both get caught up in all the madness. *Los Angeles Times*, March 30, C3.

U.S. Commission for the Study of Civil Rights. 1977. *Window dressing on the set: Women and minorities in television.* Washington, D.C.: U.S. Government Printing Office.

U.S. Department of Labor: Office of Policy Planning and Research. 1965. *The Negro family.* Washington, D.C.: U.S Government Printing Office. Reprinted in 1981 by Greenwood Press.

U.S. Riot Commission Report. 1968. *Report of the national advisory commission on Civil Disorders.* New York: Bantam.

Wilson, W. J. 1987. *The truly disadvantaged: The inner city, the underclass, and public policy.* Chicago: University of Chicago Press.

Wolff, A., and Stone, C. 1995. Backscratchers. *Sports Illustrated.* April 3, 22.

Wonsek, P. L. 1992. College basketball on television; a study of racism in the media. *Media, Culture, and Society* 14: 449–61.

Wright, K. 1998. Redemption; Harrick, Odom shed checkered past, aim to lift Rhode Island to prominence. *The Washington Times,* November 11, B1. Retrieved from Lexis-Nexis database.

Zillman, D. 1991. Television viewing and psychological arousal. In J. Bryant and D. Zillman, eds., *Responding to the screen: Reception and reaction processes,* 103–34. Hillsdale, N.J.: Lawrence Erlbaum.

Zweig, M. 2000. *The working class majority: America's best kept secret.* Ithaca, N.Y.: Cornell University Press.

# III

---

# CONSTRUCTING CLASS GROUPS

As I wrote in the introduction, perhaps at its most basic level class is a way in which we humans divide up the world, often in order to make distinctions between *us* and *them*. This part of the book looks at the way in which news media may construct or contribute to cultural constructions of class groups.

The *us*, in American terms, is most often expressed as middle or upper middle class. For those who grew up with *Life* magazine, that may not be a coincidence. In this section Sheila Webb offers a sophisticated and multifaceted analysis of the content of *Life*.

Next we'll see that class may well influence whether a story is considered newsworthy; even if it reaches newsworthy status there may be a gap between the amount and quality of coverage given to a story, based on class considerations. Carol Liebler compares two stories, both about missing college women, and how the press played each story.

When we think about *them*, a label that may resonate is "trailer park trash." Using this label as a sign, Joseph Harry uses semiotics to discuss how newspapers use the term and what it can tell us about media operating in a capitalist economy.

# 9

# "America Is a Middle-Class Nation": The Presentation of Class in the Pages of *Life*

*Sheila M. Webb*

Today we live in an overwhelmingly visual culture. The television, the computer, the animated billboard—they all demand our attention. It is hard, if not impossible, to imagine the days before our present state of image saturation, when the newspaper was the main source of printed images; when movies were available only in theaters, not at the touch of a button in one's living room; and when picture books and catalogs were the main source of visual material on art or interior design. The appearance of *Life* in November 1936 in the mailbox must have been exhilarating. Here was a visual treasury, sometimes in color, of the variety of American lifestyles and products. In perusing *Life*'s pages, one could see inside the workrooms at *Harper's Bazaar* as the staff put together the fall fashion issue, be taken on a visual tour of America's "typical" Midwestern town, gain insight into the daily life of coeds, see Helen Hayes relaxing at her New England estate, contemplate Joan Crawford's taste in furniture as she sat in her settee with her dachshund Baby beside her, take a peek at how the wealthy amused themselves at the El Morocco, peer over a debutante's shoulder as she examined a social registry to choose which eligible young men to invite to her ball, or decide which model house, with the design commissioned and sold by *Life,* to order.

The first successful pictorial journal, *Life* created a visual worldview that resonates today. The way *Life* magazine presented America to Americans in the magazine's first decade, from the first issue in 1936 to the entry of the United States in World War II, hit a chord with its audience. During a time of social and political upheaval, the editors presented the American way of life as profoundly middle class. That way of life was centered on educational advancement and proper consumption. The dominant assumptions of American life were visualized weekly in *Life*, yet so was the way to the future. The themes, subjects, and framing developed in this period continued throughout its long run as a weekly, from 1936 to 1972, and then again as a monthly from 1978 until the spring of 2000. In the spring of 2003, convinced that *Life* offers something no other journal can, the editors positioned the magazine for yet another revival, this time as a Sunday supplement to newspapers.

In the first decade of its long run, *Life*'s presentation of class was explicit: the class standing of the subjects pictured was marked in the text, the editors addressed their middle-class audience directly, and they expected the stories they published to define and improve middle-class life. To explore that thesis, this chapter begins with an overview of the increasing importance of visuals in the American media which helped set the stage for *Life*'s phenomenally successful launch. Next, an investigation of archival material documents how the editors aimed to identify and understand their readers. How this effort affected the stories the editors chose is revealed in the discussion that follows. A textual analysis, which identified emergent themes that dealt with class, is woven into a content analysis designed to quantify *Life*'s presentation of class. Finally, a look at a seminal photo-essay will show how *Life* tied middle-class consumption to the definition of what it meant to be an American citizen.

## BEFORE *LIFE* MAGAZINE

In the decades that preceded that first issue of *Life*, social and cultural factors helped promote the rise of mass-marketed magazines. As the country moved from an agrarian to an industrial economy, low-priced magazines that explained this new environment could now be distributed. Along with the rise of branded products, magazines, part of the expanding market for all goods around the turn of the century, provided the perfect venue for national marketing. Also spurring the establishment of the mass-marketed magazine were population growth, an increase in leisure time, and higher levels of education. Between 1910 and 1929, with purchasing power going up by 40 percent, a ready market was available to learn about new leisure pursuits and new consumer goods. *Life* was able to capitalize on the major changes that had taken place in mass media structures between 1910 and 1940—changes that included a rise of advertising; the increasing number and changing use of visuals—illustrations, color, and photography; and the targeting of middle-class audiences to reach the demographics advertisers preferred.

In the course of these changes, how the media saw and presented class changed as well. In addition to institutional sites, including museums, symphonies, and fairs, in the media we also find evidence for the segmentation of popular taste publics, one in which visual imagery played a major role. In the 1930s, powerful cultural factors were at work that helped foster the immediate success of this first pictorial narrative presentation. The country was in the midst of the Depression that people hoped to soon escape. *Life*, which hardly mentioned the Depression in its pages, showed the way beyond the economic crisis to a vision of the American dream, one in which hard work and proper purchasing led to class advancement. Coverage of art, fashion, and housing functioned as taste education. The entertainment sections offered insight into the cultural worlds centered in New York and Hollywood. The text described the endless possibilities inherent in the U.S. capitalist system and showed their readers how to achieve them. That path was through education and then the fulfilling of a professional role that would contribute to scientific or cultural knowledge. In every section of the magazine, the surety of the editors of their vision of the promise and responsibility of being an American citizen is clearly seen.

The photo-essays published by *Life* allow us to address how visuals and text helped create and reinforce class boundaries at the same time they argued for the possibility of a harmonious community that embraced all Americans. The editors were both speaking to and helping to define a middle-class audience. They valorized the middle-class lifestyle and presented that lifestyle as one that typified America. The photographs, and the accompanying text, helped define the norms and behaviors of both the middle and upper class, and provided a blueprint for those hoping to join them. The editors intended those norms and standards to knit the country together not only politically but also culturally. For the editors, participating in this lifestyle was what it meant to be an American. The editors shared this view with social thinkers of the time. Historian David Oshinsky writes that "Progressives like Walter Lippmann and Herbert Croly stressed the importance of material abundance in producing a more comfortable and egalitarian society. They argued that as people earned more and purchased more, class struggle would disappear and ethnic tensions would eventually disappear. In a sense, the rights and responsibilities of citizenship extended to shopping— the duty to buy goods at low prices. Mass consumption not only produced prosperity, it also democratized wealth."[1] The photos in *Life* showed the accouterments and standards of the desired lifestyle in all its tantalizing, realistic detail.

## FINDING THE AUDIENCE

To create *Life*, staff were pulled from other Time Inc. publications to test for interest and to prepare various prototypes, often to conform to Henry Luce's daily memos and proposals. During this "Experimental Period," the potential audience for *Life* was debated. According to Ralph Ingersoll, editor-executive, in 1935 Luce viewed the potential magazine as one for the carriage trade. Unlike the Time Inc. executives, Ingersoll's view was that *Life* should not be "a magazine designed for a sophisticated audience (like *Time*), or a specialized audience (like *Fortune*), but for a mass audience, the "gum chewers."[2]

Ingersoll wrote Luce that "for the whole world . . . such pictures are for rich or poor, without regard for race, class, creed or prejudice . . . you use one vernacular to a truck driver, another to a bank president, but bank president and truck driver will stand shoulder-to-shoulder to watch a parade."[3] Interestingly, the operating assumption was that a photo magazine *must* be for the masses since it would not present information textually but in easy-to-digest pictures. A contemporary writer claims that friends cautioned Luce, "*Time* and *Fortune* are not edited for mass readership. You don't know how to edit for the masses!"[4] Indeed, it was not the truck driver that Luce wished to reach. Luce is quoted as saying, "We do not intend to appeal to the mob, but we do hope that the magazine will appeal to a million or more people who are not all of them high brow."

After the magazine's launch, due to its record-breaking circulation, Luce viewed *Life* as Time Inc.'s "mass" magazine. Yet the magazine reached a middle-class and upper-class audience.[5] For example, a 1939 survey identified *Life*'s readers as at least comfortable: a mere 62,000 of 2.3 million subscribers had incomes under $1,000 a year; 1.27 million had incomes of over $3,000 a year.[6] Setting actual income aside, the presentation in *Life* reached the goals and dreams of the great majority of Americans. This can be seen in Americans' differing self-placement of social as opposed to economic class. In 1939, a Gallup poll asked Americans to place themselves in terms of "income class": 31 percent replied they were in the lower class, 68 percent said middle, 1 percent said upper. Yet when asked what "social class" they belonged to, 88 percent said middle class.[7] As Loren Baritz points out, this self-promotion of 20 percent of the respondents from an economic to a social class reflects the complex mix of economic factors as opposed to attitudes and values in class identification.[8] Even though 68 percent viewed themselves as middle class economically, 88 percent, or the great majority of Americans, viewed themselves socially as members of the middle class. This was the audience *Life* was designed to attract.

Luce was very concerned about counting, reaching, and knowing *Life*'s audience. As early as April 1937, he had lunch with John Shaw Billings, soon-to-be managing editor, to determine "how people read *Life*, are they devoted to it, would they miss it?"[9] To find out about who was reading its pages, *Life* turned to public opinion polls, following in the footsteps of both *Time* and *Fortune*. A study published in the spring of 1940 reported that *Life* reached 40.9 percent of the A group, the group that represented "the cream of those people with money to spend." *Life* reached 32.3 percent of the B group, those who were comfortable. The magazine reached 24.8 percent of the C group, those that constituted the "nation's stiff backbone." Finally, *Life* reached 15.9 percent of the D group, "the great mass of working people," the one that "manages to maintain a decent standard of living but lacks some of the things we commonly call necessities."[10]

The primacy of the middle-class experience as the editors' preferred frame is evident throughout the run of the magazine, seen over and over again in the choice of topics, the shaping of textual material to present the middle-class experience as the norm, and the insistent tone of the captions. Typical narratives included the tying of consumption to patriotism, the primers on what to buy via consumption scenarios, and the idealization of the professional as the one most able to lead, all narratives devices that continue to be prominent in the news today.

The *Life* editors viewed themselves as charged to speak to, and for, the middle class, at the time some 20 million readers. They addressed their middle-class reader directly and encouraged that reader to follow their exhortations on leisure, sports, fashion, and art. To today's reader, the explicit use of class markers may seem surprising. Yet at the time, the editors were open and explicit about which class the pictured subject belonged to and issued pronouncements on what that membership meant. As with the narrative devices they devised, this framing of what it means to be middle class still resonates today.

A magazine, of course, can direct its content and presentation to its chosen audience. The *Life* editors professed to speak to all of America. Yet an accurate representation of the United States is not one portrayed in *Life*'s pages. Rather, one finds an overwhelmingly white subject, usually middle to upper class, busy at sports, leisure, or art activities. We see the professional class going about its worthy work and the haute bourgeoisie at play. If we grant Alan Wolfe's point that democracy is inclusive, we can say that, despite *Life*'s mythologizing about the democratic system, the magazine did not present an inclusive view. Rather, it was an exclusionary one in which the poor and blacks for the most part disappeared. In addition, the magazine engaged in active and obsessive boundary creation as it outlined the habitus of the nobility and the upper class. However, for the group *Life* showed and addressed—the white middle class—we can characterize *Life*'s overall approach as this: "Boundaries are both here to stay but also here to be crossed."[11] In *Life*'s pages, we find the persistent theme that, through proper training and education, anyone could join the middle class in America. The editors made it their mission to provide that training.

## METHODOLOGY USED TO ANALYZE THE IMAGES IN *LIFE*

In order to discuss the worldview presented by the editors as reflected in the pages of *Life,* this study combined three methodological approaches: an investigation of archival material, a textual analysis of 262 issues from the first issue in 1936 to the beginning of World War II, and a content analysis. Archival resource materials included the diaries and scrapbooks of John Shaw Billings, managing editor of *Life* from 1936 to 1944. His diaries offered a rich source of material by a primary actor in how *Life* defined its audience and strove to meet that audience's needs during its first decade. An inveterate diarist, Billings made diary entries every night when he got home from work. Recounting his day at the office, he described his often frustrating dealings with Luce, mused about layouts he had done, and wondering about Luce's often cryptic comments.

I then conducted a textual analysis of each of the issues during the period—262 issues including more than 52,000 photographs—to determine their connotative social meanings and to relate them, as cultural artifacts, to larger issues at work in American culture of the 1930s and 1940s. Textual analysis also allowed me to discuss how these texts created positions for the editors and their audience and to identify how the editors addressed their reader.

Out of this grew the themes and categories for the content analysis, the third methodological approach. The seventy-six coded categories were reflective of the way the editors organized their material, and thus are directly related to the editors' construction of subjects and values. These included the standard demographic categories; themes that grew out of the departments the editors devised, such as science, technology, art, and entertainment; and themes that grew out of the text and photos, such as leisure.

Even given the great variety in the stories *Life* told in its pages, the presentation was often of a piece, including a tremendous and unrelenting effort to define class. This effort was done with great refinement, through focus on material objects, leisure activities, art activities, sports, and the description of a social circle. Often the text was a significant aid in coding since the editors made a point of noting the professional standing, and through association, the class, of their photographic subjects. The prevalence throughout *Life*'s pages of remarking not only on profession but class served to cultivate difference.

The text as the embodiment of the editors' worldview provided the way to identify the mythmaking that the editors engaged in. Just as Roy Stryker framed the hundreds of thousands of photographs in the Farm Security Administration and the Office of War Information files in a way that offered a comforting view of America at the same time it highlighted what he felt needed to be changed, so the editors of *Life* sifted through the 10,000 odd photographs that crossed their desks each week to arrive at a vision of the United States that drew on familiar themes yet educated their audience on how to face the future. After they chose the images, they then wrote the text to control and direct how the reader interpreted them. In doing so, they helped create a sense of seeming stability of the midcentury. This dominant ethos required both illusion and exclusion, as the prevalence of class markers throughout *Life*'s page served to both unite and to cultivate difference.

A critical aspect of the text form was the constant setting up of the typical, which the editors present as a common sense form with which the reader would concur. An example comes in a two-page profile of Thomas Dewey which shows him at home with his wife and two sons on Fifth Avenue. The text block describes Dewey's charming family as one of his "political assets" and notes that "Americans, at the polls and elsewhere, like to think that such handsome, well-bred, affectionate, happy families are typically American."[12] We can also attribute *Life*'s early approach as one that comes with the assumed mantle of the burden to judge, the surety of the importance of one's opinion, and the self-assumed stature to make pronouncements. A magazine historian noted the authorial style of Time Inc.: "Even the superficial reader cannot help being impressed by the studied omniscience of both *Time* and *Life* . . . if the intelligibility they offer is an illusion, it is at least a comfortable one to have."[13]

In addition to the *Time*-style captions, the stance toward the reader is also critical to an understanding of how the editors framed the photographs. In her book, *Hope and Ashes: The Birth of Modern Times, 1929–1939*, Alice G. Marquis relates the tone of captioning to the creation of a new taste community as she describes as educational the role of advertising of the 1930s: "Beneath its overt, often blatant message was a subtle invitation to join a community of the elect, the tasteful, and the discriminating, just as *Time*'s format and jargon and *The New Yorker*'s supercilious tone conveyed the ambience of an exclusive club."[14] In *Life*, often the text would address the reader directly, an approach in which the reader is addressed as "You." This approach encouraged the reader to enter *Life*'s world, to interpret the images the way in which the editor dictated, and to become part of the imaginary community portrayed in *Life*'s pages.

The following table summarizes the findings of the content analysis. It lists the 76 categories used, organized by demographics and content areas; shows the total number of images present in each category out of the 4,522 total; and gives the percentage of images that appeared in that category. The last column shows the percentage of images that showed people; based on that figure, I cross-coded for demographic categories in order to refine *Life*'s presentation race, class, and gender.

The class definition I chose to apply is based on refining and extending the production model to the functionalist one in which classes are organized in terms of prestige.[15] Thus I treated professionals as a separate category based on their privileged status in the pages of *Life*. Two categories may strike the American reader as strange: aristocracy and servants. During this period, the magazine devoted almost one tenth of its images to royalty and their lifestyles.

The content analysis shows that the world *Life* represented was very different than the one their reader inhabited. The editors were inclined to reproduce the world they themselves either lived in or felt to be most valuable. Much as the advertising executives described by Roland Marchand in *Advertising the American Dream* cared only so much for their audience's needs and preferred to present their own life view, so we can find a similar dynamic at work on the *Life* staff.[16] This tendency helps explain the prevalence

**Table 9.1.   Summary of Content Analysis**

| Categories | Total<br>N = 4,522 | Percentage Total<br>Percentage of 4,522 | Percentage People<br>Percentage of 3,706 |
|---|---|---|---|
| *Race* | | | |
| White | 3,387 | 75 | 91 |
| Black | 152 | 3 | 4 |
| Asian | 293 | 6 | 8 |
| Hispanic | 27 | 0.60 | 0.70 |
| Arab | 9 | 0.20 | 0.24 |
| Native American | 21 | 0.50 | 0.56 |
| *Class* | | | |
| Aristocracy | 332 | 7 | 9 |
| Bourgeoisie | 474 | 10 | 13 |
| Managerial | 148 | 3 | 4 |
| Professional | 1,826 | 40 | 49 |
| Middle Class | 821 | 18 | 22 |
| Working Class | 770 | 17 | 21 |
| Servants | 73 | 2 | 2 |
| Poverty | 105 | 2 | 3 |
| *Gender* | | | |
| Male | 2,991 | 66 | 81 |
| Female | 1,817 | 40 | 49 |
| Family | 880 | 19 | 24 |
| Role of Women | 993 | 22 | 27 |
| Male/Individual | 1,622 | 36 | 44 |
| Male/Group | 1,300 | 29 | 35 |
| Female/Individual | 1,005 | 22 | 27 |
| Female/Group | 788 | 17 | 21 |
| Male/Professional | 1,512 | 33 | 41 |
| Female/Professional | 767 | 17 | 21 |
| Male/Family | 627 | 14 | 17 |
| Female/Family | 625 | 14 | 17 |
| Male/Sports | 310 | 7 | 8 |
| Female/Sports | 148 | 3 | 4 |
| Male/Leisure | 390 | 9 | 11 |
| Female/Leisure | 333 | 7 | 9 |
| *Government* | | | |
| Government | 1,020 | 23 | |
| Monarchy | 168 | 4 | |
| Democracy | 633 | 14 | |
| Comm/Socialism | 129 | 3 | |
| Fascism | 350 | 8 | |
| *Geographic Area* | | | |
| United States | 3,252 | 72 | |
| Europe | 1,224 | 27 | |

| Categories | Total<br>N = 4,522 | Percentage Total<br>Percentage of 4,522 | Percentage People<br>Percentage of 3,706 |
|---|---|---|---|
| Asia | 333 | 7 | |
| S. America | 113 | 2 | |
| Africa | 43 | 1 | |
| Australia | 13 | 0.30 | |
| Canada | 32 | 0.70 | |
| Near MidEast | 37 | 0.80 | |
| *News/Lifestyle* | | | |
| Military | 842 | 19 | |
| Impending War | 635 | 14 | |
| Religion | 295 | 7 | |
| Nature | 747 | 17 | |
| Crime | 165 | 4 | |
| Violence | 479 | 11 | |
| Business | 283 | 6 | |
| Labor | 64 | 1 | |
| Depression | 104 | 2 | |
| Sports | 410 | 9 | |
| Fashion | 263 | 6 | |
| Science/Ed | 423 | 9 | |
| Education | 276 | 6 | |
| Technology | 537 | 12 | |
| Network | 483 | 11 | |
| Leisure | 513 | 11 | |
| Commodification | 759 | 17 | |
| Cheesecake | 142 | 3 | 4 |
| *The Arts* | | | |
| Painting | 371 | 8 | |
| Sculpture | 76 | 2 | |
| Architecture | 325 | 7 | |
| Photography | 98 | 2 | |
| Music | 161 | 4 | |
| Dance | 109 | 2 | |
| Theater | 301 | 7 | |
| Books/Author | 96 | 2 | |
| Movies | 389 | 9 | |
| Level of Reality | 621 | 14 | |
| Pt, Theater, Sculpt | 748 | 17 | |
| *Photo Presence* | | | |
| Photo Practice | 577 | 13 | |
| Aerial/Maps | 184 | 4 | |
| Group | 1,411 | 31 | 38 |
| Individual | 2,313 | 51 | 62 |
| Presence of People | 3,706 | 82 | 100 |

of images of the Ivy League in these years, along with the photo-essays on yachting and the new ski resorts in Idaho.

That world was defined by class. Consistently and obsessively in *Life*'s pages, the editors noted the class of a subject and explained how lifestyle, clothes, sports, and leisure marked the class under discussion. Often the presentation gets so detailed as to be strange. Particularly in the coverage of British royalty and the haute bourgeoisie in the United States, the approach is like that toward an exotic species. Following in the footsteps of the tabloids of the time or like *People* magazine today, the editors ran such copy expecting that their middle-class audience, many of whom were squeezed by hard times, would pore over images of the menu served to the king and queen on a court visit to France or delight in the many failed marriages of Doris Duke, the undeserving heir to the Woolworth fortune.

The editors made a point of noting the professional standing, and through association, the class, of their subjects. One page summarizes this approach very succinctly. A story on a Bach Choral Festival in Bethlehem, Pennsylvania, describes the choir as made up of "ordinary people" whose performances are attended by "well-to-do" music lovers. The captions that accompany the photos of the nine participants mention the role of each in the choir and their occupation, and for the working class man, his hourly salary. We are informed that "Professor Arthur W. Klein sings bass in the Bach Choir, teaches mechanical engineering at Lehigh University. Mr. Klein was No. 1 man in Lehigh's class of 1899."[17]

## LIFE'S PRESENTATION OF CLASS

### The Rich Are Different from You and Me

A high number, 9 percent, of the coded images showed royalty. This can be ascribed to several reasons. Primarily, the editors were Anglophiles. Second, news events of the day helped increase the appearance of royalty. The Wallis Simpson scandal was heavily covered by all news outlets. *Life* was proud to be the first news outlet with photos of the coronation of Queen Elizabeth. The captions worked hard to explain the norms and behaviors of this select group, as, for example, an explanation of the minute differences in dress that distinguish peers from other sorts.

A similarly high number in terms of the demographics of the American public is the depiction of the bourgeoisie, at 13 percent. Just as Marchand found in his analysis of ads of the 1920s that advertisers had no qualms about flaunting images of an opulent, exclusive, and elite class, so *Life* spent time portraying the activities of the rich in its pages. Further, just as in ads of the period, the elite class was presented in *Life* as organized, with boundaries and standards of admission which conferred on its members the status of nobility. Constant boundary marking in the magazine is seen in how the text ranked, characterized, described, and fawned over such bourgeois as the Vanderbilts, Fords, Rockefellers, and Doris Duke. Many of these stories appeared in the "Private Lives" section.[18] In what Loudon Wainwright, in his insider's look at *Life*, calls a very "un-Presbyterian talent for titillation," publisher Henry Luce conceived of this section as a "combination of the very human and snob appeals. A sort of cross between Dorothy Dix (much concerned with consideration of life's problems) and Cholly Knickerbocker (very knowing about the snobs)."[19]

Weddings, debutante balls, and coming-out parties merited much ink. This type of coverage, which showed the middle-class reader, often squeezed by circumstances, the norms and habitus of the wealthy, appears consistently throughout the first decade of *Life*. For the most part, the opulent lifestyle is framed within the duties and responsibilities that, although exhausting, must be met. The lavish season of parties and events must be carefully prepared for, requiring an entire group of professionals to support. The most highly regarded are the responsible bourgeois, as, of course, each debutante performs some sort of social service as part of her debut. Other than that mention of the possibility of others in more strained circumstances, for the most part in these stories, no clouds appear.

The language of distinction runs rampant in such stories, as the editors educate the reader on status markers. For example, a story on "high-grade" polo, attended by an "exclusive group" of Long Island socialites, is now open to the public at the request of one of the players at the Meadow Brook Country Club. The fifty-cent audience, "nice but not socialite," is getting a deal because they get to watch well-known players such as Peter Bostwick, "a slim, horsy and likable young millionaire who inherited a Standard oil fortune from his father." A justification for the story is made based on the sport's increasing popularity—even the middle class might want to participate: "Although high-goal polo is very expensive, the game has attained nationwide popularity in the last ten years."[20]

Perhaps the best example of the cultivation of difference for this class is in a photo of opening night at the Metropolitan Opera taken from the stage, where "a visiting soprano can see most of New York Society in one sweeping glance." In this photo, class is visualized, as notables are arranged in order of importance. The first row of boxes, costing $500, is the "famous Diamond Horseshoe," where sit such worthies as Mrs. Sara Delano Roosevelt and J.P. Morgan. Directly behind is the Grand Tier, costing $60, "less swank but still good enough for Edward R. Stettinius of U.S. Steel Corp." Below in social prestige is the orchestra, where seats are $10 and "white tie is distinctly preferred though a black one will get you by." A balcony seat can be had for $4; called the Dress Circle, its occupants don't always take the hint. Finally, "above the Dress Circle, in the Balcony proper ($2.50–$4) and in the Family Circle ($2) sit the real music lovers."

# The Opera

## (CONTINUED)

FROM the stage of the Metropolitan Opera House on opening night a visiting soprano can see most of New York Society in one sweeping glance. She would begin with a good look at the first row of boxes, for this is the famous Diamond Horseshoe. On opening night a box in the Diamond Horseshoe would cost $500 if you could get one. You could not, because all are rented by the season, most of them to families which have held them for years. In the second box from the left in the picture sits Mrs. Sara Delano Roosevelt, mother of the President, guest of Mr. & Mrs. Pierre C. Cartier. A few feet away in the next box to the right is Mrs. Ogden L. Mills, in black dress and tiara. The next box to hers is vacant in respect to the memory of its late owner, Mrs. W. Seward Webb. Three boxes further along, facing the camera in black dress, is the wife of the new Ambassador to Russia, Mrs. Joseph E. Davies. The box in dead center belongs to J. P. Morgan, whose silver-bearded brother-in-law Herbert L. Satterlee may be seen chatting to his guests. Further on, the third box from the right of the picture contains Mrs. H. Edward Manville (*see p. 19*), with back to camera. The Astor and Vanderbilt boxes are out of the picture. Directly above the Diamond Horseshoe is the Grand Tier, less swank but still good enough for Edward R. Stettinius of U. S. Steel Corp. He was a guest in the fifth box from the left, occupied in the picture by a young lady who is inspecting the audience through opera glasses. Grand Tier boxholders pay $60 for their party on opening night.

Slightly below the Grand Tier in social prestige is the orchestra. Seats cost $10 and a white tie is distinctly preferred though a black one will get you by. Here sit unattached socialites, and rich non-socialites. You can sit in the balcony directly over the Grand Tier for $4. The name of this balcony, the Dress Circle, is a broad hint to occupants to dress but not all take the hint. Above the Dress Circle, in the Balcony proper ($2.50–$3) and in the Family Circle or "Nigger Heaven" ($2), sit the real music lovers.

This remarkable picture was made with a wide-angle lens by three photographers of the New York *Times*. Fifteen seconds before the curtain went up for the second act of *Die Walküre* one photographer poked the camera through the curtain, a second set off flash bulbs and a third squeezed the bulb.

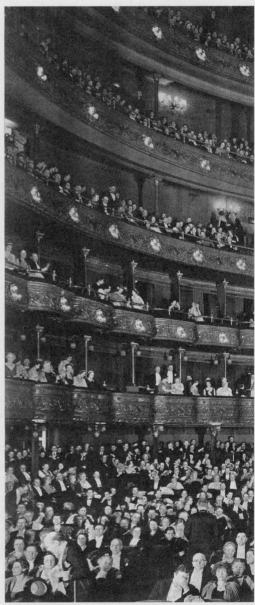

Figure 9.1.  *Life* portrays the strata of society

## The Ill Housed, Ill Clad, and Ill Fed

Even though the magazine premiered during the Depression, the plight of the poor was not covered in great detail. Instead, this group was for the most part ignored: only 3 percent of the images in my study showed this group, despite the fact that, as FDR said, one-third were "ill housed, ill clad, and ill fed."[21] This simply was not *Life*'s defined audience and was not the group *Life* either wished to reach or even discuss. Also, by the end of the 1930s, the Depression was less of a story and many felt that the economy had begun to turn around.

In the little coverage that does appear, some stories dovetailed with coverage either in other media or in governmental sources. And, the framing puts the crisis in a context of hope. For example, the reproduction of photographs of the dustbowl from the FSA is accompanied by copy that presents the dust bowl farmer as a "new pioneer" who, through no fault of his own, has been driven from his farm by the dust blight. Like others seeking a new start and like his forebears who trekked to Oklahoma, he leaves for greener pastures, with battered Chevrolets as the new prairie schooners. On his way to California, his "courageous philosophy" is quoted: "I figured that in a place where some people can make a good livin' I can make me a livin."[22]

## Business and Labor

Given Luce's strong support of the free market system, the contemporary discussions of regulation of the business world by the New Deal, and the continuing Depression, I expected to find more stories on business and businessmen. As a category, business accounted for 6 percent of the coverage. It may be that Time Inc. covered this aspect to the full in *Fortune* and *Time*, but one could also argue that given those vast resources, one would expect to see more synergy between the publications. Still, Luce viewed *Life* as more of an entertainment vehicle than *Time,* which may account for the small number of mentions of business during this period. In the stories that do appear, the pro-business stance of all the Time Inc. publications is seen in the pages of *Life*. In a story on a slump in the Stock Market, the editors offer some possible reasons, but note that "complex causes & effects aside, businessmen were feeling gloomy and hesitant. And no small part of their uncertainty was due to the fact that, with Government strongly personal, exercising unprecedented control over Business, no one can be sure of what Government is going to do next."[23]

However, the editors did not advocate unregulated business practices of the sort that led to the Depression. Their confidence in the growing role of professionalism in all fields led them to applaud the increasing role of the government in the rationalization of the market through the supervision of the SEC. They recognized the need to bring ordinary investors back into the market and that "the New-Deal hating Old Guard" was blocking progress. Progress is signaled by the appointment of William McChesney Martin Jr., as the first nonmember paid president of the New York Stock Exchange. Martin, Yale '28, meets the ideal standard of the editors who describe him as "hard-working, scholarly, public spirited," someone whose career is a "spectacular success story." His appointment means the end of the rule of the Old Guard and the election of a slate of new thinkers: "The job now well begun is to change the Exchange from a private club run for the profit of its members into a public institution run for the benefit of the investing public and the nation's business."[24]

As for the coverage of laborers, 21 percent of those shown in *Life*'s pages were working class.[25] During the early years of the magazine, when the struggle between management and labor reached its height, labor as a category accounted for only 1 percent of images. Although not heavily covered, labor issues did force themselves into *Life*'s pages due to the sit-down strikes which reached "epidemic proportions" in February-March 1937.[26] Although the copy always asserts that such strikes were illegal and that owners such as Walter Chrysler were generous in wage structure and in providing jobs, during this early period, the coverage was fair, even positive.[27] In general, *Life*'s coverage reflected that attitude of the nation as a whole. In the beginning of 1937, the majority of Americans, 76 percent, favored unions. When the sit-downs began, the CIO lost middle-class support. Most people deplored the violence and felt the government should crack down. Two years later, 75 percent believed sit-downs should be illegal and 70 percent opposed closed shops.[28] Michael Parent identified a number of features in press coverage of strikes: strikes can be avoided; they are inconvenient to the public; the government is seen as a neutral party; more ink is given to management offers than to take backs.[29] In this respect also, *Life*'s approach dovetailed with that of other news outlets.

Labor unrest was associated with the urban East with immigrants such as Italians and left-leaning Jews. Thus a strike in Iowa is presented as "a remote dream beside the noble realities of corn and hogs." The editors quote Maytag's own advertising which claims that its workers are the "best-cared for factory worker in Middle West." *Life* adds that "no Iowan doubts that the late Fred L. Maytag was a just and considerate employer who earned the good will of the thousands he pleased to call the 'Maytag Family.'"[30]

The representations of the working and business classes were joined in *Life*'s pages. Businessmen were presented as benevolent entrepreneurs who had the right to regulate their own business. Workers were shown sympathetically as long as they strove to improve and did not disrupt the factory floor. The editors came to accept the growing power of unions as part of the equation that helped build the new economy, but only if demands were made without violence.

## The Typicality of the Middle Class

For coding, 22 percent of those shown in *Life*'s pages were considered middle class. By far the greatest number shown, 49 percent, were *defined* as professionals.[31] I consider professional and middle class to essentially be the same group as conceived by the editors. These are the groups that *Life* viewed as its audience, the group *Life* portrayed in its pages, and the group around whom the editors framed their stories. This is the group that represents both the *Life* staff itself and the editors' ideal group. During this period by far the greatest focus is on those who have advanced through their own efforts.

In *The Good Life: The Meaning of Success for the American Middle Class,* Loren Baritz describes the importance of the middle-class ethos to the mythology of America: "America's spirit and tone, its historical mythology and official aspirations, political bent, educational arrangements, the centrality of business enterprise, as well as the dreams of the vast majority of its people, derive from the psychology of the great imperial middle. Although by no means have all Americans been middle-class, that is what most have wanted to be, and they have conducted themselves in ways acceptable to the norm before they had or even after they had lost the price of admission."[32]

The primacy of the experience as the editors' preferred frame for any experience is seen throughout the run of the magazine. We see this over and over again in the choice of topics, in the shaping of narrative material to present the middle-class experience as the norm, and in the insistent tone of the text. This presentation occurs in editorials as well. For example, in coverage of a speech by labor leader Sidney Hillman at the Democratic convention of 1944, an editorial criticizes his backers for their "arrogant resentment against America's middle-class nature." The editorial calls Hillman's proposals "foreign," not because his fellow members of the American Labor Party are immigrants, because immigrants are "overwhelmingly in voluntary agreement with the common purpose of America." Rather, his proposals are foreign because they go against norms. The editorial articulates a difference in occupation versus status (in the same parsing found in a contemporary Gallup study) as the editors claim that "in the field of economic function there are managers and workers and farmers in this country, just as everywhere else. But in the field of civilization and, particularly, politics, this is a middle-class country. And whoever tries to change this fundamental fact of American life touches explosives." Calling the United States a "small-town nation," the editors chide Hillman for trying to start a third party in New York, in effect, trying to pit New York against the nation: "Whoever tries to lead the city against the farm, class against class, New York against Middletown, will inescapably burn his fingers."[33]

*Life* presented the middle-class lifestyle as the "typical" American experience. A close look at a story, a profile of a Jewish garment worker, Yetta Henner, that represents a vastly different life experience from the typical *Life* reader will illustrate the editors' framing of life as *the* standard to measure others against. The profile of Yetta Henner, one of 250,000 members of the ILGWU, is part of larger story on American unions. Miss Henner is shown playing basketball, at a health clinic, at a union class, out dancing, at Sabbath dinner with her parents, and entering her apartment, which is described as being in "a tenement in New York's lower east side ghetto." All of the activities Miss Henner is shown at are union supported and are captioned as worthy: the classes the union offers give the women "food for their eager minds"; the health clinic is staffed by "top-notch specialists"; the Local 62 basketball game gives Yetta "plenty of good, vigorous exercise."

What is most intriguing in the story is that this immigrant Jewish union working-class girl from the Lower East Side is presented in the frame of the ideal American. The profile begins: "If she lived in some small American town, a middle class Yetta Henner might play basketball on the high-school alumni team, go to a church dance, listen to a ladies' club lectures. But Yetta Henner lives in New York City, is poor, works as a finisher (she snips loose threads off rayon panties) in the Mitchel Schneider shop and belongs to the ILGWU Local 62. So, Yetta . . . exercises, learns, dances within her union."[34]

Thus the standard to which she is compared is a girl from a small Midwestern town, a middle-class Protestant. This use of the middle-class life experience as a touchstone goes beyond the personal realm to the social realm. The text tells us that the union-sponsored basketball game Miss Henner plays "builds up union spirit the same way a college team builds up college spirit." In this story, we see positive converge of a woman who is normally not seen in *Life's* pages. Miss Henner is profiled, which is unusual, yet she is not enough on her own. Her activities must be sifted through another experience. No doubt the editors were trying to make Miss Henner's life relevant to their reader. The norm the editors are here proposing, and the only one they can imagine their reader can relate to, is one of a small town experience. Thus, despite the unusual content in the focus on a lower-class immigrant Jewish woman who is a Union member, the text serves to reinforce the overall preponderance of coverage of middle-class American life.

## The Professional Shall Lead Us

The decades of the 1920s and the 1930s as those in which the modern consumer society was consolidated and then assumed its central place. A new social class, those who worked for salary, not wages, was directly tied to the new culture. Citizens of this new environment were made to be aware of themselves as consumers, a new role that required "active adjustment to material and spiritual conditions of life."[35] The new ideology that this group articulated was one of abundance, not scarcity, personality, not character.[36] To educate the citizen in the quest to fit into this new life, elites served a role. The professional class, one made up of social scientists, sociologists, doctors, and educators, and government bureaucrats became important "purveyors of advice." This view of the middle-class professional grew out of the Progressive Era in which professional positions expanded, the professional class

**UNION SPORT**

**Local 62's basketball team** gives Yetta plenty of good, vigorous exercise. It also builds up union spirit, just as a college team builds up college spirit.

**UNION HEALTH**

**At I.L.G.W.U.'s health center**, which cost $250,000, Yetta pays little for medical and dental care. The center's staff includes top-notch specialists.

**UNION EDUCATION**

**Yetta studies** Public Speaking & Social Psychology in an I.L.G.W.U. classroom (*above*), takes Boy Friend Hy Stofsky to a union dance (*below*).

**UNION SOCIAL LIFE**

(continued)

# I. L. G. W. U.   ONE OF THE 250,000 WHO SPENDS MOST OF HER LIFE WITHIN HER UNION

**YETTA HENNER TRIMS PANTIES**

If she lived in some small American town, a middle-class Yetta Henner might play basketball on the high-school alumni team, go to a church dance, listen to a ladies' club lecture. But Yetta Henner lives in New York City, is poor, works as a finisher (she snips loose threads off nylon panties) in the Mitchel Schneider shop and belongs to I.L.G.W.U.'s Local 62. So Yetta, as shown at left, exercises, learns, dances within her union. Yetta is 21. She joined the union in 1933 when she took her present job. Her Russian-born father, a presser, has been a member since the general strike of 1910. Her earnings average $17. She pays 35¢ a week dues to her local, easily gets her money's worth. Not all I.L.G.W.U. members are as close to their union as Yetta. Someday most may be. Yetta herself shows promise as a union *organizer*.

**YETTA BELONGS TO AN ORTHODOX JEWISH FAMILY. SABBATH EVE, MENFOLK WEAR HATS AT TABLE**

**YETTA LIVES AT 210 RIVINGTON ST., A TENEMENT IN NEW YORK'S LOWER EAST SIDE GHETTO**

**Figure 9.2.    Profile of Yetta Henner**

began to articulate its own ideology and to associate in institutions that furthered their advance.[37]

Maren Stange describes a historic backdrop to this increasing role. She notes the "experience during the First World War of successful cooperation among business, the academy, and the military, had greatly reinforced the pre-war tendencies toward nationally centralized, high-level decision making."[38] In the postwar years, as mass production expanded, corporations grew and living standards went up. Advertising and communication networks worked to sustain the rate of consumption; public opinion polling began to assess not only political views but consumption patterns. In sociology, specialties grew, such as industrial management, as did the use of industrial psychology by those such as Taylor. Along with these new professions, new media outlets were created to address this new landscape and to explain the new work world.

*Life* strove to create a community of citizens who, with the proper training and knowledge, could thrive in the new society. The magazine profiled the jobs of professionals such as scientists and artists, and explained and promoted new products and techniques. The increasingly important role of this new group, its work life, leisure activities, and buying habits, is also reflected in *Life*'s pages. But the editors of *Life* not only explained the new professional environment, they participated in it was well. Certainly they viewed the findings of the new social sciences as stories to cover. But they also created their own studies, paving the way for the analysis of demographics in the news business. They commissioned such figures as George Gallup, who in his study on readership in newspapers claimed that his new methods were "reliable, definite, and capable of statement in quantitative terms," to conduct a study on *Life*'s audience which they then outlined in *Life*'s pages.[39] *Life* presented this new class as the creators and bearers of the norms of this modern society, and we can count the editors as among that group.

The way *Life* presented the role of the professional in American life was directly tied to Luce's view of meritocracy. In a discussion that Luce had with reporter Kenneth Stewart for an article in *PM* magazine in 1944, Luce recounted his educational experience, which included Oxford. He mused that although there were a few very bright fellows there, that he supposed that "in America the broad general average is higher." When Stewart suggested that "a high general level was a better medium for democracy than an elite of scholars," Luce countered with the query, "Why can't you have both?" Stewart then asked Luce to explain a quotation attributed to him: "without the aristocratic principle no society can survive." Luce explained that he had meant "aristocracy" in its Latin sense, as defining "those who have an appreciation of excellence or the best, whether in art, morals or intellect—the contrary to the dangers of mediocrity."[40] Luce expressed a similar sentiment when asked to define "tycoon," a word coined by *Time*. Luce defined the word as meaning a "gentleman owing his fortune to a genius adaptable to the age and a careful education and rigorous apprenticeship; a cultivated citizen of the world [who] will take in a few less leg shows and a little more literature."[41] Here again we see the Luce virtues—raw talent, hard work, and the educated appreciation of art and literature—all seen as leading to a fortune.

*Life* regarded the professional class as fit to lead. The editors contrasted the trained professional to the "ordinary citizen." They valorized the university life and hoped more young Americans could obtain that life. Once educated, the professional deservedly stood apart—trained and capable, the professional was meant to lead. A fascinating example of this theme comes in the coverage of the NBC radio show *Information Please,* one of the quiz shows so popular at the time. The text describes the program as unlike others then the rage, those in which "ordinary citizens are herded before a microphone and made to display their ignorance under a barrage of brain-teasers." This show, "probably the best" on the air, features "experts" who answer questions mailed in by the public. The text does not tell us why this format is better. Perhaps it is so obvious—that the experts can humorously answer questions sent in by ordinary folk—that it is not necessary to point it out.

In 1949, Russell Lynes, the managing editor of *Harper's,* coined the terms *highbrow, middlebrow,* and *lowbrow* as a way to describe Americans' standings based on cultural knowledge and activities. According to Lynes, "gone are the days . . . when class distinction was determined by wealth, birth, or political eminence. Instead . . . true prestige now belongs to scientists, writers, critics, commentators and thinker of global thoughts. We have a society of the intellectual elite, run by the high-brows." Although we might argue his point, this is just the social structure the *Life* had framed for over a decade. With the appearance of the article in *Harper's,* the editors asked Lynes to create a "guidance chart" so readers could locate themselves in this new order.[42]

Marchand devised the terms *social tableaux* and *parable* to capture the way in which advertisers presented material visually in the 1920s. Marchand views both as the advertisers' guideposts for the reader to modern life. The tableaux reflect upper-class society, showing products, the progress of technology, and styles. Marchand conceives of these as a sort of fantasy "slice of life" that captures not reality but shows a setting to which the consumer would aspire.[43] The parables are stories told with no apparent author that "lure the reader into active involvement." They include, among others, "The Parable of the Democracy of Goods," which presented the wonders of the market culture in which the middle class could participate in the "exclusivity of elites."[44]

In a similar dynamic, *Life* presented its version of the Horatio Alger story over and over. Directly related to the role of education and the creation of a professional class, these stories are numerous and appear so frequently that they constitute a classic form of *Life's* presentation during this period. In these "tales of advancement," the editors construct the myth of American success based on biographical sketches of prominent Americans.

These stories of success must have been both reassuring and inspiring in the midst of the Depression. However, it is not my view that they were intended by the editors to function primarily in this way. Of critical importance is the absence of the lucky break, a trope of the Alger myths. In the *Life* tales, men and women succeeded through raw talent, hard work, and application. These presentations were meant to applaud the profiled individuals and to prove, with varying details, the possibilities provided by the American democratic system as these individuals lived out the American Dream. It is the paradox of *Life* coverage that at the same time the editors created difference in selecting and identifying the specifics that placed someone in a particular class or group, they also believed these boundaries, particularly as they related to professionals, were mutable and that others could succeed in the same way their subjects had. All one had to do was follow the well-described path.

Subjects chosen were those most admired by the editors—professionals who worked to better American life, whether it was Charles F. Kettering and his invention of the self-starter; Helen Hayes and her status as the consummate stage professional; Donald Budge who, born humble, perfected his skills to win Wimbledon; Grant Wood, who used his education in Europe to further his art but came home to make his name documenting the American prairies; or Irving Berlin, the Russian Jewish immigrant whose popular songs made him a millionaire at the same time they proved the value of assimilation. Further, these stories fit the life experience of Luce and Billings—the attainment of great success and influence based on ingenuity, hard work, perseverance even in the face of naysayers, and natural talent. If the benefits of a proper birth helped, such benefits were valuable only in the sense that they gave the professional the training needed; and people who had such benefits were expected to make some form of socially active contribution and to justify their good fortune.

## *Life:* A Middle-Class Primer

The fact that *Life* was a pictorial magazine allowed the magazine to show in great detail what products and subjects it considered noteworthy, giving the magazine, as well as its advertisers, a significant advantage in the creation of a taste public due to its manipulation of visuals. The creation of a taste public depended not only on that public possessing the necessary funds, which *Life*'s audience did, but on taste education. The coverage of the lifestyles of various classes was part of that visual education. Also important was the coverage of fashion as well as the weekly coverage of new styles, the noting of various preferences of coeds for bobby socks at eastern schools, and so on. Another important element was the weekly coverage of art; the pages of *Life* were full of art intended to educate the reader's taste, always accompanied by pronouncements that helped the reader correctly interpret what was reproduced. The text focused on teaching the reader not a sophisticated appreciation of form, but rather who were the important figures and schools to know. Finally, people were typecast and placed socially by their possessions in an explicit way that clearly was meant to indicate class. This textual approach encouraged the reader to make distinctions and provided cues to interpreting the visual information the magazine presented. In claiming that these photo-essays created a common community of consumption, one could claim that consumerism democratizes by providing a way to participate in national culture. Still, the positive portrayal of modern goods can be interpreted as designed to create an educated and differentiated set of tastes as opposed to presenting hegemonic norms about what to consume.

By the 1930s, popular taste segments and been identified, both in the media and in institutional sites. Like the director of the Metropolitan Museum of Art, Luce took on the role of taste maker to his audience. Cultural knowledge and selective purchasing led to class stratification; the coverage of issues such as leisure in *Life* helped define that stratification. Along with advertising, *Life* played a critical role in tying consumption to the American way of life, as a new definition of citizen was developed that related active consumption to participation in democracy.

A seminal photo-essay will provide the basis of a discussion of this thesis. The essay was based on sociological findings drawn from the new methods of empirical survey. The editors were pioneers in using survey research to discover and appeal to their audience. Believing that such findings provided rigorous, accurate, scientific insight into the American scene, they made it their duty to disseminate them. What is of interest here is the framing of the findings visually, as various groups are defined by class and possessions.

When the Robert and Helen Lynd published *Middletown in Transition* (1937), *Life* sent Margaret Bourke-White to Muncie, Indiana, to do a photo-essay of the town. The text tells us that her photos give the reader "the truest, sharpest picture of this age" for Muncie typifies "every small U.S. city from Maine to California." Bourke-White's photos document the work of the Lynds: "Here, set down for all time, you may look at the average 1937 American as he really is."[45] The editors claim the photos they chose to publish are representative of the four different economic classes: the rich, the middle class, the working class, and the poor. The text describes the physical surroundings of the subjects and calls attention to objects in the photos that each family owned as a way to typecast and understand these folks. The characterization that the editors present is no doubt based on the Lynds' categories, but it is in keeping with *Life*'s overall coverage. Each subject is shown in the living room, much in the manner of the WPA photos of the time. Attention is called to the objects in each setting and the objects the reader is encouraged to peruse are meant to stand for their class. The text calls attention to the American glass Mrs. Bunch, the mayor's wife, collects and the chicks in the homemade brooder in the family "at the bottom of the social strata." The reader is told that the leisure activity in the Ball family signifies "the emergence of an upper class to whom certain leisure activities have value, not in relation to work, but quite independently as a symbol of status." *Life* boasted that Bourke-White's pictures "were acclaimed an important American document."

In this photo-essay we see how the editors functioned as boundary makers for class. They did this through the application of class labeling to their subjects and with commentary that tied material objects to status. This is true not only for this example, but for a wide range of articles throughout this period, from the essays on small town parades and country fairs, to the coverage of sorority rush at college campuses, to the paeans to polo.

## CONCLUSION

In the photo-essays it published, *Life* not only covered and explained events, but, through the deliberate effort of the editors, it also worked to create a sense of national unity in social and cultural terms. At a time when the American way felt under threat, *Life* was one of the new communication mediums of the period that played a part in creating an impression of coherence. The Depression, which threatened to tear the country apart, did not, due to, among other factors, "the gigantic effort to document in art, reporting, social science, and history the national life and values."[46] *Life* magazine played a critical and influential self-appointed role in the creation of what national life and values were through the editors' promotion of a middle-class lifestyle centered on consumption and educational advancement.

We can first attribute *Life*'s immediate success to its ability to reaffirm the "dominant assumptions" in American culture in the 1930s. Many of these dominant assumptions were visualized weekly in *Life*, including the assumptions that individualism is the key to America's greatness; that everyone should try to be successful; that life would not be tolerable if we did not believe in progress and know that things are getting better; that America is a land of unlimited opportunity; and that science is a fine thing it its place and that our future depends on it.[47]

In addition to affirming common beliefs, we can also attribute *Life*'s immediate success to its ability to point the way to the future. The growing role and prestige of professionals to interpret modern life, a major theme of this study, is also critical to how we view the impact of *Life* during this period. The 1930s is the decade when we see the development of the "therapeutic society": personal health, self-absorption, domestic patterns, interpersonal relations—all became social sciences in which the professional held the key. Professionals became the purveyors of advice to the new society. Further, the burgeoning use of polling data revealed values, attitudes, and buying patterns. By publi-

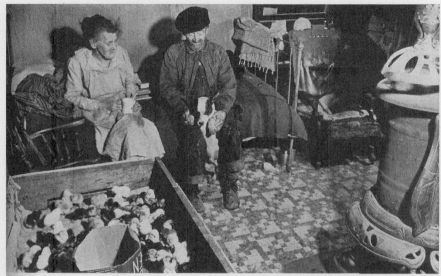

bottom of Muncie's social strata live Scott and Liza-
Brandenberg. Scott is the second husband of Lizabelle,
is from Fiat, Ky. Their home, lined with paper car-
toms, is a one-room clapboard shack in "Shedtown." In
a homemade brooder, consisting of a wooden tray, an oil lamp
and a paper box, they are raising chickens "for eatin'," not
for sale. Mrs. Brandenberg talks with the Kentucky hillbilly drawl heard in many midwest industrial towns from
southerners migrated north to work in the great auto plants.

of Muncie life is the Ball family. Here is the West
of William H. Ball. Son of one of four handy
who founded Muncie's dominant glassworks, he typifies, for Dr. Lynd, a significant new development. This is "the
emergence of an upper class to whom certain leisure activities have value, not in relation to work, but quite independently as a symbol of status." The first pink-coated fox hunt
ever to astonish an Indiana landscape was held on William
Ball's Orchard Lawn Saddle Horse Farm in April (turn page).

## Figure 9.3.   The Brandenburgs and the Balls

cizing this new information, the mass media helped establish a national community of beliefs.[48] Due to these forces, Americans became increasingly self-conscious about what it meant to be an American. Pictorial magazines that published realistic photographs depicting the upper and middle classes at work and leisure played a key role in forming that self-definition. *Life* in particular played a crucial role, not only as a conveyor of news about this new community, but as a guide to how one should fit into this new community.

## NOTES

1. David Oshinsky, "A Nation of Shoppers," review of *Why the American Century?*, by Olivier Zunz, *New York Times*, February 21, 1999, 26.
2. Hoopes, "Birth of a Great Magazine," 35.
3. Hoopes, "Birth of a Great Magazine," 38–39.
4. Edwards, "One Every Minute," 18.
5. Roland E. Wolseley defines "masses" as middle class, of moderate income, at least high school education. *The Magazine World: An Introduction to Magazine Journalism* (New York: Prentice-Hall, 1951), 34.
6. "A General Presentation of *Life*," September 1939, Time Inc.
7. George H. Gallup, *The Gallup Poll* (New York, 1972), I, 148.
8. Loren Baritz, *The Good Life: The Meaning of Success for the American Middle Class* (New York: Knopf, 1989), 105.
9. Billings Diary, April 1, 1937, Billings Collection.
10. "Bigger'n We Thought!" self-promotion in *Life*, April 15, 1940.
11. Alan Wolfe, "Democracy versus Sociology: Boundaries and Their Political Consequences," in *Cultivating Differences: Symbolic Boundaries and the Making of Inequality*, ed. Michele Lamont and Marcel Fournier (Chicago: University of Chicago Press, 1992), 323.
12. "Is Young Tom Dewey The Republican Man of Destiny?" *Life,* November 15, 1937, 24–25.
13. James Playsted Wood, *Magazines in the United States*, 2nd ed. (New York: Ronald, 1956), 214.
14. Alice G. Marquis, *Hope and Ashes: The Birth of Modern Times 1929-1939* (New York: Free Press, 1986), 138–39.
15. Robert Perrucci and Earl Wysong, *The New Class Society* (Lanham, Md.: Rowman & Littlefield, 1999), 7
16. Roland Marchand, A*dvertising the American Dream: Making Way for Modernity 1920–1940* (Berkeley: University of California Press, 1985).
17. "These are Some of the Bach Choristers of Bethlehem," *Life*, June 14, 1937, 59–60.
18. This section was dropped as the editors decide that the lives it showed were "snide and unpleasant." Otha C. Spencer, "Twenty Years of *Life*: A Study of Time Inc.'s Picture Magazine and Its Contributions to Photojournalism," Ph.D. diss., University of Missouri, 1958, 249.
18. Loudon Wainwright, *The Great American Magazine* (New York: Knopf, 1986), 12.

20. "Fifty-Cent Polo Is A Big Bargain," *Life,* July 26, 1937, 51–52.

21. The census data for 1940 lists the unemployed at 5,795,786. For purposes of comparison to my study's findings, I added domestic, service, and farm laborers who totaled 7,367,700 in this group, for a total 13,163,486, or 10 percent of the U.S. population that was poor.

22. "Dust Bowl Farmer Is New Pioneer," *Life,* June 21, 1937, 65.

23. "Fear of New American Depression Causes 25-Billion-Dollar Stock Market Crash," *Life*, November 1, 1937, 29.

24. "A New Deal Starts As Stock Exchange Booms," *Life,* July 11, 1938, 11.

25. This corresponds closely with the census data if one adds up the following categories—male and female operatives; male and female clerical and sales; male and female craftsman; and male and female nonfarm laborers for a total of 23,618,963, or 18 percent of the United States population.

26. "Sit-Down Strikes," *Life,* April 5, 1937, 18.

27. Henry Ford was so angry about *Time's* coverage of the sit-downs at the River Rouge plant in Detroit in May 1937 that he pulled all advertising from the Time Inc. publications for eighteen months.

28. George H. Gallup, *The Gallup Poll* (New York, 1972), I, 31, 143.

29. Deepa Kumar, "Mass Media, Class, and Democracy: The Struggle over Newspaper Representation of the UPS Strike," *Critical Studies in Media Communication,* Annandale, September 2001, 286.

30. "Troops Close Iowa's Maytag Plant," *Life,* August 8, 1938, 11–15.

31. The 1940 census contains data on professional men and women, semiprofessional men and women, and male and female employers and owners account for a total of 12,944,136 or 10 percent of the population. One could count only the group labeled "professional" in this category. Still, even with the larger figure, one can see that *Life's* coverage of this group far outweighed its size.

32. Loren Baritz, *The Good Life: The Meaning of Success for the American Middle Class* (New York: Knopf, 1989), xii.

33. "The Education of Sidney Hillman," *Life*, August 21, 1944, 30.

34. "I.L.G.W.U.: One of the 250,000 Who Spends Most of Her Life Within Her Union," *Life*, August 1, 1938, 46–47.

35. Richard Wightman Fox, "Epitaph for Middletown: Robert S. Lynd and the Analysis of Consumer Culture," in *The Culture of Consumption: Critical Essays in American History, 1880–1980* (New York: Pantheon, 1983), 103–229.

36. Warren Susman, *Culture as History: The Transformation of American Society in the Twentieth Century* (New York: Pantheon, 1973), xxi.

37. Barbara Ehrenreich and John Ehrenreich, "The Professional-Managerial Class," *Radical America*, 20.

38. Maren Stange, *Symbols of Ideal Life: Social Documentary Photography in America, 1890–1950* (Cambridge: Cambridge University Press, 1989), 89.

39. George Gallup, "A Scientific Method for Determining Reader-Interest," *Journalism Quarterly*, March 1930, 1.

40. Kenneth Stewart, "The Education of Henry Luce," *PM*, August 2, 1944, 8.

41. Jessup, *Ideas of Henry Luce*, 222–23.

42. "In Defense of the High-Brow," *Life*, April 11, 1949, 102.

43. Marchand, *Advertising the American Dream*, 167.

44. Marchand, *Advertising the American Dream*, 233.

45. "Muncie, Ind., Is the Great U.S. 'Middletown,'" *Life*, May 10, 1937, 15.

46. Stanley Coben and Lorman Ratner, eds., *The Development of an American Culture* (Englewood Cliffs, N.J.: Prentice-Hall, 1970), 8–9.

47. Robert S. Lynd, *Knowledge for What? The Place of Social Science in American Culture* (Princeton, N.J.: Princeton University Press, 1939), 60–62.

48. Warren Susman, *Culture as History: The Transformation of American Society in the Twentieth Century* (New York: Pantheon, 1984).

# REFERENCES

**Primary Sources**

The John Shaw Billings Collection, South Carolina Library, University of South Carolina, Columbia, South Carolina. This collection includes the seventy volumes of daily dairies kept by the first managing editor of *Life* magazine.

The Time-Life-Fortune Collection, South Carolina Library, University of South Carolina, Columbia, South Carolina. This collection is composed of the scrapbooks kept by John Shaw Billings throughout his life and includes both personal material such as photos of Redcliffe, the Billings plantation in South Carolina, and professional material, such as clippings of press coverage of *Life* and photos of Billings and the *Life* staff at work.

From the Scrapbooks: Two reports dated March 15, 1953, prepared by Time Inc. staffers at the request of Henry R. Luce:

   *The Ideology of Time Magazine Part I: A Study of the Political Attitudes and Positions Taken by Time during the years 1935–1945,* by Elsa Wardell.

   *The Ideology of Time Magazine Part II: A Research Report on Time during the period 1936–1944,* by Patricia Divver.

*Life* magazine: All issues between November 23, 1936, and December 7, 1941; 262 issues in all.

*Life's* Continuing Study of Magazine Audiences, Time Inc. Archives:

   Researchers: Paul T. Cherington, independent marketing consultant; Archibald M. Crossley, President of Crossley, Inc.; Samuel Gill, Director of Research, Crossley, Inc.; Darrell B. Lucas, associate professor of marketing, New York University (Reports 1–4); Theodore H. Brown (report 5).

   Contributors: Elmo Roper, S. S. Wilks, professor of statistics, Princeton University; Paul Lazarsfeld, Report 5.

      Report 1: December 1, 1938
      Report 2: May 1, 1939
      Report 3: January 1, 1940
      Report 4: September 1, 1940
      Report 5: October 1, 1941

Brown, J. L. "Picture Magazines and Morons." *American Mercury,* December 1938, 404–8.

"The Current Fad for Picture Mags." *Literary Digest,* January 30, 1937, 20–22.

Dutton, William S. "Prophets of Industry Prepare to Open a New Box of Wonders." *American Magazine,* May 1931.

Edwards, Jackson. "One Every Minute." *Scribner's,* May 1938, 17–23, 102–3.

Gallup, George. "A Scientific Method for Determining Reader-Interest." *Journalism Quarterly,* March 1930, 1–13.

Hurlin, Ralph G., and Meredith B. Givens. "Shifting Occupational Patterns." In *Recent Social Trends in the United States*, chap. 6. New York: McGraw-Hill, 1933.

Judd, Charles H. "Education." In *Recent Social Trends in the United States*, chap. 7. New York: McGraw-Hill, 1933.

Keppel, Frederick P. "The Arts in Social Life." In *Recent Social Trends in the United States,* chap. 19. New York: McGraw-Hill, 1933.

Kerr, W. A., and H. H. Remmers. "The Cultural Value of 100 Representative American Magazines." *School and Society,* November 22, 1941, 476–80.

Kerrick, Jean S. "The Influence of Captions on Picture Interpretation." *Journalism Quarterly*, Spring 1955, 177–82.

McLean, Malcolm S., Jr., and William R. Hazard. "Women's Interest in Pictures: The Badger Village Study." *Journalism Quarterly*, Spring 1953, 139–62.

"One Every Minute." *Scribner's,* May 1938, 17–23, 102–3.

"The Presses Roll." *The New Republic*, February 10, 1937, 5–6.

Rayfield, Stanley. *How* Life *Gets the Story: Behind the Scenes in Photojournalism.* Garden City, N.Y.: Doubleday, 1955.

Spencer, Otha C. "Twenty Years of *Life*: A Study of Time Inc.'s Picture Magazine and Its Contributions to Photojournalism." Ph.D. diss., University of Missouri, 1958.

Steiner, Jesse F. *Research Memorandum on Recreation in the Depression*. New York: Social Science Research Council, 1937. Reprinted by Arno Press, 1972.

Stewart, Kenneth. "The Education of Henry Luce." *PM*, August 2, 1944, 6–9.

———. "Henry Luce Talks about His Brand of Journalism." *PM*, September 1944, 6–10.

Swanson, Charles E. "What They Read in 130 Daily Newspapers." *Journalism Quarterly*, Fall 1955, 411–21.

Vaile, Roland S. *Research Memorandum on Social Aspects of Consumption in the Depression*. New York: Social Science Research Council, 1937. Reprinted by Arno Press, 1972.

Vitray, Laura, John Mills Jr., and Roscoe Ellard. *Pictorial Journalism*. New York: McGraw-Hill, 1939.

Whiting, John R., and George R. Clark. "The Picture Magazines." *Harper's*, July 1943, 159–69.

Woodburn, Bert W. "Reader Interest in Newspaper Pictures." *Journalism Quarterly*, September 1947, 197–201.

## Secondary Sources

Adatto, Kiku. *Picture Perfect: The Art and Artifice of Public Image Making*. New York: Basic, 1993.

Baldasty, Gerald, J. *The Commercialization of News in the Nineteenth Century*. Madison: University of Wisconsin Press, 1992.

Baritz, Loren. "The Culture of the Twenties." In *The Development of an American Culture*, edited by Stanley Coben and Lorman Ratner, 150–78. Englewood Cliffs, N.J.: Prentice-Hall, 1970.

———. *The Good Life: The Meaning of Success for the American Middle Class*. New York: Knopf, 1989.

Batchen, Geoffrey. *Burning with Desire: The Conception of Photography*. Cambridge, Mass.: MIT Press, 1999.

Baughman, James L. *Henry R. Luce and the Rise of the American News Media*. Boston: Twayne, 1987.

———. "Who Read *Life*: The Circulation of 'America's Favorite Magazine.'" In *Looking at* Life *Magazine*, edited by Erika Doss. Washington, D.C.: Smithsonian Institution Press, 2001.

Becker, Howard S. "Visual Sociology, Documentary Photography, and Photojournalism: It's (Almost) All a Matter of Context." *Visual Sociology* 10, no. 1–2 (1995): 5–14.

Berger, John. *Ways of Seeing*. London: Penguin, 1972.

Bornet, Stephen Folwell. "Missionary Photojournalism: Luce and *Life*, 1936–1947." Master's thesis, Southern Oregon College, 1972.

Bourdieu, Pierre. *Distinction: A Social Critique of the Judgment of Taste*. Cambridge, Mass.: Harvard University Press, 1984.

Brandt, Kristin Anne. "The Application of *Life*-Style Photojournalism to the Metropolitan Daily Newspaper." Master's thesis, University of Wyoming, 1973.

Brinkley, Alan. "To See and Know Everything." *Time*, March 9, 1998, 90–91.

Coben, Stanley, and Lorman Ratner, eds. *The Development of an American Culture*. Englewood Cliffs, N.J.: Prentice-Hall, 1970.

Coleman, Renita. "The Visual Communication of Public Journalism: A Content and Textual Analysis." Master's thesis, University of Missouri, 1997.

Curtis, James, and Sheila Grannen. "Let Us Now Appraise Famous Photography: Walker Evans and Documentary Photography." *Winterthur Portfolio*, Spring 1989, 1–23.

Curtis, James. *Mind's Eye, Mind's Truth: FSA Photography Reconsidered*. Philadelphia: Temple University Press, 1989.

Denning, Michael. "The End of Mass Culture." *International Labor and Working-Class History* 37 (1990): 4–18.

DiMaggio, Paul. "Cultural Entrepreneurship in Nineteenth-Century Boston: Part I." *Media, Culture, and Society* 4 (1982): 33–50.

———."Cultural Entrepreneurship in Nineteenth-Century Boston: Part II." *Media, Culture, and Society* 4 (1982): 303–22.

Doss, Erika, ed. *Looking at* Life *Magazine*. Washington, D.C.: Smithsonian Institution Press, 2001.

———."Looking at Labor: Images of Work in 1930s American Art." *Journal of Decorative and Propaganda Arts* 24 (2002): 230–57.

Editors of Time-Life Books. *Life Library of Photography, Photojournalism*. New York: Time-Life Books, 1971.

Ehrenreich, Barbara, and John Ehrenreich. "The Professional-Managerial Class." *Radical America*, 7–31.

Elson, Robert T. *Time Inc.: The Intimate History of a Publishing Enterprise*. New York: Atheneum, 1968.

"The End of a Great Adventure." *Time*, December 18, 1972, 46–55.

Fleischhauer, Carl, and Beverly W. Brannan. *Documenting America, 1935–1943*. Berkeley: University of California Press, 1988.

Guillory, John. *Cultural Capital: The Problem of Literary Canon Formation*. Chicago: University of Chicago Press, 1993.

Hamblin, Dora Jane. *That Was the Life*. New York: Norton, 1977.

Hardt, Hanno. *In the Company of Media: Cultural Constructions of Communication, 1920s–1930s*. Boulder: Westview, 2000.

Harman, Jeanne Perkins. *Such Is Life*. New York: Crowell, 1956.

Harris, Neil. *Cultural Excursions: Marketing Appetites and Cultural Tastes in Modern America*. Chicago: University of Chicago Press, 1990.

———. *Humbug: The Art of P.T. Barnum*. Chicago: Chicago University Press, 1973.

Haynes, Dixon Grant. "A Study of the Effectiveness of Photography as an Editorial Tool." Master's thesis, University of Georgia, 1969.

Herzstein, Robert E. *Henry R. Luce: A Political Portrait of the Man Who Created the American Century*. New York: Macmillan, 1994.

Hoopes, Roy. "Birth of A Great Magazine." *American History Illustrated*, September 1985, 35–41.

Horowitz, Daniel. *The Morality of Spending: Attitudes toward the Consumer Society in America, 1875–1940*. Chicago: Elephant, 1985.

Huck, Karen F. "White Minds and Black Bodies in the War for Democracy: Race, Representation, and the Reader in *Life* Magazine, 1938–1946." Ph.D. diss., University of Utah, 1993.

Hurley, Gerald D., and Angus McDougall. *Visual Impact in Print*. Chicago: American Publishers Press, 1971.

Isaacson, Walter. "Luce's Values: Then and Now." *Time*, March 9, 1998, 195–96.

Jessup, John K., ed. *The Ideas of Henry Luce*. New York: Atheneum, 1969.

Kennedy, David M. *Freedom from Fear: The American People in Depression and War, 1929–1945*. New York: Oxford University Press, 1999.

Kerber, Linda K. "The Meanings of Citizenship." *Journal of American History*, December 1997, 833–54.

Kingston, Paul W. *The Classless Society*. Stanford: Stanford University Press, 2000.

Kobler, John. *Luce: His Time, Life, and Fortune*. Garden City, N.Y.: Doubleday, 1968.

Kozol, Wendy. "Documenting the Public and Private in *Life*: Cultural Politics in Postwar Journalism." Ph.D. diss., University of Minnesota, 1990.

———. Life's *America: Family and Nation in Postwar Photojournalism*. Philadelphia: Temple University Press, 1994.

Kumar, Deepa. "Mass Media, Class, and Democracy: The Struggle over Newspaper Representation of the UPS Strike." *Critical Studies in Media Communication*, September 2001, 285–302.

Lamont, Michele. *Money, Morals, and Manners: The Culture of the American and French Upper-Middle Class*. Chicago: University of Chicago Press, 1992.

Lears, Jackson. "Mastery and Drift." *Journal of American History*, December 1997, 979–88.

Lebergott, Stanley. *Pursuing Happiness: American Consumers in the Twentieth Century*. Princeton N.J.: Princeton University Press, 1993.

"The Lesson of *Life*." *New Republic*, December 23, 30, 1972, 12–13.

Levine, Lawrence, W. "The Historian and the Icon: Photography and the History of the American People in the 1930s and the 1940s." In *Documenting America, 1935–1943*, edited by Carl Fleischhauer and Beverly W. Brannan, 15–42. Berkeley: University of California Press, 1988.

———. "William Shakespeare and the American People: A Study in Cultural Transformation." In *Rethinking Popular Culture*, edited by Chandra Mukerji and Michael Schudson, 157–97. Berkeley: University of California Press, 1991.

*LIFE: The First Decade*. New York: Time Inc., 1979. Exhibition catalogue, with an introduction by Robert R. Littman.

Lutz, Catherine A., and Jane L. Collins. *Reading National Geographic*. Chicago: University of Chicago Press, 1993.

Lynd, Robert S. *Knowledge for What? The Place of Social Science in American Culture*. Princeton N.J.: Princeton University Press, 1939.

Lynd, Robert S., and Helen Merrell Lynd. *Middletown in Transition: A Study in Cultural Conflicts*. New York: Harcourt, Brace, 1937.

Marchand, Roland. *Advertising the American Dream: Making Way for Modernity, 1920–1940*. Berkeley: University of California Press, 1985.

Marquis, Alice G. *Hope and Ashes: The Birth of Modern Times, 1929–1939*. New York: Free Press, 1986.

Marzio, Peter C. *The Men and Machines of American Journalism: A Pictorial Essay from the Henry R. Luce Hall of News Reporting*. Washington, D.C.: Smithsonian Institution, 1973.

McGarth, Edward Gorham. "The Political Ideals of *Life* Magazine." Master's thesis, Syracuse University, 1961.

Meyerowitz, Joanne. "Beyond the Feminine Mystique: A Reassessment of Postwar Mass Culture, 1946–1958." *Journal of American History*, March 1993, 1455–83.

Miller, Daniel. *Material Cultures: Why Some Things Matter*. London: University College London Press, 1998.

Mott, Frank Luther. *A History of American Magazines*. Vol. 5, *Sketches of 21 Magazines, 1905–1930*. Cambridge, Mass.: Harvard University Press, 1968.

Mullen, Bill, and Sherry Lee Linkon, eds. *Radical Revisions: Rereading 1930s Culture*. Urbana: University of Illinois Press, 1996.

Nesbit, Gretchen Kerry. "Visual Communication in Print." Master's thesis, University of North Carolina, 1980.

Ohmann, Richard M. *Politics of Letters*. Middletown, Conn.: Wesleyan University Press, 1987.

———. *Selling Culture: Magazines, Markets, and Class at the Turn of the Century*. London: Verso, 1996.

Oshinsky, David. "A Nation of Shoppers." Review of *Why the American Century?* by Olivier Zunz. *New York Times*. February 21, 1999, 26.

Peeler, David P. "America's Depression Culture: Social Art and Literature of the 1930s." Ph.D. diss., University of Wisconsin, 1980.

Pells, Richard H. *Radical Visions and American Dreams: Cultural and Social Thought in the Depression Years*. New York: Harper & Row, 1973.

Perrucci, Robert, and Earl Wysong. *The New Class Society*. Lanham, Md.: Rowman & Littlefield, 1999.

Peterson, Theodore. *Magazines in the Twentieth Century*. Urbana: University of Illinois Press, 1964.

Pollack, Peter. *The Picture History of Photography*. New York: Abrams, 1969.

Pulda, Arnold H. "Better Todays: The American Public Culture in the 1930s." Ph.D. diss., University of North Carolina, 1978.

Recken, Stephen L. "Fitting-In: The Redefinition of Success in the 1930s." *Journal of Popular Culture*, Winter 1993, 205–22.

Rosenblatt, Roger. *Consuming Desires: Consumption, Culture, and the Pursuit of Happiness*. Washington, D.C.: Island Press/Shearwater, 1999.

Rosler, Martha. "In, Around, and Afterthoughts (On Documentary Photography)." In *The Contest of Meaning: Critical Histories of Photography*, edited by Richard Bolton, 303–41. Cambridge, Mass.: MIT Press, 1989.

Rubin, Joan Shelley. *The Making of Middlebrow Culture*. Chapel Hill: University of North Carolina Press, 1992.

Scanlon, Jennifer. *Inarticulate Longings:* The Ladies' Home Journal*, Gender, and the Promises of Consumer Culture*. New York: Routledge, 1995.

Scharf, Aaron. *Art and Photography*. London: Penguin, 1968.

Schmidt, Dorothy (Dorey). "Magazines, Technology, and American Culture." *Journal of American Culture*, Spring 1980, 3–16.

Schmidt, Leigh Eric. "The Commercialization of the Calendar: American Holidays and the Culture of Consumption, 1870–1920." *Journal of American History*, December 1991, 887–916.

———. *Consumer Rites: The Buying and Selling of American Holidays*. Princeton N.J.: Princeton University Press, 1995.

Schneirov, Matthew. *The Dream of a New Social Order: Popular Magazines in America, 1893–1914*. New York: Columbia University Press, 1994.

Schuneman, R. Smith, ed. *Photographic Communication*. New York: Hastings House, 1972.

Schwartz, Dona. "To Tell the Truth: Codes of Objectivity in Photojournalism." *Communication* 13 (1992): 95–109.

Squiers, Carole. "Looking at *Life*." *Artforum* 20, no. 4 (1981): 25–32.

Stackpole, Peter. "Luce Raised the Level of Photographic Art." *U.S. Camera*, June 1967.

Stange, Maren. *Symbols of Ideal Life: Social Documentary Photography in America, 1890–1950*. Cambridge: Cambridge University Press, 1989.

Stein, Sally. "The Graphic Ordering of Desire: Modernization of a Middle-Class Women's Magazine, 1914–39." In *The Contest of Meaning: Cultural Histories of Photography,* edited by Richard Bolton, 145–46. Cambridge, Mass.: MIT Press, 1993.

Stott, William. *Documentary Expression and Thirties America*. New York: Oxford University Press, 1973.

Suchar, Charles S. "The Sociological Imagination and Documentary Still Photography: The Interrogatory Stance." *Visual Sociology Review*, Fall 1989, 51–62.

Susman, Warren, I. *Culture as History: The Transformation of American Society in the Twentieth Century*. New York: Pantheon, 1984.

———. "The Thirties." In *The Development of an American Culture*, edited by Stanley Coben and Lorman Ratner, 179–218. Englewood Cliffs, N.J.: Prentice-Hall, 1970.

Swanberg, W. A. *Luce and His Empire*. New York: Scribner's, 1972.

Swartz, David. *Culture and Power: The Sociology of Pierre Bourdieu*, Chicago: University of Chicago Press, 1997.

Trachtenberg, Alan. "From Image to Story: Reading the File." In *Documenting America, 1935–1943*, edited by Carl Fleischhauer and Beverly W. Brannan, 43–73. Berkeley: University of California Press, 1988.

Wainwright, Loudon. *The Great American Magazine: An Inside History of* Life. New York: Knopf, 1986.

Ware, Susan. *Holding Their Own: American Women in the 1930s*. Boston: Twayne, 1982.

Weeden, Kim A., and David B. Grusky. *Do Big Classes Really Matter?* Report for the National Science Foundation, January 2003.

Williams, Raymond. *The Sociology of Culture.* New York: Schocken, 1982.

Willumson, Glenn G. *W. Eugene Smith and the Photographic Essay.* Cambridge: Cambridge University Press, 1992.

Wolfe, Alan. "Democracy versus Sociology: Boundaries and Their Political Consequences." In *Cultivating Differences: Symbolic Boundaries and the Making of Inequality*, edited by Michele Lamont and Marcel Fournier, 309–25. Chicago: University of Chicago Press, 1992.

Wright, Erik Olin. *Class Counts: Comparative Studies in Class Analysis.* Cambridge: Cambridge University Press, 1997.

Zunz, Oliver. *Why the American Century?* Chicago: University of Chicago Press, 1998.

# 10

# Tales Told in Two Cities: When Missing Girls Are(n't) News

*Carol M. Liebler*

The summer of 2002 saw a flurry of press reports about missing girls. Elizabeth Smart, Danielle van Dam, and Samantha Runnion made news in local and national media outlets around the country. Indeed, a Lexis-Nexis search elicits over 1,000 hits for each girl's name. Yet not all missing girls achieve such notoriety. Alexis Patterson, of Milwaukee, Wisconsin, went missing during the summer of 2002, but media coverage of her disappearance was scant outside of her hometown—her name results in fewer than 100 Lexis-Nexis hits, most from the Associated Press or Milwaukee papers. Why the difference?

There have been numerous "theories" about the disparity in coverage, and oddly enough some originate with the media themselves. For example, several newspapers ran stories or columns about why many media covered Elizabeth Smart and not Alexis Patterson. A story in the *Boston Globe* (June 19, 2002) was one of the few to explicitly point to race and class, going so far as to suggest a link in its subhead: "Two Missing Girls, But Only One Big Story. Some See Race, Class Affecting Coverage." Five days earlier the *Milwaukee Journal-Sentinel* (June 14, 2002) ran a story querying whether race was why white, upper middle-class Elizabeth Smart became big news. And while the story quoted Bob Steele, director of the ethics program at the Poynter Institute, as suggesting that media may be "prone to the vagaries of racial bias, compounded by class bias," it also sourced spokespersons from various media outlets who argued just the opposite, claiming that the news value of the situation was what mattered.

This chapter centers on the influence of class on media coverage of missing girls, and how class interacts with race and gender. I argue not only that class is manifested in media coverage, but that class influences the news production process itself. Middle-class, media-savvy parents help shape media portrayals of their daughters, resulting in inequitable media treatment across class lines. My research focuses on two missing cases, employing a multicase study approach. One weekend in May 1996, two young college women from two different universities went missing. They share only those facts, coming from vastly different backgrounds and life experiences. In this regard, these two cases provide an excellent opportunity for comparison and contrast. My analysis centers primarily on content and textual analysis of the print coverage but also includes interview data. The time frame is from May 25, 1996, when the two young women went missing, to May 25, 1997, the one-year anniversary of their disappearances.

The FBI reported ninety-three children abducted by strangers in 2000, but some dispute their data, suggesting the figure is actually much higher (Maier 2002). Regardless of how many kids are abducted, when a private citizen goes missing, media decisions about their newsworthiness have serious implications. As with any other issue, media coverage translates to public awareness. In its publication, *When Your Child Is Missing: A Family Survival Guide*, the U.S. Department of Justice (1998) emphasizes the importance of media attention, particularly during the first forty-eight hours: "Media publicity is the best way to generate leads from the public concerning your child. . . . Intense, early media coverage ensures that people will be looking for your child." People may not realize they hold a clue to the puzzle until they hear or see something on the news. For this reason the Department of Justice recommends that parents contact the media themselves or encourage law enforcement to do so. If the media miss the story or play it down, then the public will know little or nothing about the missing person. What's more, how the media play the story will affect public perceptions. A front-page story with an accompanying photograph communicates importance and will attract attention. A small story inside the paper is less likely to do so. Similarly, the portrayal of the missing person and the circumstances of his or her disappearance may influence how much the public responds, how much people care. A woman depicted as "loose" or to blame for her own disappearance is less likely to garner public sympathy than one portrayed as a model citizen. Law enforcement officials, family members, friends, and others may serve as sources for news stories. But it's the media who have the real power to construct the public image of the missing person, although this power is mediated by the constraints of daily newsgathering.

It is not only during the initial reports that media coverage is important, however. Keeping a missing person in the news will help to sustain efforts to find her. Some cases will be inherently newsworthy and will result in continuing news coverage. Naturally, a plethora of events compete each day for the limited news hole in a newspaper, or for airtime during a newscast. For instance, as journalists look for a "peg" on which to base a story, the discovery of an important clue, a community search, or identification of a suspect will attract their attention. But with some disappearances there are very few such events, and such cases seem doomed to fade from the media agenda and therefore from the public consciousness.

Female crime victims may be particularly disadvantaged when it comes to media coverage, regardless of public relations efforts or the circumstances of the crime. Society often blames women for their own victim status and this attitude is reflected in crime coverage. This problem is compounded for poor women or women of color because the media do not consider them newsworthy (Meyers 1997). As illustrated in table 10.1, Madriz has created a typology of female victims, identifying attributes of "innocent" and "culpable" victims. She argues that "Since the representations of the victim mirror multiple and overlapping social hierarchies—hierarchies of race, gender and class—it is no coincidence that the images of the innocent victim are more concordant with the characteristics of the white, middle class female" (1997, 90).

## THE RESEARCH CONTEXT

I was en route from Paris to Detroit when the column in the *International Herald Tribune* caught my attention. Reprinted from the *New York Times*, the column by Evelyn Nieves questioned why missing Syracuse University student April Gregory wasn't bigger news. The column resonated with me because I live in Syracuse and had been pondering the same question. Why was it that April's disappearance hadn't been reported in the Syracuse media until nearly a month after her disappearance? And in the days, weeks, and months following her disappearance, why hadn't it caused more of an uproar on the

**Table 10.1. Typology of Female Victims**

| *The Innocent Victim* | *The Culpable Victim* |
|---|---|
| She is a respectable woman. | She is a woman of dubious reputation. |
| She was attacked while she was engaged in a respectable activity. | She was attacked while engaged in activity considered improper for women. |
| The time and place of her attack are considered appropriate for a woman. | She was at a place and/or time considered unsafe for women. |
| She is weaker than her attacker. | She is strong and she could have protected herself. |
| She wears conservative or modest clothes and jewelry. | She dresses in a provocative or revealing manner improper for a decent woman. |
| She associates with other respectable women and men. | She associates with the wrong crowd. |
| She was attacked by an "ideal criminal," a stranger. | She was attacked by one of her disreputable friends or by a disreputable stranger. |
| The attack was vicious, resulting in serious injury or death. | Even if she was hurt, she exaggerated or fabricated the nature of the attack. |

*Source:* Madriz 1997.

campus and in the community? As a teacher and researcher of diversity and media, I had noted two factors in particular: April was African American and came from a working-class background.

I couldn't help but contrast the lack of attention to April's disappearance with the media coverage of California Polytechnic State University student Kristin Smart in San Luis Obispo, California. Kristin disappeared the same weekend as April. For whatever reason, the San Luis Obispo media had devoted a lot of time to covering her disappearance—enough so that during a brief stay in the area I had become familiar with the case and with Kristin's blond-haired, brown-eyed image. But I also knew the amount of coverage could be deceiving: Were the San Luis Obispo media helping local law enforcement officials find Kristin, or was her disappearance a chance to sensationalize a story that would help sell newspapers and increase ratings? More coverage doesn't necessarily mean better coverage.

## MISSING

### April Gregory

> Somebody snatched my baby.
>
> —Herman Gregory, April's father (*New York Times*, April 7, 1997)

April Gregory was last seen by her brother, who dropped her off at her Syracuse University dormitory. It was late Friday evening, May 24, 1996. Lamar escorted April to her room and as he left April began to unpack the clothes she would wear during the upcoming summer session. April was due at her job at McDonald's, a short walk from campus, at 5 A.M. the next day. She never arrived.

April, who had worked at McDonald's for three years, was a reliable worker, so when she didn't show up for work, coworkers called her parents who lived nearby. Herman and Brenda Gregory assumed April was running late, and didn't become truly concerned until 24 hours later, when McDonald's again called them: still no April.

Eighteen-year-old April had left cash and other belongings in her dorm room, but there were very few clues as to what had happened to her. Police could not tell whether she had disappeared from her dorm room or en route to McDonald's. And despite flyers (belatedly) posted around campus and the community, and a $20,000 reward offered by Syracuse University, police had few answers for the Gregory family beyond the fact that they suspected foul play.

Syracuse University, in Syracuse, New York (population 160,000), was founded in 1871 and today has an enrollment of 15,000. SU, while proximate to downtown, is a community and culture unto itself. But SU and its sports teams are points of pride in the city, attracting some 40,000 fans to Orangemen football games. Commonly known as "the Hill," the 200-acre private university borders hospitals, student neighborhoods, and "M" (Marshall) Street, home to student-oriented shops, bars, and restaurants. Like April, 65 percent of students live in university-owned dormitories.

Eighteen months after she disappeared, April's dismembered body was discovered in her former boyfriend's home. Terrance Evans, who lived next door to April's parents, confessed in November 1997, to killing April. He says he and April argued, he struck her, and she hit her head and died. He is serving a 25-year to life term for second-degree murder. These developments, of course, resulted in much local media attention. It took April's death for her to *really* become news.

The Syracuse media first reported April Gregory missing nearly a month after she failed to show up for work. The evening of June 20, 1996, station WTVH, the CBS affiliate, ran stories about April on its 5, 6 and 11 P.M. newscasts. The newsroom had been given a tip by a Syracuse University intern. The next day, the *Herald American*, the daily afternoon paper, ran a column by Dick Case on the front page of the metro section. The following week, on June 26, the summer edition of the student paper, the *Summer Orange*, ran its first story about April.

## Kristin Smart

Kristin would never, ever leave without saying good-bye.

　　—Denise Smart, Kristin's mother (*Telegram-Tribune*, May 22, 1997)

Kristin Smart was nearing the end of her freshman year when she disappeared from the California Polytechnic State University. It was that same Friday night, and Kristin, like many college students, had been partying off-campus with friends. After the party, around 2:00 A.M. the morning of May 25, 1996, Kristin headed back to her dorm room walking with two other students—one male, one female. As they neared the dorm complex, the students split. The other young woman headed to her own dorm while Kristin and her companion, Paul Flores, continued on their way toward Kristin's dorm.

It was Kristin's habit to call her parents every Sunday, and when she failed to do so they became concerned. Denise and Stan Smart, of Stockton, California, became increasingly alarmed when there continued to be no sign of Kristin over the next 48 hours. The Cal Poly police remained relatively unconcerned, despite the facts that Kristin had disappeared without her purse (which held her identification) and that such behavior was said to be uncharacteristic of her. According to the campus police at the time, Kristin most likely had disappeared under her own volition. It was perhaps for this reason that an investigation didn't begin until 72 hours after Kristin's roommate reported her missing. And local, non-university authorities were not called on to the case until four weeks after Kristin's disappearance.

Cal Poly, with an enrollment topping 16,000, is located on the central coast of California, nestled in the hills of the city of San Luis Obispo (population 42,000). The city and university appear to enjoy an amicable, mutually supportive relationship, which is perhaps unsurprising given that Cal Poly is the second largest employer in the area. Both city and campus have a quiet charm, and the environs exude a friendly atmosphere. The city enjoys a relatively low crime rate, reporting no murders in 1995. It is simply not the sort of setting in which people expect a college student to go missing. But Kristin Smart has not been seen since the early hours of May 25, 1996.

Authorities now suspect foul play, and although there is not enough evidence to charge him with the crime, they suspect that Paul Flores killed Kristin. The reward for information leading to what happened to Kristin has climbed to $75,000. But few, if any, answers have been forthcoming although the Smart family continues its search to find out what happened to Kristin. Her mother and father remain convinced that Paul Flores is responsible for her disappearance and have actively sought to publicize this fact via the Internet and other mass media. Their story has received national media attention from such disparate sources as *Sightings* and *20/20*.

Kristin Smart's disappearance became news much more quickly than April Gregory's did. KSBY, the San Luis Obispo NBC affiliate, ran a brief report on May 29th, with more in-depth stories following over the next two days. The daily paper, the *Telegram-Tribune*, first covered the story in the police blotter section on May 30th, and the student paper, the *Mustang Daily*, ran a front page story the next day. In neither case did the media run the stories as quickly as the Department of Justice recommends as necessary to truly alert the public. In April's case, 27 days had passed without her disappearance becoming news. For Kristin, the time lag was much shorter, but critical days were lost nonetheless.

## WHO'S NEWS, WHO ISN'T

Some missing people receive so much attention that they permeate the public consciousness, their faces and names as familiar to strangers as they are to friends . . . April Gregory has received no such attention.

—Evelyn Nieves (*New York Times*, March 6, 1997)

The amount of coverage devoted to April Gregory and Kristin Smart was significantly different in the year that followed their disappearances. The San Luis Obispo newspaper, the *Telegram-Tribune*, ran a total of forty-seven stories during the first year of Kristin's disappearance. This number contrasts sharply with the Syracuse newspapers, which covered April in twenty-four stories—just about half the attention that Kristin received. Kristin was also covered more prominently. Fourteen stories about her appeared on page 1, whereas April made front-page news only once. Similarly, stories about Kristin were longer than those about April, averaging 534 words to 351.

Kristin's disappearance attracted even more coverage from the broadcast media in the San Luis Obispo market. KSBY-TV, the only network affiliate located within city limits, ran sixty-seven different stories in the first year after she went missing. Syracuse TV news largely ignored the disappearance of April Gregory, delivering only a handful of stories. Thus there is little question that the *amount* of media coverage privileged the white, middle-class young woman.

The disparity in the amount of coverage devoted to Kristin Smart and April Gregory is telling. One girl's community valued her life; the other's did not.

Yet the amount of coverage reveals only part of the story. It is necessary to examine how the news media portrayed each young woman and her family in order to reach an understanding of how class, race and gender each manifest in media coverage, and how this varies contextually.

## MEDIA PORTRAYAL OF APRIL GREGORY

If we consider indicators of class as including education level, employment (or one's relation to the means and mode of production), income, and assets, the Syracuse newspapers seemingly went to great efforts to remind readers of April's working-class background. Sometimes these references were explicit, sometimes subtle. And sometimes, oddly enough, they were cast as compliments of April's character.

By far the most pervasive reference to April's class status was the nearly constant mention of her employment at McDonald's. A Syracuse University student working at McDonald's immediately indicates lower-class status than most undergraduates at this relatively elite private institution. To a large extent, however, this reference was justified; after all, it was on her way to work that April disappeared. Nonetheless, April was situated within a particular class location from the very earliest media reports, and stories occasionally mentioned April's employment when it really wasn't necessary. For example, in Dick Case's column in the *Herald-Journal* on June 21, 1996, "She had been working at McDonald's since 10th grade." Or as reported in a *Post-Standard* column from March 1997, "She was attending the university's summer session and working part-time at McDonald's." In all, fifteen of twenty-four stories mentioned McDonald's, with multiple references in some of them.

As time went on, and the media apparently became more self-conscious about how they portrayed April, stories complimented her work ethic and strength of character. While manifestly positive in tone, the coverage bordered on patronizing. Moreover, the stories continued to emphasize her class, making it clear she came from a family with limited financial means. Readers learned that grants, loans, and paychecks covered April's college expenses, and that she was hoping to contribute to her family's well-being:

> She had worked for a paycheck since she turned 16. She used the money to buy her own clothes and a television for her bedroom. In the days before she disappeared, she was collecting cash for a surprise birthday gift for (her mother) Brenda. April dreamed of buying her mom a new washing machine to replace their battered old one. (*Post-Standard*, June 1, 1997, B1)

Sean Kirst, a columnist for the *Post-Standard,* wrote a year after April disappeared: "He (Lamar Gregory, April's brother) drives the neighborhood and sees the street corner faces, kids without hope who are living day by day.

April had fire. She was in school, and holding down a job, and dreaming big dreams about doing social work" (May 24, 1997, A2).

Others in April's family and social circle were portrayed in less glowing terms. These descriptions drew upon a variety of stereotypes—characterizations of loose, lazy, and drunken black people—and helped to insinuate April's family and friends into a particular social context. For example, one *Post-Standard* story mentioned, "her friends became teenage mothers" (January 1, 1997). In another her brother lamented that he had not gone to college. Reported even were the problems April's father faced with alcoholism. One paragraph was particularly striking, nearly blaming April for his troubles: "Herman Gregory tried to focus on his alcoholism when he entered a treatment center May 28, but the pull from his daughter was too strong" (August 3, 1996).

In other stories were hints that April was "culpable" in her victim status. She walked to work at the unusual hour of 5:00 A.M. She hung out with girls who had gotten pregnant. She even seemingly had a boyfriend (Terrence Evans) who couldn't keep a job: "Gregory helped Evans get the job last fall. He worked for a few months, but then he missed several days. He stopped going, figuring he'd been fired" (*Post-Standard*, August 6, 1996, B1). Yet such descriptions were juxtaposed with those of April as a good, hard-working student.

## MEDIA PORTRAYAL OF KRISTIN SMART

Newspaper descriptions of Kristin indicated her middle-class standing. The *Telegram-Tribune* reported that Kristin had worked as a lifeguard at a camp in Hawaii the previous summer, and had returned there for a reunion during a semester break. Several stories mentioned that Kristin loved to travel, and particularly liked to spend time near the ocean where she could surf. All such references point to a girl with some financial resources.

These indicators, which were sprinkled across a year's worth of coverage, were crystallized in the front-page story marking the first-year anniversary of Kristin's disappearance. *Telegram-Tribune* reporter Danna Dykstera identified Kristin as a "world traveler," and wrote that she had been a summer exchange student to Venezuela when she was sixteen (May 27, 1997, A4). Kristin's education level is also highlighted: "Kristin Smart was born in Germany to two educators who instilled early on the importance of a college education. For Kristin, it was never a question of whether she would go to college. It was simply a matter of where" (May 22, 1997, A4). The story also clearly identified the family as suburban. Wrote Dykstera: Denise Smart "finds it increasingly difficult to remember that a year ago she was a typical suburban mom consumed with the daily demands of growing teens." With that same story ran a front-page photo of the Smarts in Kristin's bedroom in Stockton, showing spacious, nicely furnished quarters.

News stories made other references to the Smart family's class location. Stan Smart was repeatedly identified as the principal at Vintage High in Napa, California. Coverage depicted him as a caring father who had the ability to pick up and relocate to San Luis Obispo to search for his daughter. According to news accounts, Stan Smart spent a lot of time distributing fliers, meeting with law enforcement officers, and organizing searches. The *Telegram-Tribune* reported a month after Kristin went missing that her father had been granted a leave of absence from work (June 20, 1996), thereby further legitimizing his presence in San Luis Obispo. While it was apparent that the Smarts were not rich—press coverage reported that local businesses helped defray the costs of searching (June 20, 1996)—they were clearly a family with resources on which to draw. A group of colleagues and friends from Napa and Stockton came to help search. Billboards appeared around the county, the family retained a private investigator (November 2, 1996) and attorney, and later filed a wrongful death suit. Similarly, the Smarts offered $5,000 in reward money, the amount of which eventually increased to $75,000 with help coming from sources such as Crime Stoppers, Cal Poly, and the California governor's office.

Yet, contrary to what might be expected, while Kristin and her parents were clearly cast as a middle-class family with resources, press coverage portrayed Kristin Smart as culpable in her own disappearance. Setting the tone for much of the early coverage was the brief in the police blotter on May 30, 1996:

CAL POLY—A 19-year-old Cal Poly student has been missing since about 2 a.m. Saturday, when she was walking back to her dormitory from a sorority party.

Kristin Denise Smart, who goes by the nickname "Roxy," was last seen by friends near the Muir Residence Hall as they were walking back to separate dorm halls.

She is about 6 feet, 1 inch tall, has blonde hair and brown eyes, weighs 145 pounds, and was wearing a black skirt and a gray shirt when last seen.

Smart did not have her purse or any identification with her, and she may have been under the influence of alcohol, according to campus police. She has not contacted her roommate, friends or family since she was reported missing.

Anyone with any information about Smart is asked to call the Cal Poly University Police Department at 736-2281.

There are several notable references here, many of which fit Madriz's (1997) conceptualization for how women crime victims are characterized. According to Colleen Bondy, who initially covered Kristin's disappearance, the Cal Poly police were largely responsible for this characterization (Bondy 1998). Indeed, the Cal Poly police report stated, "Smart does not have any close friends at Cal Poly. Smart appeared to be under the influence of alcohol on Friday night. Smart was talking with and socializing with several different males at the party. *Smart lives her life in her own way, not conforming to typical teenage behavior*" (emphasis added).

The local paper did little to question this description, as Kristin is repeatedly referred to as either drunk or a party girl. Examples include a *Telegram-Tribune* story in June in which Cal Poly police chief Tom Mitchell states that Kristin had been "fairly intoxicated." The story also included a quote by Mitchell that clearly pointed to Kristin as having had agency in her own disappearance: "This is kind of a funny age—things are done without much thought sometimes." He is granted further credibility by reference to his having a child Kristin's age (June 1, 1996, B2). Another story headlined "Witnesses describe last night before Kristin Smart disappeared" on August 8, 1996, depicted Kristin as "flirty," with one source claiming she had passed out at the party.

Reporter Colleen Bondy reflected on the use of the nickname Roxy:

> It seems to me that Roxy is a more colorful nickname . . . I don't know any other way to put it other than just racy. Roxy, I had a dog named Roxy. There's a bar in LA named Roxy. It rhymes with foxy. If that's the name people knew her by, then it might be useful for that to be in the story if people are still looking for her. But I no longer believed we were looking for someone who was running away. So what was the point of putting that name in here? To me, subconsciously or consciously, I thought it was part of the push to make her look promiscuous and all that. And I just didn't think that had anything to do with the story. (Bondy 1998)

The nickname was dropped in later stories, largely because it seemed no one had ever really called Kristin by this name. According to her father, Kristin, who liked to surf, wore clothing with the brand name of Roxy (Smart 1998). Early *Telegram-Tribune* reports, however, emphasized this nickname, which seemed to fit a party girl like Kristin: "Smart, who goes by the nickname Roxy, loved to surf at the beach. She didn't have a driver's license and often she hitchhiked to get around" (June 12, 1996).

In the early coverage, then, it was Kristin's gender that most influenced how the media covered her disappearance. The attractive blond was cast as responsible for her own troubles, in a manner largely consistent with Madriz's typology of culpable victims. Ironically, early on Kristin was not considered a victim at all—it was only as the investigation continued that law enforcement officers began to consider foul play.

## CLASS MATTERS

Given early media constructions of Kristin Smart's character, it may appear somewhat surprising that her disappearance remained such big news. However, analysis of the coverage, as well as interviews with three reporters who covered the story and with Stan Smart, indicate that it was Kristin's parents who made the difference.

*Telegram-Tribune* reporter Danna Dykstera referred to Kristin Smart as a "white blond principal's daughter." But she said she didn't think race or class were really the reason this became such a big story. "Had it not been for the parents it (the story) would have just died" (Dykstera 1997). Former colleague Colleen Bondy agreed: "Her parents were trying to keep it in the news as much as possible. I worked with them on what I thought would make it into the paper. What was actually newsworthy . . . They were really aggressive about it" (Bondy 1998).

Indeed, at least sixteen stories in the *Telegram-Tribune* are pegged to "news" driven by Stan and Denise Smart. Whether it was another search, a direct appeal for help, or some other "newsworthy" event, Kristin's parents worked hard to keep her name and face in the news. Their class granted them privilege. Stan and Denise Smart were able to obtain the attention of reporters and law enforcement officials, as well as that of members of the San Luis Obispo community. Telling is Stan Smart's extensive rolodex with names of journalists from around the state of California, as well as of Cal Poly and law enforcement personnel (Smart 1998). The Smart's family class location provided them access, and this translated into ongoing media coverage and an increasingly favorable image of their daughter, culminating in the first-year anniversary story discussed above.

Class mattered in another significant manner as well. In San Luis Obispo there was little criticism of local stakeholders who represented the community's elite. Donohue, Tichenor, and Olien (1995) call this tendency the "guard dog perspective," and argue that media serve as sentries for powerful groups in a community. San Luis Obispo media did little to challenge local law enforcement. Nor did they take to task one of their community's largest employers—the local university. So while Cal Poly police arguably mishandled the case by treating Kristin as a runaway, the *Telegram-Tribune* glossed over Smart family criticisms. It was not until eight months later, when the Smarts filed a wrongful death suit against Cal Poly in January 1997, that the *Telegram-Tribune*'s coverage reflected any disapproval of how the university had handled Kristin's disappearance: "The suit . . . also claims that Cal Poly did not provide a safe environment for Smart, and then botched the investigation into her disappearance" (January 24, 1997). A month later, a Superior Court judge dismissed Cal Poly from the lawsuit, and Denise Smart expressed her dissatisfaction at the end of a story that ran on the inside of the local section:

> I find it real difficult that Cal Poly can hide under this umbrella of failing to act correctly—it's hard to except that . . . It's kind of like firefighters who don't go to a fire. Sure the house can burn down after they've done everything they can do. But what happened here is comparable to firefighters not even bother to respond. If they don't go to the fire, that's a liability. (February 27, 1997)

With the lawsuit out of the way, the paper returned to its "sentry" coverage of Cal Poly, consistent with its approach to local law enforcement.

In contrast, local Syracuse media—albeit belatedly—questioned how April's case had been handled and were quick to place the blame on others than themselves. The *Herald-Journal* ran a story on August 2, 1996, head-lined, "Father Angry SU Didn't Do More to Find Daughter," in which Herman Gregory maintained that April would have received more attention had she been white and wealthy. The same story reported that the Urban League was stepping in to "create some awareness to try to help locate her. . . . The com-munity really didn't respond early on." Indeed, Syracuse University failed to publicize that April Gregory was missing until June 15, 1996, when the Uni-versity posted fliers about her disappearance.

Later that week on August 7, 1996, the *Post-Standard* followed-up in an editorial which not only pointed to race and class as factors in the amount of attention the case attracted, but included the media as part of the problem: "Picture her as the daughter of a wealthy Cazenovia, Skaneateles or Fayet-teville businessman. Now picture her as a cute little blond. How differently would SU, the police agencies and the media have handled the situation?"

A month later, when *Unsolved Mysteries* aired an episode that included April's disappearance, a *Post-Standard* editorial again questioned the lack of attention, but this time failed to find the media culpable:

> Thus far, law enforcers and university officials have been stymied in their search. Their failure has invited some to ask: Have authorities proceed with due diligence? Is there a double standard—unintentional perhaps—in the energy de-voted to the case of this missing young African-American woman, in contrast to missing persons who happen to be more affluent, or white? (*Post-Standard*, September 20, 1996, A10)

At the news conference that SU held when police discovered April's body on November 19, 1997, a local reporter once again raised this issue with the university's public information officer:

> Reporter: Questions are being raised about the intensity. That it wasn't as in-tense as if this person had been white or had lived in the suburbs, or if she had been from out of state living at SU. But the perception is that because she was an African-American living in the city attending SU, somehow it wasn't given the positive attention that it would have otherwise.
> SU PIO: You mean by the PD (Police Department)?
> Reporter: By the PD and SU.
> SU PIO: SU, as I indicated, did everything within its authority to try and locate this young woman. In so far as the behavior or activities of the PD, are better di-rected there. But from the outset, we had a very cooperative relationship with them.

Despite questioning how SU and the Syracuse police department handled the case, the Syracuse newspapers engaged in no enterprise reporting that would have challenged the dominant power structure. For example, Herman

Gregory, April's father, maintained throughout that he had tried to notify police of her disappearance. Yet no police report was filed until June 2, 1996. The disparity left readers wondering.

## CONCLUSION

It is apparent from the above analysis that local media treated the disappearances of April Gregory and Kristin Smart very differently. In these two instances, class appeared to influence the coverage of the missing girls in three respects: (1) the amount of coverage varied with class location, (2) the mediated image of each girl was constructed in keeping with her class location, race, and gender, and (3) while the media outlets analyzed here exhibited little enterprise reporting, media in the smaller media market were particularly loath to question the dominant power structure.

Of significance, analyzing media content, while helpful, tells only part of the story. A look at what is happening behind the scenes helps to illuminate how class influences the reportage. Media savvy parents are able to capitalize on their class location and influence the media agenda because reporters want to help them. While this tendency may be most apparent in a relatively small media market such as San Luis Obispo, California, it is noteworthy that the Smarts were successful in obtaining state and national coverage as well. Moreover, we witnessed this same phenomenon with the disappearance of Elizabeth Smart (no relation) six years after Kristin Smart went missing.

However, this analysis highlights the inaccuracy of pointing to a single factor as responsible for whether a missing girl becomes news, and how she is characterized once she does. Rather, while it is indisputable that class matters, the media coverage and practices analyzed here further reflect the intersectionality of race and gender. "Race and gender oppressions do not build on each other in any simple additive way"; each woman is "positioned" in her race (Brenner 2000, 294). Perhaps inevitable, then, is that media workers and audiences view a missing girl (and her family) through the lens of her *social* location. For example, not only was April Gregory's employment at McDonald's consistent with a working class location, it was also consistent with the labor history of black women. Similarly, not only is Stan Smart a school principal, he is first white and male. These factors conjoin to place him in a particular social location that grants access to media workers and law enforcement.

Brenner (2000) calls for the inclusion of class in intersectional analyses of race and gender; the opposite is comparably necessary. Class location alone will not predict whether media coverage of a missing child parallels that the Department of Justice (1998) stipulates as so critical. The social hierarchies that confront crime victims are inclusive of race, gender, and class (Madriz 1997). When it comes to covering missing girls, it appears news media are inclined to reproduce these hierarchies.

# REFERENCES

Bondy, Colleen. Personal communication to author, August 17, 1998.

Brenner, J. 2000. *Women and the politics of class*. New York: Monthly Review Press.

Department of Justice. 1998. *When your child is missing. A family survival guide*. Retrieved January 27, 2003; http://ojjdp.ncjrs.org:80/pubs/childismissing/contents .html.

Donohue, G. A., Tichenor, P. J., and Olien, C. N. 1995. A guard dog perspective on the role of the media. *Journal of Communication* 45: 115–32.

Dykstera, Danna. Personal communication to author, August 17, 1997.

Madriz, E. 1997. *Nothing bad happens to good girls: Fear of crime in women's lives*. Berkeley: University of California Press.

Maier, T. W. 2002. Data missing on missing children. *Insight*, September 23, 16.

Meyers, M. 1997. *News coverage of violence against women: Engendering blame*. Thousand Oaks, Calif.: Sage.

Smart, S. 1998. Personal communication to author, August 10, 1998.

# 11

## "Trailer Park Trash": News, Ideology, and Depictions of the American Underclass

*Joseph C. Harry*

As a newspaper reporter in central Florida during the 1980s, I once wrote a story about a mobile home development being built on land formerly used to mine phosphate. I characterized the development as "basically a trailer park being built over reclaimed phosphate pits." The story was published and a few readers, including the mobile home park developers, complained of my characterization of their development as a trailer park. That terminology, they said, carried negative connotations associated with the low class, the uneducated, and the unemployed that stereotypically evoke an association with a widely used term in media discourse, "trailer trash" or "trailer park trash." The complainers didn't actually use those phrases, but the implication was clear. The publisher of my newspaper was concerned. He reminded me that mobile home ad sales in our newspaper were at risk. I was required to run a correction characterizing a mobile home park as *different* from a trailer park. I thought at the time that my (mis)characterization was purely descriptive, not evaluative. And though I never thought much about this episode afterwards, on reflection it seems a clear example of how news-media depictions pertaining (accurately or not) to an element of a particular social class were discursively deployed and culturally contested.

People who live in trailer parks have long been derided as the lowest socioeconomic group, defined by their perceived social standing—as members of the "underclass"—and by what are believed to be a set of corresponding cultural habits and interests. A scan of any number of newspaper articles in recent years will give a flavor of the particular kind of stereotyping related to trailer park residents. For example, the *Atlanta-Journal and Constitution* of November 1991 begins: "For a generation, tin-walled homes

hoisted onto stacks of concrete blocks were the definitive homestead for the
rural South's rednecks. The modern-day version of the shotgun shack, trailers were considered magnets for tornadoes, poor white trash, and macaroni
and cheese."

Although the above article uses this imagery to then discuss how "mobile homes" are coming into their own as acceptable housing, it nonetheless differentiates a mobile home from a trailer. By so doing, it upholds a
derisive cultural stereotype even as, through objective reporting, it attempts to explain and in some ways even defend such a lifestyle. Trailer
park trash, in the standard usage, is a code word for low-class white
people.

In this chapter I perform a class analysis of newspapers by using "trailer
trash" as a textual *marker*, or indicator, of class bias in newspaper stories.
The phrase functions, in other words, as a class-generated metaphor that
motivates a certain stereotyped perception about a typically reviled class-
segment in America. In my analysis, the trailer trash phrase serves as a discursive entry point for class analysis (Resnick and Wolff 1987) as it occurs
within a segment of the mass media—daily newspaper accounts. I qualitatively analyze roughly one hundred American and British newspaper stories
from the past few years as a way of understanding how the trailer trash
metaphor is currently deployed, although these are part of nearly 1,000 news
articles (available through the Lexis-Nexis search engine) that use the same
terminology, which stem back as far as 1979.

The chapter attempts to demonstrate how class as a discursive-economic
category—class as metasign (Hodge and Kress 1988)—is useful in theorizing
the complex, contradictory, overdetermined relationship between class and
news-media interpretations of class issues. I take the position that class,
however else it might be understood, is fundamentally (though by no means
reductively) an *economic* category that, as entry point for textual analysis,
also functions as a *discursive*-economic category, overdetermined by and
articulated within other discursive frameworks of *cultural* (meaning centered), *political* (legal-juridical), and *natural* (personal, environmental)
social relations (Resnick and Wolff 1987; Diskin and Sandler 1993).[1] Because
a class analysis of newspaper articles is centered most fundamentally in the
texts themselves, a major determining force in the analysis will be the cultural category, the domain of meaning and sense making.

In the above sense class can be read as a *metasign*, a lens through which
trailer trash as key metaphor, deployed via a series of textual markers (related terms, phrases, images, and assumptions), constructs a consistent
stereotype and ideology about American "low-class" culture. Largely through
humor and irony, news discourse about "trailer park" life works as an ideological marker of class difference, providing journalists and columnists a
shrewd, socially sanctioned means of sustaining ideological domination
against a wildly caricatured class fraction.

## NOTIONS OF CLASS

Class as explanatory concept is notoriously resistant to any stable definition. From a broadly sociological standpoint it tends to function as both economic determinant and a way to categorize persons as belonging to certain social levels (Clark and Lipset 2001). Given the postindustrial nature of contemporary capitalism, and the ability of members of a lower-class order moving "higher up" the economic scale to middle or upper-middle classes, debates continue as to whether class analysis even remains relevant—whether classes are still even meaningfully definable (Clark and Lipset 2001; Hout, Brooks, and Manza 2001). From a postmodernist or post-Marxist viewpoint, class is but one category (and not necessarily the most important one) among other categories such as gender or ethnicity (Laclau and Mouffe 1985). In this latter framework, class, gender, and ethnicity are not clearly differentiated but rather function as hegemonic and counterhegemonic discursive points or "sutures" of contestation, each working sometimes against and sometimes within a ruling political order, the latter of which itself is seen as a discursive, hegemonic force. Class in this perspective is at best a problematic category. In traditional Marxist analysis, classes are seen as being created by a capitalist social formation's exploitative economic base (infrastructure), which functions as the determinant force dictating ("in the last instance") the formation and flow of ideas in corresponding cultural, political, and ideological spheres of the social superstructure. Here, the exploitative nature behind the capitalist extraction of surplus value from workers (who labor well beyond the amount of time required to supply their own needs for subsistence wages, thus working to supply owners with excess profits) is seen to lead to social class differences, thus social fragmentation and discord. The result, on this view, is social alienation and the commodification of social life itself, in which everything, from common products to the most sacrosanct social beliefs, is for sale as yet another market commodity.

The news media, as large-scale, for-profit companies in the business of selling a cultural product, *news*, are in this sense not dramatically different from any other capitalist organization. However, cultural products have an added dimension—they are meaningful commodities; they carry with them a specifically ideological quality. The communications media function as ideological signifying forces (alongside others, such as the school system, churches, the family, the legal and political systems) that collectively serve as superstructural social forces, each one of which is, however, relatively autonomous in how it may articulate its own ideological messages within a given social formation (Althusser 1972; Hall 1985). Hall (1985), accepting Althusser's model of overdetermination (if not his full-blown theory of ideology) reminds us that there is "no necessary correspondence" between any particular element of a social formation (economic, political, ideological) and corresponding forms of consciousness (Hall 1985). This idea is important to keep in mind, because it means that even though we may read class as *economic*, a person's relative class position does not guarantee he or she will think or act in ways that can be reductively explained by some alleged class position. Class can be theorized as a fundamentally economic category and thus as the defining feature of social analysis, but should also be viewed as a *discursive* category, not necessarily more determining in social analysis than are other analytical categories with which it interacts, such as the *political*, the *economic,* or the *natural* (Resnick and Wolff 1987). Such an overdetermined form of social analysis will therefore not render a causal explanation of a given social phenomenon. Instead, the attempt is to bring out the dominant features of a social phenomenon, as an overdetermined, contradictory form of explanation.

Within this analytical framework class can most succinctly be defined as "not a name for a particular form of consciousness but a way to produce a coherent structure of the economic space" (Diskin and Sandler 1993, 31). Class analysis via textual interpretation, then, can be viewed as a process of identifying meaningful classifications or textual markers for class, the analysis of which will also reveal the exploitation and alienation existing between different class segments. Such textual analysis can reveal how one class can be seen (linguistically) as dominating another, or even how members of one class can work (intentionally or not) to promote their own domination within their own perceived class segment. When class is linked in this way, discursively, to structures of power and domination, then class analysis also becomes a form of ideological analysis (Thompson 1990; Althusser 1972), or what Bakhtin characterized as the "class struggle in language" (Hall 1985).

## A SEMIOTIC PERSPECTIVE

Class analysis in this chapter is joined with a related, text-based method known as social-semiotics, which views meaning as reflective, and a refraction of, social structure, which itself is assumed to be conflictual, contradictory, and always in flux. Social semiotics takes this as the state of reality behind the production of social discourses and texts, made evident in Voloshinov's notion of the "multi-accentuality of the sign" (Hodge and Kress 1988). "He sees language as normally dialogic, as the site of competing voices and competing interests" (83). Within this perspective, semiosis is defined as the social production of meaning that functions by linking discursive reality (the semiosic social world) to a designated referential reality (a world referred to), the latter of which exists materially in the form of a mimetic text or texts (Hodge and Kress 1988). Within the social-semiotic construct, a text is simply a string of social discourses pertaining to one or more related topics, and brought together (articulated) in a certain format or genre. Any text or set of texts must be generally situated within an immediate (synchronic), and sometimes historical (diachronic) social context, either one of which constitutes a text's logonomic plane (Hodge and Kress 1988)—the practical, cultural, and ideological domain of the "known categories and rules" (266), related to and forming any genre or text type. Additionally, within any text one will find instances of metasigns, a class of sign composed of transparent markers, or "signifiers of classifiers and classifications" (264), existing as a "cluster" of related terms (79). Once these textual markers are identified as corresponding to a certain metasign, then the analysis of ideology is possible because in the social-semiotic view, texts are strings or traces of social discourse constituted by and within an identifiable social structure, the latter of which is, by definition, ideological. The text can then be seen as "declaring a specific version of social relations. The meanings they communicate are an important instance of the ideology of the group concerned" (79).

Texts contain and express ideological schemas (individual perspectives), articulated as ideological "complexes" (266). An ideological complex is "a set of different and contradictory ideological schemas which serve and express the interests of a single group," generated by the discursive (social-structural) plane and expressed in the "mimetic" (textual) plane ( 266). We can view class, then, as the metasign-in-dominance in newspaper stories about "trailer trash," and the latter phrase, as well as a variety of synonyms, functioning as textual markers—similar metaphors serving as classifiers for the metasign, *class*.

Trailer trash, as a phrase, functions as what might be called the chief textual marker of the class metasign, with related phrases, imagery, and assumptions serving a support function, as code words for the same class-based social construction. (Trailer park trash designates, it should be noted, only one of many class fractions under the class metasign—in the present case, a lower or underclass—but the metaphor cannot be understood without its overdetermined and contradictory relation to, and differentiation from, other class designations, such as upper or middle class.)

In what follows I sketch out, synchronically, the immediately sociocultural and ideological framework within which trailer park trash as a key metaphor for the class metasign can be more fully understood. I then describe distinct but interrelated thematic categories within which textual markers for the trailer trash metaphor were deployed in newspaper articles.

## SOCIAL, CULTURAL, IDEOLOGICAL CONTEXT BEHIND "TRAILER PARK TRASH"

The trailer park is a "culturally marginal site in America," associated with the low class as "white trash," and those who consider themselves of the middle class tend to use the "white trash" designation to distinguish themselves from the "lower orders" (Thomas and Enders 2000). Trailer park trash is more or less synonymous with white trash, the latter term linked to a vision of "unpopular culture," a domain existing apart or outside of "mainstream" culture

(Hartigan 1997). White trash and, by extension, the trailer trash metaphor also can serve as coded forms of racism (Wilson 2002), in that both terms designate a certain fraction of people as fundamentally different from upper-echelon groups. Race and class exist almost invisibly to shape constructions of whiteness and to promote the idea of America as a classless society, when in fact the exact opposite is true (see, e.g., the collection of essays exploring this theme in Wray and Newitz 1997). The seeming invisibility of race (at least in relation to whiteness), and especially the putative invisibility of class, provides an especially fertile ground from which ideological, stereotyped notions of race and class spring.

Trailer park residents and "white trash" are frequently given a regional, specifically, a Southern character (Bouson 2001). This was quite evident in newspaper depictions, where "white-trash" and trailer park residents often are portrayed as virtually synonymous with being a Southern "redneck," and with other stereotypical markers of a decidedly Southern kind of poverty, linked thematically to certain bodily and behavioral characteristics as well as to a limited range of musical, food, fashion, and general lifestyle preferences. For example, a movie review in the University of California-Berkeley *Daily Californian* student newspaper (April 16, 2001) begins: "What do you think of when you think of trailer trash—the smell, the filth, the inbreeding, the stupidity, the lack of teeth, the abject poverty, the horrible hair . . . country music, needless fist fights, infidelity, unwanted children, deadbeat dads, jalopies, or the fact that they cannot for the life of them find actual homes." This depiction is a nearly perfect microcosm of the range of interrelated discourse markers regularly found in hundreds of newspaper stories framed within the trailer trash/class metasign.

The real-world referent for trailer park is actually an overdetermined discursive phenomenon. What are often called trailer parks are better described as "mobile homes" or, the most current usage, "manufactured housing"—the latter of two forms of housing generally not being set on wheels. Thus estimates of how many people live in manufactured housing will include those living in mobile homes or trailers. An estimated 8 percent of the U.S. population lives in "manufactured housing," and the industry represents a nearly $37 billion-a-year business (*Financial Times*, July 28, 2000). A brief examination of this article by the *Financial Times*—a London-based newspaper—provides useful context for understanding the larger discursive terrain within which most news depictions of mobile home life thrive.

This article, a well-sourced, expertly reported piece, details how the Arkansas governor was planning to move into a "triple-wide mobile home" while the governor's mansion was being repaired. The article focuses, nevertheless, on a range of common stereotypes that produce an uneasy mix of objective reporting and cultural derision, almost in the same breath. The writer refers to the "age-old stereotype that Arkansas trailer parks are full of backward hillbillies who will do anything for a quick buck." The story then introduces the phrase "trailer trash" as if it is well known: "The 'trailer trash' tag has now been resuscitated with the news that Mike Huckabee, the current Republican governor" will be moving into a mobile home, the article reports. It then goes on to report that Arkansas residents "are getting slightly tired of the characterization that trailer parks are filled with uneducated, low-income transients who can only afford to live in the tin-can shelters." "Tin-can shelters" is the reporter's own word choice, not that of any quoted source at this point in the article. The reporter quotes a 1996 study by the Michigan-based Foremost Insurance Company in which the average manufactured home buyer is said to be between 40 and 49, and is a white-collar professional. This functions, in the news discourse, as a way of contrasting the stereotypical trailer park resident from what, it appears, is a changing socio-political landscape of more upscale, better-educated "manufactured home" dwellers. This is one of several newspaper articles written in just the last few years that in some ways attempts to correct an "age-old stereotype" about manufactured-home residents, but which simultaneously invokes those same stereotypes as a means of shooting them down.

About 20 percent of the roughly one hundred articles analyzed for how they deploy the class metasign were of the above nature, that is, examples of the "objective" news reporting subgenre, in which the reporter is expected to remain relatively anonymous. In these types of articles, objectivity and neutrality function as class-based, professional norms that shape news writing and delimit it as standardized, routine practice (Tuchman 1978; Fishman 1980) in which sources are gathered and quoted, without the overt evaluative intervention of the reporter's own views. However, reporters can rhetorically, and covertly, insert their own views by having them voiced by official, quoted sources as "verbal reactions" (van Dijk 1998). This form of objective reporting can also be seen as a mechanism of social control (Tichenor et al. 1980; Ericson et al. 1989) in that an "official" world is constructed from sanctioned, authorized sources. In these ways the journalism profession, following its own ideology of objectivity, itself sustains a class-based division, constructing a world where middle- and upper-class sources, for the most part, do the talking—in this case about a lower-class fraction.

The rest of the news articles using the trailer trash metaphor were feature and entertainment-page stories or opinion pieces. Unlike objective news reporting, these "soft news" subgenres allow writers (especially columnists) relatively free rein to insert their own caricatures, commentary, and colorful evaluations as a means of deploying any number of trailer trash stereotypes. Regardless of the news genre, class divisions are systematically constructed by journalists, who represent middle- and upper-class fractions (depending on their respective economic and cultural circumstances) and work for newspapers that represent a range of overdetermined class positions, depending on a newspaper's given audience and set of advertising interests.

## HOW TRAILER TRASH WAS USED: NEWSPAPER EXAMPLES

The trailer trash marker, as key metaphor for the class metasign, was discursively deployed in what can be thought of as three different types of cultural markers, or classifiers: personal characteristics, cultural characteristics, and cultural icons. The first (personal characteristics) is linked to someone's general appearance and fashion choices. The second (cultural characteristics) is associated with lifestyle and behavior practices, and a generalized cultural environment, typically including violence markers (guns, fights, wife beating); being jailed; being on welfare; being Southern and a hillbilly or redneck; liking country or heavy metal music; being fond of alcohol or drugs, souped-up cars, and unhealthy food. The third category (cultural icons) refers to such things as famous media and pop music personalities, television shows, movies, restaurants, and certain upscale fashion items—all of which serve as cultural standard-bearers for the stereotyped projection of a kind of low-class, kitsch culture. These three broad categorizations can and typically do function in two ways, and often simultaneously in the same article: either as straightforward derision by one class-fraction toward another (as a spatial metaphor, from the top looking down); or as high irony or farce, as a wry celebration and appropriation of perceived lower-class characteristics by a higher-class fraction (as a spatial metaphor, bringing a lower-level element upward toward a higher cultural use).

Personal characteristics were grouped into a relatively small number of markers pertaining to both physical and fashion appearance. Specifically, the most frequent fashion markers were hair (big, bleached, mullet), clothing (tight, tacky, gaudy, skimpy, cheap), makeup (too much, bright colors), and head gear (caps); the most often used personal markers were teeth (missing), filth and dirt, stupidity or slowness, craziness, deceitfulness, sex obsession, and incest.[2] Fashion markers were most often linked to women, especially in the context of a kind of sexualized femininity associated with tight-fitting or gaudy clothing overexposing a woman's bodily features. More personal characteristics were linked to both genders, but missing teeth and dirt were associated only with men. An interesting difference in the way women and men generally were depicted is that women tended to be lampooned as tawdry sex objects, desirable only in a perverted hyperreal sense, as fast-talking, flaming red-lipped, big-bosomed, bleach-haired plastic dolls, while the standard construction of trailer park men was as dumb, fat, dirty and slovenly, as the exact opposite, in other words, of the "done-up" look linked to the caricatured trailer park woman.[3]

In an opinion piece in the March 5, 2001, *New York Observer*, the writer, through irony tinged with derision, attempts to defend life in trailer parks by claiming that trailer park residents he's familiar with "all had either their own teeth or reasonable facsimiles; nobody was married to a blood relative; their clothes were clean (although unfashionable enough to inspire screams of disdain on Seventh Avenue); and they spoke with great fondness about organized labor and the need for unions."

The hypersexualized nature of the trailer trash woman comes through clearly in an entertainment feature about actress Robin Wright Penn's role in the film *White Oleander.* The September 23, 2002, *Chicago Sun-Times* quotes Wright's characterization of her own character: "Literally, I had five days to prepare to play the character of this trampy trailer trash mom named Starr."

She characterizes her role as a busty, lusty woman: "Blame it on the tight clothes and the big hair and makeup . . . I also have a theory that anytime a woman is wearing white high-heeled pumps that you just think certain things on her are bigger than what might be true."

The writer then offers her own characterization, saying Penn "plays a trailer trash type to the hilt with flimsy shirts cut down to her navel and skirts hiked up to her underwear." The class metaphor here equates low-class women with cheap sexuality, while with respect to depictions of men, the rhetorical tactic is to tie low class to "low life." In either case the result is the same: Men and women living in mobile home parks equate with trashiness—trashy sexuality in the case of women, and trash as dirt or filth when associated with men. Here the *Sun-Times* writer engages in another frequent rhetorical tactic, in which "trailer trash" is offered unproblematically, without quote marks or further explanation; thus ideologically the phrase stands on its own as an already unified, coherent, commonsense category, already full of meaning—a generalized marker of the class metasign.

The May 5, 2002, edition of the *Los Angeles Times Magazine*, in a style column, begins with the headline: "For Decades a Certain Eye Shadow was for Teens and Trailer Parks. But Things are About to Change." The writer comments that today, "even" women of "style and maturity" are wearing blue and other brightly colored makeup. Perhaps more interesting is that nowhere else in the article is the "trailer park" phrase used—only in the headline, which, combined with a lead sentence, collectively serves the linguistic function, in journalistic copy, of signaling importance and framing a reader's thematic entrance into a story (van Dijk 1988). Thus another example (one of dozens) of use of the trailer trash metaphor as a stand-alone, ideological category, a divisive marker of class difference.

A *Wall Street Journal* lifestyle article about the advertising "recession," and how lower television ad rates make possible the selling of "lowbrow" products, begins with the lead sentence: "The ad recession is making television's beachfront property available at trailer park prices." Nowhere else in the story is the key discursive marker used, yet it is connected to synonymous markers: "Second-tier commercials of all sorts are getting ample play, even during time that had been the exclusive selling field for blue-chip brands such as Ford, Coca-Cola and Kraft. NBC executives have privately joked about the tacky ads on its nightly news program."

The American trailer trash stereotype travels globally, as many examples were available from papers in Great Britain, such as the following from the *Scotsman* (November 18, 2001): "It wasn't so long ago that country music was the genre that dared not speak its name outside the trailer park. Confessing to liking it was akin to admitting to a taste for wife beating and bumper stickers that read, 'They'll take my gun when they prise it from my cold dead fingers.'"

Other than in the lead sentence, "trailer park" appears nowhere else in the story. The headline "Wild in the Country" associates trailer park life with a kind of craziness or bizarre lifestyle that was a frequent image in many other reports.

References to pop stars, TV shows, and other popular culture phenomena were some of the most prevalent uses across articles, and these markers were frequently linked with stereotyped cultural practices, behaviors, and personal characteristics. Jerry Springer, Rikki Lake, and the Jenny Jones daytime talk shows were common code words for low class. A movie review in the New York *Daily News* (November 16, 2001) says the movie characters would have been more enjoyable to watch on a real-world talk show: "But watching this lowlife couple smack each other up on the Jerry Springer Show would have been far more entertaining."

A book review in the *Tampa Tribune* (October 21, 2001) begins: "Florida's own special literary genre, full to the brim with the down and dirty, bizarrely populated, weird and wonderful world of trailer parks, seedy motels, motorcycle mamas and tattered remnants of Old South aristocracy, needs to shuffle over a notch to make room for another contender for the Trash Tiara."

A favorable review of a documentary ("People Like Us: Social Class in America"), in *The Gazette* of Montreal, states in the reporter's own words, "The rich have more money, better teeth, nicer manners, dogs, horses, Madras pants and a house in Nantucket." "Southernness" as a class marker was often used in articles, especially ones featuring former President Bill Clinton and Paula Jones, who sued him for sexual harassment. An opinion piece in the lifestyle section of the *Boston Herald* (November 15, 1998) notes that Jones was "excoriated" by "the Beautiful People" as "trailer park trash." The article is written as a sustained piece of Southern-accented irony. The author notes, sardonically, that without Jones, Clinton's critics would have had little to complain about—"none of them could have turned this presidency into a maudlin country-music song."

A column in the London *Guardian* (January 20, 1998) begins in the second paragraph: "Look at Paula Jones. Ever since some snobby little oik said she looked like trailer park trash, with all the big-haired, short-skirted, overpainted, promiscuous and 'common' connotations that phrase carries in the famously class-free United States of America, she has been trying hard to be someone else."

The column is interesting in its sarcastic assessment of America as a class-free society, even as it relies on some of the most common discursive markers that prove just the opposite. A column in the *New York Observer* (February 25, 2002) that criticizes Bill and Hillary Clinton's behavior in the White House concludes, "For all their self-righteous oratory, their actions are pure trailer trash. Do these people have no shame?" As is so often the case, the writer uses the trailer trash metaphor as a transparent marker of class difference—comparing how one is supposed to act (in the White House) with how another class (never otherwise mentioned in the article) *always* acts.

Tonya Harding, the former ice-skating star who fell from grace, was one of many celebrities thematically linked to the trailer trash class marker, as in the *Boston Herald* (March 6, 1994): "Say this about Tonya Harding. She never lived down her media image as the trailer park trash trollop who could do no right."

Along with Harding, many other cultural standard-bearers for trailer trash as a key class-based metaphor emerged, such as Eminem, Jerry Springer, Kid Rock, Britney Spears, Jenny Jones, Rikki Lake, and Dolly Parton. Whether referring to daytime talk shows, auto shows and other cultural events, or pop stars, the surrounding imagery evokes a consistent sense of cultural cheapness or tackiness—on the one hand, as a purposeful cultural ploy embraced by the celebrities themselves, or on the other hand as the essential, natural state of their millions of fans. Here, self-identification seems to function simultaneously as a defensive badge and as ironic self-mockery, or sometimes just as self-defensiveness alone, as in numerous articles where writers mention that manufactured-housing residents (as well as industry representatives) want to make it clear that they are not "trailer park" residents. As one writer noted, passing along the standard industry defense: "Please don't call them trailer parks." Sometimes residents or representatives of manufactured housing expressed surprise and bemusement at how they perceived themselves. The *Chicago Sun-Times* (February 9, 2001) does a lengthy, well-researched news report on the higher-quality, higher-priced kind of manufactured housing emerging in the Chicago area. The article quotes a single mother, Terry Nelson, who's commenting on her fourteen-year-old daughter: "I asked her if she ever got teased about living in a mobile home and she said no, but the kids expressed surprise that she was so smart and well-dressed," said Nelson.

Later in the article another woman, Darla Gomez, is quoted about her hesitancy in taking up residence in a mobile home park: "I was very hesitant because I have to admit I had this preconceived idea of trailers and the kind of people who live in trailers," she said.

Here residents confront their own long-standing class-based stereotypes and express surprise at the different reality they encountered after living in manufactured housing. Interestingly, the article—for all its comprehensive reporting and objective tone—does not avoid falling into derisive stereotyping. The article's headline frames the story with a "low-class" tinge by purposely using bad grammar: "Ain't what they used to be; now called manufactured housing, mobile homes are bigger, sturdier." The lead sentence completes the stilted image: "Comedians still refer to them as places where trailer trash live."

As was the standard practice in many other articles, the trailer trash key metaphor was used nowhere else in the story. Thus it could ideologically conjure a derogatory image without a hint of irony—made more potent, in the above case, by the bad grammar of the headline. In this way, even when residents of manufactured homes attempt to shoot down damaging class stereotypes, a newspaper can (intentionally or not) revive them.

Ironic self-deprecation was a more common response. An article about the annual "Redneck Games" in the London *Mirror* (August 4, 2001), quotes a colorful source: "You wanna know what a real redneck is?" demands Big Papa Plump, a 41-year-old, 24-stone, sweating man mountain. "It's a guy who loves beer and loves the South, whose grass has grown so high he can't see his lawnmower, mosta his truck is hanging from a tree and his dog cusses at you instead of barks."

The writer describes the event as the "Trailer Trash Olympics," and its participants as follows: "The men who gather here love their guns and fishing almost as much as they love their sisters. They have few teeth, large tattoos, droopy-arsed jeans, oily caps and oilier mullets."

Others are described as "slow-drawling Southerners who have come from all over the state for one reason only—to get drunk and throw themselves face first into a mud pit."

> The women—big ladies with even bigger hair—have come too . . . many are decked out in tight denim shorts, Dixie flag bikinis, hefty rings and garishly-painted long nails. Several have gone for bleach-blonde perms teamed with Farrah flicks, while slack bellies spill over short shorts and cleavages hang somewhere around the midriff. All the women overflow with Southern friendliness.

This overt stereotyping finds a more coolly ironic telling in writers commenting on various restaurants, cookbooks, movies, stage shows, nightclubs, and fashion pieces that all have acculturated "trailer trash" as a chic marker of upper-class irony. An article in *Cleveland Scene* magazine (December 25, 2002) declares in its headline, regarding how hip the drinking of Pabst beer has become in fashionable Cleveland neighborhoods: "A trailer trash beer wins over the ultra-hip crowd." Nowhere else in the article is "trailer trash" used, but it goes on to make the familiar linkages: Pabst, the article tells us, is sold as a "low-life special," "there's a sense of authenticity to it," and drinkers value the beer "for its 'retro' and 'white trash' vibe."

The print media featured many articles about a new Christian Dior "trailer trash" handbag collection, in bright red and green colors and in the shape of Cadillacs and other objects, each one selling for hundreds or thousands of dollars, and which function as an ironic appropriation of a stereotyped low-class lifestyle. A writer in the *Los Angeles Times* (February 1, 2002), notes that critics attended a fashion show where the handbags were on display: "Critics unfamiliar with the trappings of lower-class America had missed the wonderful irony in the show, which glorified the unheralded status symbols of an often invisible class."

## CONCLUSION: SPECULATIONS TOWARD THEORY

The examples selected above from American and British newspaper reports, mainly written in the past few years, collectively provide a common set of class-driven themes devolving around the trailer park trash key metaphor, all of which connote associations with the class metasign. The goal was to focus on more recent cases of the sign and its markers as a means of giving a sense of contemporary usage. As such, these examples provide a selective, partial, historically limited but telling set of ideas about how newspapers sustain class divisions in America.

Several conclusions can be drawn from the selected evidence. Although an economic category, the class metasign is itself invisible. Trailer park residents and their perceived lifestyles are depicted principally through a cultural lens, in the form of caricatured habits, beliefs, and practices. Cultural categorization, deployed via tropes of irony, the ridicule of parody, or the farcical, carnivalesque mode of pastiche, work to strongly overdetermine the underlying economic reality of class. Indeed, the carnival in Bakhtin's (1968) sense, as a collapsing within usually distinct social classes of official barriers between upper and lower, between high and low culture, may help explain how, for example, "trailer park" or "trailer trash" class markers can today be reappropriated as hip, chic markers of more middle- or upper-class style. The carnival mentality, embodied by its central feature—laughter—is among other things "ambivalent: it is gay, triumphant, and at the same time mocking, deriding. It asserts and denies, it buries and revives. Such is the laughter of carnival" (Bakhtin 1968, 11–12). Whereas prior to the establishment of the Roman state, carnival and its purposeful, parodic transversal of serious and comic values was celebrated by everyone at all social levels, in the later "consolidated state and class structure" of society, carnival and its "comic forms" have gradually been transferred to a "nonofficial level," to become the expression of "folk culture" within a marketplace atmosphere (Bakhtin 1968, 6). Contemporary journalism's place as an essentially oral form of everyday communication, perhaps the most pervasive and important form of popular-cultural expression within the postmodern marketplace of ideas (Hartley 1996), would seem to provide a narrow but culturally sanctioned space for journalists to document trailer park life in all its carnivalesque guises, as various cobbled-together versions of real life in comic form, both through the voices of quoted sources and through a metaphoric chain of related terminology. In this way, journalists are allowed to temporarily cast aside much of their professional detachment to gleefully take part in the transgressive festivities of the carnival, while at the same time masking the bulk of their news discourse in the more-or-less official language of objective reporting, thereby marking themselves off from the "lower" classes and thus upholding their own putatively superior class position.

Rhetorically, the trailer trash key metaphor also functions as what Aristotle called an enthymeme, which masks a whole series of largely unspoken assumptions and propositions drawn from "everyday affairs" (Martin and Andersen 1968, 25). This is most evident in the repeated use of trailer trash or trailer park trash as stand-alone phrases marking an already understood and accepted state of affairs, as terminology not requiring supplementation and distancing through quote marks or even source attribution. Headlines or lead sentences often use the metaphor to frame a reader's entry into and understanding of the story, but never use the phrase again anywhere else in the story—instead relying on various synonymous textual markers. This recurrent feature of the news discourse, namely, that so many stories offer no special explanation, no quotation marks, no attribution when invoking "trailer trash" as a stand-alone phrase, whether in headlines or in reporters' or columnists' articles, is a troubling reminder that class antagonism is a cultural and political reality alive and well in journalistic practice. The stand-alone status of trailer trash as key metaphor is also an example of how the objective rhetorical form of contemporary journalism may provide protective cover not only for irony— which for journalism can have both positive and negative effects (Glasser and Ettema 1993)—but for unquestioned assumptions to creep into depictions of reality, in the thinly veiled form of destructive tropes of parody, which serve mainly to ridicule and deride. In such a discursive move the reporter, unwittingly or not, maintains already long-standing class divisions that, one would hope, a more ethical journalism would seek to diminish rather than enlarge.

Trailer trash as class metasign is made visible only through its presence in metaphor, through its dispersions and inversions as discursive characteristics— via skewed cultural markers such as food, clothing, and behavior, and personal and media habits all linked garishly, stereotypically to a specific group of people—white people—unproblematically marked off as magically having these and a host of other clown-like characteristics, assumed class positions, and attendant views. In this way, journalists make the mistake (equating class position with mental beliefs) that the class analyst working within the overdetermination model should resist. As Grossberg and Slack remind us: "Subjectivity is endlessly displaced and the individual is continually fractured into multiple subject positions" (1985, 89). But in newspaper reports, "trailer park trash" always points directly to a certain kind of devalued, ridiculed character whose beliefs and practices are seen to flow directly from their perceived class roots.

The capitalist economy itself—class in its material presence, as the engine of exploitation, alienation, social division, and fragmentation within the social structure—always lurks quietly on the fringes, deployed, dispersed, and inverted only in and through its cultural markers. Class functions much like what

Jameson (1981) calls, in a related context, the political unconscious, the ghost-like "absent history" animating social life, present through its absence. As Althusser famously remarked, the economy may ultimately be determinant in the last instance, but the lonely hour of the last instance never quite seems to arrive.

The news media represent a variety of mostly white-dominated class fractions and related professional, economic interests—owners and key investors, national and multinational partners and subsidiary businesses, local and national advertisers, publishers, editors, reporters, and others—all collectively responsible for shaping and influencing the daily commodity, a good story. Thus news media depictions of a lower-class strata—even when those reports are framed in the rhetorical form of objective storytelling—reflect an uneasy discursive tension between the professional mandate for accuracy, balance and fairness, and the reality of commodification: the reality that cultural stereotypes are hard to avoid and may even be entertaining storytelling devices that will help generate audiences—at the risk, however, of targeting a more or less imagined community for systematic derision and ridicule. From an ideological-psychological view, the operational reality would seem to be one in which mostly white media owners and relatively well-off white journalists, in concocting blithely ironic and occasionally serious stories about trailer park life, end up trashing their own counterparts, the poor white trash, setting them up for a punishing run through the symbolic gauntlet—all in good fun. American and British news stories don't differ dramatically on this score, although the British papers are, if anything, even more prone to over-the-top caricatures, perhaps because of their greater geographic and cultural difference, and because the class system in Great Britain has always been more openly acknowledged.

Evidence in recent years shows manufactured housing is growing in popularity, quality, and respectability, due in part to a contracting U.S. economy, and this fact is often noted in many stories. But that line of thought is too often just as quickly abandoned in the rush to codify this type of housing in a convenient, derogatory framework that serves ultimately to sustain age-old, damaging class divisions at the heart of American life. The journalists' typical ploy, often perhaps unconscious, is to take a fragment of reality and make it a full-color cartoon.

In the end, such journalistic discourse of derision and ridicule—sometimes playful and ironic, sometimes straightforward, sometimes a conflicted mixture—is disturbing evidence of what may be the last gasp of official, class-generated prejudice in America.

## NOTES

1. "By economic processes we mean the production and distribution of the means of production and consumption for communities of human beings. By political processes we mean the design and regulation of power and authority in such communities. By cultural processes we mean the diverse ways in which human beings produce meanings

for their existence" (Resnick and Wolff 1987, 20). The "natural," for Resnick and Wolff, means everything from immediate life forces such as breathing and eating, to the surrounding environment, such as one's neighborhood, the air one breathes, and so forth. Each one of these categories must be constructed in discourse, and in analyzing a social phenomenon one attempts to discover which categories seem *most* determinant within the overall complex of *all* determining forces.

2. See Newitz and Wray (1997, 1–12) for a historical overview of how "white trash" as a cultural marker for lower-class whites evolved in America. The phrase historically has been a connotation for "poor, dirty, drunken, criminally minded, and sexually perverse people," and the "stereotypes of rural poor whites as incestuous and sexually promiscuous, violent, alcoholic, lazy, and stupid remain with us to this day" (2).

3. See Kipnis (1997) for a fanciful but interesting account of how "white trash" as cultural pastiche can function as ironic, parodic, hyperreal female sexuality within popular culture.

# REFERENCES

Althusser, L. 1972. *Lenin and philosophy and other essays*. New York: Monthly Review Press.

Bakhtin, M. 1968. *Rabelais and his world*. Cambridge, Mass.: MIT Press.

Bouson, J. Brooks. 2001. "You nothing but trash": White trash shame in Dorothy Allison's *Bastard out of Carolina: Southern Literary Journal* 34: 101–23.

Clark, T. N., and Lipset, S. M. 2001. Are social classes dying? In *The breakdown of class and politics: A debate on post-industrial stratification*, 39–54. Baltimore: Johns Hopkins University Press.

Diskin, J., and Sandler, B. 1993. Essentialism and the economy in the post-Marxist imaginary: Reopening the sutures. *Rethinking Marxism* 6, no. 3: 28–48.

Ericson, R.V., Baranek, P. M., and Chan, J. B. L. 1989. *Negotiating control: A study of news sources*. Toronto: University of Toronto Press.

Fishman, M. 1980. *Manufacturing the news*. Austin: University of Texas Press.

Glasser, T. L., and Ettema, J. S. 1993. When the facts don't speak for themselves: A study of the use of irony in daily journalism. *Critical Studies in Mass Communication* 10, 322–38.

Grossberg, L., and Slack, J. D. 1985. An introduction to Stuart Hall's essay. *Critical Studies in Mass Communication* 2: 87–90.

Hall, S. 1985. Signification, representation, ideology: Althusser and the post-structuralist debates. *Critical Studies in Mass Communication* 2: 91–114.

Hartigan, J. 1997. Unpopular culture: The case of "white trash." *Cultural Studies* 11: 316–28.

Hartley, J. 1996. *Popular reality: Journalism, modernity, popular culture*. London: Arnold.

Hodge, R., and Kress, G. 1988. *Social semiotics*. Ithaca, N.Y.: Cornell University Press.

Hout, M., Brooks, C., and Manza, J. 2001. The persistence of classes in post-industrial societies. In T. Nichols Clark and S. M. Lipset, eds., *The breakdown of class politics: A debate on post-industrial stratification,* 55–76. Baltimore: Johns Hopkins University Press.

Jameson, F. 1981. *The political unconscious: Narrative as a socially symbolic act.* Ithaca, N.Y.: Cornell University Press.

Kipnis, L. 1997. White trash girl: The interview. In M. Wray and A. Newitz, eds., *White trash: Race and class in America*, 113–30. New York: Routledge.

Laclau, E., and Mouffe, C. 1985. *Hegemony and socialist strategy.* London: Verso.

Martin, H. H., and Andersen, K. E., eds. 1968. *Speech communication: Analysis and readings.* Boston: Allyn & Bacon.

Newitz, A., and Wray, M. 1997. Introduction to *White trash: Race and class in America*, 1–12. New York: Routledge.

Resnick, S., and Wolff, R. 1987. *Knowledge and class.* Chicago: University of Chicago Press.

Thomas, J. B., and Enders, D. 2000. Bluegrass and white trash: A case study concerning the name "folklore" and class bias. *Journal of Folklore Research* 37, no. 1: 23–52.

Thompson, J. B. 1990. *Ideology and modern culture: Critical social theory in the age of mass communication.* Stanford: Stanford University Press.

Tichenor, P. J., Donohue, G. A., and Olien, C. N. 1980. *Community conflict and the press.* Beverly Hills, Calif.: Sage.

Tuchman, G. 1978. *Making news: A case study in the construction of reality.* New York: Free Press.

Van Dijk, T. A. 1988. *News as discourse.* Hillsdale, N.J.: Lawrence Erlbaum.

———. 1998. *Ideology: A multidisciplinary approach.* London: Sage.

Wilson, J. Z. 2002. Invisible racism: The language and ontology of "white trash." *Critique of Anthropology* 22, no. 4: 387–402.

Wray, M., and Newitz, A., eds. 1997. *White trash: Race and class in America.* New York: Routledge.

Wright, E. O. 1997. *Class counts: Comparative studies in class analysis.* Cambridge: Cambridge University Press.

# IV

# LABOR, WORKERS, AND NEWS

Class and labor are two topics that seem inexorably linked. In the United States many unions were founded to battle against long working hours, intolerable working conditions, and low wages. News organizations themselves are sites where workers toil and in some cases where workers have unionized. No volume on class and news would be complete without some consideration of these ideas. Historian Bonnie Brennen offers a history of the formation of the American Newspaper Guild, probably America's most successful union made up of journalists. Her study reveals something about the way in which news workers conceptualize their own class standing.

How journalists cover labor issues can also be telling when it comes to determining news organizations' stance toward class and class disputes. Christopher Martin examines how news organizations framed the UPS strike in 1997, and Laura Hapke uses a more recent event, the attack on the World Trade Center, to examine how the press constructs ideas about workers and unions.

# 12

## The Emergence of Class Consciousness in the American Newspaper Guild

*Bonnie Brennen*

Far from going too far, we haven't gone far enough in fighting for the guild. We cannot exist half slave and half-free. We cannot exist half-union and half non-union.

—Heywood Broun 1936

During an era of economic turmoil, daily newspapers in the United States confronted the pressures of standardization, through consolidations, mergers, and buyouts. Morning daily newspapers dwindled and by the 1930s many U.S. cities were left with a single daily newspaper. Newspaper content became increasingly standardized as chain newspapers shared story material and press associations and syndicates supplied many newspapers with identical news and feature information. Technological advances and changes encouraged the dissemination of news and information on a scale never previously available and the new medium of radio began to challenge the dominance of daily newspapers. Responding to the challenges of the Depression, journalists specialized in politics, business, labor, and economics and offered readers background information, interpretation, and commentary. Although reporters provided a critical link between the coverage of labor and economics and public perceptions of these issues, as a class of workers they had little power and lacked the economic benefits of other professions. Within this specific context, an emphasis on the development of the American Newspaper Guild provides insights into the class-based cultural, political, and economic realities of journalism during the 1930s and helps to understand the practice of news under the institutional constraints of corporate media control.

233

## COURTING THE BLUE EAGLE

Created to increase employment, enhance purchasing power, and aid economic recovery, Franklin D. Roosevelt's National Recovery Administration's (NRA) National Industrial Recovery Act of 1933 required industries to work with the federal government to set up maximum working hours, minimum wage standards, and fair practice codes. Employees were given the right to organize and bargain collectively, "free from the interference, restraint, or coercion of employers of labor, or their agents" (*A Handbook of NRA Laws, Regulations, Codes* 1933, 327). Those businesses in compliance with NRA regulations were given a stamp of approval symbolized by a Blue Eagle logo that could be publicly displayed. In negotiations with the newspaper industry, the Roosevelt administration bent to pressure by members of the American Newspaper Publishers Association (ANPA), and the daily newspaper section included key modifications to the temporary New Deal code.[1] Most notably, editorial workers who earned more than $35.00 a week were considered "professional persons" (*NRA Laws* 1933, 326) and were summarily exempted from hour and wage provisions (MacDougall 1941, 68).

Outraged at the inequities of the newspaper section of the code, journalists throughout the country spoke out at NRA hearings and met to organize protests against the publishers' actions to exempt editorial workers from the provisions of the code. Reporters questioned the arbitrary differentiation between reporters earning $34.50 as laborers and those earning $35.50 as professionals. They also suggested that some newspaper jobs such as radio editors, aviation editors, and advice to the lovelorn editors, came with "high-sounding titles" and no "executive authority" but could be categorized by publishers as executives and exempted from the benefits of the code.[2]

Amid discussions of the NRA code came developmental meetings for a national organization of editorial workers held at the home of *New York World Telegram* columnist Heywood Broun. Although there was general agreement among the journalists that action should be taken against the inequities of the code, there was considerable disagreement as to whether a national organization should be framed as a union or as a professional organization (Leab 1970, 59–60). According to newspaper critic Lewis Gannett, at early planning meetings, journalists expressed concern over the name of a national organization. "Most newspapermen at that time were afraid of the word 'union,'" and therefore the "safer word 'Guild'" was chosen.[3] The choice of the term "guild" was also a compromise that helped to bring together in one organization two fundamental ideological positions, trade unionism and professionalism. This chapter examines both positions and focuses on understanding how these two schools of thought ultimately helped to create a sense of class consciousness among editorial workers, during the development of the American Newspaper Guild from 1933 to 1937. Overall, this research suggests that an emphasis on the history of class consciousness in terms of the development of labor and news workers is an essential component of the history of American journalism.[4]

The notion of class consciousness used in this research is based on E. P. Thompson's (1968) definition of class as a historical phenomenon that occurs in human relationships over periods of time and through which patterns develop in ideas, relationships, and institutions. Thompson's concept of class does not exemplify a structure or category but represents real people who are involved in actual cultural contexts that are primarily determined by the productive relations they are born into. Class consciousness develops from cultural strategies "embodied in traditions, value-systems, ideas, and institutional forms" (9) that individuals use to handle their real-world experiences. Thompson suggests that when class is considered a structure or thing, the notion of class consciousness becomes static and limiting. From this perspective, the term class consciousness is often used pejoratively to indicate individuals who disturb the "harmonious co-existence of groups performing different 'social roles'" (10). Yet, when class consciousness is seen as a historically specific series of relationships, it articulates a shared identity of common interests of a group of people that is distinct from other classes, groups, or interests.

## PROFESSIONALISM VERSUS TRADE UNIONISM

On August 7, 1933, Heywood Broun, in his column "It Seems to Me," included a letter from an unemployed reporter who was concerned about the lack of class consciousness of news workers to see themselves as they actually were: "hacks and white-collar slaves" (Broun 1933a, A1). Responding to the NRA classification of editorial workers as professionals, the reporter maintained that such terminology as "professionals," "journalists," "members of the fourth estate," and "gentlemen of the press," obscured reporters' actual working conditions "by falsely dignifying and glorifying them and their work" (A1). In 1933, Broun was a well-paid and respected newspaperman with a reputation as a "gin-drinking, poker-playing, wicked old reprobate" (Swope 1940, 14). A liberal thinker, with a "burning lust for justice" (Jackson 1940, 16), Broun felt challenged by the reporter's comments and vowed to start planning a "newspaper writers' union" (1933a, A1) by 9:00 A.M. on October 1, 1933.

Two lines of thought quickly emerged at early organizational planning meetings; one group argued for a professional association while the other group lobbied for a trade union. Initially both perspectives were openly and freely debated.[5] Broun and other early leaders realized that if a guild were to be successful that it was necessary to avoid an internal fight over the professional vs. trade union issue. Believing that a national guild could become an association large enough to accommodate all points of view, organizational leaders left initial definitions of the guild flexible and open (Kuczun 1970, 21). For example, in the first issue of the *Guild Reporter* (1933), New York guild Secretary Jonathan Eddy explained that a national guild would function "as a labor union only insofar as the collective spirit of today calls upon it to do so" (*Guild Reporter* 1933, 1).

The American Newspaper Guild (ANG) was officially founded in Washington, D.C., on December 15 1933, in order to raise journalistic standards, represent the "vocational interests of its members and to improve the conditions under which they work by collective bargaining."[6] Broun, representing the New York guild, was elected president, Lloyd White, from the Cleveland guild, first vice president, Andrew McClean Parker, a Philadelphia guild delegate, second vice president, and Eddy, secretary.[7] In his history of the development of the American Newspaper Guild, Daniel Leab explained that at its inception the new national organization was little more than a "hollow shell" (1970, 103) that needed time to develop. The initial ANG bylaws and constitution, valid only for six months, created a decentralized organization with virtually no financial stability or power.

Editorial workers who initially envisioned the guild as a professional club or organization where reporters could interact with one another, similar to those in law and medicine, focused on enhancing the quality and dignity of the field of journalism. The rationale for considering newspaper work a profession was that it required considerable on the job training, an extensive apprenticeship, and continued ethical decision-making strategies. Russell McLauchlin, an early advocate for the creation of a professional-style guild, suggested that during the 1930s, some reporters considered themselves "a privileged lot"[8] who wanted to share their values and training with the entire field of editorial workers. There were other proponents of a professional guild who felt superior to blue collar workers and were openly antagonistic toward the labor movement. They did not want to create a union "that would put them in the same class as the mechanical workers they scorned" (Leab 1970, 83), and felt that they could improve working conditions for journalists through the use of "gentlemanly tactics." In addition, some editorial workers felt that unionization would eventually compromise the integrity of journalism. *New York Daily News*, rewrite man Nelson Robins explained this perspective: "A thoroughbred can work in plow harness, but it makes him a plow horse to keep him there."[9]

During this era many news workers were caught up in the romance of journalism that stressed rugged individualism and encouraged a belief that the excitement and attractiveness of reporting more than compensated for the low pay and poor working conditions (MacDougall 1941, 532). Wary of organized labor, many reporters refused to seem themselves as workers. A 1930s media critic explained the logic of this prevailing view: "They cherished their individualism like a white plume and accepted at face value the legend that they would never organize for mutual benefit" (Keating 1935). A general impression of the average reporter as a "dashing sort of individualist" (Brown 1935) and societal crusader pervaded news rooms and was also perpetuated in popular culture.[10] The romance of journalism was such a pivotal element in understanding the mind-set of editorial workers in the 1930s that Broun repeatedly addressed the romance of journalism and its relationship to the founding of the American Newspaper Guild. In an *Editor & Publisher* column, Broun suggested that the romantic nature of journalism was a fundamental reason why editorial workers must be organized. "In times past there has been a disposition to say 'Why, you boys don't care how long you work or how much money you get, look at the fun you're having'" (Broun 1933b, 8). Broun explained that organizing efforts were initially difficult because many reporters felt they were artists, not workers. Yet he maintained that his extensive experience in the newspaper business, and the inconsistent pay that he received, convinced him that he was a worker rather than an artist. Ultimately Broun insisted that the newspaper business remained "just as romantic" (quoted in Mann 1933, 7) when he was overpaid as when he was underpaid.

Editorial workers who encouraged the development of the guild as a professional association initially received support from the trade publication *Editor & Publisher (E&P)*.[11] The December 23, 1933, issue of *Editor & Publisher* included a column by Heywood Broun on the need for an editorial workers' national organization and a two-page news article on the American Newspaper Guild's founding convention, held December 15, at the National Press Club in Washington, D.C. It also reprinted the full text of the ANG constitution and ran an editorial (1933) welcoming the guild and wishing it success. Noting that there were some "glaring instances of economic injustice" (Editorial: Made to Order 1933, 22) in the newspaper industry, the editorial also mentioned the role of individualism in journalism and expressed confidence that the guild would use its powers as a professional organization wisely to correct those problems:

> There is a system, crusted all over with the rugged individualism and ruthless competition of 150 years, which has exploited editorial honor and sensitiveness sometimes to the limit of endurance. The Guild will demand some alterations, looking to improved working conditions, job security, arbitration of disputes, pay and hours which will recognize faithful and valuable service and yet be consistent with the special requirements of the city room. (22)

A professional focus for the American Newspaper Guild was also favored by publishers who emphasized the romance of journalism and spoke of journalism as a profession "too fine to be deadened by the fetishes of maximum and minimum pay."[12] For example, *Topeka State Journal* editor Henry J. Allen insisted that reporters were professionals educated as "gentlemen of self control and independent action" (1937, 12). Media mogul William Randolph Hearst maintained that if the guild functioned as a union that it would attempt to determine editorial policies, which would result in efforts to negate the public interest and might "deprive the reporter of the character which makes a newspaper man a romantic figure" (quoted in Lee 1937, 684). Hearst, who at this time was the single largest employer of editorial workers (Leab 1970, 243), called himself a romanticist and felt that if necessary reporters should be expected to work all day and all night on a story just "for the love of it" (Lee 1937, 684).

In contrast, advocates for a union-based guild maintained that the primary objective of the American Newspaper Guild was to "obtain economic advantages for its members through collective bargaining" (Brant 1937, 13). Insisting that journalists were workers who should form alliances with employees in other fields, pro-union guild members argued that before journalism could become a profession that the working conditions for editorial workers must become equivalent to those of other professionals (MacDougall 1941, 551). Wary of the designation of professional, many editorial workers were disillusioned about the motivation of newspaper publishers to pay them a living wage.[13] They showcased the publisher-inspired NRA definition of editorial workers as professionals as an example of how titles could be used to abuse and manipulate editorial labor. Pro-union guild members suggested that most news workers did not feel like professionals but instead felt like "underpaid, precariously situated employees."[14]

Two key founding members of the American Newspaper Guild, Broun and Eddy clearly favored the trade union perspective, in part because they were concerned that a national professional organization would not be able to negotiate effectively with publishers. They also pointed to the failure of earlier professional newspaper organizations to improve working conditions for editorial workers, and they wondered how such an organization might actually be successful in the Depression era.[15] ANG treasurer Garland Ashcraft hoped that guild members' common sense would help them to understand that the guild would eventually have to become "a hard-boiled labor union or a flop."[16] Support for a union based national guild also came from local guilds, some of which were explicitly founded on trade union principles. For example, during organizational meetings, Cleveland guild members discounted the possibility of creating a professional organization as an unworkable alternative and organized as a trade union.[17] For a few founding members of the American Newspaper Guild, the distinction between professionalism and trade unionism was merely a matter of semantics. As C. C. Gilfillan of the *Minneapolis Tribune* explained, the issue was not if the guild was a professional organization or a labor union. From Gilfillan's perspective, it was actually a combination of the two: "We all know we labor for a living; we also know we have at least a quasi-professional status. The left handed attempt to classify us is just humbuggery" (Gilfillan 1935, 56).

## BECOMING A UNION

Initially the American Newspaper Guild functioned as a loose federation of local guilds, "a hybrid professional society with a dash of debating club and a touch of press clubism" (Kuczun 1970, 191), without any direct ties to labor unions. Guild-sponsored economic studies were soon undertaken which showed that in most U.S. cities, the majority of editorial workers earned less than mechanical employees. As a result of these findings, salary issues quickly became a major focus for the American Newspaper Guild (Scribner 1934, 699). Within months of its founding the guild's emphasis on collective bargaining became clear to newspaper publishers. In response, publisher resistance began to escalate (Leab 1970, 124) and they began to reject the guild as if it were actually a part of organized labor (Kuczun 1970, 22). Publishers refused to negotiate with the guild for collective bargaining purposes, and in some cases they would not recognize it as a representative for editorial workers. For example, *New York Times* publisher Arthur Hays Sultzberger felt that guild membership was not conducive to intellectual freedom and objective reporting and he refused to negotiate with the local guild (Leab 1970, 275). Roy W. Howard, publisher of the *New York World-Telegram*, broke off all negotiations with the guild and insisted that journalism would "no more flourish and develop in the straitjacket of trade-unionism than an orchid on an iceberg" (quoted in Kuczun 1970, 33). In direct opposition to the NRA code that insisted on the right of employees to organize, the Rochester, New York, *Journal American*, a Hearst newspaper, posted notice that it did not recognize the American Newspaper Guild. Comparing the guild to the KKK, *Journal American* management said that it would only negotiate with its own employees and would not negotiate with any outside organization (Scribner 1934, 698). Guild members were intimidated, fired, and given the least desirable beats and assignments. Publishers gave selective pay raises to nonguild members and editors warned news workers that if they joined the ANG that their jobs would be in jeopardy. As Leab noted, "It took extraordinary bravery for a newsman to join a guild in the face of an editor who made it clear that 'no guild member would retain his place on my staff. A guild member always can be fired for incompetence'" (1970, 135–36).

The final NRA code, approved by President Roosevelt on February 17, 1934, nullified wage and pay protections for editorial workers earning more than $35 a week; as in the initial newspaper code submitted by publishers, these journalists remained classified as professionals. Shocked to learn that the final code reflected none of their concerns, news workers felt that the government had failed them and that they had been "left in the cold" (Bordner 1933, 6). Guild members realized that they could not count on governmental support and in response organizational efforts increased and negotiating tactics began to change. Understanding that the guild alone would focus on economic advances for journalists, a sense of class consciousness, as described by Thompson (1968), began to emerge among editorial workers. Leab maintained that if the final NRA code had been responsive to the needs of editorial workers, that support for the guild might have eventually faded away. Instead the final code aided the development of the guild and helped to create a sense of group allegiance among ANG members (Leab 1970, 77).

As a sense of class consciousness began to emerge among guild members, newspaper publishers grew increasingly alarmed at the potential power of the American Newspaper Guild and they began to put pressure on the ANPA to help fight the guild. At the first annual American Newspaper Guild convention, held June 5–8, 1934, in St. Paul, guild members emphasized economic goals including a minimum wage, maximum hours, paid vacations, and dismissal notice. In addition they approved a code of ethics and passed a freedom of conscience resolution that considered freedom of the press a right of readers and a responsibility of news producers (Brandenburg 1934, 7). Following the guild convention, ANPA counsel Elisha Hanson offered publishers legal advice and suggested strategies to avoid negotiating with the guild (Kuczun 1970, 46). The ANPA board of directors also advised its members not to enter into any agreement that restricted a publisher's control of the news and editorial departments (120).

Publishers were furious with the guild's freedom of conscience resolution and *Editor & Publisher* called the code of ethics "class-conscious propaganda" (Editorial: Speaking of Ethics 1934, 24). Publishers responded to the code of ethics by asserting that guild activities were actually subverting press freedom. Fearful of losing control of the news and editorial departments, publishers suggested that if all editorial employees were guild members that it would "lead to biased news writing" (Kuczun 1970, 120) that would destroy freedom of the press. Harry J. Grant, publisher of the *Milwaukee Wisconsin Journal*, maintained that guild membership led to "partisanship in political and labor affairs" (Publishers See 1937, 6), which would compromise newspapers' independence and prohibit the primary function of newspapers, "impartial service to the general public" (6). Grant and other publishers consistently equated guild membership with political partisanship, warning that the American Newspaper Guild was affecting editorial workers' independence and seriously compromising freedom of the press. Yet Alfred McClung Lee found that instead of discussing actual guild demands such as wages, hours, and employment security, publishers chose a strategy of focusing on the guild as a menace to freedom of the press. Unable to provide any concrete evidence to support their contention, publishers "convinced themselves by repeating these catch phrases over and over, much like primitives do some holy ritual" (1937, 684).

Editorial members failed to understand how better working conditions could impair press freedom and they suggested that because journalists fought for integrity of the news that they had a greater stake in freedom of the press than publishers (Kuczun 1970, 135).[18] Responding to reports of editorial employee intimidation, Broun said the press was not free when it "rests upon the fears and apprehensions of reporters who are frightened and who feel that they have good reason to be frightened" (quoted in Lee 1937, 680). Overall, news workers felt that the recognition of their right to build an organization that would represent their economic needs as well as their responsibility to society would enhance press freedom far more than publishers' anti-guild commentary (Gilfillan 1935, 55).

In the summer of 1934, facing a precarious financial situation, escalating publisher resistance to the American Newspaper Guild, and greater publisher pressure on editorial workers not to join the guild, ANG leaders realized that they needed to take action to help foster pro-guild sentiment among journalists. When the Samuel Newhouse–owned *Long Island Daily Press* fired nine journalists, eight of whom were guild members, and pressured remaining staff members to disband the local guild chapter, editorial workers picketed the newspaper. The use of trade union tactics, considered a first in the history of American journalism, according to *Editor & Publisher* (Guild Pickets 1934, 8), were intended to win the sympathy of readers and embarrass Newhouse into settling with the guild. Actively participating in the picketing, Broun's presence boosted editorial workers' morale, helped to settle the conflict, and ultimately helped to cement news workers' commitment to a more union oriented guild.

The picketing of the *Long Island Daily Press* also served to solidify publishers' rejection of the American Newspaper Guild. In addition to charging that guild membership was severely compromising freedom of the press, publishers focused on the development of a class conscious affiliation among guild members. Utilizing the concept of class consciousness as an epithet, publishers maintained that the guild had "fostered a deleterious class consciousness" (MacDougall 1941, 545) that impinged on editorial workers' loyalty to newspaper management and led to the "coloration of the news, especially news of labor" (545). Publishers compared guild policy with the ideology of the Communist party and the journalism of the ANG newspaper, the *Guild Reporter,* with that of the Communist *Daily Worker.* Overall, publishers maintained that guild actions were antithetical to the ideals and traditions of journalism within a democratic society (Editorial: No Closed Shop 1937, 30).

During a University Press Club of Michigan talk, *Editor & Publisher* editor Marlen E. Pew announced that editorial workers' class conscious affiliation was destroying the viability of the American Newspaper Guild. Finding the guild "too fine a fat pigeon for greedy hands to resist" (1934, 6), Pew warned that union affiliation would negate every pretense of free and independent journalism. He defined a pro-union guild as a "grotesque incongruity" (13) that would disrupt press independence and idealism, and hoped that professional editorial workers would join together to curb the power of the radical elements in the guild. According to Pew, "the trades union method, dependent as it is on class conscious propaganda, violence, regimentation, time-clocks and standardization of human effort can hold no lure for the creative newspaperman who is, or should be, the enemy of propaganda, violence, and time-clock standardization of mankind" (18).

Just nine months after *Editor & Publisher* came out in support of the founding of the American Newspaper Guild, *E&P* charged that the guild was no longer "an independent body of responsible professional news writers and editors" (Editorial: Humiliating 1934, 24), but had become a radical class conscious trade union. Dismissing complaints that publishers refused to cooperate with the guild, *E&P* insisted that it was guild leaders' "brutal cynicism [and] reckless disregard of the sensibilities and responsibilities of the rank and file of editorial workers" (24) that was to blame for the lack of negotiations. Calling the American Newspaper Guild a failure, *E&P* determined that Broun, who was "desperately bent on an adventure in martyrdom" (24), had misled guild members and had allowed power-hungry guild leaders to abuse the support of editorial workers. The tone and word choice in editorials appearing in *Editor & Publisher,* between 1934 and 1937, strongly illustrated their shift of opinion regarding the guild. The guild was repeatedly described as a "destructive force," that was increasingly "menacing" the existence of newspapers. Guild policy was referred to as "guild dogma," liberal guild members were called "guild pinkos," "extremists," and "radicals," and newspaper managers were told they "must have defensive plans," because to guild members, a publisher was considered a "tribal enemy."[19]

Newspaper publishers insisted that they still welcomed a professional organization of editorial employees (MacDougall 1941, 547). Yet their lack of cooperation with the guild helped to convince news workers that trade union techniques of collective bargaining, supported by strikes and boycotts, and backed by affiliated unions, would be needed to ensure the rights of journalists. Broun explained that initially guild organizers were willing to attempt a "semi-organized, semi professional set-up" (quoted in Robb Attacks Guild 1938, 5) that would work with publishers to improve working conditions for journalists. When that strategy failed, the organization resorted to using trade union procedures. Ultimately, ANG secretary Jonathan Eddy noted, "F.D.R., the NRA, and above all the ANPA gave us the choice of either being a union or being quietly laughed out of existence."[20]

## CLASS-CONSCIOUS NEWS WORKERS

Initially opinion was split among guild members regarding the issue of professionalism versus trade unionism. Yet the lack of government support combined with the extremism of newspaper publishers against organizational attempts by the guild actually strengthened the organization and encouraged a shift of opinion along with the development of a sense of class consciousness among guild members (Nicolett 1936, 190). Each time a publisher fired editorial workers for joining the guild, or tried to destroy a local guild by intimidating news workers, or refused to negotiate with a local chapter, American Newspaper Guild members grew stronger in their resolve to succeed. Cleveland guild president, Bruce Catton explained that guild members soon became distrustful and cynical regarding the actions of newspaper publishers. "We had completely lost confidence in the publishers and considered them an extremely reactionary group of people. As a result, we were so anxious to get a really militant labor union started."[21]

The idealistic notion of journalism as a romantic endeavor began to retreat as news workers came together to work for the improvement of economic conditions through collective bargaining. Under Broun's guidance, the American Newspaper Guild was becoming a "democratic, militant trade union of newspaper workers, a union determined that the history of exploitation in the newspaper industry shall not repeat itself" (Crawford 1940, 48). As the guild began to rely more on labor union techniques, some guild members who had favored a professional organization became less involved in the organization. Others, like Luther Huston (1959), a reporter with International News Service, disliked the collective bargaining strategies and resigned from the guild. Huston, who explained that he had no thoughts of strikes and picket lines when he first joined the guild, ultimately decided to leave the ANG because he felt that strikes were professionally wrong and economically wasteful (13). While guild membership dropped for a brief time, the news workers who remained in the guild became more focused and united in their commitment to the organization (Leab 1970, 142).

Picketing, walkouts, and strikes "resulted in a unprecedented display of collective action by the normally individualistic American news workers" (Leab 1970, 164). This collective action in turn cemented a feeling of class consciousness among guild members and a common social, political, and cultural relationship emerged among guild members. Trade union tactics also gave the American Newspaper Guild much needed publicity and afforded guild leaders the opportunity to strengthen ties with organized labor. As early as the 1934 St. Paul convention, changes to the American Newspaper Guild constitution had begun to give the national organization additional collective bargaining authority. In 1935, a new constitution strengthened the guild "by centralization and by a rearrangement of [the] internal structure."[22] The initial professionalism versus trade unionism debates gave way to two new positions: guild affiliation with the American Federation of Labor (AFL) or guild cooperation with the AFL.

Guild members who favored cooperation feared that AFL affiliation would offer unwarranted security to the incompetent and could plunge guild membership into the "brick-layer level of the social stratum" (Leab 1970, 207). Those who favored affiliation maintained that since the guild was already a labor union that it would benefit from AFL support during organizing campaigns and strikes. Although Broun clearly favored affiliation from the beginning, he was initially worried that the issue of trade unionism might destroy the fledgling organization, and he delayed action on the issue of affiliation until the vast majority of delegates supported it (Kuczun 1970, 82). By the end of 1935, most guild members favored affiliation and on the third anniversary of Broun's column calling for a newspaper union, the American Newspaper Guild received a charter from the American Federation of Labor.[23]

Not surprisingly, guild affiliation increased publishers' antagonism toward the ANG and gave them yet another reason not to negotiate with the guild. Editorial director of the *Detroit Free Press*, Malcolm W. Bingay, insisted that a labor union defeated the actual intent of a professional guild: "It destroys the spiritual essence of our work, lowers the levels of personal achievement and makes the day's job a thing of factory routine" (1937, 12). Bingay maintained that union affiliation would eventually reduce journalistic excellence and compromise editorial standards and working conditions. *Topeka State Journal* editor, Henry J. Allen, believed that journalism was an individualistic profession that did not need "the protection of a mob union, which gains its ends through force and massed action" (1937, 12). *Editor & Publisher* maintained that journalism was not a trade and that affiliation with organized labor was a "mistaken and futile move" that destroyed an understanding of editorial work as "a blend of the arts and professional skill" (Editorial: Futile Move 1936, 24). By 1937 *E&P* was actually predicting the death of freedom of the press and democracy at the hands of the American Newspaper Guild (Editorial: No Closed Shop 1937, 6).

Some guild observers have suggested that left on their own, editorial workers were confused individualists who would never have organized. But Depression-era salary cuts, long hours, and poor working conditions instituted by newspaper publishers may have pushed news workers into the guild. According to the writer Ferdinand Lundberg, "publishers should be given credit for organizing the Guild."[24] Without their active resistance to the American Newspaper Guild, fueled by their own class conscious organization, ANPA (Lee 1937, 697), editorial workers might not have come together to fight newsroom wage and hour inequities.

Finally, it was the shared identity of common interests of guild members that ultimately joined them together to fight for the economic rights of editorial workers. Continually inspired by Broun, a tireless leader of the labor movement, news workers developed cultural strategies, based on their actual lived experiences, which helped them to create a united class of workers. As Curtis MacDougall explained, "until the guild began to create it, there certainly was nothing which might be called class consciousness in the average reporter's outlook" (1941, 533). Reporters might have been hardboiled, cynical, or disillusioned, but it took the development of a sense of class consciousness as members of the American Newspaper Guild to show them that they belonged to the ranks of organized labor.

# NOTES

1. Following the release of the temporary newspaper code, the government held open hearings to determine the final applicability of wage and hour provisions to editorial workers.

2. Andrew McClean Parker, statement before the public hearing on the Newspaper Code, Washington D.C., September 22, 1933; Daniel J. Leab Collection, Archives of Labor and Urban Affairs, Walter Reuther Library, Series I, A Union of Individuals, Box 7, File 7-1.

3. Lewis Gannett to Daniel Leab, January 5, 1965; Daniel J. Leab Collection, Archives of Labor and Urban Affairs, Walter Reuther Library, Series V, Daniel Leab's Research Correspondence, Box 9-13.

4. For an extended discussion of the role of labor in the development of media history, see Hardt and Brennen 1995.

5. Ferdinand Lundberg to Daniel Leab, July 7, 1967, Daniel J. Leab Collection, Archives of Labor and Urban Affairs, Walter Reuther Library, Series V, Daniel Leab's Research Correspondence, Box 9-16.

6. "Constitution of the American Newspaper Guild, December 15, 1933, Daniel J. Leab Collection, Archives of Labor and Urban Affairs, Walter Reuther Library, Section I, A Union of Individuals, Series I (A-C), File 1-3.

7. Minutes, Washington Meeting, December 15, 1933, Founding Convention, Daniel J. Leab Collection, Archives of Labor and Urban Affairs, Walter Reuther Library, Section I, A Union of Individuals, Series I (A-C), File 1-11.

8. Russell McLauchlin to Daniel Leab, June 11, 1965, Daniel J. Leab Collection, Archives of Labor and Urban Affairs, Walter Reuther Library, Series V, Daniel Leab's Research Correspondence, Box 9-16.

9. Nelson Robins, quoted in "Reporters and Labor Unions" *Publishers Service Magazine* October 19, 1933, 1, Daniel J. Leab Collection, Archives of Labor and Urban Affairs, Walter Reuther Library, Series IV, Ancillary Material 1933–1962, Box 8, File 24.

10. For an extended discussion of journalists in fiction, see Brennen 1995.

11. *Editor & Publisher* supported the American Newspaper Guild for a short time. By mid-1934, the trade publication was vocal in its opposition to the guild and insisted that it was destroying the credibility and independence of journalism.

12. Nelson Robins, quoted in "Reporters and Labor Unions," *Publishers Service Magazine,* October 19, 1933, 1, Daniel J. Leab Collection, Archives of Labor and Urban Affairs, Walter Reuther Library, Series IV, Ancillary Material 1933–1962, Box 8, File 24.

13. Bruce Catton to Daniel Leab, April 25, 1968, Daniel J. Leab Collection, Archives of Labor and Urban Affairs, Walter Reuther Library, Series V, Daniel Leab's Research Correspondence, Box 9-8.

14. Ferdinand Lundberg to Daniel Leab, July 7, 1967, Daniel J. Leab Collection, Archives of Labor and Urban Affairs, Walter Reuther Library, Series V, Daniel Leab's Research Correspondence, Box 9-16.

15. For an extended discussion of previous efforts to form a professional editorial workers association, see McDougall 1941; Lee 1937.

16. Garland Ashcraft, "Dues and Professionalism Were Early Guild Issues. Board Member of Mid-Thirties Recalls ANG Life-or-Death Struggle," *Guild Reporter,* December 25, 1953, 10, Daniel J. Leab Collection, Archives of Labor and Urban Affairs, Walter Reuther Library, Series IV, Ancillary Material 1933–1962, Box 8-22.

17. I. L. Kenan to Clyde Beals 1938, Daniel J. Leab Collection, Archives of Labor and Urban Affairs, Walter Reuther Library, Series IV, Ancillary Material 1933–1962, Box 8-23.

18. See, for example, Nicolett 1936.

19. See, for example, *Editor & Publisher* editorials in 1934, 1936, and 1937.

20. John Eddy to Daniel Leab, May 19, 1966, Daniel J. Leab Collection, Archives of Labor and Urban Affairs, Walter Reuther Library, Series V, Daniel Leab's Research Correspondence, Box 9-11.

21. Bruce Catton to Daniel Leab, April 25, 1968, Daniel J. Leab Collection, Archives of Labor and Urban Affairs, Walter Reuther Library, Series V, Daniel Leab's Research Correspondence, Box 9-8.

22. Report of the Constitutional Committee, I. L. Kenan, committee chair 1935, Daniel J. Leab Collection, Archives of Labor and Urban Affairs, Walter Reuther Library, Section I, A Union of Individuals, Series 1, File 1-6.

23. Garland Ashcraft, "Dues and Professionalism Were Early Guild Issues. Board Member of Mid-Thirties Recalls ANG Life-or-Death Struggle," *Guild Reporter*, December 25, 1953, 1, Daniel J. Leab Collection, Archives of Labor and Urban Affairs, Walter Reuther Library, Series IV, Ancillary Material 1933–1962, Box 8-22.

24. Ferdinand Lundberg to Oliver Pilat, October 24, 1963, Daniel J. Leab Collection, Archives of Labor and Urban Affairs, Walter Reuther Library, Series IV, Ancillary Material 1933–1962, Box 8-18.

# REFERENCES

*A Handbook of NRA Laws, Regulations, Codes.* 1933. Washington, D.C.: Federal Codes.

Allen, H. J. 1937. This Conflict between Publishers and Guild. *The Quill*, December, 12.

Bingay, M. W. 1937. An Editor's Case against the Guild: Unionism in Editorial Rooms Will Not in Long Run Raise Wages, Will Glorify Mediocrity, Destroy Loyalty, Reduce Journalism to Machine Shop Formula. *Editor & Publisher*, June 26, 12.

Bordner, R. 1933. Why We Organized. *The Quill*, October, 6.

Brandenburg, G. A. 1934. Newspaper Guild Adopts Ethics Code. Broun Is Re-Elected President—Following Rebuff from Gen. Johnson, Organization Decides to Put Buckley Dismissal Plea Up to President Roosevelt—New Constitution Approved. *Editor & Publisher*, June 16, 7.

Brant, I. 1937. This Conflict between Publishers and the Guild. *The Quill*, December, 13.

Brennen, B. 1995. Cultural Discourse of Journalists: The Material Conditions of Newsroom Labor. In H. Hardt and B. Brennen, eds., *Newsworkers: Toward a History of the Rank and File*, 75–109. Minneapolis: University of Minnesota Press.

Broun, H. 1933a. It Seems to Me. *New York World Telegram,* August 7, A1.

———. 1933b. Broun Interviews Broun on Guild. *Editor & Publisher*, December 23, 8.

Brown, L. 1935. The Press Faces a Union. *New Republic*, January 23.

Crawford, Kenneth K. 1940. In *Heywood Broun As He Seemed to Us*. New York: Random House.

Editorial: Made to Order. 1933. *Editor & Publisher*, December 23, 22.

Editorial: Speaking of Ethics. 1934. *Editor & Publisher*, June 16, 24.

Editorial: Humiliating Failure. 1934. *Editor & Publisher,* September 15, 24.

Editorial: Futile Move. 1936. *Editor & Publisher*, June 6, 24.

Editorial: No Closed Shop. 1937. *Editor & Publisher*, June 26, 26, 30.

Gilfillan, R. S. 1935. Guild Viewpoint. *Journalism Quarterly* 12 (March): 56.

Guild Pickets L.I. Daily, Crying "Intimidation." 1934. *Editor & Publisher*, July 14, 8.

*Guild Reporter*. 1933. November 23, 1.

Hardt, H., and Brennen, B., eds. 1995. *Newsworkers: Toward a History of the Rank and File*. Minneapolis: University of Minnesota Press.

Huston, L. 1959. Professional Ideal Lost Out in Guild. *Editor & Publisher*, January 3, 13.

Jackson, G. 1940. In *Heywood Broun As He Seemed to Us*. New York: Random House.

Keating, I. 1935. Reporters Become of Age. *Harper's*, April.

Kuczun, S. 1970. *History of the American Newspaper Guild*. Ph.D. diss., University of Minnesota.

Leab, D. J. 1970. *A Union of Individuals: the Formation of the American Newspaper Guild 1933-1936*. New York: Columbia University Press.

Lee, A. M. 1937. *The Daily Newspaper in America: The Evolution of a Social Instrument*. New York: Macmillan.

MacDougall, C. D. 1941. *Newsroom Problems and Policies*. New York: Macmillan.

Mann, R. S. 1933. National Guild Asks Five-Day Week. Heywood Broun Chosen President at Washington Meeting: Constitution Calls for Collective Bargaining, But Sentiment Is Against Any Affiliation with A.F. of L. *Editor & Publisher*, December 2, 7.

Nicolett, C. C. 1936. The Newspaper Guild. *American Mercury*, October, 186–92.

Pew, M. E. 1934. Professional vs. Trades Union News Departments. Address Before the 16th Annual Convention of the University Press Club of Michigan, November 8.

Publishers See Economic Havoc Arising out of Guild Demands. 1937. *Editor & Publisher*, June 26, 6.

Robb Attacks Guild Tactics: Broun Defends in Debate. Editor Also Hits Guild Shop and Leadership . . . ANG President "Not a Dictator Calling Strikes," Says He's for Sanctity of Contracts. 1938. *Editor & Publisher*, April 16, 5.

Scribner, J. 1934. The News Writers Form a Union. *The Nation*, June 20.

Swope, H. B. 1940. In *Heywood Broun As He Seemed to Us*. New York: Random House.

Thompson, E. P. 1968. *The Making of the English Working Class*. Harmondsworth, U.K.: Penguin.

# 13

## Writing the Workers' World Trade Center: An Analysis of Reportage on Ground Zero in the Aftermath of September 11, 2001

*Laura Hapke*

Where was the line between exuding confidence and being a fool?

—Construction worker at Ground Zero (Chivers 2001, A1)

The business world appears as the only world.

—George Lipsitz (Lipsitz 1981, 2)

Between the Great Depression and September 11, 2001, New York City's labor force was been portrayed as heroic. The Giuliani administration was a case in point. Prior to 9/11, the Republican mayor was careful to attend funerals for slain policemen and fallen firefighters. But he as carefully avoided terms like blue collar, worker, manual laborer, or even everyday, average, and common. If anything, his customary rhetoric at such solemn events invoked the sacrifice of these members of the "bravest" and the "finest." Yet he made no reference to the powerful municipal unions to which these "heroes" belonged or the increasingly frequent battles of the mayor to force union concessions in the name of budget cutbacks (Greenhouse 1996; Jay 1995).

Restricted to isolated events rather than commemorations of deceased workers, these mayoral appearances belied rather than reasserted the rich working-class heritage of the city. Joshua Freeman and others have eloquently catalogued the many ways that prior to the Cold War, and briefly in the mid-1960s and 1970s, New York City was a place of union gains and majorities, mass transit, affordable public housing, and a site of working-class political activism and heritage (Freeman 2000). Despite its reputation as a working-class town, from the late 1970s onward a steady series of fiscal crises and corporate victories perennially stalled negotiations with the various administrations "had succeeded in at least partially prying the city away from its working-class, social democratic heritage" (Freeman 2000, 87). Even as the labor movement claimed some victories in the 1980s and 1990s, it never regained its Depression-era reputation as the premiere urban home of the American salt of the earth (Finder 1995, B2; Uchitelle 1994; Hacker 1999, 45).

When September 11 hit, tragedy and emergency reaffirmed national strengths. Construction workers from a nearby job stood side-by-side with affluent citizens of Brooklyn Heights on the promenade across from Lower Manhattan. Cross-class bonds of countless number were formed at ground zero. The local construction workers who were models of bravery for the work they did at ground zero were joined by tradesmen as part of the 10,000 to 15,000 who spent months digging for remains and sifting through debris. They merged into the mass of those, from management to operators, all known as "engineers" (The cranemen's job designation happens to be "operating engineer," but that obscures rather than clarifies differences with management-end engineering staff.)

Municipal disaster united those often divided in recent corporate and mayoral battles, and temporarily silenced some of labor's influential corporate critics. But the bewildering attack also hardened antilabor attitudes. Even as "ordinary" people were celebrated in the metropolitan press for their efforts on the days and months following the terrorist onslaught, reportage returned to the familiar animus against manual workers that had informed the city's history (Freeman 2000).

One of the most obvious erasures of laboring people issued from the journalistic reluctance to distinguish among the classed work categories of the day before. This chapter will argue that *New York Times* was an unofficial but flawed leader of mainstream American journalism in reporting to the nation on the aftermath of 9/11. Like many other papers that sought inclusive coverage of the tragic day and its events, the *Times* instead virtually ignored labor issues and diminished the role of workers.

This erasure of workers is hardly surprising to students of labor. For one thing, the term "working class" is contested. Theoretically it can encompass workers from lower-tier white-collar workers, many union members, who were the majority of the World Trade Center's casualties.[1] Working class as well were the many municipal fire and police union members who engaged in the first response phase of the ground zero rescue and cleanup. These labor movement people, for that matter, would probably define themselves as middle-class people who paid often unreasonably high union dues.

Despite the ambiguity attached to and denial of working-class status among most office workers employed prior to September 11 at the World Trade Center and most union workers employed outside of it, it is still widely agreed that even in an officially classless society such as the United States, "blue-collar" is a synonym for a class of workers who toil with their hands. Such work often, though not always, requires little or no secondary or postsecondary schooling.

Obviously blue-collar jobs, particularly those protected by craft and municipal unions, can be highly skilled, as the salaries of construction union upper-tier workers, such as the many iron welders crucial to the ground zero operation, demonstrate. The old industrial unions of late have recruited in nontraditional venues as diverse as the restaurant, janitorial, hospital, word processing, and university clerical sectors in order to retain a membership base. This patch-work quilt of workers alone suggests why there is such imprecision in jour-nalistic pieces on "blue-collar" or "white-collar." However, none of this negates the fact that the "average" EMS, firefighters, police, carpenters, ironworkers, and sanitation people who joined the many other laboring personnel at the cleanup site lose socioeconomic identity by being bundled into the term "mid-dle class" or the now equally bourgeois phrase "working families."

This chapter investigates how September 11 similarly failed to inaugurate a "new reportage" about working people in the city and instead reaffirmed a middle-class set of values as normative and representative of the World Trade Center experience. I rely on a sample of fifty articles, predominantly but not exclusively from the first three crucial months at ground zero. The majority appeared in the *New York Times,* the most complete city source for detailed print information on disaster. The *Wall Street Journal, Newsday,* and the *Daily News,* referred to here as well, also offered some fully researched reportage al-though not usually with the breadth or depth of the *Times* coverage.

Despite obvious class distinctions among victims, survivors, and rescuers, such coverage raised morale even as it provided factual data when it char-acterized those affected by the World Trade Center collapse as similar. Those who died were oblivious to class distinctions; those who rescued came from varied socioeconomic backgrounds. Those picking through the rubble and experiencing the dangers of ground zero were doing a job that in the early weeks was often volunteer work, even if they were salaried union members in their pre-WTC lives.

There is little dispute that from a mass media perspective, September 11 was the first time workers have been heroic since the Great Depression. By American news standards they were enduringly heroic: After a year's view-ing, subway posters, magazines, CNN, MTV videos, even fashion magazines picture heroes in uniform, municipal workers, EMS, blue-collar men, and even some women. Dennis Smith's *Report from Ground Zero* (2002) helped institutionalize the "first responders" vision of police, Port Authority workers, and firefighters. Subordinating the languages of labor and class to that of warfare, the narratives of the massive cleanup effort replace depictions of la-boring people with those of the operation's difficulty, financial expense, and emotional cost. What follows is a brief analysis of the rescuers, victims, en-vironment, and missing; the diffusion of the old-left labor rhetoric in dis-courses of war and religion; and the way even the most prolabor mainstream journalists renders rescuers heroic replace and displaces interest in the labor issues and by implication the very dignity of labor itself.

## NARRATING GROUND ZERO: LABOR AS A REPRESSED CATEGORY

Despite a kind of journalistic lip service to that truth that ground zero was a site of hard labor directed at replacing devastation with reconstruction, newspapers repressed the issue of class in their minimal coverage of the rescue as a work experience. Labor figures emerge in *Times* reportage soon enough, but the focus is on self-abnegating war work. From September 12 onward, the very enormity of the labor mission canceled out its drudgery in mainstream reportage. Bringing out the dead for many weeks dominated this missionary enterprise. Laboring was a matter of protecting the national pride.

At a certain point, though, the hard job of removal, demolition, and cleanup had to replace the recovery work. There was more to the ground zero story than respect for the unearthing of human remains. Articles had to address working conditions.

More popular in front-page coverage was the continuation of the "altruistic task" narrative. A number of pieces adopted a language of brotherhood: "thousands work together, hundreds of firefighters, police and National Guardsmen add to the mix. For weeks, some of them have been climbing underground through ventilation shafts and emergency stairwells to survey damage to the seven-story basement below the Trade Center."

This narrative language is, to be sure, a tribute to the rescue workers' solidarity. But the distinction between work and sacrifice was omitted. Workers extensively used martyrdom language themselves and pointed to a ground zero village of equal toilers (Chivers 2001, A1). Nevertheless decoupling firefighters from other workers occurred when no longer directly linked with self-sacrificial tasks. In *Times* reportage and interviews alike, this was not the language of cross-trade solidarity for other key reasons. For one thing, those who used such solemn rhetoric either masked or were minimizing the clear municipal imperative to finish the job as quickly as possible: the project astonishingly finished under budget and ahead of schedule. For another, in ways reminiscent of early American Federation of Labor history, elements of the workforce divided along craft lines. And management used the issue of workplace safety to reinforce such divisions. And perhaps most important, the protocol was not a labor one.

## "IT'S ALL ABOUT IRONWORKERS NOW"

From the opening days of ground zero reportage, response to the unprecedented workload undertaken by members of the city's unions inspired veneration in the mainstream press. Many of their pieces echo the admiration expressed by the crowds of New Yorkers and visitors to the city who in the early weeks lined the exit routes along which debris-filled trucks left and supply-laden ones returned to the site. Chroniclers joined the praise for the selfless labor of emergency service personnel and volunteers whose hazardous jobs now seemed almost sanctified. The attention to the labor of the ground zero workers, reported on in great detail, seems on one level to challenge that assertion. Certainly even as hopes for trapped survivors waned, as the dead were brought out or their remains searched painstakingly for victims, the rhetoric of selfless toil was invoked repeatedly. There was no ambiguity, apparently, for the truck drivers and other laborers who returned wearily from the site or stayed in nearby makeshift shelters after marathon days.

The monumental nature of the task, 1.2 million tons of debris by conservative estimate, including 300,000 tons of structural steel, compelled a solidarity of sorts among all who undertook it. With the Chambers Street home front now a post–battle war zone, the press conflated the person and the job itself, representing the ground zero workers as a crucial cadre in a nation suddenly under attack. The WTC dead had been mostly civilians; but the downtown that had once seemed immune to attack from foreign terrorists was now home to military and peacetime personnel alike.

In the earliest days and then weeks of the rescue effort, the *Times* depictors, from the few staff labor reporters to its feature writers, evinced a surface respect for work, both volunteer and paid. Yet if one scrutinizes the descriptions of sacrifice, laboring as itself a valuable activity, whether in peacetime or under attack, dropped almost completely out of the discussion.

The now familiar rhetoric was of the fire and police workers who rushed to help their fallen comrades. So did those in other professions. The *New York Times* permitted one of its few labor commentators, Charlie LeDuff, to point out that truck drivers were union members usually paid almost thirty dollars an hour and were volunteering their services in the days immediately following the Tuesday massacre (LeDuff 2001a, A1). It was not always clear whether men and women were volunteering their expertise or paid overtime to pry "at the ground with shovels and crow bars to free body parts, bits of human flesh, and rubbery patches of skin" (Barry 2001, A1). In the solemnity of the shared experience a sacral respect for "soot-covered, weary rescue workers" the reportage concerned the tight-lipped comments of traumatized salvage teams; the cold details of the injuries; even the way canine searchers were overwhelmed by the smell of flesh "just coming out of the cracks . . . everywhere" (A1).

As days became weeks in the nightmarish landscape on West Street and its environs, and, in the *Times* framing of that late-September period, "Hundreds, then thousands, of people converged at ground zero." The "village" that emerged was a combination of behind-the-lines command center, smoldering battlefield, postterror war zone, and unprecedented New York City site of industrial wreckage (Chivers 2001, A1).

In this context, the reportage of self-abnegating work of the two weeks following September 11 continued. *Times* writers usually more detached from mass tragedy echoed the tone of awe reported as used by interviewees like the

National Guardsman, "It's all about truckers and ironworkers now" (LeDuff 2001a, A1). In an unusual piece of journalism, "Ground Zero Diary," one author even doubled as a reporter himself while serving in the guard cleanup (Chivers 2001, A1). It is not surprising that those on the site, including case-hardened reporters, would join in the near veneration of the working-class rescuers. Even LeDuff's transformation of white working-class patriotism, the object of satire during the Vietnam War confrontations between workers and students, is understandable given the pressure of the historical moment. The way the early cadre of ironworkers and truckers seized the narrative should not obscure the way that even in the opening days of the rescue/cleanup, representations of these men (women were hardly mentioned) were made culturally palatable.

Le Duff's is not true labor reportage. He provides virtually no coverage, and none of a substantial nature, of the work of the site in terms of daily difficulties, job descriptions. He is alert to the "eerie green vapor" illuminated by the powerful lighting and produced by the devastated buildings as if part of the decompositions within. Apparently unwilling to risk desacralizing the honored dead or the courageous ones still trapped in the wreckage, he positions the work in and of itself as unimportant. The recovery of human beings is at once too energetic to do justice to the graveyard quality; the ancillary efforts and cleanups conversely are too monotonous to be worth extended examination. Contrast these assumptions with those of the more proletarian (but hardly leftist) *Daily News*. It did withhold labor sympathies in its reliance on unflattering clichés of "brawny hardhats" whose strength and muscle were implicitly opposed to their deep intelligence (Gittrich 2001, 20). Still a few *News* articles, appearing in the month after September 11, did readdress the labor balance:

Vesey St. is passable between Broadway and West Broadway. But it remains blocked where 7 World Trade Center and 6 World Trade Center collapsed onto each other.

Sections of the wrecked roadways, especially closer to the fallen towers, are covered with uneven mounds of soil and capped with a crude form of asphalt.

In many places, debris, timber and steel columns from the charred towers have been placed under the soil to distribute the loads of hulking demolition machines across a wider path . . .

The passageways first allowed rescue workers to venture safely into the ruins. They are now crucial to the unprecedented cleanup and recovery effort.

Backhoes, bulldozers, excavation machines, flatbed trucks, dump trucks and all-terrain vehicles that look like souped-up golf carts come and go constantly.

There is so much activity that construction workers stand at intersections directing traffic.

"Sometimes we make six to seven trips a day," said trucker Luis Torres, 39, who hauls debris from the site . . .

Just inside the perimeter of the disaster area are . . . laborers wearing credentials from the Office of Emergency Management. They wash windows, scrape ash off parking garages . . . lower garbage bags . . . and mop up asbestos-tainted dust. (Gittrich 2001, 20)

In its somber tone, the *Daily News* piece here abandoned its usual hyperbole of dramatic and tragic events. Instead ironically it was the seasoned labor reporters of the *Times* whose version was as sensationalized as it was cursory. It was as if they too questioned the value of the working class in a time when the official truth was that this classless nation needed to come together.

Historically labor coverage by the *Times* ranges from outright criticism of labor's motives to a minimization of labor reportage. Steven Greenhouse long had covered unions and doggedly reported on management's "cost-cutting" initiatives in the aftermath of the tragedy; Bob Herbert brings his considerable moral sensibility to the lowest-wage, including sweatshop workers.

But it was Charlie LeDuff who was assigned the working-class ground zero. Part Native American, Le Duff was born into the Detroit working class and did cannery and carpentry work prior to joining the *Times* in 1995 (LeDuff 2001b). He became a veteran reporter who held down some of the most unsavory blue-collar jobs such as those in racially job segregated slaughterhouses to nail down his workerist stories. With this vita, he was the ideal candidate to narrate the discomforts of those in the ground zero trenches.

LeDuff's forte was the human interest anecdote, part interview, part impressionism. His earlier essays on meat industry workers relied on his ability to bond (and drink) with the guys. He would no doubt have agreed with his fellow reporter Jim Rasenberger, who in the winter of 2001 dubbed them "Cowboys of the Sky" and depicted them in the "risky, glorious calling" of erecting steel frames for Manhattan's skyscrapers (Rasenberger 2001, 14:1).

Rasenberger's piece appeared only in the "City" section of a Sunday *Times*, a special repository of human interest pieces on the New York toiler and his work world. Le Duff's article took the World Trade Center article on ironwork out of the soft news, back sections of the paper Given the importance of the rescue, LeDuff's December 10, 2001, *Times* article, "At the Pit: A Night Shift to Numb Body and Soul," is granted rare front-page status. Unusual for its attention to the nonmunicipal union men, the piece foregrounds ironworkers who take the night shift though they receive no extra pay for the choice. "The workers . . . do not count their success in metal or tonnage, but in bodies. Despite pressure from the contractors [and City Hall] it is still a recovery effort for them" (LeDuff 2001c, A1).

Yet in the article as a whole they emerge far less ennobled than in the Rasenberger piece or the many articles on the uniformed personnel at the site. One reason is obvious: these workers are all too aware of the unfamiliar risk taking generated by the toxic WTC site. Somewhat out of step with the fraternal sacrifice narrative, they question not only the futility of the many casualties among the uniformed personnel but also point to the "the civilians who died here and those who lost them. Who salutes them?" one man inquires bluntly. Such skepticism in the trenches heralds the "undramatic things familiar only to the ground zero crew." As iron welders dismantle burned metallic structures and ensure structural stability for recovery of bodies, they evidence the grueling and inglorious nature of the work itself. This is the labor underside of fraternal solidarity.

The men's manner of coping with the job, described later in the article, does justice neither to their frayed nerves nor to the recovery itself. At the mealtime break, they misbehave with a vengeance. They are already frightening enough to passersby because of their faces pockmarked by "slag sparks from burning metal have smoldered into their necks and arms and eyelids." They then taunt passersby and act out the sex-obsessed construction worker: "Haw, haw, did you see that?" [they say] laughing, screaming. LeDuff's expertise is the repartee of proletarian buddyship, and he seems here to trade objectivity for admiration. "The size and volume [noise] of the ironworkers," LeDuff remarks ironically, "upsets a man in white shoes and clean overcoat who is walking out of the Pink Pussycat" (LeDuff 2001c, A1).

As if to justify the impulse-driven conduct of the ironworkers, LeDuff transforms them into figures in a short story. They are wanderers in a gothic landscape where "gnarled beam[s] . . . jut out over the pit like a gangplank." Their redemption is as much in rowdiness as in the amulets from the site made from bits of iron welded together into small crosses.

Half of the LeDuff paragraphs are not about the work at all. As if fearing readership boredom, he offers behavior that alienates rather than impresses.

Ironworkers' participation in the cleanup, then, as well as that of crane operators, demolition experts, carpenters, welders, construction workers attached to the five firms responsible for it, were underreported. So too was the degree of union involvement; workers and management were even conflated in their worry over a threatened government contract shift to an out-of-town firm, Bechtel (Bagli 2001, D10).

## RHETORICAL EXCHANGES: SAFETY FIRST, CHOOSING SIDES

What so many articles in the *Times* and elsewhere backgrounded or ignored altogether was that any attempt in post-WTC times to demystify labor can only reaffirm its centrality both to the ground zero operation and the history of the nation. Recent discussions of labor violence on prolabor sites such as the scholarly H-labor listserv have swirled around workers as instigators and perpetrators of violence. Those explaining the necessity of labor violence have sought to redefine injuries and fatalities on the job as a kind of violence perpetrated by the industrial order. Whether one embraces that logic or not, no one could fail to label the site as a hazardous one: protective gear, even if worn religiously, did not guarantee protection. Improperly stored fuel tanks and dangerously assembled cranes (workers in a sense imperiling other workers), hot steel, gas cylinders, unstable debris piles, cranes swinging back and forth. All of the preceding was the stuff of early-cleanup articles in the *Times* by seasoned labor reporters (Lipton and Johnson 2001, 1: 5). Yet while it was straight reportage to limn this industrial war zone work environment, the causes of actual injuries were left uninterpreted in the fascination with ground zero's daily operations. In the chart "How They Were Hurt: Week-by-Week Reports of Five Classes of Injuries, Mid-September to November 4" (Lipton and Johnson 2001, 1:5) it appears that worker error combined about equally with faulty equipment. This air of haste could have been the subject of inquiry about efficiency at the site. Yet the perception that workers were rightly martyring themselves by spending ten or twelve hour days preempted criticism of them or their brothers for inadequately designating warning zone, storage tanks, or reporting inadequate equipment, all routine safety checks in the far less mine-filled terrain of the factory floor.

In early November, firefighters reinforced the martyrdom in a surprising way: they began to protest a cutback of rescuers that made the remaining workers' jobs more difficult. When it was time for city hall to curtail the recovery phase, safety rather than the greater imperative efficiency was invoked by Mayor Giuliani. Feeling that this was desecrating hallowed ground, firemen themselves responded and were quoted in early November 2001 *New York Times* pieces, with an alternative rhetoric: that of fraternal/military duty. The phrases "bring them home" and "respect the dead" filled their speech (McFadden 2001, B8).

The *Times* explored the firefighters' rage and frustration through the coverage of their melees with the police. One recent retrospective, unable to fathom the internecine battles between police and firefighters, continued to dub it divisive on labor's part (Rasenberger 2001, 134:1). In these sometimes violent confrontations, there was an implicit separation between labor and management. One firefighter queried the police who were hemming him in, "whose side are you on?" a variant on the old coal miners' protest song by Aunt Molly Jackson. The fracas also partook of the World War II internal labor arguments about wildcat protests in which the dockworkers and laborers in basic industry, agreeing to put grievances on hold, went back to work while their more militant brothers decided to strike.

Accusing police of being agents of the state recalled other labor protests to a degree, even though the few demonstrators arrested were high-level union officials rather than the rank and file. The very fact that police responded to protesters "we're not your enemies" suggests blurred boundaries as well. And it dramatizes the difficulty of separating the WTC site labor discourse from a wartime one. The verbal exchanges between two sets of union men, firefighters, and police, represented at best a quasi-labor rhetoric, not the language of lockout or strike march or picket line. City hall's response to the demonstrations distanced the mayor himself from labor language of any kind. He argued the pullback of personnel protected workers and maximized the efficiency of those left at the site. Yet he neglected to note that in the cleanup operation, safety was not prioritized until December. (The safety argument, moreover, can be a scrim for other concerns. A similar lag of months before invoking the danger of industrial accidents occurred in the recent lockout and subsequent dock strike of the ILWU in Los Angeles, in which management was concerned with another, if far less dangerous, site than ground zero: the many unopened containers on the docks of Los Angeles. Employers worried publicly as the strike became more proactive about the safety of the work crews who would eventually return after the protest.)

The firefighters' demonstrations were, at least on a symbolic level, a protest against labor conditions. These people were proclaiming that the needs, aspirations, and cherished ideas of working people should not simply be construed as a "problem" for the mayor and the New York City businessmen to whom he had ties.

## AFTER GROUND ZERO: FROM HEROES TO HANDS

One media source critical of *Times* reportage especially in the early months commented recently:

> Everyone is praising NYC workers for their resilience after the 9/11 crisis. But, praise won't pay the bills. A year after the Sept 11th tragedy, NYC workers are still suffering the economic aftershocks. Over 100,000 workers lost their jobs due to this calamity. Unemployment is hovering around 7% but unemployment compensation has not been extended even for those initially covered. The NYS and NYC budget crises deepen but 911 funds cannot be to balance the budget. The city government has a jobs freeze with attendant speedups and service cutbacks and is contemplating layoffs. And through it all the immigrant community is hardest hit, denied much of the 911 relief aid, unemployment, welfare, and, as is the case with the airport screeners, even the rights to certain jobs. Massive rebuilding plans are announced and contemplated but most of the federal aid is still only en route and workers have to wait for this to trickle down. (Rosenberg and Nash 2002)

The demythologizing of labor in the wake of the return to normality one year after the World Trade Center continues. Over 130,000 jobs have been lost to a recession greatly impacted by the ground zero devastation, and blue-collar losses loom particularly large. For the salt of the earth, then, there are clear links to the Depression era that popularized the term. There is high unemployment (at this writing, the highest in 7 years). Many layoffs are without severance pay (Greenhouse 2001, A1). Large-scale layoffs occurred after September 11 in many industries, but one year later Verizon workers, members of the Communications Workers of America, advertised in November 2002 to point out that the cuts proliferate and ask if "anyone is listening" (CWA 2002, A27).

Several patterns emerge, most notably that workers again are just "hands."
The dangers of the job tend to preempt working-class consciousness of a
cross-trade nature: the bravest, the finest reinforced craft consciousness
among those in "elite" unions. At the same time the culture has rejected the
average worker by confusing it with the vague rubric "everyday person." The
instability of the term "working class" was evident in the coverage com-
memorating the yearly anniversary of the bombing tragedy. Rather than indicate a socioeconomic group, however, now that working class had been
paired with "hero" by the print media for a year, it was as unstable and ambiguous as ever. Nowhere was this more evident in the *Newsday* headline for
Labor Day 2002. Earlier years had seen at least a survey of New York's labor
heritage in "soft news" pieces in weekend section, "New York City, Cradle of
American Labor" (*Newsday* 1996, C1). The event was an occasion to employ
the term with dual potency. "Working-Class Heroes" read the September 2,
2002, headline, with an African American female firefighter and a Slavic
baker smiling into the camera for their photos on the front page. Yet the subtitle and the largest photo on the headline page contradicted the proworker
message. "New Yorkers Express Appreciation for Life, Work and Colleagues
since Sept. 11: Defiant Labor Force Empowers City" it read, and beneath it was
a photo of two workers posed in an office setting. Although they were casu-
ally attired and their ethnic identifications were nonwhite, non-Protestant—In-
dian and Hispanic—their occupation was vaguely listed as "analysts" without
further clarification. Taken as a composite, the title, subtitle, and trio of photos
moved attention away from notions of class and classed work in ways that the
article itself solidified.

The article continued by quoting Constantin Tsirbos, "The best answer to
give those people [the terrorists] is to go on working" (*Newsday* 2002, 8). Included among interviewees were electrician IBEW Local 3 ("our local lost 16
or 17 men") and president of NYC Central Labor Council, Brian M. McLaughlin. Yet Tsirbos was the chief spokesman of the piece. Although a small business tradesman not connected with the rescue or its cleanup, he was now
the voice of the labor force at the 2001 rescue site.

In a similar vein, September 2002 saw dismal mainstream print media reportage of Labor Day. WTC references completely replaced those honoring
the history of labor or the dignity of labor (The parade itself, if there was one,
was a back-page affair.) The focus, as usual, when it was on workers, was
restricted to lively human interest stories.

Still stranger, the *Times* editorial, as if rewarding the exhausted ground
zero workers, exhorted the U. S. workforce to "take it easy." The subtext,
however, was don't complain, workers (On Taking It Easy 2002, A15).
Steven Greenhouse's small paean, "Where Hands Still Labor," reminded
readers of people who work with their hands in low-wage jobs. But he too
engaged in half-truths by excluding those in skilled trades in favor of a
generic "salt of the earth" (Greenhouse 2002b, A15).

Sifting through dirt and rubble and debris as ironworkers did was no longer hailed. What was retained were not calls from employers of iron welders or carpenters or crane or operating engineers employers to join up but heroic luster used to recruit potential police and firefighters. Making labor capital from ground zero images, the union strengthened the salaries of New York's firemen and policemen arguing the "bravery . . . displayed during the September 11 terrorist attack" (Greenhouse 2002a, B4). In so doing, they joined the many nonunion and antiunion elements in the city who backgrounded New York's traditional working class.

## NEW DIRECTIONS FOR RESEARCH

The ground zero site was a labor space but still not so perceived not only because of the enormity of the tragedy but also because of the traditional erasure of labor unrest. The financial center, for all its glitter and Wall Street aristocratic citizenry, is as working-class a part of New York City as one can imagine. This is particularly true with the dissolution of many factories, the flight of entrepreneurs to offshore venues, and the downsizing of business with middle-management employees. The renovated WTC area employs service, lower-rung white-collar, blue-collar unionist, illegal day workers, and nannies to rich coop and condo residents in classic numbers. As Orwell taught us, those who work with their hands are invisible. Workers breathe the same air as senators, but while White House buildings are evacuated for senators, post offices as of this writing remain anthrax risk centers. Yet workers are the majority of those who must report to work, drink the water, breathe the air, eat the employee cafeteria food, and the like. Any study of environmental quality post–September 11 is necessarily a document important to the labor movement. In considering the continued hazards to working people, here are some questions to consider: What about those working class men and women who are still alive today, and are heroes in their own right? How many detailed stories are there of the people who toil each day in the toxic, dangerous rubble that makes up the World Trade Center site today?

What the reportorial majority studied here failed to discern was that the Twin Towers were not just symbols of global capitalism (though they were that). They were also workplaces. While we have heard a great deal about the traders and bankers, we have heard far too little about the janitors, maintenance workers, and others who make buildings—and cities—work. Still missing from reportage is any extended attention to the over sixty Windows on the World workers, many illegal aliens, killed on September 11.

This chapter has attempted to insert itself into a new dialogue by narrowing what has necessarily become a rather broad focus. The attention to a small body of news reportage can serve as a reintroduction to the hidden history of American labor at a time when issues of nationhood and patriotism again seem at odds with workplace democracy and self-empowerment. In examining the state of emergency's impact on the perception of the workforce, research needs to be done comparing worker readiness and resistance to excessive labor conditions in other situations of post "war" cleanup: Pearl Harbor as a key site. Wildcat strikes abounded in the Second World War, it should be noted too (Lipsitz 1981). What kinds of injunctions, admonitions, and directives against challenging federal, state, city, and private management existed in the days and weeks after September 11? To what extent did reportage honor workers for what they did rather than what they were thought to so selflessly symbolize?

I have not made extravagant claims for a survey of articles or considered these implicitly antiworker pieces as a microcosm of U.S. labor reportage in times of national crisis. I have not addressed memoirs by workers (Larry Boyles, *Fallen Heroes*), left-of-center reportage, or *American Ground*, the new book on the mechanics of the cleanup process). But I have opened the inquiry on the ways antilabor attitudes in the nation's past, mirrored in mainstream press coverage, persist, endure, and take contemporary forms. Issues of blue-collar "narratives" of the WTC experience also await other students. (Oral histories collected by nonworkers and editors including the recent Joe McNally book exclude working-class people almost entirely.) Returning to the "sacrifice narrative," scholars might ask how the American drama as played out erases class distinctions.

Future writing, in addition to the *Times* coverage, will need to parse more counterculture venues, on and off the Web. The moderately liberal *Nation* and *New Republic*, the leftist *People's Daily World*, the African American *Amsterdam News*, and the feminist *Ms.* magazine might be touchstones as well. As an oral-historical ancillary source, conversations and interviews with people working at or near the site seem unquestionably important. Finally, the subject of a completely other inquiry: labor press self-reportage (*Labor Notes, Southern Exposure, Against the Current, Building Bridges: Community Labor on WBAI*) and the prolabor contributions in left-liberal journals.

George Lipsitz has observed that mainstream journalism rarely acknowledges the existence of a labor perspective (Lipsitz 1994, 2). To better honor the 3,000 laboring people in the restricted zone of the former World Trade Center (LeDuff 2001a, A1), as well as the many other workers who perished in the months following September 11, labor studies scholars must engage in their own recovery efforts.

## NOTE

1. Cornell's Industrial and Labor Relations program in labor studies in New York City organized a special one-day conference on Saturday, September 14, 2002, entitled Changing Realities: The Mexican Worker in New York and Beyond. The conference was cosponsored by the Mexico-America Workers Association (AMAT) and the Hispanic Labor Committee, as well as other labor bodies.

# REFERENCES

Bagli, C. 2001. Fears of New Company at Ground Zero. *New York Times*, November 8, D10.

Barry, D. 2001. A Few Moments of Hope in a Mountain of Debris. *New York Times*, September 13, A1.

Chivers, C. J. 2001. Ground Zero Diary: 12 Days of Fire and Grit. *New York Times*, September 30, A1.

Communications Workers of America. 2002. Advertisement. *New York Times*, November 12, A27.

Defiant Labor Force Empowers City. 2000. *Newsday*, September 2, 8.

Finder, A. 1995. New York Builders Flaunting Wage Law to Increase Profits: Builders Flouting Wage Law on Nonunion Workers Pay. *New York Times*, June 5, B2.

Freeman, J. 2000. *Working-Class New York: Life and Labor since World War II*. New York: New Press.

Gittrich, G. 2001. Slow but Steady Progress amid Ground Zero Rubble. *Daily News*, October 15, 20.

Goldberg, J. 2002. Review of *American Ground*. *New York Times Book Review*, October 20, 9.

Greenhouse, S. 1996. [Job] Security a Top Issue in Municipal Pact. *New York Times*. January 4, B3.

———. 2001. Unions at Airlines Assail Management for Denying Benefits. *New York Times*, September 26, A1.

———. 2002a. Workers Are Angry and Fearful This Labor Day. *New York Times*, September 2, B1.

———. 2002b. Firefighters' Union Accepts Nearly Same Deal as Police. *New York Times*, November 14, B4.

Hacker, A. 1999. Who's Sticking to the Union. *New York Times Review of Books*, January 18, 45.

Jay, S. 1995. Of Industrial Things Past: The Ancient Relics of Williamsburg Testify in Silent Eloquence. *New York Times*, September 3.

LeDuff, C. 2001a. Hauling the Debris, and Darker Burdens. *New York Times*, September 17, A1.

———. 2001b. Interview. www. journalism.jobs.com/interviews_leduff.cfm.

———. 2001c. At the Pit: A Night Shift to Numb the Body and Soul. *New York Times,* December 10, A1.

Lipsitz, G. 1981. *Rainbow at Midnight: Labor and Culture in the 1940s*. Urbana: University of Illinois Press.

Lipton, E., and Johnson, K. 2001. A Nation Challenged, The Site: Safety Becomes Prime Concern at Ground Zero. *New York Times*, November 8, 1:5.

McFadden, R. 2001. The Firefighters: Second Union Leader Is Charged with Trespassing in Demonstration at Ground Zero. *New York Times,* November 5, B8.

On Taking It Easy. 2002. *New York Times*, September 2, A15.

Rasenberger, J. 2001. Cowboys of the Sky. *New York Times*, January 28, 14:1.

Rosenberg, M., and Nash, K. 2002. The Current Crisis: New York City, the U.S., and the Labor Movement. WBAI, November 18. Archived at www.buildingbridgesonline.org.

Uchitelle, L. 1994. Insecurity Forever: The Rise of the Losing Class. *New York Times*, November 20, 4:1, 5.

# 14

# UPS Strike Coverage and the Future of Labor in Corporate News

*Christopher R. Martin*

The casual television viewer in the United States in the first quarter of 2002 could have hardly missed the pervasive buzz about the color brown. The occasion celebrating this rather unsung color was the rollout of a new $45 million advertising campaign by United Parcel Service. Breaking with their long-running promotion as "the tightest ship in the shipping business," a campaign that featured the heroic efforts of UPS delivery workers, the new ad campaign (the largest in the corporation's ninety-five-year history) obliquely asked, "What can Brown do for you?" In the television (and print) ads, actors portraying the mailroom guy, the shipping manager, the logistics manager, the customer service manager, the CFO, and the CEO talk about what brown does for them. Dale Hayes, the UPS vice president for brand management and customer communications, said the campaign is a "more aggressive way" to portray the company's employees "as a strong team working together, to bring solutions to customers" (Elliott 2002).[1] But, strangely enough, the UPS workers who wear the brown uniforms and drive the brown trucks were completely missing from the ad campaign.

Perhaps the absence of worker images from the most extensive UPS corporate branding campaign ever is not so surprising. The year 2002 marked five years after the high-profile 1997 Teamsters strike against UPS, and the expiration (on July 31) of the five-year National Master Agreement that ended the strike. As talks between the union and the corporation geared up, the fact that UPS corporate managers aggressively attempted to supplant the image of the heroic worker with the brown brand color makes sense after losing a hard-fought strike in which the majority of the United States unexpectedly—at least according to mainstream news coverage—supported the workers, not management.

The success of the Teamsters strike can be measured not only in the final contract signed between the workers and management, but also in the substance of the strike coverage in the mainstream news media. The traditional frames used by the news media to cover labor reflect the consumer-oriented ideological environment in which the U.S. corporate mass media operate. In most cases, these frames result in stories that prioritize consumer objectives, obscure union messages, and disdain collective action. But, as this analysis of news coverage of the 1997 UPS strike illustrates, the consumer-oriented frames of the news may be turned to labor's benefit with democratic social activism and a message that reveals the connection between production and consumption.

## NEWS FRAMES AND STORIES ABOUT LABOR

When the news media cover labor, they don't do so by communicating "neutral" facts, but by telling us stories about labor, especially stories that shape and reflect our culture's commonsense ideas about labor, management, and capital (Parenti 1986; Puette 1992; Tasini 1990; Gans 1979). Like any good story, news stories can be engaging, and the way in which the story is told can encourage the news audience to understand and experience the story in a certain way. Media historian James Carey explains that "news is not information but drama. It does not describe the world but portrays an arena of dramatic forces and action; it exists solely in historical time, and it invites our participation on the basis of our assuming, often vicariously, social roles within it" (Carey 1989, 21).

Thus the narrative story form in news gives meaning to individual events and circumstances. The particular structure of a story is its frame. As W. Lance Bennett and Murray Edelman explain, "the who, what, where, why, how, and when . . . give acts and events a narrative *frame*. A choice among alternative settings or among origins of a political development also determines who are virtuous, who are threats to the good life, and which courses of action are effective solutions" (1985, 159). Similarly, Todd Gitlin has called media frames "persistent patterns of cognition, interpretation, and presentation, of selection, emphasis, and exclusion, by which symbol-handlers routinely organize discourse, whether verbal or visual" (1980, 7). The act of framing is largely an act of common sense on the journalist's part. Unfortunately, common sense leads back to the familiar and traditional, and often cuts off creative thinking and imagination in news coverage.

Peter Golding and Graham Murdock suggest that there are two general ways in which cultural forms, such as news, work as mechanisms regulating public discourse. First, the form itself provides certain limitations on the range of discourses possible, from solely official discourses to the articulation of counterdiscourses. News tends to operate in the parameters of a consumer sphere, addressing its audience as consumers. Second, discourses within the form can be treated in various ways, from being arranged in a "clearly marked hierarchy of credibility which urges the audience to prefer one over the others" to "a more even-handed and indeterminate way which leaves the audience more open to choice" (1991, 27). These two ways of regulating discourse are similar to the concepts of inclusion of coverage and the kind of portrayals in the coverage.

Ralph Miliband concurs with the notion that the media regulate public discourse. He notes that the mass media have the power to "foster a climate of conformity . . . by the presentation of views which fall outside the consensus as curious heresies, or, even more effectively, by treating them as irrelevant eccentricities, which serious and reasonable people may dismiss as of no consequence" (1969, 238). Jimmie Reeves and Richard Campbell describe this journalistic function as "policing" the boundaries of reason and nonsense, or the normal and abnormal:

> In the ongoing representation of authority and the visualization of deviancy, the well-informed journalist mediates two symbolic horizons of common sense . . . on one horizon the journalist bridges the knowledge gap between 'expertness and the lack of it'; on the other, the journalist guards the frontier between 'normalcy and the lack of it,' between 'reasonable people' and 'deviant nonsense.' (1994, 59)

We might then expect similar policing of the boundaries of common sense in news stories of labor relations, where stories are framed to suggest who are the virtuous and threatening actors, what are the most effective solutions to labor disputes, and whose interests are paramount.

Thus when journalists frame a story, they deploy a structure to the narrative that helps us, the audience, makes sense of the events. Because the vast majority of the U.S. population has little direct contact with labor unions—only 13.5 percent belonged to labor unions by 2000, down from a peak of 34.7 percent in 1954 (Department of Labor 2000)—the news media exist as a primary storyteller of the labor experience. By studying the frames of mainstream news narratives, we can hope to understand how the news media represent the institution and members of labor unions in the United States.

Unfortunately for labor, the news media's coverage of labor has a decidedly pro-capital bent. One of the earliest studies of such news coverage found that unions are usually portrayed as the "wrong" party in workplace disputes (Sussman 1945). More recent studies have come to similar conclusions. For example, the extensive Machinists Union Media Monitoring Project of television entertainment and news broadcasts in 1980 and 1981 found that "television typically casts unions as violent, degrading, and obstructive" (Rollings 1983, 135). Although class structure is more pronounced in Britain, media coverage of labor-management conflict is often similar. Studies by the Glasgow University Media Group (1976; 1980; 1982) and David Morley

(1976) on British television's coverage of industrial news consistently demonstrate poor coverage of labor issues. The Media Group found that events reflecting negatively on management, such as industrial accidents, were systematically underreported, whereas labor's reasons for striking were reported irregularly or not at all. The British studies also show that the credibility of labor's position is always in question in the description of industrial conflict: "the traditional *offers* of management are inevitably countered by the *demands* of workers to the point where the nouns and verbs describing management actions are generally positive while the matching vocabulary for worker's actions is negative" (Glasgow University Media Group 1976, 401). In the United States, Parenti (1986) and Puette (1992) catalogued comparable representations and stereotypes of labor unions and workers as inefficient and greedy, and unwilling to negotiate in good faith.

Even suggesting that labor gets a bad rap in the U.S. press risks countercharges that the U.S. news media are liberal lapdogs. For example, Lichter, Rothman, and Lichter (1986) suggest an elite, liberal East Coast media biased against business. But, even by their own standards, the myth of an antibusiness bias is problematic, not the least because they also find that the media elite are broadly supportive of policies and ideas about America's capitalist system. In Litcher, Rothman, and Lichter's own surveys, large majorities of the journalists responded that they believe "people with more ability should earn more," "private enterprise is fair to workers," and "less regulation of business is good for the U.S." (1986, 29). Apparently the elite media worker's liberalism doesn't extend to the concerns of labor. The news watchdog organization FAIR (Fairness and Accuracy in Reporting) came to a similar conclusion when it found that on a wide variety of economic issues—including the expansion of NAFTA, taxing the wealthy, concern over corporate concentration of power, and government guaranteed medical care—the press was to the right of the public's views (Croteau 1998).

The key to interpreting the news media's framing of labor news is to consider how the corporate news might frame labor stories in a way that harmonizes with the media corporation's own economic priorities and also make sense to the audience without the appearance of an obvious bias, which would undermine credibility. The news media do so by framing stories in the common sense of the consumer-oriented media system (in an advertising- and corporate sponsor-based media system, this is the familiar ideological environment in which all media stories are framed).

## Five Central Labor Frames

The stories about labor that emanate from such a system of framing are outlined below. In a larger study of how the mainstream news media covered major labor stories of the 1990s, I found five central frames continually emerged (Martin forthcoming). These frames are consistent with the generalizations and stereotypes listed by Parenti (1986) and Puette (1992), but go further in explaining the "commonsense" consumer-oriented ideological environment in which the U.S. corporate mass media structure news stories about labor unions:

1. *The consumer is king.* Because the consumer is fundamental to the U.S. economy and culture, treating the individual consumer as a hallowed entity is the unstated assumption of all news. Likewise, this is a consumer's democracy. Americans are told they are blessed with an abundance of choices and can "vote" with their pocketbooks. But caveat emptor: in this news frame, the consumer is valued when acting individually but seen as a menace when acting collectively on behalf of a social purpose (see frame 5 below). As economist Juliet Schor explains, "Ours is an ideology of non-interference—the view that one should be able to buy what one likes, where one likes, and as much as one likes, with nary a glance from the government, neighbors, ministers, or political parties. Consumption is perhaps the clearest example of individual behavior which our society takes to be almost wholly personal, completely outside the purview of social concern and policy" (2000, 452).

2. *The process of production is none of our business.* The role of the consumer is to decide whether or not to buy a product or service, not inquire about the production process. Yet, aside from a few government labeling laws, it is nearly impossible to know anything about the means of production of a product or service. In fact, it is a main function of advertising and public relations to avoid discussing the actual collective process of production (which would entail the stories of workers and their conditions) and instead create a substitute meaning that typically has little or nothing to do with material production (see Goldman and Papson 1996). The news treads lightly on the topic of production because to undermine advertising/PR myths and images of production would be to undermine the work of their sponsors.

3. *The economy is driven by great business leaders and entrepreneurs.* This news frame is the flip side of the hidden production process. Why bother talking about the workers, the news seems to say, when the embodiment of production can be portrayed by individual CEOs and entrepreneurs? The heroic CEO and entrepreneur were staples of journalism in the 1990s, an era that witnessed an explosion of growth in business reporting (Henriques 2000). Yet more business journalism was not necessarily better journalism, as the news more often glorified the developing information economy with sycophantic features on the new "Culture Trust" (Frank 1997) and celebrated the ultrawealthy's outrageous fortunes so excitedly that a writer for the *Columbia Journalism Review* dubbed the genre "wealth porn" (Poole 2000). A corollary of this frame is that anyone with the gumption can become a superrich entrepreneur/CEO—the myth of the self-made man. In fact, those in power are there because, according

to the business cliché, they work harder and smarter—thus denying any advantages to being born into the right social class or having access to cultural capital.

4. *The workplace is a meritocracy.* This frame derives from an individualist vision that doesn't include unions. It basically suggests that "you get what you deserve" in the workplace. Similar to the corollary of frame 3 above, the myth here is that good people rise to the top and are compensated correspondingly. Those who don't rise to the top probably aren't working hard or smart enough. Moreover, working is like consumption—an individual choice. If people don't like their job, they should get another. This kind of frame deflects any responsibility for the workplace by the employer and preempts collective action, as noted in frame 5 below.

5. *Collective economic action is bad.* The notion here, developed historically in the corporate assault against unions and liberalism (Fones-Wolf 1994), is that collective action by workers, communities, and even consumers will upset the well-functioning, democratic American consumer economy, and the decisions of great business leaders and entrepreneurs. The news media disapproves of collective action—including strikes, slowdowns, boycotts, and protests—with a number of standard canards: it is inflationary, un-American, protectionist, and naive; it causes bureaucratic red tape, disrupts consumer demand and behavior, foments fear and violence, and so on. The frame carries an interesting underlying assumption: economic intervention by citizens should happen only at the individual level (e.g., tell your boss to "take this job and shove it" if you are dissatisfied or "vote with your pocketbook" if you don't like something). Individual action preempts collective action, which is more democratic and potent. But politics outside of the reigning corporate-political structure is largely disdained, if not usually ignored, by the press.

These five dominant frames resulted in news coverage throughout the 1990s that was often severely critical of labor's actions and enthusiastically supportive of capital's actions. With such framing, the news media's stories have continually undercut a legitimate social institution—labor unions—that might serve as a useful remedy to millions of U.S. workers who want independent representation in their workplace for collective bargaining and dispute resolution, as well as a voice in the economy (Freeman and Rogers 1999). Of course, one could argue that labor unions, especially in the second half of the twentieth century, have often failed to adequately communicate their case to the mass media. Even the AFL-CIO charged in 1985 that "efforts should be made to better publicize organized labor's accomplishments," "union spokespersons need training in media techniques," and "efforts must be made at every level to better inform reporters about unions and trade unionism" (AFL-CIO 1985).

But the dominant news frames back labor into a tight corner. Especially in the 1990s, even with the best public relations, labor was left with little possibility for framing its story in a way that would both represent its mission and somehow fit into the typical consumer frames of coverage. However, in the following case study, we will see an instance where, with advanced planning, collective action, and a widespread and consistent public message, labor unions engaged these same consumer frames to define the news story to their benefit, publicizing issues in ways that are difficult for a corporate, consumer-oriented press to ignore, and that are salient to both consumers *and* citizens.

## UPS WORKERS ADJUST THEIR MESSAGE TO FIT THE CONSUMER LOGIC OF THE NEWS

The UPS strike of August 1997 is commonly cited as labor's greatest success of the 1990s, as 185,000 Teamster workers brought the nation's largest parcel delivery service to a standstill and won most of their demands, despite the fact that millions of consumers were inconvenienced. The strike was one of the top stories of 1997, with 77 *USA Today* reports, 139 *New York Times* stories, and 70 network news packages (ABC, CBS, NBC) during July-August 1997. Network news stories were acquired through the Vanderbilt Television News Archive. Newspaper reports were obtained via the Lexis-Nexis full-text database, supplemented with microfilm copies. This case study is based on a critical analysis of all of those reports.

The UPS strike story received significant mainstream news coverage and gained the nation's attention. The Pew Research Center monthly News Interest Index nationwide surveys ask people how closely they follow certain news stories. The UPS strike was the fifth most closely followed story (in terms of "very closely" responses) of all news stories in 1997, and was the most closely followed labor story of the entire decade, with 76 percent of respondents following it closely—a combined 36 percent "very closely" and 40 percent "fairly closely" (Craighill 2001).[2] The unique feature of the strike is that by the account of the news media's own surveys, the striking workers gained a majority of the nation's support. In the next section, I'll provide some examples of how mainstream national news organizations began to deploy a limited narrative of the strike via the five traditional frames, and then how specific factors of the UPS strike forced the news media to reframe the story and present a more open forum of the issues surrounding the labor dispute.

### The News Deploys the Traditional Frames

On Monday, August 4, 1997, nearly 185,000 Teamsters working for United Parcel Service went on strike. The workers' primary concern was to reverse the fast growth of part-time positions, which had undercut the creation of new full-time jobs at the global parcel delivery company. The dual wage structure of the Teamster union workers at UPS was similar to that of the American Airlines flight attendants. In 1982, the Teamsters agreed to a two-tier wage scale that paid part-timers less than half the wages of full-time workers. By 1997, with the company taking full advantage of the dual-wage system, more than 60 percent of the Teamster workers at UPS were part-time (up from 42 percent in 1986), although many of them worked thirty-five or more hours a week (Brecher 1997).

The day the Teamsters walked out, the story led all network newscasts. Even with the improving economy at the time, the earliest stories on the strike featured hand-wringing consumer-oriented news frames. ABC's veteran reporter Dean Reynolds wrapped up his August 4 report from Dallas by warning, "And economists say one thing is certain. The longer this strike lasts, the higher will go the prices for everything UPS *was* shipping."

NBC's report by Mike Jensen on the same day waved a red flag of inflationary fears:

> JENSEN (voice-over): When all this is over, shipping charges for packages are likely to go up, says consultant William Dean.
> DEAN (in office): UPS is such a dominant carrier that they're gonna have to raise their rates, and almost all the other private carriers are going to inch up at the same time.
> JENSEN (voice-over): Another worry for the million and a half customers who use UPS every day. For them, it's only going to get worse for each day the strike goes on.

After the first day of the strike, the stories peddling the myth of inflation had largely ended. The subsequent events of the fifteen-day UPS strike, which often couldn't be fit to typical labor news frames, seemed to baffle the consumer-oriented news media. One of the most unusual developments of the strike was the considerable public favor won by the workers. By the second week of the strike, the public support of the striking workers was legitimized by news surveys; a *USA Today*/CNN/Gallup poll showed that 55 percent of Americans supported the strikers, while only 27 percent supported UPS (Field 1997). Similarly, an ABC News/Nightline poll conducted in the second week also found that 40 percent of respondents supported the union workers, while 30 percent supported the company [with 16 percent supporting neither, and 13 percent with no opinion] (Langer 1997).

The results of the surveys defied the news media's conventional wisdom and framing strategy—many consumers were inconvenienced, yet the bulk of Americans supported the strikers. For example, a long *New York Times* story on August 17, 1997, announcing the *USA Today*/CNN/Gallup Poll data stated:

> Even though the 13-day-old walkout by the teamsters is inconveniencing far more Americans than most strikes have, the American public strongly . . . supports the workers in this high-stakes showdown, the largest strike in the nation in two decades.

That is a surprising switch because the public sided with management in most other recent work stoppages that grabbed the nation's attention, including the 1994 baseball strike, the 1982 football players' strike and the 1981 air controllers' strike. (Greenhouse 1997, A1)

Likewise, the *USA Today* story on the pro-worker poll seemed rather perplexed, as it noted "Public support for the Teamsters comes even though 31% disapprove of unions" (Field 1997, A1). An ABC News.com story on the ABC News/Nightline poll results took a similar tone, highlighting the unusual fact that although people were inconvenienced by the strike, most people didn't want the president to step in and end it (Langer 1997).

The poll results undermined the potential for the disgruntled consumer to be the primary frame of the UPS strike story. In fact, the unexpected poll results created the possibility for untraditional strike narratives. For example, a *USA Today* story on York, Pennsylvania, entitled "Town finds strike is inconvenience but not calamity" took a more measured, less alarmist view of the impact on consumers (Parker 1997).

Still, there were the fairly typical consumer-problem stories: by August 5, the second day of the strike, reports focused on an electronics business hampered by missing shipments (on *CBS Evening News*), fresh flowers going unshipped (*ABC World News Tonight*), and Lobstergram and cheesecake deliveries at a standstill (*NBC Nightly News*). Before the strike ended, the television news reports also covered the impact on fish deliveries, a wedding (an undelivered wedding dress), blood supplies, pricey Nieman Marcus department store goods, espresso, and frozen yogurt.

The news media also attempted to discredit the 185,000 striking workers by painting them as violent unionists. For example, the Big Three television networks ran seventy package reports between August 3 and August 20, 1997, in their strike coverage. No fewer than ten of the reports, all between August 5 and August 10, noted violence on picket lines and showed police shoving picketers back to make way for UPS trucks rolling through the UPS gate. A typical report was the August 5 lead-in by *ABC World News Tonight* anchor Diane Sawyer:

SAWYER (on camera): Tempers flared at UPS plants today, in a second day of the Teamsters strike against the shipping company.
SAWYER (now voice over video of Chelmsford, Massachusetts police pushing picketers): Two strikers were arrested at this Massachusetts site after a scuffle with police left one person injured (shift to video of an older male UPS worker lying on the pavement, with his head cradled by an emergency medical worker).

The assumption, of course, is that the striking workers were at fault, since they were the ones arrested. But there never were (and typically never are) follow-up reports to such stories that tell the consequences of the arrests, nor were there reports investigating police conduct or responsibility for the worker's injury.

In fact, the peaceful nationwide work stoppage of 185,000 workers defied the news media's stereotype of violent picketers. Nevertheless, during the first week of coverage, the network television news media returned again and again to the images of police physically pushing back and arresting workers attempting to nonviolently block UPS gates in a few Boston suburb locations. Even after such isolated incidences of "violence" had ended, CBS still stoked fears of more striker-induced violence by recycling the same video that CBS use earlier in the week. On August 10, 1997, CBS reporter Diane Olick filed a news package that included this content:

> OLICK (voice over trucks leaving UPS gates through a crowd of people): There is also growing concern that as the possibility of negotiations cools, tempers will heat up on the picket lines . . .
> OLICK (voice over file footage of six police officers pulling a striker away from the front of a UPS truck): . . . as they did already in Boston.
> RON CAREY (from *Face the Nation*): I have made it very clear that there will be no violence.
> UNIDENTIFIED PICKETER: Some people are getting fed up—that may go violent.

Even when no violence exists (the video CBS used had nothing to do with strikers becoming inflamed by slow negotiations but instead showed police breaking a blockade with force), the news media seem irresistibly compelled to use it as a narrative element for labor stories.

## The Unique Factors Behind Reframing the Story

Despite the news media's hyping of a violence angle and befuddlement over public support of the workers, in several reports the news actually did what news is supposed to do: inform the public and be a medium for the open discussion of relevant public issues. Almost surprisingly, many reports on the UPS strike presented varying opinions about the status of part-time workers in the American economy, the years of downsizing at U.S. corporations, and the question of fair wages. There were four unique factors behind the Teamsters victory and the widespread public support of the workers.

First, there was a new democratic environment at the International Brotherhood of Teamsters. Under the direction of Teamster President Ron Carey and the organizational help of the Teamsters for a Democratic Union (TDU), a reform movement in the union, the Teamsters improved democracy in decision making and maintained a very high degree of solidarity among its UPS workers (West 1997). Almost a year in advance, the Teamsters leadership developed the kind of internal communication campaign that contrasted highly with the corrupt, secretive Teamsters leadership style of earlier decades. In advance of the contract talks, the Teamsters:

[H]ired rank and file activists from UPS centers as coordinators; mapped out an extensive one-on-one communications network; surveyed members on the issues; published flyers; prodded locals to hold before-work rallies; and put some rank and filers on the national bargaining committee. International officers and staff traveled to local meetings around the country; some attended the TDU convention last fall. (West 1997, 14)

Well-paid, full-time UPS workers willingly risked their positions by striking for the benefit of their fellow UPS workers who were part-time and low-paid. The Teamsters persuasively convinced their drivers earning about $20 an hour to go on the picket line to support full-time jobs for part-timers who were starting at $8 an hour. UPS pilots also honored the strike, in return for support later in the year from other UPS workers when the pilots entered contract negotiations. The new democracy meant that only a few thousand union members failed to join the strike, so the Teamsters' public front was almost completely united (Witt and Wilson, 1998).

Second, the Teamsters effectively turned the news media's consumer orientation to their benefit. The main issue of the strike was fairness to workers and the ability to make a living wage, the kind of wage that allows workers to enjoy the fruits of their wage labor in the consumer economy (Glickman 1997). As Jim West observed in *Labor Notes*, this was a salient issue. "Fighting for full-time jobs that can support a family resonated with workers throughout the country, many of whom have similar problems" (West 1997, 14). The work stoppage successfully struck a chord with Americans disturbed by the trend of downsizing: well-paid, full-time, family-wage jobs being replaced with low-paying positions with no benefits and little security—while corporate profits soar. In fact, the ABC News/Nightline Poll found that 65 percent of respondents agreed that part-time workers should get the same health insurance as full-time workers, and 82 percent felt that part-timers should get the same pay as full-timers for equal work (Langer 1997).

The idea that workers should get paid enough to be good consumers is an old one in the United States, and was popularized in 1914 by Henry Ford's offer to pay his auto plant workers at least $5 a day, enough of a wage to be able to buy the cars they built and the new, corresponding consumer lifestyle (Gartman 1986). The idea of decent living standards was renewed for labor's efforts when the new head of the AFL-CIO, John Sweeney, declared in 1996 that "America needs a raise" (Kusnet 1998). A year later, the Teamsters had a similar slogan for the UPS strike: "Part-time America won't work." The Teamsters had prepared for nearly a year to communicate the idea of a living wage to the news media, and trained their rank-and-file workers to speak effectively on the topic (Manheim 2001). As a result, mixed in with stories that exaggerated worker violence and the strike's threat to the U.S. economy were at least two network television packages that investigated the use of part-time workers in the economy.

After a story lamenting the slowdown in car parts deliveries to mechanics (on August 4, the first day of the strike), Dan Rather introduced a second report, which offered context for one of the strike's central issues:

RATHER: We want to give you a closer look now at one of the key issues in the strike because its one that goes beyond the Teamsters and UPS. It's the use of part-time, as opposed to full-time, workers. As CBS News economics correspondent Ray Brady reports, it's a trend in this country that is growing fast.

BRADY (voice over picket lines and file footage of UPS workers quickly sorting boxes along the conveyer belt lines of an immense facility): UPS employs more part-time workers than any other company—fully two-thirds of its workforce. And that's the problem. Some part-timers get just three hours of work a day, for a starting salary that hasn't been raised since 1982.

UNIDENTIFIED FEMALE WORKER (on picket line): We're guaranteed three hours. We're begging for more. We cannot live on three hours.

BRADY (voice over picket lines): Even part-timers who get more hours say they're paid half as much as full-timers.

UNIDENTIFIED MALE WORKER: They got us working like forty hours a week and still keeping us at a part-time rate.

Brady's package for CBS continued with the story of a sixty-three-year-old woman who had worked at Woolworth's for twenty-seven years when she was fired and replaced with part-timers who earned less money and no benefits. Brady's on-camera conclusion focused on the sobering reality of business's increasing use of part-time labor: "Unions may feel that this is the time to make an issue of low-paid part-timers. As the ranks of these workers grow, more Americans may be wondering, could I be replaced by one of them?"

On the second day of the strike, August 5, NBC broadcast a package that also investigated the problem of part-time work.

TOM BROKAW (anchor): Of course, one of the issues at the heart of this strike is the practice of hiring part-time workers for long-term jobs. It's a practice in which UPS is certainly not alone in this country . . .

MIKE JENSEN (reporter, voice over picket line): Six out of ten workers at UPS are part-timers, and a lot of them want full-time jobs.

CECELIA FRETS, UPS WORKER (on picket line): I would like to make full-time, but they're not going to give it to us.

JENSEN (voice over picket line, shots of man on line): Anthony Diaz gets only four hours of work a day. He'd like eight.

DIAZ: I live with my three sisters and my grandmother, and help them and support them.

JENSEN: (voice over images of waitress, Wal-Mart store, and hotel doorman working): It's a sign of the times. Almost every company in America hires temporary or part-time workers in the name of efficiency—UPS because its work comes in spurts.

JIM KELLY, UPS CHAIRMAN (voice begins over shots of UPS workers sorting, then goes to a head shot of him): We have three or four hours where we have to sort packages, and there's no work before that, and no work after that, *in many cases*.
JENSEN: The number of temporary workers is up 400 percent in the last fifteen years. And one out of every five workers is part-time. Some labor experts defend part-time work.
PROF. JEFF SONNENFELD, EMORY UNIVERSITY: An awful lot of people got new footing into the world of work in a very important way in a critical time in their lives. And that's through part-time work.

If Jensen were a more enterprising reporter, he might have taken Kelly to task for the suggestion that there is nothing more than a few hours of work a day for workers classified as part-time at UPS. Kelly's use of *in many cases* obscured the fact that more than 10,000 UPS "part-time" workers put in over thirty-five hours a week (Slaughter 1997). If Jensen were a more accurate reporter, he would have better described the background of his expert labor source Sonnenfeld, who curiously seems to be an apologist for part-time jobs. In fact, Sonnenfeld was not a "labor expert," but a management professor—who had worked professionally as a consultant for UPS executives (Myerson 1997; Associated Press 1997).

Despite the report's shortcomings and inaccuracies, Jensen's package still made clear that part-time work was destroying the full-time job market:

PONCE, UPS WORKER (on picket line, with his young son on his shoulders): I got two kids and a wife. What I take home after taxes is about $120.
PONCE (new shot, with Jensen nodding slightly as he stands beside Ponce): You can't survive. It's impossible, impossible.
JENSEN (voice over shots of picket line, including Ponce and son): A part-time job can be a stepping-stone. But if you want to work full-time and can't, part-time is more like a dead end.

In these reports, the message planning of the Teamsters was clearly effective. Within the constraints of consumerism, the Teamsters were able to show that UPS was denying its thousands of part-time workers a living wage for them and their families, and that this was part of a national trend affecting millions more.

A third element that aided the UPS workers in their struggle with UPS was the workers' existing goodwill with millions of Americans. An ABC News.com timeline reflecting on the major stories of 1997 captured the American sentiment toward UPS workers: "In early August the nation learned—through sudden deprivation—just how completely dependent we have become on the armada of brown UPS vans and their ever-friendly drivers" ("UPS strike starts" 1997). Unlike laborers in so many sectors of the American economy, UPS workers have daily contact with people—a lot of people, since each UPS driver delivers up to 500 packages a day ("UPS story" 2002). Because UPS delivery drivers work regular routes, they build personal relationships with their customers. The *New York Times* in an August 17, 1997, story related one such anecdote:

> In Brooklyn, Michael Rodriguez, owner of Open Road Cycles, said he sympathized with the Teamster strikers partly because he was so fond of his brown-suited U.P.S. driver. "The workers do work hard," he said. "I have some feelings for my regular guy. They do deserve something." (Greenhouse 1997)

It is a fact of the consumer-based economy that most people don't have knowledge of a worker's daily life or the process of production. Through its framing of labor stories, as noted in frame 2, the news characterizes this lack of disclosure as normal. The UPS case is unique because it's a rare situation where the public didn't rely on the news media to communicate the experience of the worker. Moreover, UPS advertising portrayed its delivery people as noble, courageous workers—the dedicated people who made UPS "the tightest ship in the shipping business."

Fourth, the economy was good. The American economy was doing well for businesses, with high profits and low unemployment in 1997. UPS too was extremely successful, with 80 percent of the nation's parcel business, $1.15 billion in profits in the previous year, and a profit rate of 19.4 percent, which dwarfed competitors like Federal Express and the U.S. Postal Service. Yet UPS workers—like workers in many industries—did not completely share in the fruits of the economy. Given the good economy, it was hard for UPS to make the argument that they were in a precarious fiscal situation or that they were highly pressured to stay competitive.

The strike, the largest walkout since the 1983 AT&T strike, lasted fifteen days. The resulting settlement created 10,000 new full-time jobs, reduced the wage differential with raises for full-time workers and larger raises for part-timers, prohibited UPS from taking control of the workers pension fund, and limited subcontracting of labor. Thus, with their advance planning, the Teamsters were able to turn to their favor every one of the five major frames used by the consumer-oriented news media:

- *The consumer is king.* The Teamsters plainly showed that UPS denied part-timers a living wage and the ability to be normal, everyday consumers.
- *The process of production is none of the public's business.* The Teamsters trained their workers to be articulate on the issues and traded on their uniformed workers' long-term goodwill with the public, as well as the public's knowledge of their hard work.
- *The economy is driven by great business leaders and entrepreneurs.* Although the typical news framing of labor stories suggests that great business leaders and entrepreneurs drive the economy, the nucleus of UPS operations is their brown-clad workers, and the company's own advertising heralds their contributions.

- *The workplace is a meritocracy.* It was quite evident that the UPS workplace wasn't a meritocracy. Full-time and part-time workers performed the same tasks but earned grossly disparate wages.
- *Collective economic action is bad.* It was hard to argue that this collective action was bad. Although the strike inconvenienced some people (which the news pointed out many times), the public largely supported this strike. Moreover, holding 80 percent of the parcel business and earning more than a billion dollars in profits the previous year, it was hard for UPS to claim it was under attack.

Although the Teamsters were able to engage the typical news frames to their advantage, the limits of consumer-oriented frames were also apparent in the UPS case. The other important issue for the Teamsters was control of the union's pension fund. UPS wanted to withdraw from the union's multi-employer pension plan and administer its own pension fund for workers. It wasn't until an August 17 report by CBS—about two weeks into the strike—that any of the television news reports even attempted to explain why workers might not want their pension in the hands of their employer. As the package by correspondent Troy Roberts explained, retired Pan Am airline workers continue to suffer from underpayment of their pensions after Pan Am went bankrupt in 1991 and ceased operations.

### Back to the Same Old Frames

Many observers hailed the Teamster victory as a victory for all of labor, and a milestone that would mark labor's resurgence. On the network television news, an NBC report on August 18, an ABC report on August 19, and a CBS report on August 20 all covered the new life in the U.S. labor movement, after years of decline. Yet, for the corporate news media, any levity that might be associated with broad public support for the Teamsters and a possible upswing in fortunes for working people was strongly tempered with worry about Corporate America's bottom line. Clearly, the prophets of Wall Street get the final word on whether or not anyone beyond the Teamsters should be pleased by the UPS settlement. On Sunday, August 17, a day before the resolution of the work stoppage, CBS News weekend anchor Russ Mitchell speculated on the causes of a stock market drop at the end of the previous week:

> MITCHELL (voice over video of Teamsters picketing): Another problem may be the UPS strike. Even though polls show most Americans are siding with workers in the dispute, some investors think labor's demands in the strike could spill over into contract talks at other companies and cut into corporate profits.

At *ABC World News Tonight* on Tuesday, August 19, the day the strike ended, ABC carried its report on labor's new momentum. Immediately afterward, anchor Peter Jennings cheerily reported that "the stock market seemed genuinely pleased with the UPS settlement," and noted the upturn in the Dow Jones index and the NASDAQ market. The same day, economics correspondent Ray Brady filed his final report on the UPS strike for the *CBS Evening News*. In his on-camera summary, Brady concluded:

> BRADY: There have been concerns this settlement might set off a whole new round of wage increases in other industries and heat up inflation. But that's not likely for now. There are no big labor contracts like rubber, autos, or steel coming up until next year.

Even after labor's biggest victory in two decades, the mainstream news media slid back into the same old consumer-oriented news frames. The good news, it would seem, is not that working people might get a well-deserved raise in an era of rising profits, but that Corporate America's profits (and, of course, the prices of consumer goods) wouldn't again be threatened for at least a year.

## WHAT SHOULD WE EXPECT?
## THE FUTURE OF LABOR IN THE CORPORATE NEWS

Consumerism can sometimes be the basis for coverage in labor's interest when the consumption-production link is apparent. Some of the most powerful news stories of recent years have developed when consumption gets linked back to production. (Of course, the mainstream news media, which don't regularly cover a labor beat, and rarely use investigative reporters, rarely shed light on production and labor. The impetus for such stories usually begins with social activism by labor or other organizations.) For example, the production-consumption link was visible in much of the UPS story. In some ways, it was undeniable, since many people were personally acquainted with the 185,000 striking UPS workers across the country. In other words, the consumers knew the people who did the work and identified them as regular people with valid concerns—not as the faceless, potentially demonized members of organized labor. The reform-minded Teamsters also did an excellent job of communicating their message of a living wage to the media and the people.

The story of Wal-Mart and its use of sweatshop labor—which used the narrative hook of Kathie Lee Gifford's Wal-Mart clothing line—was another major news item that linked the often invisible process of production to consumption. As historian Lawrence Glickman explains, the recent and historic campaigns for a "living wage" have been ways in which labor has advantageously linked consumerism—the ability earn a wage so that one can live in a comfortable fashion—to production (Glickman 1997). By March 2002, more than eighty local living wage ordinances had been passed in the United States (Kern and Luce 2002).

The news media, though, generally don't portray the link between consumption and production, often because the production process and treatment of labor doesn't reflect very favorably on their advertisers or own corporate parents. In fact, it scares the hell out of businesses when they can't control the image of production (witness Phil Knight's and Nike's discomforts over charges of sweatshop labor). Businesses don't want to call attention to production, which is exactly what labor and consumer advocates do. (The World Trade Organization protests in Seattle are an example of such unwanted publicity.) Businesses often fight to control or hide the image of production through public relations and advertising. GM's efforts to make Saturn a "different" people-friendly auto company and Wal-Mart's advertised "Buy American" policy are both approaches (rather transparent approaches to the keen observer) that try to mask the true modes of production. Recent books from the left (e.g., Thomas Frank, *The Conquest of Cool: Business Culture, Counterculture, and the Rise of Hip Consumerism*) and the right (e.g., David Brooks, *Bobos in Paradise: The New Upper Class and How They Got There*) detail how business, through advertising and PR, now sells consumption as hip and countercultural, and business entrepreneurialism as equally radical. This is only possible, though, by obscuring labor and class relations, and true radical social action.

Thus there is a constant battle between corporate interests defining consumerism in one fashion—buy, buy, buy, and let business do as it wishes—versus labor, which asks for a living wage to participate in a consumer economy, and also fair, safe modes of production. The major news media are commercial, corporate media, and generally frame news stories in ways that favor corporate interests. But, in cases of widespread public activism by labor and other social groups, news cannot afford to be *seen* as acting as lackeys of corporate capitalism. In these instances, the news media are unable to frame labor news from their typical consumer economy perspective, and must report the story that presents clear criticism of the production side of the economy to sustain their own credibility. In other words, the mainstream news media won't cover labor news, and won't cover it with favorable frames, unless the stories are thrust on them. Then, of course, corporate damage control teams work to reestablish corporate-friendly framing of news events. The UPS "brown" branding campaign of 2002 was one part of this effort, publicizing the corporate processes and obscuring the company's former symbol—the people who do the work.

## NOTES

1. The TV ads also ran during broadcasts of the NCAA men's basketball tournament, the Academy Awards, and on CNN, CNBC, Fox News Channel, and Discovery in 2002. The print ads appeared in the *Wall Street Journal, Business Week, Forbes, Fortune, Newsweek, Sports Illustrated*, and *Time*.

2. Craighill, project director of the Pew Research Center for the People and the Press, supplied News Interest Index data for all labor stories in their surveys from the 1990s.

# REFERENCES

AFL-CIO Committee on the Evolution of Work. 1985. *The changing situation of workers and their unions*. Washington, D.C.: AFL-CIO.

Associated Press. 1997. Star business professor falls amid vandalism allegations. *Augusta Chronicle* Online, December 23. www.augustachronicle.com/stories/122397/biz_dean.shtml.

Bennett, Lance, and Murray Edelman. 1985. "Toward a new political narrative." *Journal of Communication* 35, no. 4: 159.

Brecher, Jeremy. 1997. *Strike!* Cambridge: South End.

Carey, James W. 1989. *Communication as culture: Essays on media and society*. Boston: Unwin Hyman.

Craighill, Peyton M. 2001. E-mail to the author, August 15.

Croteau, David. 1998. Challenging the "liberal media" claim. *Extra!* July-August, 4–9.

Department of Labor. Bureau of Labor Statistics. 2000. Union members in 2000. ftp://ftp.bls.gov/pub/news.release/union2.txt.

Elliott, Stuart. 2002. "Going big on brown." Advertising newsletter, *New York Times* on the Web, February 19, 2002. www.nytimes.com/email.

Field, David. 1997. Poll: 55% support strikers at UPS. *USA Today*, August 15, A1.

Fones-Wolf, Elizabeth. 1994. *Selling free enterprise: The business assault on labor and liberalism, 1945–60*. Urbana: University of Illinois Press.

Frank, Thomas. 1997. *Commodify your dissent*. New York: Norton.

Freeman, Richard B., and Joel Rogers. 1999. *What workers want*. Ithaca, N.Y.: Cornell University Press.

Gans, Herbert J. 1979. *Deciding what's news: A study of* CBS Evening News, NBC Nightly News, Newsweek, *and* Time. New York: Pantheon.

Gartman, David. 1986. *Auto slavery: The labor process in the American automobile industry, 1987–1950*. New Brunswick, N.J.: Rutgers University Press.

Gitlin, Todd. 1980. *The whole world is watching*. Berkeley: University of California Press.

Glasgow University Media Group. 1976. *Bad news*. Vol. 1. London: Routledge and Kegan Paul.

———. 1980. *More bad news*. Vol. 2. London: Routledge & Kegan Paul.

———. 1982. *Really bad news*. Vol. 3. London: Readers & Writers.

Glickman, Lawrence B. 1997. *A living wage: American workers and the making of consumer society*. Ithaca, N.Y.: Cornell University Press.

Golding, Peter, and Graham Murdock. 1991. Culture, communications, and political economy. In *Mass media and society*, edited by James Curran and Michael Gurevitch, 11–30. London: Edward Arnold.

Goldman, Robert, and Stephen Papson. 1996. *Sign wars*. New York: Guilford.

Greenhouse, Steven. 1997. Strikers at U.P.S. backed by public. *New York Times,* August 17, A1, A16.

Henriques, Diana B. 2000. Business reporting: behind the curve. *Columbia Journalism Review*, November-December, 18–21.

Kern, Jen, and Stephanie Luce. 2002. Living wage movement greets the recession with new victories. *Labor Notes*, March, 1, 14.

Kusnet, David. 1998. The "America needs a raise" campaign. In *Not your father's union movement: Inside the AFL-CIO,* edited by Jo-Ann Mort, 167–78. London: Verso.

Langer, Gary. 1997. Poll: Keep Clinton out of U.P.S. ABC News.com, August 12, 1997. http://more.abcnews.go.com/sections/us/upspoll812/index.html.

Lichter, S. Robert, Stanley Rothman, and Linda S. Lichter. 1986. *The media elite.* Bethesda, Md.: Adler & Adler.

Manheim, Jarol B. 2001. *The death of a thousand cuts: Corporate campaigns and the attack on the corporation.* Mahwah, N.J.: Lawrence Erlbaum.

Martin, Christopher R. Forthcoming. *Framed! Labor and the corporate media.* Ithaca, N.Y.: ILR Press.

Miliband, Ralph. 1969. *The state in capitalist society.* London: Weidenfeld & Nicolson.

Morley, David. 1976. Industrial conflict and the mass media. *Sociological Review* 24, no. 2: 245–68.

Myerson, Allen. 1997. Fracturing U.P.S. image of labor peace. *New York Times,* August 10, A16.

Parenti, Michael. 1986. *Inventing reality: The politics of mass media.* New York: St. Martin's.

Parker, Laura. 1997. Town finds strike is inconvenience but not calamity. *USA Today,* August 15, 6A.

Poole, Gary Andrew. 2000. "'Wealth porn' and beyond." *Columbia Journalism Review,* November-December 2000, 22–23.

Puette, William J. 1992. *Through jaundiced eyes: How the media view organized labor.* Ithaca, N.Y.: ILR Press.

Reeves, Jimmie L., and Richard Campbell. 1994. *Cracked coverage: Television news, the anti-cocaine crusade, and the Reagan legacy.* Durham, N.C.: Duke University Press.

Rollings, Jerry. 1983. Mass communications and the American worker. In *Labor, the working class, and the media.* Vol. 1 of *The critical communications review,* edited by Vincent Mosco and Janet Wasko. Norwood, N.J.: Ablex.

Schor, Juliet B. 2000. Towards a new politics of consumption. In *The consumer society reader,* edited by Juliet B. Schor and Douglas B. Holt, 446–62. New York: New Press.

Slaughter, Jane. 1997. Teamsters may strike UPS for full-time jobs. *Labor Notes,* August 1, 14.

Sussman, Leila. 1945. Labor in the radio news: An analysis of content. *Journalism Quarterly* 22, no. 3: 207–15.

Tasini, Jonathan. 1990. Lost in the margins: Labor and the media. *Extra!* 3, no. 7: 2–11.

UPS. 2002. The UPS story. 25 March 25. www.ups.com/about/story.html.

UPS strike starts. 1997. ABC News.com, August 4. http://more.abcnews.go.com/sections/world/1997/97_ups.html.

West, Jim. 1997. "Big win at UPS!" *Labor Notes,* September 1, 14–15.

Witt, Matt, and Rand Wilson. 1998. Part-time America won't work: The Teamsters fight for good jobs at UPS. In *Not your father's union movement: Inside the AFL-CIO,* edited by Jo-Ann Mort, 179–87. London: Verso.

# V

PROSPECTS FOR CHANGE

A book can be considered successful if it clearly lays out tenets of a problem. But often there's little regard for what might be done to work toward a solution to that problem. Class differences, by almost any definition, will continue to be with us into the indefinite future. But how the news media deal with class is another matter.

In this final section authors look at one of the more interesting developments in journalism that has emerged in the past decade or so: civic or public journalism. James Ettema and Limor Peer revisit a groundbreaking study they did concerning coverage of two Chicago neighborhoods. Along with recapping some of their original quantitative findings, they add results from qualitative interviews and examine what role public journalism might play in newspaper coverage of neighborhoods with significantly different economic profiles.

Paul Jones and Michael Pusey contribute an international perspective with their study about talk radio in Australia and how radio programs help produce an informed citizenry, largely along class lines. David Kurpius, who's work has centered on examining civic journalism, weighs in with some observations about portrayals of class in broadcast programs recognized for excellent adherence to principles of civic journalism.

# 15

## Good News from a Bad Neighborhood: Urban Journalism and Community Assets

*James S. Ettema and Limor Peer*

Using an evermore elaborate language of social pathology to describe lower-income urban neighborhoods—poverty-stricken, crime-ridden, violence-prone, welfare-dependent, drug-infested, gang-ruled, predator-haunted—America has come to understand these communities entirely in terms of their problems. Guided by such terms, government agencies, educational institutions, and philanthropic foundations have responded with what urban sociologists John Kretzmann and John McKnight characterize as "deficiency-oriented policies and programs." And as a result, these neighborhoods have become "environments of service" in which residents may to see themselves as "fundamentally deficient, victims incapable of taking charge of their lives and of their community's future" (1993, 4).

These problem-focused descriptions and the resulting deficiency-oriented mind-set must be replaced, Kretzman and McKnight insist, by a conception of the urban community that recognizes "the capacities, skills, and assets of lower income people and their neighborhoods" (1993, 5). Such a capacity-focused description would direct the attention of agencies, institutions, and the neighborhoods themselves to what is present in the community, "the capacities of its residents and workers, the associational and institutional base of the area," rather than what is absent (9). The authors go on to define what might well be understood as a basic vocabulary for asset-based community development that specifies the meaning for social planning and action of large institutions such as education and health care and small organizations such as neighborhood-based associations and block clubs as well as individual citizens.

## JOURNALISM AS A VOCABULARY OF ASSETS

The search by community development practitioners for new terms in which to conceive the community clearly parallels the search by some journalists for new terms in which to cover it. That search, often conducted under the rubric of public journalism, is a quest not merely for a new approach to reporting but a new role for journalism in the democratic process. More than just dissemination of information about public affairs, civic journalism seeks citizen participation in public life. To accomplish this, news organizations must establish relationships with communities that allow journalists to carefully and systematically listen to citizen concerns, to continuously report in depth on those concerns and to facilitate public deliberation on how those concerns are to be addressed. "Public journalists have to look for ways to strengthen their community's goodwill, cooperative habits, insights into where other social groups are coming from," writes Arthur Charity concluding that these are "the groundwork factors of democracy" (1995, 11).

Civic journalism, according to leading proponent Jay Rosen is a search for nothing less than a new "theory of credibility," a reconception of news that would emphasize community connection over objective detachment and substantive dialogue over official pronouncement. Under the ideal new theory, Rosen tells journalists, "Credibility follows because you're concerned, because you care, because it matters to you what happens in the community" (Rosen 1993, 53). As an actual newsroom practice civic journalism has often taken the form of a special project: candidate forum, opinion poll, interpretive series. Although a new theory of credibility would continue to inspire major projects from time to time, it could also inform ordinary newsgathering from day to day. Routine coverage of community affairs, no less than extended coverage of major campaigns and crises, could be revised and renewed by a theory of journalism that recognizes the importance of community care.

The search for such a theory might well proceed by assessing the ability of journalistic language to express concern to, and for, communities. This study critiques the discourse of urban pathology, but at the same time it disputes the common contention of community leaders that all the "bad news" from urban neighborhoods should be, or even could be, balanced with more "good news." As an alternative, this study promotes a vocabulary of assets. Terms in this vocabulary are already familiar to reporters, but they take on expanded meanings in the context of concern for communities. For example, a term such as "neighborhood-based citizen association," understood as a basic element of community building, may come to mean greater credibility as a community information source. Thus this study begins with the conviction that the vocabulary of community assets can enhance the language of journalism just as it has begun to enhance the language of community development. And indeed our interviews show that journalists readily acknowledge the relevance of asset-oriented language to lower-income neighborhoods. Journalists also recognize the tensions that such language creates within the conceptual system of urban affairs reporting; but that is precisely the point of our project—to challenge conventions of journalistic practice.

## The Research Project

For this study, we returned to an urban laboratory that for more than a century has been a crucible of civic thought and action—the city of Chicago. We conducted a quantitative content analysis using Kretzmann and McKnight's ideas about pathologies versus assets to compare news coverage of two very urban but very different neighborhoods: Austin, a lower-income neighborhood on the city's Far West Side, and Lincoln Park, a higher-income neighborhood on the Near North Side.[1] Stories concerning these neighborhoods appearing in the city's two metropolitan newspapers, *Chicago Tribune* and *Chicago Sun-Times*, during 1993 were located in an electronic search and screened to eliminate those that mentioned the neighborhood only in passing (e.g., restaurant reviews). This procedure yielded 161 stories about Austin and 324 stories about Lincoln Park—an interesting finding in its own right. One-half of the stories about Lincoln Park were then randomly selected for analysis, yielding a sample of 162 for that neighborhood. Items less than one paragraph in length (e.g., photo captions) were then deleted, yielding 161 stories for Austin and 155 stories for Lincoln Park.

With the individual story as the unit of analysis, thirteen undergraduates enrolled in a senior seminar examined the coverage of the two neighborhoods. A coder determined whether or not each story was framed in terms of a social problem (i.e., whether the story analyzed a problem or reported a situation or event readily attributable to a problem). Whether or not the story was so framed, the coder determined what the story was about (e.g., crime, education) and whether the story concerned a positive situation or development from the point of view of neighborhood residents or a negative development or something in between. Using a list adopted from Kretzmann and McKnight, the coder also checked the story for any mention of community assets.[2]

The content analysis revealed some unexpected features of neighborhood coverage and raised some interesting issues about the possibilities for a journalistic vocabulary of community assets. To further explore these issues, we discussed our findings with editors and reporters at a *Tribune* news huddle. We also discussed them in a series of on-the-record interviews with urban affairs journalists conducted in mid-1995. For the *Tribune* these discussions came at a pivotal moment. Earlier in 1995 the paper had begun to reorganize—indeed, to rethink—its coverage of the city. It had created the urban affairs team and had assigned members to each of the nine zones into which the city had been divided. The task for the reporters would not be to cover all community meetings and events as would a neighborhood paper but to gather information from diverse, often nontraditional sources and with that information to produce stories of interest beyond a single neighborhood.

"Rather than being the outside observer, standing way back, looking at the city, finding these huge problems and talking at people, our goal is to make sense of things from the standpoint of people's daily lives," Byron White, assistant metro editor, told us in 1995. "There are a whole lot of folks who we write about but never talk to." As succinctly summarized by reporter Patrick Reardon, the goal of the team would be to "move away from the press conference attitude." And as we shall hear from Reardon and his colleagues, the vocabulary of community assets is not unutterably foreign to journalists willing to relinquish that attitude. Such a vocabulary does, however, strain established conventions—perhaps enough to matter.

In late 2002 we returned to the *Tribune* newsroom for another series of on-the-record interviews with reporters and editors. We found that in the intervening years, the newspaper's urban affairs approach, along with its urban affairs staff, had changed. "Our thinking today is much different," said Hanke Gratteau, associate managing editor for metropolitan news, noting the demise of the nine-zone system. "We're trying to push the organization of subject matter toward more thematic approaches." A key feature of this push is greater use of temporary reporting teams on major stories. "If we have an urban affairs team, who should be on it? And if you think about that thematically the answer is: my city hall reporters, my education reporters, my transportation reporters," she said. "Almost everybody at the paper should play a role in shaping our urban affairs coverage."

Another feature of the new approach according to Gratteau is a region-wide perspective on major stories. "We used to think of urban affairs coverage as stopping at the city's geographic limits; but its clear from all sorts of signs and symbols, the census being one of them, that a lot of topics thought of as urban affairs coverage don't end at the city's borders," she said. "We need to reach out, to get our reporters at bureaus throughout the region to think about housing stories or integration/segregation stories or community building stories."

In this chapter, we juxtapose the content analysis results with reporters' reaction in 1995 to those findings. Thereby we recreate a dialogue on the limits to, and the opportunities for renewal in, contemporary journalistic practice conducted at the moment that these journalists were embarking on a new venture in urban journalism. (We also include brief excerpts from interviews with Austin community leaders conducted in 1995.) To conclude this chapter we move on to the interviews conducted in 2002. And as we learn from Gratteau and her colleagues, the vocabulary of community assets still strains established conventions.

## In a Bad Neighborhood

As Kretzmann and McKnight would have expected, the content analysis reveals that newspaper coverage of the lower-income Austin neighborhood is largely a discourse of urban pathology. More than two-thirds (69 percent) of the stories about Austin in the *Tribune* and *Sun-Times* are framed in terms of a social problem. In contrast, less than one-quarter (22 percent) of the stories about Lincoln Park are framed in that way. For readers of either newspaper, Austin is a bad neighborhood.

In the terms of urban pathology, Austin is "crime-ridden" and "drug-infested." As table 15.1 indicates, crime (which includes drug dealing and use as well as gang violence and domestic abuse) not only leads the list of the five most frequently reported problems in Austin, it is the topic of more than half of all problem-oriented stories from that neighborhood. Far behind crime are assorted social, political, and economic topics that could not be categorized elsewhere, such as a boycott against the state lottery. Behind those are the topics that might well be understood as the underlying problems of any lower income area: business activity, housing, and education.

In Lincoln Park, crime also leads the list of the most frequently covered social problems, though crime does not dominate the list as it does in Austin. While Lincoln Park actually had slightly more reported criminal offenses

**Table 15.1.   Five Most Frequently Cited Problems in Stories about Austin and Lincoln Park, *Chicago Tribune* and *Sun-Times*, 1993**[a]

| Rank | Austin<br>n = 111 | Lincoln Park<br>n = 34 |
| --- | --- | --- |
| 1 | Crime<br>51%<br>n = 57 | Crime<br>24%<br>n = 8 |
| 2 | Social/political/<br>economic<br>11%<br>n = 12 | Infrastructure<br>21%<br>n = 7 |
| 3 | Business<br>10%<br>n = 11 | Neighborhood life<br>12%<br>n = 4 |
| 4 | Housing/real<br>estate<br>7%<br>n = 8 | Social/political/<br>economic<br>12%<br>n = 4 |
| 5 | Education<br>7%<br>n = 8 | Education<br>12%<br>n = 4 |

[a]The reliability coefficient for FRAME is k = .81.

than Austin (10,550 compared to 10,370 in 1992), it had far fewer violent crimes. Austin, therefore, is more likely to generate a true-life crime story (e.g., "Boy, 8, fatally shot during squabble between 2 drivers") that offers a gripping narrative and, in turn, broad-based reader appeal (McWhirter and Poe 1993, 3).

Journalists who cover these neighborhoods are no more surprised than their critics at the level of attention to social problems in general and crime in particular. "We struggle to find ways to cover what's *not* a social problem," said Byron White, noting that most reporters are more interested in covering problems. "The reaction you get is: 'if its not a problem, why cover it? What's the story?'"

Specifically in regard to crime, Patrick Reardon noted that "it's easy and cheap to cover," citing what he called "the source infrastructure" that interlocks with "the journalistic infrastructure" to move crime information quickly and easily from police to press. But in addition to the well-established institutional arrangements for covering crime, Reardon cited the apparent conceptual simplicity of crime stories in comparison to stories about most other problems confronting neighborhoods. "Crime is easy for us also because it's a clear-cut thing. A guy's dead and you only need to talk to one source: the cops," he acknowledged. Conversely Reardon attributed the relative inattention to neighborhood schools to the lack of infrastructural support as well as conceptual complexity. "If it were easier to cover schools, we would have more coverage," he said. "If every week there were reading scores for every school and you could chart them; and if they were in a computer bank and you could just press a button, then we would probably have more coverage."

Despite the lingering grip of traditional practices, these reporters affirmed the possibility of, and their commitment to, a new kind of urban affairs reporting. One of their goals, White said, was to "cover the city from the grassroots" rather than rely entirely on institutional infrastructures to identify news. "Often times what happens is that there's a story that comes out of some institution—whether a government study, a police investigation, a court case or university research—and reporters put a human face on the story by going out into the community to verify the findings," he said. "We're trying to turn that on its head—to get the story before it rises up to city hall. When it's necessary, we'll find experts to verify what we've learned at the grassroots level." These journalists, in other words, recognize that they can—and should—transcend the routinized discourse of urban pathology.

### Good News versus Bad

The level of attention to social problems in the Austin neighborhood was no more of a surprise to community group leaders than to the reporters. "The downtown papers, *Sun-Times* and *Tribune*, cover more of the negative, drug-related issues of the community," said Glenda Cunningham-Ross, a community organizer. "They don't highlight enough of the good things or the strengths of the community." Cunningham-Ross's sense of overemphasis on negative stories—bad news—and lack of attention to more positive stories was echoed by Jackie Reed, the executive director of a community-based health organization, who wanted a more evenhanded portrayal of the neighborhood. "Generally, I think the community is portrayed as a very bad place for people to live," Reed said. "If the *Tribune* was my paper, and if I could look at it not only in terms of entertaining suburban people who buy it but also real service, I think I would make sure there was more balance."

In light of such comments, the results of the content analysis may hold something of a surprise after all; as table 15.2 reveals, a majority of the stories from Austin were coded as a positive situation or development—good news—for the community. Indeed, the percentage of positive stories from Austin is twice that of the negative stories and is even slightly higher than the percentage of positive stories from Lincoln Park. Austin also generates more negative stories than Lincoln Park, however, and sometimes that news, especially crime, can be very bad, as well as very dramatic. Those are often the instances to which complaints about overemphasis on bad news refer.

Reporters are sensitive to such instances but still may find the complaints annoying. "I don't like to use 'positive' and 'negative' to discuss stories," said reporter Janita Poe, "but if we're going to use those terms, then there are some very positive stories that go unnoticed." Poe said that she has been "bashed over and over again" by other African Americans about certain stories. "I think what happens is that people clip them and circulate them and, all of a sudden, the *Tribune* is this terrible monster," she said. "No one seems to be clipping those 'positive' stories that we do all the time." Poe thought many of her critics simply didn't read the paper very carefully. "But then I do understand," she concluded, "that maybe they are not reading us on a regular basis because, historically, we didn't serve them well."

Table 15.2.   Good News and Bad News, *Chicago Tribune* and *Sun-Times*, 1993[a]

| Type of News[b] | Austin n = 161 | Lincoln Park n = 155 |
|---|---|---|
| Good | 57% | 52% |
| | n = 91 | n = 80 |
| Bad | 27% | 9% |
| | n = 44 | n = 14 |
| Mixed | 11% | 13% |
| | n = 17 | n = 20 |
| Neither | 6% | 27% |
| | n = 9 | n = 41 |

[a]$\chi^2$ = 36.8474, d.f. = 3, $p <$ .0000.
[b]The reliability coefficient for GOODBAD is k = .90.

If more than two-thirds of the Austin coverage is framed in terms of social problems, and yet more than half of the coverage is "good news," then much of that coverage must concern positive developments in regard to problems. Among stories cast in terms of social problems, as table 15.3 shows, Austin does generate more positive stories (52 percent) than negative stories (34 percent). Among such stories, Austin even generates more good news than Lincoln Park (41 percent). And among the smaller number of stories *not* cast in terms of social problems, Austin is absolutely brimming with good news (66 percent) even when compared to Lincoln Park (55 percent). Thus the good news from this bad neighborhood is largely that somebody seems to be responding in some way to some symptom of urban pathology.

Community leaders might greet all of this good news with surprise; but as Poe's comments suggest, reporters greet it with professional unease. Several reporters wondered aloud whether the results of the content analysis could indicate a lack of tough-mindedness. "Here's this plucky block club that's fighting the gangs. Well, that story is worth doing, but often it's just as inaccurate a picture of the place as a story about, you know, 'crime-ridden Austin,'" said Patrick Reardon. "So the 'good news' can be just as unthoughtful or as inaccurate as the bad news."

"Austin isn't Lincoln Park," argued Ron Grossman, "and if there are too many nice stories, I think it means that we are trying to paint too comfortable a picture of it." Grossman, the most veteran of the reporters interviewed, worried that the sympathies of younger reporters are "naturally on the side of the underdog" and also that editors might try to "artificially" balance bad news with good. "No editor goes to a reporter and says, 'Kid, go to Lincoln Park and get me a good news story,'" Grossman said. "But lots of times, they look at how much bad news they've had about an inner-city community and say, 'Can you get a lighter story from out there?'"

**Table 15.3.   Social Problems: Good or Bad News?** *Chicago Tribune* **and** *Sun-Times*, **1993**

| | Problem[a] | | No Problem[b] | |
|---|---|---|---|---|
| Type of News | Austin $n = 111$ | Lincoln Park $n = 34$ | Austin $n = 50$ | Lincoln Park $n = 120$ |
| Good | 52% $n = 58$ | 41% $n = 14$ | 66% $n = 33$ | 55% $n = 66$ |
| Bad | 34% $n = 38$ | 18% $n = 6$ | 12% $n = 6$ | 6% $n = 7$ |
| Mixed | 12% $n = 13$ | 32% $n = 11$ | 8% $n = 4$ | 8% $n = 9$ |
| Neither | 2% $n = 2$ | 9% $n = 3$ | 14% $n = 7$ | 32% $n = 38$ |

[a]$\chi^2 = 13.4242$, d.f. $= 3$, $p < .005$
[b]$\chi^2 = 6.6614$, d.f. $= 3$, n.s.

Byron White too expressed concern about an inclination to balance crime or tragedy with "a superstar story—you know, the exceptional kid who has beaten the odds and has made it." White added, however, that in any community "there are awful things going on, wonderful things going on, and there is the stuff in the middle—just daily life." He acknowledged that the urban affairs team was struggling with the question of how best to cover "just daily life" in certain neighborhoods. "We do a much better job of it in suburban communities and affluent neighborhoods," he concluded. And indeed, the content analysis indicated that of the stories from Lincoln Park *not* framed in terms of a social problem, 35 percent were categorized as "neighborhood life"—interesting people, places, and events—but of stories from Austin, only 12 percent were so categorized. "Just daily life," it seems, is more newsworthy in Lincoln Park than in Austin.

In sum, the journalists were very reluctant to evaluate, or even discuss, their work in terms of negative versus positive stories, and they were adamant in their rejection of any notion that they should systematically attempt to balance bad news with good. "If we do nice, soft, warm, and fuzzy features about people in the suburbs, we should do them in the city too, but I don't think we should do them just for balance," said Poe. "I think what we want to do is help people see these communities as real, with all of the things communities have—all of the wonderful things, all of the problems, everything in between." For Poe and her colleagues, the term "balance" does not mean an even number of positive and negative stories, but rather more in-depth reporting from more diverse sources. Thus, while community leaders may be tempted to demand a more favorable "balance" of "good news" with "bad news," they should recognize these are not terms in which journalists are willing to think about the community or their connection to it.

## Accounting for Assets

If journalism is to transcend the discourse of urban pathology without resorting to a simplistic balance of good news versus bad, then the vocabulary of community assets offers an alternative. As table 15.4 indicates, a majority of stories from both Austin and Lincoln Park (though more from Lincoln Park) refer to at least one resource found on Kretzmann and McKnight's list of community-building assets. Although most stories from Austin are framed in terms of problems, assets are often mentioned, if only in passing. Community assets, in other words, seem to be terms with which journalists already work— even if those assets are not always recognized and reported as such.

If the descriptions of the two neighborhoods in terms of social problems seem quite different, the descriptions in terms of community assets seem rather similar, as shown in table 15.4. Local institutions and agencies— whether economic, governmental, or cultural—are the most often mentioned assets in both Austin (39 percent) and Lincoln Park (63 percent). The

24 percent difference might seem to suggest simply that Lincoln Park has more assets; but the discrepancy is accounted for largely by mentions of a single institutional asset: the lakefront park that gives the neighborhood its name. Twenty percent of all stories about the Lincoln Park neighborhood mention the park while only 1 percent of the stories about Austin mention any park.

The green expanse of Lincoln Park, located between a palisade of sky-scrapers and the Lake Michigan shore, provides an excellent example of a metropolitan newspaper's vested interest in the "symbolic capital" of its core city. Such capital includes any feature of the urban environment that has come to symbolize the city and, according to Kaniss (1991), can help unite the fragmented suburban audience into a market for the downtown paper. "If we're doing a story about springtime," Janita Poe said sardonically, "we'll go right to Lincoln Park, though there are people enjoying the warm weather

**Table 15.4.　Primary Assets Mentioned in Stories about Austin and Lincoln Park, *Chicago Tribune* and *Sun-Times*, 1993**

| Assets[a,b] | Austin $n = 161$ | Lincoln Park $n = 155$ |
|---|---|---|
| No assets mentioned | 34% | 21% |
| Local institutions | 39% | 63% |
| Businesses | 9% | 9% |
| Schools | 12% | 9% |
| Parks | 1% | 20% |
| Libraries | 1% | 1% |
| Hospitals | 4% | 1% |
| Cultural institutions | 1% | 4% |
| Real estate / housing | 8% | 12% |
| Other institution | 3% | 7% |
| Citizen Association | 21% | 8% |
| Churches | 2% | 1% |
| Block clubs | — | — |
| Cultural groups | 2% | 2% |
| Other citizen association | 17% | 5% |
| Gifts of individuals | 8% | 10% |
| Youth | 2% | — |
| Elderly | — | 1% |
| Artists | 1% | 4% |
| Volunteers | 2% | 1% |
| Other individual gift | 3% | 4% |
| Total | 102%[c] | 102%[c] |

[a]Based on Kretzmann and McKnight 1993.
[b]The reliability coefficient for ASSETS is k = .88.
[c]Percentages may not equal 100 due to rounding.

in Austin too." Ironically, then, stories about the Lincoln Park neighborhood's greatest asset serve much the same news commodification function as stories about the Austin neighborhoods most heavily covered social problem: crime.

Disregarding parks, neighborhood-based institutional assets still account for the largest number of assets mentioned in both neighborhoods. Given the propensity of news to reflect institutional "infrastructures," however, the number of stories citing institutional assets (about two-fifths in both neighborhoods) does not seem particularly high. And in the same way, the number of stories citing the "gifts of individuals," about one-tenth in both neighborhoods, does not seem particularly low. Such stories concern the talents and skills of individual residents; and while these may be especially important resources for community building in lower-income areas, they are not often deemed newsworthy for a downtown newspaper.

Where the asset descriptions of these two neighborhoods most differ is in mentions of neighborhood groups. These groups, listed as "other citizen associations" in table 15.4, include neighborhood groups organized around either specific issues or the general interest of the community. In Lincoln Park, only 5 percent of the stories mention this sort of asset; but in Austin, 17 percent of the stories mention it. In neither neighborhood, however, do churches or block clubs make much news. Like the gifts of individuals, these assets are especially important to lower-income community building but do not fit the traditional definition of newsmakers.

In both Austin and Lincoln Park journalists find community assets and mention them in some way in many stories. Table 15.5 indicates how assets are mentioned. Overall, assets are cited in the context of both positive and negative developments, though somewhat more often in a positive context. Among institutional assets, schools in both neighborhoods and hospitals in Austin are examples of assets that are more often mentioned when the news is bad. A closer examination of these stories suggests that schools and hospitals, particularly in Austin, are often characterized less as assets than merely as the site at which the symptoms of urban pathology emerge, for example, a story headlined: "Shooting that leaves Austin teen brain dead apparently accidental" (Johnson 1993, 3). On the other hand, mentions of businesses and real estate in Austin are more often found when the news is good. Moreover, these sorts of institutional assets are often explicitly framed as valuable community resources, for example, a story reporting: "Avenue Bank announced it would open a branch in the West Side Austin neighborhood and would lend $40 million in the area during the next five years" (Chandler 1993, 62).

Neighborhood groups ("other citizen associations") in Austin are mentioned about equally in regard to negative and positive developments (16 percent and 17 percent, respectively). One function of these groups is to focus attention on social problems. Thus they may be called on, often in reports of negative developments, to voice the perceived threat. An interesting

**Table 15.5.   Primary Assets Mentioned in Good and Bad Stories about Austin and Lincoln Park,** *Chicago Tribune* **and** *Sun-Times,* **1993**

|  | Austin | | Lincoln Park | |
|---|---|---|---|---|
| *Assets*[a] | *Good News* n = 99 | *Bad News* n = 44 | *Good News* n = 80 | *Bad News* n = 14 |
| *No assets mentioned* | 25% | 46% | 17% | 36% |
| *Local institutions* | 45% | 32% | 71% | 46% |
| Businesses | 12% | 5% | 8% | 7% |
| Schools | 11% | 18% | 10% | 14% |
| Parks | 2% | — | 25% | 21% |
| Libraries | 1% | — | 1% | — |
| Hospitals | 3% | 7% | — | |
| Cultural institutions | 1% | — | 6% | — |
| Real estate / housing | 12% | — | 11% | 7% |
| Other institution | 3% | 2% | 10% | — |
| *Citizen Association* | 20% | 18% | 3% | 15% |
| Churches | 1% | — | — | — |
| Block clubs | — | — | — | — |
| Cultural groups | 2% | 2% | — | 7% |
| Other citizen association | 17% | 16% | 3% | 7% |
| *Gifts of individuals* | 9% | 4% | 9% | — |
| Youth | 3% | — | — | — |
| Elderly | — | — | 1% | — |
| Artists | 1% | — | 5% | — |
| Volunteers | 3% | — | 1% | — |
| Other individual gift | 2% | 4% | 2% | — |
| *Total* | 99%[b] | 100%[b] | 100%[b] | 100%[b] |

[a]Based on Kretzmann and McKnight 1993.
[b]Percentages may not equal 100 due to rounding.

example is a story that reported a positive development in regard to crime but used a representative of a neighborhood group to remind readers that whatever the good news of the moment, social problems are ever with us. "Now that the killings have decreased," a community organizer was quoted as saying, "let's do something about these guys on the corner selling drugs" (Fornek 1993, 4). In this story, as in so many others, an asset is mentioned but only in passing to highlight a problem.

Another function of neighborhood groups is to act on a problem, and so they may appear in positive stories attempting to confront the threat. For example, a story headlined "Grass-roots groups get job done," reported "grass-roots organizations have become a larger force in African American neighborhoods, covering duties as varied as mediating neighborhood-police disputes to working with gang members" (Bey 1993, 19). As this example suggests, groups are often explicitly framed as important community resources for confronting problems.

An especially poignant example of community groups in action is a story and follow-up editorial concerning one of many skirmishes between group members and drug dealers. The story describes how an organizer convinced neighborhood residents to set up lemonade stands one Saturday afternoon on the street corner where the dealers normally conduct business (Seibel 1993). Noting the symbolic resonance of this tactic, the editorial begins with the headline, "Taking a stand against drugs." It concludes with this accounting of assets: "The lemonade stand is standing in the way of drug deals which is yet further evidence that community mobilization is the best way to fight crime" ("Taking a stand" 1993, 23).

As these data and examples suggest, the vocabulary of community assets is not fundamentally at odds with journalistic practice. Reporters were quite comfortable with the idea of framing stories in terms of grassroots institutions such as local businesses that they readily recognized as assets. "Usually when we think of business, we think of corporations," said McRoberts, "but the urban affairs team is trying to paint a fuller picture of the business community, particularly small business and its role in the neighborhoods." And among citizen associations, McRoberts thought that churches deserve more coverage. "Religious organizations are such a huge part of many neighborhoods, but the coverage is miniscule," he said. "There's a whole subculture of PR agencies that push not-for-profit stories, but religious organizations just go about their work and don't get as much attention."

While the reporters were not unsympathetic to the concept of community assets, their comments did reveal a tension between the idea and professional practice, especially concerning coverage of neighborhood groups. "In terms of generating dollars from funding sources, they want to be at the center of the problems," said Grossman pointing out that groups often welcome stories focusing on problems in their area. As McRoberts's comment about PR agencies pushing not-for-profit stories suggests, reporters treat community groups with the same wariness as they treat governmental and other institutional news sources.

"'Good news' is created by neighborhood-based organizations all the time," Grossman continued. "It doesn't mean the news is good; it means that the organizations are picking up skills for touting their own cause." Grossman urged more attention to outcomes in stories about group activities. "Some group takes responsibility and the reader is left with the impression that it's all going to work. Well, two weeks later another program is announced," he said mordantly. "Whenever a program is announced, we really should give the prior history of that problem in the community and of the organizations that have tried to work on it—what their successes have been and what their limitations have been."

Another obvious tension arises in regard to the importance of the gifts of individuals. "These are always going to be low numbers," said McRoberts about the small number of stories concerning that sort of asset, "because even if you are doing good street-level reporting, you are going to be identifying the assets with some sort of group or entity as opposed to the individual." McRoberts, who was probably the most sympathetic to the idea of asset-oriented reporting, nonetheless insisted on the applicability of conventional news values to his work. "I would argue in terms of news judgment—and I make no apologies for this—it's more newsworthy if more people are doing it, if it's affecting a larger number of folks," he argued. "So I think, inevitably, even if you do a better job of covering a community's assets, it's going to be more institution- and association-based than individual-based." Thus a good example of a story about "gifts" that does make the paper is headlined, "Black men give boys someone other than Mike to be like" (in reference to basketball superstar Michael Jordan). The story describes workshops conducted by successful African American professionals for "300 antsy younger men" (Heard 1993, 1).

The community development practitioner's vocabulary of assets will not, then, be accepted uncritically by journalists. Our argument, nonetheless, is that a vocabulary of assets—some ready to be enlisted in battles against social problems, some threatened by those problems, others simply of interest in their own right—promises to be far more rich and powerful than a vocabulary in which communities can be described only in terms of social problems or only as the source of "bad" or "good" news. Community leaders, therefore, would do well to demand more stories explicitly framed in terms of community-building resources, not more "good news."

## A Good Word for Good News

The importance that community development practitioners attach to neighborhood groups, along with the skepticism that journalists express about all the "good news" emanating from those groups, invites additional scrutiny of stories deemed to be positive. As table 15.6 shows, a large majority of all stories from Austin that are framed in terms of a social problem, whether positive or negative, mention efforts to address the problem. Positive and negative stories differ dramatically, however, in regard to whether or not those efforts are reported to be working. Among positive stories, 72 percent suggest that the effort is working; but among negative stories, 29 percent of the stories suggest it. Most interestingly, positive stories are far more likely to suggest that neighborhood residents have the capacity to solve the problem (62 percent) as compared to negative stories (16 percent).

In addition to the data shown in the tables, the content analysis revealed the importance of "other citizen associations" in the making of good news from Austin. Stories that mention Austin neighborhood groups are more likely to suggest a social problem (81 percent) as compared to stories that do not mention these groups (64 percent). However, stories that mention groups are also more likely to be positive even when a social problem is suggested (67 percent) as compared to stories that do not mention groups (52 percent). Moreover, stories that mention groups are more likely to suggest that the problems are being addressed (97 percent) and that the efforts to address the problem seem to be working or promising to do so (62 percent) as compared to stories that do not mention groups (87 percent and 44 percent respectively). Most dramatically, stories that mention Austin neighborhood groups are more likely to suggest that residents have the capacity to solve the problem (80 percent) as compared to stories that do not mention groups (25 percent).

Perhaps these results will only exacerbate the skepticism of reporters who have written too many stories about promises that went unfulfilled. Grossman's point about the need to examine the effectiveness of programs is very well taken, but it is reporters themselves who should take the point. In the era of often taught but seldom practiced investigative and computer-assisted reporting, news organizations need not depend on either the claims of neighborhood groups or the reports of government agencies to assess problems and evaluate solutions. A compelling example of how journalists can check out the claims of community groups is "The Color of Money," a Pulitzer Prize-winning investigative series written by Bill Dedman for the

**Table 15.6. Some Characteristics of Good and Bad News Suggesting a Social Problem about Austin and Lincoln Park, *Chicago Tribune* and *Sun-Times*, 1993**

|  | Austin | | Lincoln Park | |
|---|---|---|---|---|
|  | Good News<br>n = 58 | Bad News<br>n = 38 | Good News<br>n = 14 | Bad News<br>n = 6 |
| Stories suggesting<br>problem addressed[a] | 98%<br>n = 57 | 79%<br>n = 30 | 100%<br>n = 14 | 100%<br>n = 6 |
| Stories suggesting<br>efforts working or<br>promising[b] | 72%<br>n = 42 | 29%<br>n = 11 | 71%<br>n = 10 | 33%<br>n = 2 |
| Stories suggesting<br>residents have<br>capacity to solve[c] | 62%<br>n = 36 | 16%<br>n = 6 | 79%<br>n = 11 | 50%<br>n = 3 |

[a]The reliability coefficient for ADDRESSED is k = .87.
[b]The reliability coefficient for WORKING is k = .70.
[c]The reliability coefficient for CAPACITY is k = .83.

*Atlanta Journal & Constitution.* Dedman's work began when a community group leader told him that lower-income housing construction was hindered by the refusal of banks to lend in particular neighborhoods. This reporter's work finally concluded when he had thoroughly documented racial bias in home mortgage lending by Atlanta financial institutions. This investigation, which drew on the expertise of university-based researchers to analyze publicly available lending data, was hardly an exercise in daily assignment reporting. The project, however, highlights intellectual resources and professional skills that, in addition to street-level reporting, can help expand the conception of urban journalism. (For an elaboration of this theme, see Ettema and Glasser 1998.)

We do not argue that the activities of citizen associations should be uncritically reported but we do maintain that those activities deserve attention. More than merely validating group efforts to funding agencies, stories of citizen associations could be part of a dialogue both within and between communities about what has been tried, what might work, and what probably will not work. Stories that emphasize the capacities of community residents themselves are most important in this regard. More than merely reporting what the community needs, these stories describe what the community is and what it has the capacity to become. Though buried in the dominant discourse of urban pathology, there is authentically good news from the Austin neighborhood: when neighbors join together in citizen associations, they develop the capacity to confront their problems and to act on their own behalf. This news deserves to make the paper.

## Terms of Care

In the discourse of urban pathology, the city's neighborhoods are described in terms of unending problems that can be overlooked for a moment with "a lighter story from out there." With the vocabulary of community assets, however, neighborhoods can be described in more constructive terms. Appropriate to the ideals of civic journalism, these are terms through which connections can be established and dialogues begun with, and within, economically distressed communities. And equally appropriate to the ideals of civic journalism, these are terms in which reporters may actually be willing to think about their tasks. Our interviews suggest that journalists can commit to the mission of establishing connections and conducting dialogues—so long as that mission can be accomplished within the fundamental requirements of contemporary professional practice. Whatever their goals for a new sort of urban journalism, these reporters expect to retain their role as the professional mediators of public knowledge about their city. Although Flynn McRoberts spoke of "giving a voice" to groups and individuals outside of formal institutions, he rejected the idea that his newspaper should be an unmediated forum for those voices. "I'm leery of the forum metaphor," he said, associating the idea with talk radio. "You [journalists] play the part of the moderator in the news-gathering process and you create dialogue by searching out other voices." These reporters also expect to retain their claim to authoritative representations of social reality. "When I say that we should be giving voice to people, I mean that our role is really to give a picture, an image, of what life is," explained Byron White. "There is some authoritative voice that newspapers ought to have, but I'm saying that we're trying to have that without all of the information." He added, "I'm saying, 'Let's go and hear from people. Let's allow their voices to shape the picture we give.'"

The vocabulary of community assets could accommodate these long-standing journalistic expectations. At the same time, that vocabulary would enable journalists to think more expansively about both urban neighborhoods and urban journalism. Urban neighborhoods would be not only a set of social problems but also an array of human resources including small groups and ordinary people as well as social institutions. And urban journalism would be less an unending list of problems than a connection to the human resources of the community and a continuing dialogue about how those resources have been, or could be, enlisted in the service of community building. This would be a dialogue composed of a few big projects, perhaps, but also many daily stories like this one from the *Tribune's* urban affairs team in 1993:

> For years Carliss Gill saved her money, dreaming of her own home in the suburbs. On Sunday, Gill celebrated the start of a new dream in her old neighborhood. Gill plans to buy a condominium at 124 N. Keeler Ave., an abandoned three-flat that will become a community group's first affordable condominium project in West Garfield Park.
>
> "I'm going to stay here and take a chance," said Gill, who will share the home with her 14-year-old son, Tyrie Anderson. "It won't help if we all keep moving out." ("Neighbors invest," 3)

In this story, the asset (not the problem) provides the frame while the problem (not the asset) is mentioned in passing. That this neighborhood has one of the worst murder rates in the city is mentioned, but the community group's redevelopment effort is the point of the story. "Not only does this represent a new kind of home ownership here," says a member of the group, "but it's part of a larger plan to rebuild the neighborhood." While this story may be one of those "lighter stories from out there," it is also an example of authentically good news from a neighborhood now a little less bad because new homes have been created there and, if journalism makes any difference at all, less bad because those homes and the people who created them have made the paper.

This story is not the result of an attempt to do something called civic journalism, though it is the result of a conscientious effort to think and write about the community in modestly expanded terms. Even if journalism never embraces a comprehensive theory of community connection and care, daily urban affairs reporting can come to recognize that stories such as this are newsworthy because they are asset-oriented news of a community in action rather than merely a little good news from a bad neighborhood.

## Returning to the Newsroom and the News

Our second set of interviews, which were conducted seven years after the first, indicated that the *Chicago Tribune's* change in approach to urban affairs reporting reflected less a judgment that the zone system had failed than simply a turnover in personnel. Reporters and editors most committed to the system were promoted to new positions or left the paper, according to Byron White, who held several positions at the *Tribune* before beginning an academic career. From his new position White professed his continuing intellectual commitment to his vision. "Stories in which the primary source of information was not an official—that's what I really wanted to see," he said. "The only way to do that kind of reporting is to spend some time to rethink: Who are your sources? How do you find them? How do you connect?" White also acknowledged that maintaining the infrastructure needed to realize this vision had always been problematic. "Managing that process was very difficult because something big would come up and the two best reporters would get pulled off to do some more traditional reporting. It's all a matter of limited resources."

As an advocate of a thematic, metro-wide conception of urban affairs, Hanke Gratteau saw benefit precisely where White saw detriment to coverage of communities: an infrastructure that focuses reporters more narrowly in terms of content but disperses them more widely in terms of geography. Gratteau cited education as a good example of the value of her approach—including the economic value of broader reader appeal. "If we thought about education as having various themes, we would still do stories specific to Chicago schools or specific to suburban schools—a teachers' strike being one example of something we would need to cover to serve our readers in that 'zone,'" she said. "But if we have reporters work together and develop various areas of expertise—the achievement gap, school funding, the curriculum—then a reporter who had responsibility for the Chicago Public Schools and was an expert in the achievement gap, for example, could be pulled in to help another reporter develop a story with a theme that appealed to readers in all 'zones.'"

To illustrate the value of a team approach to coverage of education, Gratteau pointed to a particular story that also illustrates the value of computer-assisted reporting. "We've tried to analyze what it means to students who attend schools deemed to be failing by federal standards. We've gathered a group of reporters, including a computer-assisted reporting expert who was able to crunch data for us," she said. "There were hundreds of schools deemed to be failing. But if you looked at where these kids would be able to go, to transfer to a more successful school, we came up very quickly with a story that said, well, federal law says that these kids can transfer but there aren't many options for them."

Obviously this story is framed in terms of education as a social problem and Gratteau as well as Lisa Manns, assistant city editor for courts and urban affairs, acknowledged that major urban affairs themes are often synonymous with social problems. "In lower-income areas most of the time problems are going to out weigh whatever assets the community has," Manns said echoing a point made by our interviewees seven years before. "But if there is a resource in the community that people can turn to, we need to let that be known. And if there is a need in the community for an asset, we need to look at why it's not there." As an example, Manns and Gratteau cited a series of reports on the role of churches in various neighborhoods.

More provocatively, these editors also cited stories that were written in the aftermath of well-publicized crimes in a particular neighborhood, Englewood, as examples of coverage concerned with assets. "Our attention was focused by some terrible crimes," said Gratteau, "but immediately we begin asking what assets are in the community in terms of leadership, how the community is coalescing and what the community has been doing to fight this problem." Because several murderers had taken advantage of the many abandoned buildings and vacant lots in Englewood to commit their crimes, the *Tribune's* attention eventually focused on the community's response to that aspect of its environment. "Those crimes prompted us to profile the community, to go back to the mission of introducing a community to readers who otherwise might not see it," Gratteau said. "And to do it in a way that wasn't just a buzz word: 'crime-ridden Englewood.'"

To be sure, these stories were also framed in terms of problems. One of them began:

> The painful history of Chicago's Englewood neighborhood often is measured in the number of sex offenders who live there, rape victims of suffer there and the string of women who have died there.
>
> But another telling barometer of its troubles looms quietly over the streets: more than 600 abandoned building. (Puente and Lightly 1999, 1)

This story did, however, go on to seek out voices from the Englewood neighborhood:

> Community leaders are urging the city to develop a comprehensive affordable housing plan for the area. They argue that tearing down buildings and leaving vacant, weeded lots—the kind where 11-year-old Ryan Harris was murdered last summer—are not a viable alternative.
>
> "Let's save the buildings. Let's do rehabs," Jones [spokesman for a community-based organization] said. "Demolition is not the answer. We need reinvestment."
>
> Other residents said they would like the city to convert some vacant lots into playgrounds. "If Mayor Daley could get the extra funds, could turn all these lots

into playgrounds and basketball courts. It's very simple," said Linda Walker, 35, a married mother of three who lives near two of the crime scenes where a recent serial killer struck.

Gratteau credited this and similar stories with prompting her staff to thoughtfully consider "who truly speaks for the community." She also credited the lead reporter on this story with finding the sources in Englewood who should be given voice. Gratteau characterized this as gaining "traction" in a neighborhood that the paper had infrequently covered. "Teresa Puente really became our eyes and ears in that community," she said citing the reporter's work for "very eloquently articulating how the community was coalescing and building a sense of identity and mission."

The other reporter on this story, Todd Lightly, lent investigative skills to the project. "All the things people have suspected about a slumlord, you document that so the story can't be perceived as just some whiny disgruntled people," Lightly said with regard to the value of investigative methods. Noting that much reporting done under the rubric of urban affairs is "talking to people for human interest stories," Lightly credited his paper with an emphasis on the sort of urban affairs coverage that demands accountability from both the public and private sectors for situations such as that in Englewood.

Teresa Puente's "traction" in Englewood was one example of what both Gratteau and Manns insisted is the newspaper's continuing commitment to a close connection between journalists and communities. Another example cited was the reporting of Ray Quintanilla, especially a story profiling several ex-convicts who returned home to the notorious Cabrini-Green public housing to find that much of it had been demolished for redevelopment:

> To these men, born and raised in poverty there, the infamous public housing development's doomed fate is forcing them to do what the penal system seemingly could not: Make hard decisions about their future. Ironically the demise of Cabrini-Green has offered a rare chance to break out of the pattern of life that got them locked up in the first place.
>
> "There ain't nothing here any more," said Keller, 32, standing out side a highrise where he said he once made $2000 a day selling cocaine and marijuana. "People like me have a choice to make, right now. Either we find a way to get something out of life or move on to another part of the city and make money on the streets." (Quintanilla 2002, 1)

"This was a great piece of work with the theme: If you are a product of your environment and your environment no longer exists, what problems and opportunities are created?" said Gratteau. "This was a story that did not emerge out of an agency report or press release. It came from being tuned in to the kinds of issues that were cropping up in the incredible transformation of that area." For Quintanilla, the story was interesting because it had drama. "Something hangs in the balance, those are the pieces that I like to do," he said. And along with the drama, he managed to offer some information about resources in the community, modest though they are, available to these men with important decisions to make.

This sort of community connection—traction—has new urgency at the *Tribune*, according to Gratteau. "I'm not sure we would have defined this as an urban affairs story ten years a ago, but I think part of our mission, post–9/11, is to introduce and explain the Muslim community to others in the region," she said. "We've recently hired someone who speaks Arabic for the very purpose of getting more traction in covering another community that we previously didn't cover very well."

Quintanilla for one is adamant that the *Tribune's* current approach is more effective than the previous one at meeting this mission, but he also recognizes that change will continue. "I think we do a pretty good job; but at the *Tribune*, like a lot of places, there is an eternal struggle over how we do things," he said. "We question ourselves a lot but I think ultimately we get at what's important." Lightly agrees that the previous approach, which was abandoned before his arrival, was probably unworkable; but he recognizes that the concept of "neighborhood bureaus" could still be valuable. "We don't have people who go to police beat meetings. We don't have people who go to neighborhood meetings," he said. "We have people come downtown to the Tribune Tower."

Upon returning to the newsroom we found that, although urban affairs journalism remains a discourse of social problems, these journalists can and do invoke a basic vocabulary of community connections and assets, even if sometimes self-consciously or defensively. Leaving the newsroom, we chose to take heart in the assurance that "an eternal struggle" over how reporters and editors do things continues among thoughtful journalists.

## NOTES

This chapter is extensively revised and expanded from Ettema and Peer 1996.

1. The median household income at the time of the content analysis was $24,877 in Austin and $41,016 in Lincoln Park. The population was 87 percent African American and 11 percent white in Austin and 88 percent white and 6 percent African American in Lincoln Park. The Austin police district reported six times more murders, about three times more sexual or aggravated assaults, and about four times more robberies than the district that includes Lincoln Park.

2. The students were systematically trained in the method of content analysis for this project. After a discussion and demonstration of the coding process, students were given the same set of ten stories to code individually. The data from these stories were compared and discussed, and the problems detected in the coding process were reviewed. After the training was complete, each student independently coded between 10 and 12 stories a week for six weeks. For the purpose of assessing intercoder reliability, about 20 randomly selected stories each week were coded by two coders. This procedure yielded a sample of 15 percent of all stories from which reliability estimates were made. A spot check of those stories indicates an acceptable level of reliability (coefficients range from k = .70 to k = 1.0 with mean of k = .89).

# REFERENCES

Bey, Lee. 1993. "Grass roots groups get job done." *Chicago Sun-Times*, April 11, 19.

Chandler, Susan. 1993. "Avenue Bank replaces president." *Chicago Sun-Times*, July 1, 62.

Charity, Arthur 1995. *Doing Public Journalism*. New York: Guilford.

Ettema, James S., and Theodore L. Glasser. 1998. *Custodians of Conscience: Investigative Journalism and Public Virtue*. New York: Columbia University Press.

Ettema, James S., and Limor Peer. 1996. "Good News from a Bad Neighborhood: Toward an Alternative to the Discourse of Urban Pathology." *Journalism and Mass Communication Quarterly* 7, no. 34: 835–56.

Fornek, Scott. 1993. "Murder rate down 18 percent over last year." *Chicago Sun-Times*, July 2, 4.

Heard, Jacquelyn. 1993. "Black men give boys someone other than Mike to be like." *Chicago Tribune*, February 26, Chicagoland, 1.

Johnson, Steve. 1993. "Shooting that leaves Austin teen brain dead apparently accidental." *Chicago Tribune*, September 2, Chicagoland, 3.

Kaniss, Phyllis. 1991. *Making Local News*. Chicago: University of Chicago Press.

Kretzmann, John P., and John L. McKnight. 1993. *Building Communities from the Inside Out: A Path toward Finding and Mobilizing a Community's Assets*. Evanston, Ill.: Center for Urban Affairs and Policy Research, Northwestern University.

McWhirter, C., and Janita Poe. 1993. "Boy, 8, fatally shot during squabble between 2 drivers." *Chicago Tribune*, October 3, Chicagoland, 3.

"Neighbors invest in beleaguered area." 1993. *Chicago Tribune*, September 18, 3.

Puente, Teresa, and Todd Lightly. 1999, July 26. "Giving crime a home, Englewood a victim of its landscape." *Chicago Tribune,* 1.

Rosen, Jay. 1993. "Beyond Objectivity." *Nieman Reports*, Winter, 48–53.

Quintanilla, Ray. 2002. "As Cabrini dies, news hopes born; the demise of the infamous housing complex spurs one-time hustlers to chase a better life." *Chicago Tribune*, October 10, 1.

Seibel, Tom. 1993. "Neighbors seek refreshment: West side lemonade stands put squeeze on drug dealers." *Chicago Sun-Times*, May 22, 5.

"Taking a stand against drugs." 1993. *Chicago Sun-Times*, June 1, 23.

# 16

## Class and Media
## Influence in Australia

*Paul Jones and Michael Pusey*

> When you get a television station, we'll take notice of what you say.
>
> —Kerry Packer, proprietor of Australia's leading
> commercial TV network (Masters 1995)

Australian media baron Kerry Packer's blunt retort followed a journalist's reference to criticism of one his television network's programs. Clearly Packer believes that there are extreme social class barriers to certain kinds of opinion entitlement. Packer's comment came at the height of a corporate battle with Rupert Murdoch for control of subscription television. The transparency of his allusion to the naked power broking that characterizes Australian media policy stands in stark contrast with Rupert Murdoch's frequent invocation of the rhetoric of press freedom and diversity of opinion at similar moments (e.g., Murdoch 1998).

Similar tensions have haunted normative discussion of the role of the press ever since (at least) newspaper production became heavily capitalized (Curran 1979). Yet Australia, we wish to argue, offers a kind of limit case. We begin with a somewhat heuristic distinction between two well-established topics: (1) the relation between social class and informed citizenship among all citizens of a democratic polity and (2) the social relations of production of news and other cultural production that ostensibly serve that informed citizenship.[1]

This chapter briefly addresses both these matters. We are especially interested in the various ways in which ownership has shaped media policy and structured the range of possibilities in our second field of interest and—the focus of our interest—thus restricted the possibilities of informed citizenship.

One of the legitimate concerns of informed citizens is their own economic well-being and quality of life. Here the recent empirical work coming out of Michael Pusey's Middle Australia project has something to offer (Pusey 2003). This project surveyed 400 adult Australians in five capital cities with both an interview and a self-administered questionnaire and a number of focus groups. The Middle Australian interviewees were defined as having incomes in the middle 70 percent of the household income distribution.[2] The first stage of this research was conducted in 1996–1997, the second in 1999. It aimed to establish how Middle Australians experience the economy and economic relations generally and to understand how they are adapting, coping, and, most importantly for our purposes here, *interpreting* the impacts of structural economic change on their everyday lives.

While there is a long tradition of sociological class analysis in Australia, very little of it deals explicitly with media "influence."[3] We attribute this oversight in part to the disrepute into which "influence" fell in critical media audience research internationally in the wake of the Lazarsfeld project.[4]

This is regrettable for, as we argue below, the most significant relationship between social class and media influence is perhaps not that of media on socially classed audiences, but the crude yet real influence of capitalist proprietors on media policy makers.[5]

Even though the media consumption material deriving from the Middle Australia project is peripheral to its main focus, we believe it is worthy of reportage in the context of a schematic history of Australian media policy. We will also relate a recent eruption of Australian populism to what we shall call a "virtueless circle."

## CONSTITUTIONAL AND POLITICAL CONTEXT

Given our emphasis on politics and public policy, a brief overview of the Australian constitutional and political context may be useful here.

Australia is a federation and Westminster parliamentary democracy. It is not a republic. The reigning British monarch is recognized as the Australian head of state and is represented by an appointed governor-general with considerable reserve powers. The houses of the bicameral federal national parliament are named after those in the United States rather than Britain. As we shall see, such superficial hybridity is a recurring Australian institutional pattern.

Australia has no bill of rights. This is an increasingly conspicuous anomaly; even Britain passed the 1998 Human Rights Act as part of its harmonization with the European Union. On the central issue of freedom of communication, the Australian High Court found an implied constitutional freedom of political communication in a series of decisions in the 1990s. The implications of this implied freedom for media policy are only beginning to be debated (Jones 2000, 2001).

National governments of three-year terms are formed by the party that achieves a majority in the House of Representatives but the Senate, commonly dominated by opposition parties, has considerable capacity to block legislative bills. Since World War II, national government has alternated between a conservative coalition—of the Liberal and National (formerly Country) Parties—and the nation's oldest party, the Australian Labor Party (ALP), which traditionally identified itself as the party of the industrial working class. Table 16.1 provides a brief historical summary to aid our later discussion.

Australia is also one of the few nations in the world with compulsory voting. This—and the complexities of preferential voting systems that effectively redistribute votes cast for unsuccessful minor candidates—means that minor parties can play a very significant role.

In the mid-1990s a new minor party, One Nation, led by Pauline Hanson, arose. Its platform has been defined around themes of "anti-immigration," "anti-Asianization" and, more recently, demands to "turn back queue-jumping boat people" (asylum seekers arriving by boats). This party challenged the existing degree of cross-party consensus about immigration and multiculturalism. One Nation/Pauline Hanson achieved considerable prominence and electoral success, peaking at 8.4 percent of the primary House of Representatives vote in the 1998 federal election but achieving up to 20 percent in Queensland state elections. Many political observers believe that the wooing of the votes of this constituency by extraordinary means aided the return of the federal Howard Coalition government in 2001 (e.g., Marr and Wilkinson 2003, 45).

**Table 16.1.   Australian Governments and Media Policy, 1949 to Present**

| Period | Governing Party | Prime Minister | Indicative/Major Media Policy Development |
|---|---|---|---|
| 1949–1972 | Coalition | Menzies (until 1966) | Introduction of television (1956) with ownership dominated by newspaper proprietors |
| 1972–1975 | Australian Labor Party (ALP) | Whitlam (dismissed November 11, 1975) | Australian content rules; "extra channels" (e.g., FM radio) including early "multicultural" radio broadcasting |
| 1975–1983 | Coalition | Fraser | SBS multicultural broadcaster established in television and radio; commencement of deregulation of commercial sector |
| 1983–1996 | Australian Labor Party (ALP) | Hawke/Keating | "Extra channels" and "new players;" cross-media ownership rules (1986) |
| 1996–present | Coalition | Howard | Several attempted reversals of cross-media ownership rules; significant attempts to diminish autonomy of ABC |

## AUSTRALIAN CLASS RELATIONS: FROM "FAIR GO" TO "ECONOMIC RATIONALISM"

For most of the twentieth century Australian class relations were governed by a remarkable settlement held together by a peculiarly Australian social contract, a centralized wage-fixing and arbitration system with its own industrial courts. This defining feature of Australian economic relations—that Castles famously calls "the wage earners' welfare state"—combined primary wage and salary regulation with certain protections for employers. The famous Australian ethos of the fair go was thus primarily institutionally vested in regulation of the labor market (Castles 1985). These arrangements fostered one of the most equal distributions of income in "the developed world" for some twenty years from the end of World War II (Sawer 1976).

In the 1980s the class settlement was steadily wound back as part of a major neoliberal campaign of what is (pejoratively) known in Australia as economic rationalism.[6] A once strongly regulated labor market was deregulated in several stages. Ironically, this process was started by an ALP government captured by its economic rationalist advisers, big business interests, new right think tanks, and opinion leaders and other elements of the free-trade-cum-globalizing elite (Pusey 1991). Today, the relative equity of Australian wage differentials has been replaced by one of the highest levels of income inequality and job casualization among the OECD nations (Saunders 2002). In short, the circumstances that led most Australians to identify as middle class have come under enormous challenge. This once stridently egalitarian society has been hollowed out and the distribution of power, income, and resources, polarized.

Middle Australia (as defined above) understands these changes in a non-homogeneous, uncertain, and often contradictory manner. Ironically, the class structure of the Australian media provides one of the most potent, accessible, and widely shared figurations of this understanding of class and power—namely, the media baron as archetypal greedy capitalist.

## MEDIA POLICY, PROPRIETORIAL INFLUENCE, AND AUSTRALIAN NEWS PRODUCTION

The Australian broadcasting system is often described as "the best of both worlds." This metaphor alludes to a British broadcasting system ostensibly dominated by the BBC and a U.S. free market system dominated, as it is today, by major corporations and networks.

Organizational diagrams like that from 1982 reproduced as figure 16.1 suggest just this kind of hybridity.[7] However, while the ABC was certainly modeled on the BBC, it never enjoyed the latter's long period of monopoly dominance. Likewise, the commercial broadcasting sector was never subjected to the levels of regulation expected of its counterpart in Britain nor—in the case

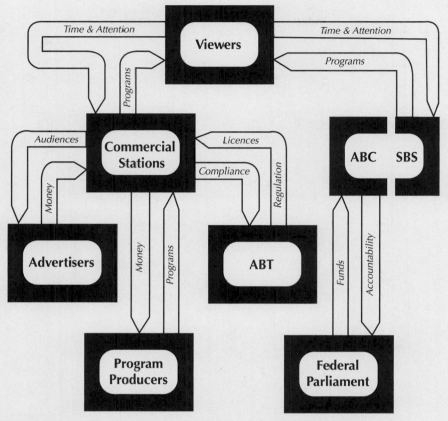

**Figure 16.1.    Major Organizational Relations of Australian Television Industry**
*Source*: Adapted from Schou (1982)

of news—even to the levels expected by the U.S. Fairness Doctrine (Jones 2001). The legitimating myth of the best of the both worlds in fact conceals the remarkable market dominance and influence of the Australian media barons (cf. table 16.2).

There has been much useful argument about terminology, periodization, and the value of calling such figures barons. In one of the most systematic formulations, Jean Chalaby contends that the press baron is primarily a nineteenth-century phenomenon and then "a *transitional figure* between pre-capitalist newspaper production and its capitalist and bureaucratized production" (Chalaby 1997, 622). However, most analysts would have the baron continuing as a dominant type of proprietorship well into the twentieth century. British and U.S. historians tend to mark a midcentury period of interruption to the power of the barons coinciding with a tendency toward greater editorial independence and a corresponding retreat, on the part of the proprietors, from their completely instrumental orientation toward some or all of their newspapers (e.g., Mott 1962, 651ff.). According to such views,

**Table 16.2. Cross-Media Control of Key Australian Commercial News Providers (Australian Holdings Only)**

| | News Corp (Murdoch) | PBL (Packer) | John Fairfax Holdings | Seven Network Ltd | Ten Network Holdings Ltd |
|---|---|---|---|---|---|
| Capital City and National Daily Newspapers (12 in all) | 67.8 percent of total circulation (7 of 12) | Nil | 21.4 percent of total circ. (3 of 12) | nil | nil |
| Sunday newspapers | 75.7 percent circ. | Nil | 22.8 percent circ. | nil | nil |
| Magazines | Negligible | 14 of top 30 titles (including the news magazine, *The Bulletin*.) (44 percent of total circ.) | 7 | 10 (6 of top 30) | nil |
| Controlling interest in free-to-air television networks | nil | 9 Network (direct ownership 4 capital city free-to-air) | nil | 7 Network (direct ownership 5 capital city free-to-air) | 10 Network (direct ownership 5 capital city free-to-air) |
| Subscription TV | 25 percent ownership of Foxtel Joint Venture Partner in Sky News channel (via B Sky B) | 25 percent ownership of Foxtel Joint Venture Partner in Sky News channel | nil | Some channels on Optus Pay-TV Joint Venture Partner in Sky News channel | nil |

*Source:* Derived from *Communications Update* (2002), Productivity Commission (2000), and corporate websites.

there has been a recent reassertion of proprietorial intervention and visibility dating roughly from the 1980s (Curran and Seaton 1998, 72ff.; Seymour-Ure 1998). Although the linkage is not always made explicit, the rise of semi-independent broadcast news services roughly coincides with the temporary decline in organizational influence of the barons.

What matters here is that the Australian domestic case stands in dramatic contrast with such subtleties. This is not so much because of relatively well-known high concentrations of ownership. Rather, it has occurred precisely because of the historical and sectoral *continuity* of such ownership dominance by press-cum-media barons—across newspapers, television, magazines (and, recently, subscription television)—from the time of their emergence to the present day. Indeed, dynastic barons and their families have never been less visible or less given to proprietorial intervention. Although strong and continuous intervention of this kind has been much debated, it has always been taken as a given.[8]

This Australian peculiarity has direct relevance for our construction of the relation between class and news. The main significance of this peculiarity is not, as one might be tempted to assert, the classical—but difficult to prove—political economy proposition concerning direct proprietorial influence upon news content.[9] As Tiffen has recently pointed out, at this level of analysis it matters little whether there is evidence that proprietorial influence—in shaping public opinion and/or directing media content—really exists. *It is far more significant that there is ample evidence that the politicians who direct media policy firmly believe in such influence and shape policy accordingly* (Tiffen 2002, 40–41).[10]

Influence in this sense might more aptly be considered a self-fulfilling prophecy. The news-producing components of the media could well be seen as the core of Australian media policy making. However, the only shortcoming of this formulation is one of understatement. The barons have so much influence that their news media are indeed present in their (increasing) absence from formal regulation. It is this curious dialectic that has massively shaped the relationship between social class and the potential for informed citizenship in Australia today.

## MEDIA MATES

The key event in the symbiotic relationship between political parties and the barons was the failure of the conservative Menzies coalition government to establish a barrier to entry by the press proprietors into television broadcasting, which commenced in 1956 (Hall 1976, 12–27). Almost all early television licenses went to newspaper proprietors (Western 1975, 10).

The formative pattern of television ownership was established during the long period of government by the conservative coalition from 1949 to 1972.

The ALP then held radically different media policies, including a planned ABC monopoly of television. One might have expected policy recognition of the relationship between social class and informed citizenship to have sprung from this source. This was not to be.

The short-lived Whitlam ALP government of 1972–1975 is legitimately characterized as one that legislated a whole raft of "progressive" policies, such as universal health care, massive innovation in education, ethnic, and community affairs and industrial relations, and variously successful regulation of several sectors of business and investment such as insurance and banking. These initiatives gave Australia its nearest—but still comparatively pale—approximation to the normal public policies of the contemporary European social democratic welfare states. However, media policy was not one of these areas of achievement. It became a contested field between the left and right wings of the ALP government. In practice broadcasting was not decommodified, although such policies formally existed; for example, through plans to set up an ABC-like newspaper, the proposed strengthening of the commercial broadcasting regulator and the related structural prevention of convergent competition along British lines. However, these policies never achieved implementation. Instead, the policy options actually achieved centered on a strategy of expanding Australian content and adding new media channels, ostensibly to increase social access (Hall 1976, 55–182). The argument for more channels was chiefly touted as a way of creating more Australian media jobs. This focus derived from an emphasis on economic class issues and a conception of citizenship construed only in terms of a national identity without any well-articulated notions of informed citizenship.

Crucially, this strongly reformist Whitlam government made few successful moves toward improving the quality of mainstream Australian broadcast journalism. This failure to address broadcast journalism was especially ironic given that the entire Whitlam ethos relied heavily on the ideals of informed citizenship. Whitlam himself, for example, attributed his rise to power to the inherent virtue of the provision of clear policy platforms to the electorate (Whitlam 1986).

In late 1975 a standoff developed between the lower house of the federal parliament—in which the ALP had a popular majority—and the upper house controlled by the conservative coalition. On November 11, the governor-general dismissed the Whitlam government, announced an election, and installed the opposition leader as caretaker prime minister in the interim. This highly controversial resolution of the deadlock by the queen's representative was followed by perhaps Australia's most divisive ever election during which the Murdoch press conducted an unprecedentedly hostile campaign against the ALP (Edgar 1979). Those most outraged by Whitlam's dismissal regarded it as a class-based constitutional coup and democracy itself to be at stake. The ALP lost the election resoundingly and out of these conflicts a republican movement was born.

The ALP reaction to the 1975 defeat did not lead to the development of a media policy that might complement Whitlam's commitment to the cultivation of informed citizenship. Instead this orientation toward the Australian public was largely abandoned with remarkable alacrity in favor of a "realistic" political strategy of news management and overt accommodation toward the barons.[11] In media policy per se the de facto Whitlam strategy of developing new channels and new players was revamped.

However, in the context of the now entrenched oligopolistic ownership structure, "new players" meant new proprietors or new capitalists. The ALP government of 1983–1996—committed, as we have seen, to neoliberal economic "reform"—found itself increasingly associated with leading 1980s *nouveau riche* entrepreneurs. Their investment capital was overgeared and hence reliant on massive (and, as we later discovered, nationally compromising) levels of indebtedness. The most notorious of these, Alan Bond and Christopher Skase, took control of two of the three major television proto-networks, Seven and Nine. Both became bankrupts following the crash of 1987.

The 1986 network takeovers by Bond and Skase were made possible by the very belated introduction of cross-media ownership rules. On the face of it the "old player" press barons were excluded from television. In reality they were offered a choice of staying in either television or newspapers. Packer initially left television but returned following Bond's collapse. Murdoch left (free-to-air) television and remains restricted to his massive newspaper ownership. The ALP media policy goal had become, as its architect, Paul Keating, revealed in 1994 after becoming prime minister, the creation of a "diversity of media power bases" (O'Brien 1994). Moreover, there was a suggestion of a secret payback in which the dynasty on which most negative impact of these rules fell, the Fairfaxes, was punished for allegedly anti-Labor news coverage in previous years.[12]

The 1986 cross-media rules did manage to slow the reduction of newspaper titles. Nonetheless, there is now, as table 16.1 shows, a near duopoly of control over the circulation of metropolitan and national dailies.

The situation of Australian commercial radio continued to spiral downward for many years, exacerbated by neoliberal policies such as the auctioning of new FM licenses. Governments' misleading and restrictive notions of media influence in general, and of the barons in particular, combined with an unthinking technological determinism. This led to the false conclusion that radio was no longer a particularly influential medium and thus less in need of regulation (Miller and Turner 2002, 141). The 1992 Broadcasting Services Act removed most public interest requirements for radio licensees, including a requirement to supply local news and current affairs (Miller and Turner 2002, 142). The possibility that the cultural form of radio talkback might evolve into the "shock jock" phenomenon was thus overlooked.

This oversight is especially ironic as talkback radio is now widely acknowledged by major political parties in Australia as the most important battleground in opinion formation (Megalogenis 2002). The parties continue to include talk-back in their news management itineraries despite revelations in 1999 that leading talkback figures had accepted "cash for comment," undisclosed payola arrangements in which major corporations bought approving comments (Australian Broadcasting Authority 2000).[13] *Realpolitik* requires continuing involvement with the shock jocks because Australia's compulsory preferential voting system renders their audiences of key electoral significance.

But cash for comment is merely part of a larger problem with radio, as Miller and Turner have argued:

> *The provision of news and current affairs on commercial radio has effectively been abandoned* in favor of the talkback hosts—John Laws, Alan Jones, Stan Zemanek. All, at various times, have abused their market power and made a mockery of the notion that such programs have anything to do with the provision of information. The redefinition of talkback as entertainment, rather than information, programming is accurate and underlines the inadequacy of the commercial sector's commitment to the provision of information. The loss of independent local news services accompanies a decline in the role of professional ethics within broadcasting organizations, and a corresponding increase in the promotion of hosts with a record for being outspoken—the spin given to reactionary, abusive and opinionated on-air personas. (Miller and Turner 2002, 142–43; emphasis added)[14]

At the New South Wales state governmental level, for example, few decisions are now taken in relation to policing without direct consultation with the dominant Sydney talkback figure, Alan Jones (Masters 2002).

More generally, these few barons and talkback demagogues hold quite pivotal roles in the formation of what Gramscians would call "ruling blocs," governing alliances of economic class fractions, political parties, and other social groups (e.g., Hall 1978). It is now difficult to imagine how any Australian political party would consider forming a government without assistance from a media mate.

## CLASS AND A VIRTUELESS CIRCLE

We saw earlier that the ALP post-1975 media policy did not adopt informed citizenship as its chief goal. Rather, constitutional reform was seen as the appropriate response to the legacy of the 1975 dismissal. Referenda to this end were put forward in 1988 but defeated. In response, a concern for active citizenship education developed within the last ALP's government, closely linked to the growing republican movement (Davidson 1997, 134–36).

In 1994 a "civics expert group" reported on educational means of improving such "active citizenship" (Macintyre 1994). While the group's chief orientation was toward a civics education program, its commissioned research established strong links between lack of informed citizenship and consumption of broadcast news media. The survey conducted for the group found extraordinarily high levels of public ignorance of democratic institutions and practices. The study listed the chief sources of information nominated by survey respondents. The media was found to be the most generally relied on source of public information, including "what it means to be a citizen" (Macintyre 1994, 159). Further, "reliance on television for news and information was highest amongst the least well informed population groups" (Macintyre 1994, 137).

This suggests that Australia's commercial broadcast news services fail to provide even the most basic civics knowledge. Two years later a small comparative content study of ABC and commercial radio in Brisbane drew similar conclusions (Turner 1996).

Such interpretations strongly resemble the arguments of those who complain of a "civic malaise" that is often identified by declining voting participation, especially in the United States. The chief culprit is usually seen as the tabloidization of news, especially in television. There is a sense of déjà vu here for the Australian observer. Insofar as tabloidization means the prioritization of one set of news values over more civic ones (Sparks 2000)—to whatever extent—such a tendency has long been dominant in Australian commercial broadcasting. Indeed, the nakedness of this pursuit of profit has a characteristically Australian signature. It constitutes a more pervasive and threatening consequence of oligopolistic baronic power than editorial intervention. The civics expert group report marked a moment in which the norm of informed citizenship finally began to emerge indigenously as a well-articulated alternative to entirely profit-driven news values.

Almost simultaneously, however, the post-1992 deregulatory environment accelerated the development of what we call a "virtueless circle."

## VIRTUOUS AND VIRTUELESS CIRCLES

The work of Pippa Norris has subjected the media malaise explanation of civic decline to the most thoroughgoing critique and empirical testing across an array of internationally comparative datasets. Norris has proposed instead that a virtuous circle exists linking television news media consumption and civic engagement (Norris 2000a). As she puts it in a recent summary:

> In the long-term through repeated exposure, like the socialization process in the family or workplace, there may well be a virtuous circle where the news media and party campaigns serve to activate the active. Those most interested and knowledgeable pay most attention to political news. Learning more about public affairs (the policy stances of the candidates and parties, the record of the government, the severity of social and economic problems facing the nation) reduces the barriers to further civic engagement. In this interpretation, the ratchet of reinforcement thereby moves in a direction that is healthy for

democratic participation. In contrast, the news media has far less power to re-inforce the disengagement of the disengaged, because, given the easy avail-ability of the multiple alternatives now available, and minimal political inter-est, when presented with news about politics and current affairs this group is habitually more likely to turn over, turn off, or surf to another web page. If the disengaged do catch the news, they are likely to pay little attention. And if they do pay attention, they are more likely to mistrust media sources of infor-mation. Repeatedly tuning out political messages inoculates against their po-tential impact. (Norris 2000b, 10)

Norris would probably be the first to admit that her virtuous circle has a definite class character that only becomes evident by implication. Her circle privileges an active—almost certainly dominantly (upper) middle-class—citizenry that might (re)include the disengaged given favorable socializing determinants. However, there is no suggestion here that somehow virtue merely adheres to social class position. Rather, the socialization Norris hy-pothesizes is virtuous in that it "represents an iterative process gradually ex-erting a positive influence on democracy" (Norris 2000a, 318). Thus:

If the pool of activists is gradually shrinking, so that society is dividing between the information-rich and information-poor, then that process legitimately should raise fears about its effects on mass democracy. But if . . . in postindustrial soci-eties the news media have become diversified over the years, in terms of chan-nels, availability, levels, and even the definition of news, this means that today information about public affairs (broadly defined) is reaching audiences over a wider range of societal levels and with more disparate interests. In this situation, the effects of the virtuous circle should gradually ripple out to broader sectors of society. (2000a, 318–19)

It is this latter optimistic scenario to which we (regrettably) wish to set lim-its below (without endorsing Norris's conception of mass democracy in her alternative). Australia has never figured prominently in Norris's comparative studies. This is unfortunate as the modest Australian research conducted so far—including now that from the Middle Australia project—suggests impor-tant potential limit case implications for the optimism of her thesis.

Norris has rightly stressed that her virtuous circle should point researchers of civic malaise away from blaming the media and toward problems arising from institutional structures and governmental systems, including changes in media regulation (Norris 2000b, 10).

Her own more recent research has already sounded a note of caution that might temper her former optimism. She recently conducted a large Europe-wide survey-study that deliberately sought out the audiences of dual system broadcasting regimes—which so share a broad similarity with the Australian system. She found crucial differences in the political knowledge held by the audiences of public and commercial channels, and further differences be-tween the audiences of news and entertainment programming. Accordingly, without abandoning her virtuous circle thesis, she cautiously concurs with the warnings of European public sphere critics of recent trends toward commercialization (Holtz-Bacha and Norris 2001).

Despite its generally modest sample size, the Middle Australia project points to unusual dimensions of civic malaise. In the first citation above, Norris argues that the virtuous circle protects the polity against the disengaged. In Australia we see two clear institutional factors that might tell against the plausibility of this claim: unregulated talkback radio and compulsory voting. Significantly for the civic malaise debate, Australian compulsory voting was introduced in 1922 with the specific purpose of addressing declining voter participation (Davidson 1997, 245).

It is the *combination* of these two factors that establishes some preconditions for a distinctive form of populism. Certainly, generic civic malaise claims have been leveled at Australian talkback radio (e.g., Kelly 2000). Murray Goot has given a very careful critique of such views based on just the kind of historical survey data favored by Norris (Goot 2000; Holtz-Bacha and Norris 2001, 3). Yet Goot acknowledges that radio is the medium, *par excellence*, that has had the greatest impact during Australian electoral campaigns since 1969 and, further, that there exists a small constituency that is susceptible to political influence by One Nation (Goot 2000, 12, 37). However, as we have seen, during those years of greatest growth in radio's influence, its news was increasingly replaced by talkback.

In this context one set of results from the Middle Australia project has some importance. We may initially speak here of media influence in the conventional sense. The Middle Australia respondents made their own assessments, on a five-point scale, of the levels of influence various media and social institutions had on their opinions about political and social matters.[15] Mean levels of influence were calculated for each type of medium/social institution. Results were then analyzed according to respondents' self-identification of their own social class, occupational class, and a scale that measures perceptions of individual control over political and economic institutions and systems. A consistent pattern emerged from this analysis. The mean level of influence of spouse/partner *significantly decreases* for individuals employed in nonmanagerial/nonprofessional services or manual work. The mean level of influence of talkback radio *significantly increases* for the same group. There is limited statistical evidence for a higher than average influence among those working in occupations broadly defined as working class.

Attitudes measuring social role conformity were then compared with the reported level of influence given to talkback radio. There is some evidence that respondents reporting *high levels of talkback radio influence* also report strong tendencies toward *very conformist social attitudes*. This trend is apparent across the political spectrum, with statistically significant results among ALP voters. These rather tenuous statistical results do, however, resonate very strongly with corroborating evidence from the Middle Australia focus groups in which talkback radio, disgust with political elites, and strong One Nation support came together very forcefully.

**Table 16.3. Mean Level of Influence of Various Media and Social Institutions on Opinions on Social and Political Matters**

*Percentage of Respondents Reporting Strong/Quite Strong Influence*

| Overall | | Middle/Managerial (n = 173) | | Working/Service Class (n = 135) | |
|---|---|---|---|---|---|
| Newspapers | 36 | Newspapers | 39 | Newspapers | 33 |
| Experts | 34 | Experts | 38 | Experts | 30 |
| Educational institutions | 27 | Spouse/partner | 28 | Educational institutions | 28 |
| Spouse/partner | 25 | Educational Institutions | 27 | Television | 23 |
| Television | 21 | Political leaders | 21 | Close friends | 22 |
| Political leaders | 20 | Television | 19 | *Talkback radio* | *21* |
| Close friends | 19 | Close friends | 17 | Spouse/partner | 21 |
| Talkback radio | 15 | Business leaders | 13 | Political leaders | 18 |
| Business leaders | 13 | Workmates | 11 | Business leaders | 13 |
| Other relatives | 11 | Other relatives | 11 | Other relatives | 11 |
| Workmates | 9 | *Talkback radio* | *11* | Workmates | 6 |
| Religious leaders | 6 | Community leaders | 7 | Religious leaders | 6 |
| Community leaders | 5 | Religious leaders | 6 | Community leaders | 2 |
| Neighbors | 1 | Neighbors | 1 | Neighbors | 2 |

*Source:* Table prepared by Shaun Wilson (statistics by T. Fattore) for Michael Pusey. Previous two paragraphs also based on text supplied by Wilson and Fattore.

Problems with the disaggregation of those reporting strong and quite strong influence caution against anything more than a heuristic interpretation of these numbers. And Norris's warning about the need for longitudinal research is also relevant here. However, Goot's research certainly provides an appropriate longitudinal context for the cautious inferences we have made. Moreover, these results are broadly consistent with the political wisdom coming from internal party polling profiling of the "million voters who matter" (Megalogenis 2002) in a total electoral enrolment of some 13 million voters.

Norris developed her virtuous circle formulation as an explicit alternative to unidirectional models of media influence. We propose to conclude similarly that one can propose the existence of a virtue*less* circle. In the Australian situation at least, it is just as plausible that a virtueless circle might prevail iteratively over a circle built around informed opinion. Moreover, where the virtuous circle of informed citizenship fails to expand, we can speak more accurately of opinion formation in terms of hegemony and moral panics.

## CONCLUSION: TWO CIRCLES IN CONFLICT?

Our conclusion may appear paradoxical: the relationship between class and news in Australia is at its plainest where news, as it is usually understood, diminishes as a cultural form as it is replaced by talkback radio. Underlying this trend we find a correlation between this cultural form and the angry, mistrustful, and reactive conservatism of a prominent fraction of the Australian working class that Pusey has dubbed "the Battler Hansonites" (Pusey 2003). In an American context they would be dubbed "industrial rednecks" much like the reactive Reagan Democrats of the late 1980s. "Battler" is an Australian colloquialism—with strong old working-class connotations—now much used by talkback figures and politicians to signify those who are struggling to make ends meet in the new "lean and mean" labor market that has developed in recent years with the erosion of the old social contract. "Hansonite" simply identifies a propensity toward acceptance of the One Nation agenda that emerged in the Middle Australia focus group discussions.

It is this class fraction that we see caught in a virtueless circle based in the cultural forms of talkback radio, the small number of tabloid press titles, and tabloid television current affairs. It is of course not the Battler Hansonites who are virtueless but rather these cultural forms. We stress "caught within" in its full sense of entrapment within an institutionalized information-poverty trap.

One of the familiar strategies to issue from the cultural forms of this virtueless circle is the turning of traditional investigative journalistic techniques upon the powerless—e.g. those on welfare. Such techniques risk fostering moral panics. Their key step is the heightening and elaboration of a *ressentiment* similar to the "initial misunderstanding" reported in Stan Cohen's classic study, *Folk Devils and Moral Panics: The Creation of the Mods and Rockers* (Cohen 1972). A moral panic is a coercive societal overreaction—or in Stuart Hall's more evocative phrase, "a societal tailspin" (1974)—based in "labeled deviance" that usually resembles scapegoating.[16] While the media and institutions of social control are crucial to Cohen's thesis, he argues that successful pejorative labeling of deviants also requires a receptive social ground, a suspicious misrecognition of the motives of some others. More specifically in a recent commentary on his earlier work, Cohen has suggested that asylum seekers have become the newest folk devils to find themselves on the receiving end of this form of stigmatization (Cohen 2002).

Australian talkback, as we have seen, has gone beyond merely seeking to mobilize *ressentiment* to embrace payola-funded overt deception. Moreover, mainstream commercial broadcast journalism, notably primetime television current affairs, has been exposed as practicing demonstrable falsification.[17]

The replacement of radio news by talkback came as a consequence of the barons' mighty influence on Australian media policy. Cynical power plays over the introduction of the cross-media rules in the 1980s created a new "diversity of media power bases" which in turn threw the Australian commercial radio industry into chaos and precipitated further content deregulation.

As we have noted, the Middle Australia project leaves us in no doubt about the existence of popular hostility toward the barons. They are seen as the epitome of all that Middle Australians most loathe about big business moguls and the abuse of power. A moral discourse has emerged among the Middle

Australia interviewees. It is laden with two inflections: "blame the victim" and "blame the big end of town." In Stuart Hall's terms, popular *ressentiment* is capable of articulation with two contradictory sets of social explanation, potentially hegemonic and counterhegemonic respectively (Hall 1978, 49). Neither of these options, however, would meet Norris's criteria of the virtuous informing of citizens. Potentially, nonetheless, the barons themselves could as plausibly be cast as the new folk devils in a limited counterhegemonic discourse. Not surprisingly, the Battler Hansonites were more susceptible to the former inflection of blaming the victim. Nor, by comparison with the tabloid exploitation of victims, have the media given much encouragement to the *ressentiment* toward the barons.

As André Métin noted more than one hundred years ago, in what he called *un socialisme sans doctrine*, Australians never had much time for sophisticated justifications of elite power (Métin 1977). Bryan Turner argues similarly that Australia never had a dominant ideology of the classical sort and that social integration was secured instead at the precognitive (nuts and bolts) economic level with such provisions as widespread home ownership and wage regulation—and a somewhat unreflective invocation of the fair go ethic (Turner 1990). That ethic issued from a generally pragmatic cast of thought with a distinctively utilitarian accent.

As that fair go ethic of the earlier Australian class settlement has dissolved, new legitimating discourses have been elaborated—especially *within* the virtuous circle—to serve the need of a new *global* balance of changed class and power relations. One of the principal conclusions drawn from the Middle Australia project is that a twenty-year attempt from above to win over Australians to a neoliberal economic rationalism—in virtually every sphere of government and daily life—is slowly failing. In Gramscian terms, this ideology has failed to become organic beyond those class fractions it helps cohere within the ruling bloc. The formation of new ruling blocs in Australia now overtly includes key sections of the media (Sklair 1996). This may be seen as a studied response of corporate (global) power to a crisis of hegemonic legitimation.

Australia thus seems to be moving through a period remarkably similar to that which Stuart Hall identified in 1970s Britain as "a crisis of hegemony" characterized by an escalating series of moral panics that shift increasingly toward the labeling of folk devils by race, with asylum seekers today the latest victims (Hall et al. 1978).[18] However, the Australian broadcast media are subject to nothing like the level of supervision and constraint that Hall took as a given in 1970s Britain.

The tragic dimension here is that while Australian media policy is so captured by ruling bloc circles—a practice sustained by a more enduring *realpolitik*—there is little prospect for an alternative strategy of actively encouraging the broadening of the virtuous circle of informed citizens beyond its current class limits. Citizens of other nation-states might reasonably view this dilemma as a warning.

# NOTES

Paul Jones drafted this piece and made me coauthor because the discussion uses some of my unpublished Middle Australia project data and incorporates my comments on his drafts. I thank him for his generosity. (—MP)

1. However, the focus on these relations will be entirely on the barons/owners, not the employees. Baron is as much a misnomer as that other predemocratic allusion commonly employed in this context, fourth estate (Jones 2000). In the absence of a widely accepted alternative, baron will be used in this chapter in conjunction with this heuristic distinction.

2. The sample was randomly drawn from householders in five capital cities with incomes above the 20th percentile of household income and below the 90th.

3. The chief exception is the sociology of media research conducted by John Western, better known for his work on social class (for example, Western and Hughes 1983). A recent Bourdieuian research project on Australian cultural consumption has produced much needed data, but news consumption is there treated peripherally and without adequate reference to informed citizenship (e.g., Bennett et al. 2001).

4. The standard critique of the Lazarsfeld project is Gitlin 1978.

5. Thus, for example, Cunningham's (1997) commentary on the concept is quite correct about audience research traditions but, despite the context of its delivery at a media policy conference, sets aside this proprietorial dimension.

6. This Australian term for supply side economics, economic reform, or neoliberalism took hold in the public debate that issued from Pusey 1991.

7. The only major updating required is renaming the commercial regulator from Australian Broadcasting Tribunal (ABT) to Australian Broadcasting Authority (ABA). The second public broadcaster, SBS, has an explicitly multicultural remit. In contrast to the other elements, it is a genuine innovation and is today partly funded by advertising.

8. Ward, however, argues that "blatant" proprietorial intervention in Australia did retreat (1995, 126).

9. See, for example, Curran's recent assessment (2000). Of course this is not to deny such direct intervention exists in the Australian case.

10. See Tiffen 1995 for historical examples and Westfield 2000 for an extraordinary blow-by-blow account of the barons' lobbying in the slow development of Australian subscription television. A more complete historical study of Australian proprietorial excesses has just been published (Griffen-Foley, 2003).

11. This strategy started almost immediately in state politics in NSW (Tiffen 1995).

12. Chadwick argues this was achieved by granting Packer and Murdoch advance notice of the rule changes (Chadwick 1989, 20).

13. Australia has no U.S.-style antipayola laws.

14. Collingwood's research (1997, 1999) suggests Turner's and Miller's opening assertion may be overstated, but the trend seems clear.

15. The exact question asked was: "We each have our own personal views about political and economic matters (about who gets what and how it should be decided). What is interesting for this research is to understand how our views change as we get older. Thinking about yourself now—what counts most in changing your views and feelings about political and economic matters?"

16. For an excellent recent account of this largely British concept that relates it to comparable U.S. research, see Critcher 2003.

17. For accounts of tabloid television current affairs excesses, see Turner 1999. For overt falsification see, for example, the cases discussed in Barry 2000.

18. For a descriptive account of the recent trend toward labeling asylum seekers as the new folk devils in both Britain and Australia, see Coole 2002.

## REFERENCES

Australian Broadcasting Authority. 2000. *Commercial Radio Inquiry: Report of the Australian Broadcasting Authority Hearing into Radio 2UE Sydney Pty Limited*, February, Sydney.

Barry, P. 2000. Peter Meakin, interview, *Media Watch*, ABC, April 24.

Bennett, T., Emmison, M., and Frow, J. 2001. Social class and cultural practice in contemporary Australia. In T. Bennett and D. Carter, eds., *Culture in Australia*. Cambridge: Cambridge University Press.

Castles, F. 1985. *The working class and welfare: Reflections on the political development of the welfare state in Australia and New Zealand, 1890–1980*. Sydney: Allen & Unwin.

Chadwick, P. 1989. *Media Mates: Carving up Australia's media*. South Melbourne: Macmillan.

Chalaby, J. 1997. No ordinary press owners: Press barons as a Weberian ideal type. *Media, Culture, and Society* 19: 621–41.

Cohen, S. 1972. *Folk devils and moral panics: The creation of the Mods and Rockers*. London: MacGibbon & McKee.

———. 2002. Introduction to *Folk devils and moral panics*. 3d ed. London: Routledge.

Collingwood, P. 1997. *Commercial radio since the cross-media revolution*. Sydney: Communications Law Centre.

———. 1999. Commercial radio 1999: new networks, new technologies. *Media International Australia* 91 (May): 11–21.

Communications Law Centre. 2002. Media ownership update. *Communications Update* 164 (April).

Coole, C. 2002. A warm welcome? Scottish and UK media reporting of an asylum seeker murder. *Media, Culture, and Society* 24: 839–52.

Critcher, C. 2003. *Moral panics and the media*. Milton Keynes: Open University Press.

Cunningham, S. 1997. Which media? How much influence? In Communications Law, ed., *Media ownership in Australia: Conference papers*. Sydney: CLC.

Curran, J. 1979. Press freedom as a property right: The crisis of press legitimacy. *Media, Culture, and Society* 1: 59–82.

———. 2000. Media organizations in society: Central issues. In J. Curran, ed., *Media organizations in society*. London: Arnold.

Curran, J., and Seaton, J. 1998. *Power without responsibility: The press and broadcasting in Britain*. 5th ed. London: Routledge.

Davidson, A. 1997. *From subject to citizen: Australian citizenship in the twentieth century*. Melbourne: Cambridge University Press.

Edgar, P. 1979. *The politics of the press*. South Melbourne: Sun.

Gitlin, T. 1978. Media sociology: The dominant paradigm. *Theory and Society* 6: 205–53.

Goot, M. 2000. Distrustful, disenchanted, and disengaged? Polled opinion on politics, politicians and parties: An historical perspective. Department of Senate Occasional Lecture, November 24.

Griffin-Foley, B. 2003. *Party games: Australian politicians and the media from war to dismissal.* Melbourne: Text.

Hall, Sandra. 1976. *Supertoy: Twenty years of Australian television.* Melbourne: Sun.

Hall, Stuart. 1974. *Mugging: A case study in communication.* Milton Keynes: Open University. Video recording.

———. 1978. Newspapers, parties, and classes. In J. Curran, ed., *The British press: A manifesto.* London: Macmillan.

Hall, Stuart, et al. 1978. *Policing the crisis: Mugging, the state, and law 'n' order.* London: Macmillan.

Holtz-Bacha, C., and Norris, P. 2001. "To entertain, inform, and educate": Still the role of public television in the 1990s? *Political Communication* 18: 123–40.

Jones, P. 2000. Democratic norms and means of communication: public sphere, fourth estate, freedom of communication. *Critical Horizons* 1: 307–39.

———. 2001. The best of both worlds? Freedom of communication and "positive" broadcasting regulation. *Media, Culture, and Society* 23: 407–17.

Kelly, P. 2000. *Paradise divided.* Sydney: Allen & Unwin.

Macintyre, S. 1994. *Whereas the people: civics and citizenship education.* Report of the Civics Expert Group. Canberra: AGPS.

Manning, P. 1975. Now you see it, now you don't. *New Journalist* 17: 15–21.

Marr, D., and Wilkinson, M. 2003. *Dark victory.* Sydney: Allen & Unwin.

Masters, C. 1995. "The Gamekeepers." *Four Corners,* ABC, May 22.

———. 2002. "Jonestown." *Four Corners,* ABC, May 6.

Megalogenis, G. 2002. The million voters who matter. *Weekend Australian,* December 21–22, 17, 20.

Métin, A. 1977. *Socialism without doctrine.* Sydney: Alternative.

Miller, T., and Turner, G. 2002. Radio. In S. Cunningham and G. Turner, eds., *The media and communications in Australia.* Sydney: Allen & Unwin.

Mott, L. 1962. *American journalism: A history, 1690–1960.* 3rd ed. New York: Macmillan.

Murdoch, R. 1998. Pluralism and diversity rule in the excitement of a brave new world. *Sydney Morning Herald,* April 13, 13.

Norris, P. 2000a. *A virtuous circle: Political communications in postindustrial societies.* Cambridge: Cambridge University Press.

———. 2000b. A virtuous circle: The impact of political communications in postindustrial democracies. Paper presented at the annual meeting of the Political Studies Association of the UK, London School of Economics and Political Science, April 10–13.

O'Brien, K. 1994. *Lateline,* ABC, October 18.

Productivity Commission. 2000. *Broadcasting.* Canberra: Ausinfo.

Pusey, M. 1991. *Economic rationalism in Canberra: A nation-building state changes its mind.* Cambridge: Cambridge University Press.

———. 2003. *The experience of middle Australia: The dark side of economic reform.* Cambridge: Cambridge University Press.

Saunders, P. 2002. *The ends and means of welfare: Coping with economic change in Australia.* Melbourne: Cambridge University Press.

Sawer, M. 1976. *Income distribution in OECD countries.* OECD Occasional Study. Paris: OECD.

Schou, K. 1982. *The structure and operation of the television industry in Australia.* Sydney: AFTRS.

Sklair, L. 1996. Conceptualizing and researching the transnational capitalist class in Australia. *Australian and New Zealand Journal of Sociology* 32, no. 2: 1–18.

Seymour-Ure, C. 1998. Are the broadsheets becoming unhinged? In J. Seaton, ed., *Politics and the media: Harlots and prerogatives at the turn of the millennium.* Oxford: Blackwell.

Sparks, C. 2000. Introduction: The panic over tabloid news. In C. Sparks and J. Tulloch, eds., *Tabloid tales: Global debates over media standards.* Lanham, Md.: Rowman & Littlefield.

Tiffen, R. 1995. The Packer-Labor alliance, 1978–1995: RIP. *Media International Australia* 77: 20–34.

———. 2002. Political economy and news. In S. Cunningham and G. Turner, eds., *The media and communications in Australia.* Sydney: Allen & Unwin.

Turner, B. 1990. Australia: The debate about hegemonic culture. In N. Abercrombie, S. Hill, and B. Turner, eds., *Dominant ideologies.* London: Unwin Hyman.

Turner, G. 1996. Maintaining the news. *Culture and Policy* 7: 127–64.

———. 1999. Tabloidization, journalism, and the possibility of critique. *International Journal of Cultural Studies* 2: 59–76.

Ward, I. 1995. *Politics of the media.* Melbourne: Macmillan.

Western, J. 1975. *Australian mass media: Controllers, consumers, producers.* Australian Institute of Political Science Monograph 9.

Western, J., and Hughes, C. 1983. *The mass media in Australia.* St. Lucia: University of Queensland Press.

Westfield, M. 2000. *The gatekeepers.* Annandale, NSW: Pluto.

Whitlam, G. 1986. *The Whitlam government.* Melbourne: Penguin.

# 17

## Television Civic Journalism and the Portrayal of Class

*David D. Kurpius*

More than a decade ago, a middle-aged, well-spoken, working-class African American woman stood up at a television civic journalism town hall meeting and asked a simple question. She wanted to know why the media knew how to find her modest neighborhood when crimes occurred, but those same journalism organizations could not find her street for a "build a snowman story." Her question resonates at the heart of the issue of covering lower- and working-class communities. When I related this story to a news director in another part of the country, her response indicated how forgotten the lower classes of individuals are in the media. She said she simply had not thought about why her station did their gardening segments only in the nicest parts of town. While the station may have had the latest Doppler weather radar that can practically tell you when it will start raining on your house, its news radar was not as sophisticated and only saw certain communities and people.

How media, particularly television, include issues of class in coverage is rarely overt. Instead the pictures and sources are often left to convey class without direct discussion. We know that television traditionally does not include lower-class people as sources because the focus is on officials, who are generally middle or upper class in stature. There are times when class is the focus of stories. The typical stories are crime coverage or portrayals of the homeless during the holiday season. These stories utilize a frame of good people and organizations helping the less fortunate. This focuses on the event and not directly on the issue and its root causes or even potential long-term solutions.

The issues at the heart of coverage of class are not new to media professionals or scholars. These include such simple questions as who is missing from the mediated conversation and what perspectives are lost as a result of the missing stakeholders? It also ties back into the norms and routines of journalistic practice. This encompasses what is considered news and how it

325

is gathered and reconstructed for presentation. In television news organizations, there is also a focus on the pictures and sounds that are integral elements in story narratives. With these elements in view, the core question focuses on how to change the structures and practices of journalistic coverage to become more inclusive of missing stakeholders and their perspectives. I believe the answer is found in connections. However, that comes with its own problems—resources and audience.

This chapter draws from my almost decade-old research focus on inclusion of missing stakeholders and communities in television news coverage. It benefits from a couple hundred interviews with television journalists and managers and content analyses of both traditional television news content and civic journalism award entries. Ultimately, the underlying focus is on how television journalism can be improved to include missing communities, more accurately and deeply reflect the portrayal of communities, and expand public affairs content on television.

## CIVIC JOURNALISM INSIGHTS

Civic journalism is a decade-old effort to improve the "news radar," alter journalists' routines to include more and deeper coverage of citizens and their communities, and strengthen the public discussions and development of potential solutions. Civic journalism, also referred to as public or community journalism, is an attempt to encourage the media to help citizens make connections to public life and to participate in the public deliberation and problem-solving process (Rosen 1996, 1999). Though it is not often framed as such, in many ways, it has also been an effort to drive back marketplace forces that have become increasingly rooted in journalism and have created a greater focus on key middle- and upper-class demographics.

Civic journalism thrives primarily in newspapers, while television stations have been slower to adopt such principles. However, some stations have found success in their attempts. KRON-TV in San Francisco, WFAA-TV in Dallas, and WISC-TV in Madison, Wisconsin, are prime examples (Kurpius 2003; Sirianni and Friedland 2001).

Civic journalism scholars widely agree that journalists should portray ordinary citizens as active participants in public life (Charity 1995; Friedland and McLeod 1996; Friedland 2000, 2001; Kurpius 2003; Merritt 1998; Rosen 1996, 1999; Sirianni and Friedland 2001). This suggests that citizens should be shown in the "working through" process of public life (Yankelovich 1991, 1999). However, it is not common to find news organizations going to working- or lower-class people to understand and solve problems facing those groups. Instead, there appears to be a heavy reliance on officials and policy makers. This follows a trend in television toward favoring official sources (Grabe and Barnett 1999; Sigal 1973).

## MISSING CLASS ON TELEVISION NEWS

America is often regarded as a class-free society. Compared to the caste systems in India and other parts of the world, this may be relatively true. However, class is a fundamental part of the society and political system in the United States. It is a key element in many of the social programs and public policy debates at the local, state, and federal levels. "There has always been a privileged class, even in America, but it has never been so dangerously isolated from its surroundings" (Lasch 1995, 4).

While sociologists have spent time documenting class through ethnography, depth interviews, and surveys, media scholars have virtually ignored the subject (Anderson 1990; Fischer 1982; Gans 1962; Liebow 1967; Wellman 1979; Whyte 1981). Holtzman wrote, "Class is a word that is rarely used in American households or school and is therefore difficult for us to conceptualize and hold concretely in our hands" (2000, 99). The lack of understanding among Americans increases the difficulty journalists face in making their stories relevant to viewers. Holtzman conceptualizes class initially as "the understanding of our socioeconomic place and life chances" (99).

Of greater interest is how class is understood and portrayed on television. Holtzman invites her readers to consider how income affects who we are and how it influences "your values, beliefs, and behavior" (99). It is beneficial to twist that invitation to consider how journalists struggle to portray class in their coverage and how routines and conventions of journalistic practice might hinder or help improve coverage of class both as an issue and as an element of coverage of other issues in society.

What journalists cover is a result of the norms and routines of their work. These have been well documented and discussed (Fishman 1990; Gans 1980; Kaniss 1991; Soloski 1989; Tuchman 1973). Tuchman, for example, developed the idea of the news net. One way to think about it is that resources and practices and routines determine the size of the holes and the strength of the net. When cast, the net does not equally capture news in its webbing. Instead, it has some areas where the web has smaller holes and stronger webbing. City hall is an example of such an area, since this is typically a place where news is generated that fits professional norms. Other areas, particularly in minority communities, are less well understood and tend to slip through the web.

When searching for portrayals of class in journalism, television is an obvious place to look. Television is the medium most Americans use as a primary source of information (Gallup 1994, 1996; Maguire and Pastore 2000; National Science Board 1998; Pew Research Center 2000). But television journalists often portray class inadvertently. The video carries much of the narrative without the reporter having to say a word. For example, a person's appearance, including his clothing and jewelry and grooming, are cues of class status. As Entman (1990, 1994, 1992) noted in his research on race and television, the video and audio separately may not carry images of race, but when combined the message can portray stereotypical coverage of minorities. It is likely that this same phenomenon is the case with class.

## TELEVISION CIVIC JOURNALISM SUCCESSES

The people journalists select to quote or use in sound bites reflect a pattern of access, credibility, and news practices across media content (Clayman 1990; Zelizer 1989). There is evidence that television civic journalism has altered this pattern in ways that allow previously ignored groups greater access and voice in content. My previous studies of 1,071 sources in the 184 television entries sent to the James K. Batten Civic Journalism Awards found that civic journalism coverage included significantly more women, minority, and ordinary citizen (unaffiliated) sources (Kurpius 2002a,b). Though these particular studies did not look at class, the dramatic change in sourcing patterns in the content suggests that classes lacking voice and position from which to speak in news stories might be included in television civic journalism content.

The Batten Awards study found improved diversity of sources in civic journalism content, particularly for African Americans (23 percent of all sources) and women (40.4 percent of all sources) (Kurpius 2002b). Scholars studying traditional journalism have found minorities, particularly African Americans, to be underrepresented (Campbell 1995; Entman 1994; Entman 1992; Smith 1993). Women are also underrepresented as sources in traditional journalism (Grabe and Barnett 1999; Liebler and Smith 1997; McShane 1995; Zoch and Turk 1998). Thus, at least in television there is mounting evidence that civic journalism can effectively alter journalists' routines and practices to improve the accuracy and fairness of the coverage. But does television civic journalism include meaningful portrayals of class and sources from the lower classes?

## EXAMPLES OF CLASS COVERAGE

Television civic journalism provides several good examples of lower- or working-class portrayals. In Charlotte, North Carolina, WSOC-TV and the *Charlotte Observer* created a partnership to focus coverage on issues in lower-class neighborhoods and efforts to revitalize these areas. The newspaper called the series "Taking Back Our Neighborhoods," while the television station insisted on branding it "Carolina Crime Solutions." The name differences demonstrate a difference in approach to the topic. Crime is a staple of local television news and framing the coverage around crime fit well with the station's news focus. However, once into the project, the station did branch out from the crime focus. Journalists spent time in the communities covering housing, community centers, and other needs, in addition to crime issues. The newspaper, in contrast, framed coverage around citizens, business leaders, government officials, and community leaders' efforts to redevelop the area to address housing, crime, community assets, and community structure. This community-building approach to coverage provided greater depth and context to the coverage. In many ways, the partnership worked well. The town hall meetings were well attended and television coverage was a vital element for increasing awareness of the problems of poor neighborhoods and the people in those communities.

Government agencies and community groups were already working on the issue of revitalization of the area before the media shined the spotlight on the problem, and solutions would likely have developed even without the media attention. However, with the media attention, some people living outside of these areas gained an understanding of the issues facing Charlotte's working poor. The media attention also helped activate financial support for the effort and likely worked to increase the focus and speed of the solution development and implementation.

Also of note is the fragility of television work in both civic journalism and coverage of the lower classes. Once the partnership with the newspaper on this project ended, the paper continued to work on other civic journalism projects, while the television station opted to end its civic journalism work. The station was the top-rated news station in town at the time of the project and there is no evidence that the civic work improved or hindered the ratings for the newscasts during the civic journalism effort.

Binghamton, New York, provides another long-term piece of evidence that civic journalism can develop coverage of class in meaningful ways. The area experienced an economic downturn when two large corporate citizens moved out of town. Endicott Johnson shoes and IBM both pulled up roots and moved. The Endicott Johnson story is more relevant to this chapter. The company moved its factory to Mexico, leaving its workers and the company community it had built over generations in its wake. The effect on the community was visible when visiting the area. In response, the *Binghamton Press* and *Sun-Bulletin* partnered with local television station WBNG-TV on a civic journalism project aimed at developing solutions for economic revitalization of the area. Business leaders joined the effort and helped create a "super" chamber of commerce for the area. A young leaders development organization provided help in leading citizen groups through the process of identifying problems and potential solutions on topics ranging from city beautification to attracting new businesses to the area. Once again the newspaper was the lead media organization, with television providing promotion of civic group work sessions and occasional summaries of the meetings. One of the striking elements about the meetings was the range of people who turned out to work in the groups. They ranged from bankers to laid-off factory workers.

This mix of people also showed through in the coverage, though the issue was not generally focused on class. Once again, television played a supporting role in focusing attention on the issue without extended, deeper coverage of class issues.

One of the best civic journalism examples focused on tapping into the conversations on issues among working-class people is rural-urban dialogue that connected residents in a working-class area of Minneapolis with the Crookston residents in rural Minnesota. Lucille's Soul Food Kitchen was the gathering place in North Minneapolis. This small restaurant serves a predominantly working-class minority clientele and regularly hosts community radio station KMOJ's live community issues talk show over the lunch hour. Crookston is a predominantly white working-class community in the northwestern part of the state. The two communities have high unemployment rates and double-digit percentages of their residents living below the poverty line.

The Minnesota Citizen's Forum, a partnership of Minnesota Public Radio, the Minneapolis *Star Tribune,* and KTCA-TV, produced a dinner and discussion program to air live on Twin Cities Public Television's *NewsNight Minnesota,* KMOJ radio, and Minnesota Public Radio using the Lucille's Kitchen/KMOJ talk show model for discussion. Internet videoconferencing technology connected the two locations, allowing for the live interaction. The program tackled issues including crime, education, and politics.

The Lucille's Kitchen and Crookston sites brought working-class views and voices into the public discussions on issues facing the state. Without these venues, lower-class viewpoints would likely have been greatly diminished, if not missing, from the public dialogue. The civic journalism focus of the newspaper, and the public television and public radio stations were central forces in providing a mediated venue for presentation of these less-visible community perspectives.

While Lucille's Kitchen provides a minimalist production quality that is almost like C-SPAN, the other end of the television spectrum also provides evidence of civic journalism creating an entry point for coverage of the working poor. One of the best ways television is able to portray complex issues (e.g., class) is through documentary work. The documentary *On the Outside Looking In* portrayed changes in welfare laws in Minnesota and Wisconsin. It focused attention on the working poor. This two-year project produced by David Nimmer and Steven Lybrand from the University of St. Thomas followed families through the changes and put a face on the enduring struggles of lower-class individuals. The documentary aired on select PBS stations. This form of civic journalism did not take the format of town hall meetings and solution-oriented efforts; rather, it gave voice to the people intimately involved in the welfare system and it worked to illuminate the daily struggles of people at or below the poverty line.

These long-term examples from television civic journalism show that television can alter its news net to capture class in meaningful ways. However, fewer than 15 percent of the Batten Award entries included class as a primary element in their coverage. While television civic journalism holds promise for more meaningful inclusion of class in coverage, class remains limited in its expression on-air.

## POTENTIAL FOR CLASS COVERAGE

The case to be made here for television class coverage is based on three factors. First, evidence that journalists cover upper- and lower-class communities differently. Second, that television journalism holds the capacity to cover class in a meaningful way. Third, that there are entry points for television journalists to understand and more accurately reflect the realities of lower-class life in their coverage.

Ettema and Peer in a previous chapter in this book make a strong case that rich and poor neighborhoods are covered differently by journalists. They found that "bad neighborhoods" were much more likely to be described in terms of social problems. Ettema and Peer suggest that journalists cover neighborhoods with a focus on "asset-oriented news" as a means for telling stories of community connection and action that goes beyond simply feel-good coverage of a bad neighborhood. This is closely related to some veins of civic journalism practice, though it is more narrowly focused. For example, the civic journalism project in Binghamton described earlier focused on identifying and activating the community assets in a variety of citizen-defined areas.

Kretzmann and McKnight (1993) spell out an asset-focused form of community organizing that could easily be adapted to help journalists understand how to cover community assets more effectively. Some, including Lewis Friedland at the University of Wisconsin–Madison and Neil Heinen from WISC-TV (CBS) in Madison, Wisconsin, are already exploring the boundaries of this form of journalism, commonly referred to by journalists as community mapping. Civic mapping is a systematic process of gathering detailed information about communities and residents that helps journalists bring context and depth to their reporting. WFLA-TV in Tampa, Florida, experimented with civic mapping techniques in its coverage of a working class neighborhood in the mid-1990s with some success. When other stations were following the official view, WFLA-TV reported that residents in the community did not want abandoned homes torn down but rather wanted help applying for community block grants to redevelop the area. The journalists' understanding of the issue and the area resulted from civic mapping efforts.

Kretzman and McKnight's study was conducted in 1993, at a time when civic journalism was just emerging. In their conclusion, they suggested that "civic-minded journalists must find new ways, not merely to *talk to* their communities, but to *think about* them." They suggested that Kretzmann and McKnight's (1993) community asset mapping might offer "a glimpse of what

David D. Kurpius

civic journalism would be if journalists referred more often to asset-based maps of their communities."

Ettema and Peer (1996) conducted their study at a time when civic journalism was developing and spreading at both newspapers and television stations. The Pew Center for Civic Journalism became one of the engines of civic journalism development, holding workshops, sponsoring experimentation, and rewarding success with the James K. Batten Civic Journalism Award. Community mapping has roots in the Kretzmann and McKnight community-asset mapping process. Community mapping is a systematic method of developing deep contextual understanding of specific areas within the coverage area. This idea is to create a sociological picture of the area, its residents, and its issues. Some community mapping efforts are now spreading to the internet in the form of interactive gaming that allow citizens to help plan their own communities.

Before that development goes much further, it is prudent to assess whether civic journalism mapped communities differently, as was suggested should occur. Of particular interest is how class was portrayed. This study looked at the television entries for the James K. Batten Civic Journalism Award to see how journalists portrayed class within the construction of the portrayals of citizens and communities within journalistic content.

While newspapers have adopted civic journalism at a much higher rate than television and it has become more of a part of journalistic conventions at newspapers, television may be the more interesting case to study. Market forces are driving television owners to focus more on segmentation of the audience for advertisers. Instead of trying to win the overall ratings, now the battle is to dominate the key demographics of interest to advertisers. This focus on age and class is likely to create gaps in coverage that neglect the old and the poor. However, in theory, civic journalism should work against these market forces to include these disenfranchised residents, reflect their realities, portray their issues, and provide opportunities for them to join the public deliberative process.

## DISCUSSION

As Yankelovich (1991, 1999) pointed out, learning other perspectives and having discussions on issues are not the end result. He wrote extensively about the "working through" process. Inherent in this process is progress toward solutions. Knowledge about differing principled positions on an issue helps form consensus by illuminating possible areas of agreement. It is generally assumed that the media are a primary source of information for people to gain the requisite knowledge. As mentioned earlier, it is logical that at least a significant portion of the information will come through television.

Television journalism holds the potential to provide citizens with good, contextual information on issues. My research found citizens and other unaffiliated sources are more likely to be given voice in television civic journalism stories than in traditional television work (Kurpius 2002a). Simply expanding the voices and perspectives in the mediated dialogue helps to expand the marketplace of ideas that is at the root of helping democracy succeed. Women, minorities, and people from all points on the class continuum are provided opportunities not only to be seen in television stories but also to express their thoughts and ideas.

Certainly television civic journalism has provided examples of deep, contextual coverage of class, from the Lucille's Kitchen/Crookston issues discussion to the documentary *On the Outside Looking In* to the Charlotte revitalization effort documented in the series Carolina Crime Solutions. These are small examples in the vast array of television coverage. Structurally, civic journalism promotes a pattern of developing understandings and connections in poorly understood communities and bringing new stakeholders and voices into the public dialogue. The question remains, though, Why are lower-class communities often missing in television civic journalism coverage?

While television civic journalism can work to improve the diversity of stakeholders and their perspectives, market forces work against it. This includes the discovery and inclusion of lower-class residents' views in television news stories. The entry points into these communities take time and effort to develop. Television journalists rarely are given the time to work on building connections due in part to the daily need to provide content for newscasts. Even if they did find ways to develop the entry points, turnover rates among reporters, particularly at small and medium-size stations, limit the effect. Since the connections created are rarely transferable to others in the newsroom when a journalist leaves, the ties to communities that the journalist developed are diminished or severed.

Market forces are not the only reason for limited coverage of class. The complexity of the issue does not lend itself to television coverage. Journalists need an educational background and experience in lower and working class communities to more fully develop an understanding of class issues. This makes reporting in that area difficult at best for many reporters. Time and resource constraints also limit the possibilities for developing coverage on such a complex topic.

Finally, professional norms of television journalism focus on good video, breaking news, and a storytelling narrative. Class coverage does not inspire journalists to seek out stories, and lower-class community story narratives are more difficult for reporters to develop. One possible reason for this difficulty is a lack of knowledge about lower-class communities, since journalists tend to be from predominantly middle-class backgrounds. Reporters could gain that knowledge by spending time in lower-class neighborhoods to gain a deeper understanding and make connections with area residents before developing meaningful story ideas. This is time television journalists rarely have at their disposal. These are not neighborhoods that journalists can simply parachute into, get a story, and get out with good contextual information that accurately portrays issues of class.

Stations have been able to spend time in communities gaining context and deeper knowledge through external grants. My long-term study of civic journalism television found that the foundation support for these efforts was particularly important for deep, contextual coverage of issues. When such funding ended, it was difficult for even the best-intentioned stations to continue the effort. A few have succeeded, though primarily through partnership agreements with other commercial and public media organizations. This in turn tends to dictate a project focus, rather than integration into daily reporting routines. Historically, these projects have focused on election campaign coverage or mainstream issues in the public dialogue, including race, transportation, and education. There is not much room for class coverage and there is likely a fear that such coverage will not attract the right demographic to the station's news audience.

The current trends toward convergence and consolidation of media entities under large corporations is troubling. Local news is becoming less local in many markets and some television ownership groups are even moving toward more regionally based newscasts. There is a loss of balance in local news coverage, which is now structured to favor entertainment and shock value over the quality information that addresses community issues and concerns.

Though I never enjoyed the paperwork in the ascertainment process when working as a news director, the demise of the FCC ascertainment requirements for license renewal removed a device that helped balance the influx of market forces. More importantly, it dictated ascertainment of the needs of the entire community, not simply the demographically significant portion. Civic journalism can provide a more careful and thoughtful ascertainment process that focuses on the journalistic outcomes and not the paperwork or threat of loss of the station's license. However, civic journalism is not an end itself. Rather, it is a way of working through the potential for expanding public affairs coverage, creating connections to communities, and bringing a wider range of stakeholders into the public mediated conversation. Still the problem is money. Without grants to encourage and support this type of work, it is less likely to develop, let alone grow. The audience must own part of the blame since viewers are not demanding journalistic work at this level.

Based on the study of what might be considered the best examples of television civic journalism, the vast majority of stations miss the opportunity to include coverage of different classes. Managers at many stations conducting civic journalism projects noted in interviews the balancing act they have to maintain between doing civic work and meeting profit and audience demographic expectations. Stations no longer consider it a winning ratings period to simply have the greatest number of people watching their newscasts. Instead, they look for wins in key demographics that advertisers find desirable.

While civic journalism is structured to increase the diversity of stakeholders for inclusion in stories, the market-force fight against the demand for specific audience demographics is most likely to win in the end. Lower-class individuals tend to be excluded from the prime demographic targets, and this potentially limits their inclusion in news stories. This is not to suggest that journalists are being told to avoid less desirable classes of citizens to please advertisers. Instead it is filtered down to employees through an emphasis on the types of stories and newscasts that attract ratings wins in the desired demographic categories. Employees know what will please the boss and protect their jobs, even if it is not overtly stated as a policy. While civic journalism efforts might open a discussion about inclusion of underrepresented stakeholders in coverage, it is likely to fail eventually when competing against the marketplace. With its very limited success in coverage of class, this points out a flaw in how complex social issues are even selected for coverage. For class to gain significant coverage on television, the issue will need to become more a part of the public dialogue.

## REFERENCES

Anderson, E. 1990. *Street Wise*. Chicago: University of Chicago Press.

Campbell, C. P. 1995. *Race, Myth, and the News*. Thousand Oaks, Calif.: Sage.

Charity, A. 1995. *Doing Public Journalism*. New York: Guilford.

Clayman, S. E. 1990. From Talk to Text: Newspaper Accounts of Reporter-Source Interactions. *Media, Culture, and Society* 12, no. 1: 79.

Entman, R. 1990. Modern Racism and the Images of Blacks in Local Television News. *Critical Studies in Mass Communication* 7: 332–45.

———. 1994. Representation and Reality in the Portrayal of Blacks on Network Television News. *Journalism Quarterly* 71, no. 3: 509–20.

Entman, R. M. 1992. Blacks in the News: Television, Modern Racism, and Cultural Change. *Journalism Quarterly* 69, no. 2: 341–61.

Ettema, J. S., and Peer, L. 1996. Good News from a Bad Neighborhood: Toward an Alternative to the Discourse of Urban Pathology. *Journalism Quarterly* 73, no. 4: 835–56.

Fischer, C. 1982. *To Dwell among Friends: Personal Networks in Town and City*. Chicago: University of Chicago Press.

Fishman, M. 1990. *Manufacturing the News*. Austin: University of Texas Press.

Friedland, L., and McLeod, J. 1996. Community integration and mass media: A reconsideration. Paper presented at the Association for Education in Journalism and Mass Communication convention, Los Angeles.

Friedland, L. A. 2000. Public Journalism and Community Change. In A. J. Eksterowicz and R. N. Roberts, eds., *Public Journalism and Political Knowledge*, xvii, 198. Lanham, Md.: Rowman & Littlefield.

———. 2001. Communication, Community, and Democracy: Toward a Theory of the Communicatively Integrated Community. *Communication Research* 28, no. 4: 358–91.

Gallup, G. 1994. *The Gallup Poll: Public Opinion 1993*. Wilmington, Del.: Scholarly Resources.

———. 1996. *The Gallup Poll: Public Opinion 1995*. Wilmington, Del.: Scholarly Resources.

Gans, H. J. 1962. *The Urban Villagers: Group and Class in the Life of Italian-Americans*. New York: Free Press.

———. 1980. *Deciding What's News: A Study of CBS Evening News, NBC Nightly News, Newsweek and Time*. New York: Vintage Books.

Grabe, M. E., and Barnett, B. 1999. Sourcing and Reporting in News Magazine Programs: 60 Minutes versus Hard Copy. *Journalism and Mass Communication Quarterly* 76, no. 2: 293–311.

Holtzman, L. 2000. *Media Messages: What Film, Television, and Popular Music Teach Us about Race, Class, Gender, and Sexual Orientation*. Armonk, N.Y.: Sharpe.

Kaniss, P. 1991. *Making Local News*. Chicago: University of Chicago Press.

Kretzmann, J. P., and McKnight, J. L. 1993. *Building Communities from the Inside Out: A Path toward Finding and Mobilizing a Community's Assets*. Chicago: Center for Urban Affairs and Policy Research/Acta Press.

Kurpius, D. D. 2002a. Source Prominence and the Unaffiliated: Testing a Primary Tenet of Civic Journalism. Paper presented at the Association for Education in Journalism and Mass Communication, Miami Beach, August.

———. 2002b. Sources and Civic Journalism: Changing Patterns of Reporting. *Journalism and Mass Communication Quarterly* 79, no. 4: 853–66.

———. 2003. Bucking a Trend in Local Television News: Combating Market-Driven Journalism. *Journalism* 4, no. 1: 77–95.

Lasch, C. 1995. *The Revolt of the Elites and the Betrayal of Democracy*. 1st ed. New York: Norton.

Liebler, C. M., and Smith, S. J. 1997. Tracking Gender Differences: A Comparative Analysis of Network Correspondents and Their Sources. *Journal of Broadcasting and Electronic Media* 41: 58–68.

Liebow, E. 1967. *Tally's Corner: A Study of Negro Streetcorner Men*. Boston: Little, Brown.

Maguire, K., and Pastore, A. L. 2000. *Sourcebook of Criminal Justice Statistics*. Retrieved December 4, 2001. www.albany.edu/sourcebook.

McShane, S. 1995. Occupational, Gender, and Geographic Representation of Information Sources in U.S. and Canadian Business Magazines. *Journalism of Mass Communication Quarterly* 72, no. 1: 190–204.

Merritt, D. 1998. *Public Journalism and Public Life: Why Telling the News Is Not Enough*. 2nd ed. Mahwah, N.J.: Erlbaum.

National Science Board. 1998. *Science and Engineering Indicators*. NSB 98-1. Arlington, Va.: National Science Foundation.

Pew Research Center for the People and the Press. 2000. *Internet Sapping Broadcast News Audience: Investors Now Go Online for Quotes, Advice*. Pew Research Center for the People and the Press. www.people-press.org/media00rpt.htm. Retrieved August 19, 2001.

Rosen, J. 1996. *Getting the Connections Right: Public Journalism and the Troubles in the Press*. New York: The Twentieth Century Fund Press.

————. 1999. *What Are Journalists For?* New Haven, Conn.: Yale University Press.

Sigal, L. V. 1973. *Reporters and Officials: The Organization and Politics of Newsmaking.* Lexington, Mass.: Heath.

Sirianni, C., and Friedland, L. 2001. *Civic Innovation in America: Community Empowerment, Public Policy, and the Movement for Civic Renewal.* Berkeley: University of California Press.

Smith, C. 1993. News Sources and Power Elites in News Coverage of the Exxon Valdez Oil Spill. *Journalism Quarterly* 70, no. 2: 393–403.

Soloski, J. 1989. News Reporting and Professionalism: Some Constraints on the Reporting of the News. *Media, Culture, and Society* 11: 207–28.

Tuchman, G. 1973. Making News by Doing Work: Routinizing the Unexpected. *American Journal of Sociology* 79: 110–31.

Wellman, B. 1979. The Community Question: The Intimate Networks of East Yorkers. *American Sociological Review* 84: 1201–31.

Whyte, W. 1981. *Street Corner Society,* 3rd ed. Chicago: University of Chicago Press.

Yankelovich, D. 1991. *Coming to Public Judgment: Making Democracy Work in a Complex World.* Syracuse, N.Y.: Syracuse University Press.

————. 1999. *The Magic of Dialogue: Transforming Conflict into Cooperation.* New York: Simon & Schuster.

Zelizer, B. 1989. Saying as Collective Practice: Quoting and Differential Address in the News. *Text* 9, no. 4: 369.

Zoch, L. M., and Turk, J. V. 1998. Women Making News: Gender as a Variable in Source Selection and Use. *Journalism and Mass Communication Quarterly* 75, no. 4: 762–75.

# Epilogue

*Don Heider*

Almost thirty years ago George Gerbner and Larry Gross argued that TV is "an agency of the established order and as such serves primarily to extend and maintain rather than alter, threaten, or weaken conventional conceptions, beliefs and behaviors" (1976, 175). James Carey has argued that news media serve a ritual function, reinforcing people's already held beliefs about the world around them (1989). The chapters in this volume make a strong case for the idea that news media often reproduce and enforce certain norms, especially ideas about class.

Social distinctions are largely arbitrary. These social boundaries can change depending on who is in power in a culture. They are situated in history but may or may not be based on concrete characteristics. Similarly, class can be defined by income, held wealth, family ties, upbringing, wardrobe, speech pattern, skin color, or an endless number of other variable characteristics. Humans decide how those distinctions are made. Humans with power in a culture select what is valued and held in esteem. As the scholars gathered here have closely examined the way in which class is manifested in news products and in newsrooms, we begin to see what role the news media play in this process.

After considering the research presented here, one is left wondering who speaks for the poor in America? Who speaks for the working class? Who speaks for those not in power? If journalism is, as some have written, the first draft of history, who is being systematically left out of the history journalists tell each day? Another old adage states that journalism should comfort the afflicted and afflict the comfortable, yet based on what this group of media scholars have found, who is really being afflicted who is really being comforted? And what are the prospects for change?

Around a century ago, American journalism was in what might be considered a golden era. Muckrakers like Lincoln Steffens, Ida Minerva Tarbell, and

338

Ray Stannard Baker were crusading against big business and unscrupulous labor bosses in the pages of such publications as *McClure's* and *Collier's*. This reporting was popularly read. Is there a place for such reporting in the current media atmosphere?

In the final few pages I'd like to grapple with these questions and discuss the outlook for meaningful change in journalistic practice.

## OWNERSHIP

In the era of muckraking journalism, some popular magazine publishers saw the value in publishing sensational exposes. Stories that portrayed the plight of the common man struck a chord with audiences. A few publishers and editors saw the value in this kind of reporting and realized there was an audience for this brand of journalism. Given that currently most mainstream press is owned by large, corporate conglomerates—the very types of huge companies the muckrakers often targeted—there is some doubt as to whether such pieces could get widely published today. Think for a moment of what now are the most popular magazines, for instance. You aren't likely to find hard-hitting stories about the plight of the poor in the pages of *Parade* or *TV Guide*.

There is an ongoing debate about the direct effects of corporate ownership on journalistic content, but there are a few points that stand as obvious. Corporate owners, often publicly held companies, have a vested interest in maintaining the status quo. There really is no such thing as a politically neutral stance. If publications are silent on issues, it is a de facto statement of support for the existing system.

Directors of publicly held media companies have a primary responsibility to maximize profits. In earlier days, family-owned media outlets doubtlessly looked to make money through their media holdings. However, I would contend that when newspapers, radio stations, and television stations were locally owned, families often had a larger view of their companies' responsibilities and obligations to the community. If you live in a community, it may be more difficult to turn a blind eye to problems in that community. At times owners were willing to settle for slightly lower profit margins to maintain larger editorial staffs and therefore better journalistic product. Stockholders, looking to make money on their investments, seem to have little interest in the public service role of companies that practice journalism. Buying Time Warner or Gannett stock, to most investors, is the same as buying stock in IBM or Microsoft. The difference is journalists don't make widgets. Journalism has as a core value the idea of trying to serve the public. This raises serious questions as to whether or not, in a free market system, journalism has a bright and robust future in the hands of for-profit companies. Even public broadcasting in the United States is heavily subsidized by major corporations, raising questions at times about journalistic independence. As much as companies may want to do excellent journalism, the bottom line is always going to dominate these considerations. What that translates into for companies is trying to do excellent journalism within certain economic parameters ensuring healthy profits. That often means more news done by fewer journalists. Excellent journalism generally takes time and resources. Investigative journalism, such as that done by some of the muckrakers, often on behalf of poor or working-class citizens, can take weeks and months to compile and is very labor intensive. It can also expose a news organization to devastatingly expensive litigation. Such journalism does not easily fit into a model of maximizing profits.

The prospects for local ownership of local media become increasingly dim. The FCC seems hell-bent on almost complete deregulation, allowing single owners to hold more and more outlets, even in the same market. Recent trends in broadcasting—with Clear Channel owning more than 1,200 radio stations, which resulted in the decimation of many of local news operations, and with Sinclair Broadcast Group's plan to consolidate news operations for its twenty TV stations across the United States—make chances for strong, independent local news outlets committed to covering local communities seem slim.

Fewer owners, except to an FCC commissioner who has never written a news story, does not bode well for the future of excellent journalism and does not bode well for the prospects of journalists telling the stories of people without considerable expendable income. The current ownership situation, I believe, lends itself to more reporting on attractive demographic groups, with others falling by the wayside.

What's needed in my view is not deregulation, but a strong move toward reregulation, or decentralization. At least on the broadcast side of the journalism equation, more owners mean more voices. Currently even entrepreneurs with millions of dollars have almost no chance of owning local broadcast stations. Local owners, whether they would be more civic-minded or not, have been virtually shut out of the business.

On the newspaper side of the journalism industry, most cities have been relegated to becoming one-newspaper towns, with almost all meaningful competition falling by the wayside. This leaves many of these organizations as placid, rarely willing to take on any meaningful fights in their local communities, often also run by managers who must keep a tight rein on expenses at the bidding of large corporate owners. Editorial pages have often been tamed to the point of offering little meaningful comment for fear of alienating advertisers. If not for syndicated columnists, we would see almost no dissent; even many columnists seem bland when compared with their predecessors from other eras.

## MANAGERS

Given the corporate climate, managers only have so much leeway to affect journalistic product. And managers in any organization often are encouraged to perpetuate norms. People who do not cause trouble or push for change are often promoted within organizations, or managers promote like-minded colleagues, ensuring stability and little change from year to year.

News workers in general and managers in particular are often fairly well paid, often college educated. These are also the people who most control the news philosophy and news decision making. If they have no contact with poor or working-class people, the chances are not good they will select stories important to this population.

In light of diminishing readership or shrinking audiences, managers have been forced to spend more time considering who their audience is and how they might attract or increase viewership and readership. This often does not involve concerted effort toward attracting people with little income. As the media audience becomes more fragmented, outlets begin looking at how to cater to viewers and readers with an attractive demographic profile, in other words, people in the upper income brackets.

As Martin Gilens pointed out in his chapter, even when news managers are well-meaning or more progressive than their audience, they may perpetuate stereotypes of the poor.

Hope for change may come in the amount of discussion and attention paid to public or civic journalism for the past dozen or so years. One tenet of civic journalism encourages journalists to become more familiar with their local communities. Some managers have embraced the philosophy and some interesting projects have emerged, as David Kurpius pointed out. But change is slow in coming and many news organizations have resisted and continue to resist change. As Jay Rosen, one of the founders of the civic journalism movement, has noted, some of this country's largest and most venerable news organizations have dismissed civic journalism completely, choosing not to even take a close look at how journalism is practiced within their own institutions (1999).

## JOURNALISTS

I began my career in journalism in 1980, and alongside me were many people who picked the career because of Watergate. As a journalism educator I look at my students now and wonder what inspires them. With its low salaries and tough working conditions, why are they choosing this field? Watergate had no impact on their lives. Many are from the suburbs. Most have never visited a poor neighborhood; they have few working-class friends. With no passion to fight for reform and no experience with people who live outside the upper middle class, what hope do we have of expecting them to comfort the afflicted? Even if they were to see that coverage is now incomplete and needs to be changed, individual journalists would face an uphill battle in fighting for change in newsrooms.

They could go to work to work for alternative publications. However, in many major cities, even the leading weekly alternatives have become vehicles to sell advertising to companies wanting to reach the progressive upper middle class. These papers' slightly left political stance makes them appear progressive, but they are so packed full with ads that the most basic political message they send to reader is: Consume! If students pick more radical publications, they often are choosing to work at the lowest end of the pay scale. Only a few may be willing to take on this crusade at great sacrifice, especially when they face paying off student loans and see colleagues from communications programs who take advertising and public relations jobs that offer much greater material rewards.

In allowing more deregulation of the broadcast industry, FCC Chairman Michael Powell and others argued that because of the plethora of new media outlets, the media landscape had changed. Perhaps young journalists could go work in these many new outlets and provide alternative news to what we see in the daily papers and broadcasts. There are two problems with this thinking, however. First, the same large corporations that own the networks and cable systems own 90 percent of all the cable channels on the air, part of that "diverse terrain." In regard to the many websites that fill the Internet, the question is, What kind of audience do they garner? Most studies have shown that when it comes to news, most viewers go to established news source websites (e.g., *New York Times,* CNN, etc.). So the alternative news sources, often with bare-bones staff, have a struggle ahead to win enough readership to be economically viable. Most Internet users still visit the Web for two reasons—to shop on commercial sites or view pornography. To even have access to Internet news, one must have access to a computer and an Internet connection, two requirements that still elude many Americans. All of this does not add up to an optimistic outlook for alternative news sources, even if those sources are dedicated to covering underrepresented segments of our society.

## CHANGE

It's not that there is no coverage of poor and working-class citizens in contemporary journalism. In 1968, a group of reporters who had covered Robert F. Kennedy organized an awards competition that each year honors the work of journalists who cover the problems of the disadvantaged. If you look over the recent winners, you see reporters and news organizations that are committed to this kind of journalism. Yet, as the authors here have indicated, the award winners may represent the exceptional rather than the everyday practice.

For meaningful change to occur in coverage, owners, managers, and journalists must be on board. Given the success of capitalism, any significant effort to cover underrepresented class groups must find an audience. Ironically, in the United States, the future success of this kind of reporting may lay in the hands of entrepreneurs with soul—creative people committed to excellent journalism, committed to telling stories, to serving the public, but also innovative enough to find a market for this kind of journalism.

A changing media terrain can offer opportunities for change. New media technology is not inherently imbued with any values, positive or negative. It's up to humans to decide how the new media are used. But it can offer openings for innovation. However, change requires a committed group of entrepreneurs, managers, and journalists with a strong vision to develop a successful journalistic product that would remain committed to cover all segments of society.

There are a few rays of light peeking through the dark clouds covering the current news media landscape. There remains, for instance, a remnant of journalists committed to public service. In recent years some of these current and former professionals have become more vocal and better organized, for example, the Committee of Concerned Journalists (www.journalism.org), a group dedicated to improving practice. If groups like this can focus attention on chronic coverage problems and if Congress would be willing to pressure the FCC into democratizing media ownership, there might be a possibility for change.

We hope this volume will spur innovation or at least help someone understand better how journalism is practiced in regard to class. In *Les Miserables* Victor Hugo wrote that "there is always more misery among the low class than there is humanity in the higher." The question these chapters raise is how much humanity remains and is allowed to remain among those working in journalism?

## REFERENCES

Gerbner, G., and Gross, L. 1976. Living with Television: The Violence Profile. *Journal of Communication* 26: 173–99.

Carey, J. 1989. *Communication as Culture*. Boston: Unwin Hyman.

Rosen, J. 1999. *What Are Journalists For?* New Haven Conn.: Yale University Press.

# Index

# About the Contributors

**Janet Blank-Libra** (Ph.D., Southern Illinois University) is associate professor of English and journalism at Augustana College in Sioux Falls, South Dakota. She has presented and published research related to the teaching of questioning in journalism courses as a way to infuse critical thinking into writing assignments and enable students to bring depth to stories, particularly those focused on social issues. As a writer, she freelances for local and area publications.

**Bonnie Brennen** is associate professor at the University of Missouri School of Journalism. She is the author of *For the Record: An Oral History of Rochester, New York, Newsworkers* (2001) and coeditor (with Hanno Hardt) of *Picturing the Past: Media, History, and Photography* (1999) and *Newsworkers: Towards a History of the Rank and File* (1995).

**Dennis J. Dunleavy** is a doctoral candidate at the University of Oregon and has completed his first year as an assistant professor and photojournalism program coordinator in the School of Journalism and Mass Communications at San Jose State University. A former photojournalist, his research interests include visual communication, interaction ritual, rhetorical studies, and critical pedadogy.

**James S. Ettema** (Ph.D., University of Michigan) is professor and chair of communication studies at Northwestern University. His most recent book is *Custodians of Conscience: Investigative Journalism and Public Virtue* (1998), written with Theodore L. Glasser. Among other citations, the book won the Sigma Delta Chi Award for research on journalism from the Society of Professional Journalists. His current research project examines applications of communication technology to the work of community-based organizations in urban settings.

**Koji Fuse** (Ph.D., The University of Texas at Austin) is assistant professor in the School of Journalism and Mass Communication at Drake University in Des Moines, Iowa. His primary research area is journalism and public opinion.

**Martin Gilens** (Ph.D., University of California, Berkeley) is associate professor of politics at Princeton University. Professor Gilens is the author of *Why Americans Hate Welfare: Race, Media and the Politics of Antipoverty Policy* (2000), and has published on media, race, gender, and welfare politics in *American Political Science Review, American Journal of Political Science, The Journal of Politics, British Journal of Political Science, Public Opinion Quarterly,* and the *Berkeley Journal of Sociology.*

**Maria Elizabeth Grabe** (Ph.D., Temple University) is associate professor in the School of Journalism at Indiana University, Bloomington. She has recently published work in *Communication Research, Journalism & Mass Communication Quarterly, Journal of Broadcasting & Electronic Media,* and *Critical Studies in Media Communication.*

**Laura Hapke** is a working-class studies scholar whose interdisciplinary focus is literature in relation to the history of U.S. labor. Dr. Hapke's most recent books include *Labor's Text: The Worker in American Fiction* (2001) and *Sweatshop: The History of an American Idea* (2004).

**Joseph C. Harry** (Ph.D., Michigan State University) is assistant professor in the Department of Communication at Slippery Rock University in Pennsylvania. A former newspaper reporter, Harry's research focuses on the ethics, rhetoric, political-economy, sociology, and ideology of mass media—especially journalism, television, and movies.

**Don Heider** (Ph.D., University of Colorado) is associate professor in the School of Journalism at the University of Texas at Austin. He spent ten years working as a reporter, producer, photographer, and manager in television news. In his book, *White News* (2000), Heider details why, in two local television markets, local news organizations did not cover communities of color, including Latinos, Native Americans, Native Hawaiians, Asian Americans, and others.

**Paul Jones** is senior lecturer in sociology at the University of New South Wales in Sydney. He is a graduate of the Birmingham (U.K.) Centre for Contemporary Cultural Studies. Jones has been an active participant in recent Australian public inquiries into media ownership and has published widely within the sociology of media and culture. His most recent work includes *Raymond Williams's Sociology of Cuture: A Critical Reconstruction* (2004).

**Deepa Kumar** teaches media and communication at Wake Forest University. Her research can be found in *Critical Studies in Media Communication* and *Television and New Media*.

**David D. Kurpius** (Ph.D., University of Wisconsin) is associate professor in the Manship School of Mass Communication at Louisiana State University. Kurpius has served as a CIES Fulbright Specialist Review Panel member for media arts. His work has appeared in leading scholarly journals, including *Journalism & Mass Communication Quarterly* and *Journalism*.

**Carol M. Liebler** (Ph.D., University of Wisconsin) is associate professor and department chair of communications at the S.I. Newhouse School of Public Communications at Syracuse University. She has published widely on issues related to diversity and the news media. Liebler teaches graduate courses in media and diversity, media sociology, and mass communication theory and research methods.

**Christopher R. Martin** is associate professor in the Department of Communication Studies at the University of Northern Iowa. He has written articles and reviews for several publications, including *Communication Research*, *Journal of Communication*, *Journal of Communication Inquiry*, *Labor Studies Journal*, and *Culture, Sport, Society*. He is author of *Framed! Labor and the Corporate Media* (2004) and co-author of *Media and Culture: An Introduction to Mass Communication* (2003).

**Gabriela Martinez** is a doctoral student in communication and society at the University of Oregon. Her research areas are international communication and ethnic studies, both with emphases in Latin America and Latinos in the United States. Martinez is also a professional ethnographic documentarian.

**Julianne H. Newton** (University of Oregon) is associate professor of visual communication and editor of *Visual Communication Quarterly,* a juried research journal. Newton's scholarship explores the impact of visual culture on society, on our ways of knowing, and on the integrity of the self. She has worked as a reporter, designer, editor, broadcast journalist, and photographer and is the author of *The Burden of Visual Truth: The Role of Photojournalism in Mediating Reality* (2001).

**Chad Okrusch** is a Ph.D. student working with Professor Julianne Newton at the University of Oregon. He is concerned with critically documenting, understanding, and evaluating the relationships among the social, cultural, and ecological realms of human existence. Specifically, his research program entails theoretically conceptualizing the mutually defining relationships between the ideal and material worlds by exploring the ecological consequences of corporate "green" PR campaigns in environmentally devastated areas.

**Limor Peer** is adjunct assistant professor in the Department of Communication Studies at Northwestern University. Her academic research interests include public opinion theory and methodology, media and democratic theory, and macro-level media effects. She is also research associate for the Readership Institute at the Media Management Center, Northwestern University.

**Jennie Phillips** is a doctoral candidate in the Department of Radio-TV-Film at the University of Texas at Austin. Her teaching and research are in the areas of media and cultural studies with emphases on television studies, the cultural industries, and processes of cultural production.

**Michael Pusey** was educated in England, France, Australia, and the United States, where he obtained his doctorate and taught at Harvard University. He is the author of *Jürgen Habermas* (1987, 2001); *Economic Rationalism in Canberra: A Nation Building State Changes Its Mind* (1991); and *The Experience of Middle Australia: The Dark Side of Economic Reform* (2003). He is an honorary visiting professor of sociology at the University of New South Wales in Sydney and a fellow of the Academy of the Social Sciences in Australia.

**James A. Rada** (Ph.D., University of Georgia) is assistant professor in the School of Communication at Howard University. His research focuses on mediated portrayals of African Americans and the effects those portrayals may have on an audience.

**Sheila M. Webb** holds a Ph.D. in journalism and mass communication and an M.F.A. in graphic design and photography, both from the University of Wisconsin-Madison. Since 1998, she has taught in the Department of Journalism in the College of Communication at Marquette University. She is also an editor and designer for the nonprofit civic journalism websites produced by ONline@UW. Previously, Webb was a museum educator and curator at the Cleveland Museum of Art and the John Michael Kohler Arts Center (among others), where she focused on twentieth-century works on paper.

**K. Tim Wulfemeyer** is professor and coordinator of the Journalism Degree Program in the School of Communication at San Diego State University. He has degrees from Fullerton College, San Diego State University, Iowa State University, and UCLA. He has taught at Iowa State University, New Mexico State University, and the University of Hawaii and has worked as a radio and television journalist. His research interests include ethics in journalism, the content of radio and television newscasts, audience interests and content preferences, mass media literacy, and sports journalism.